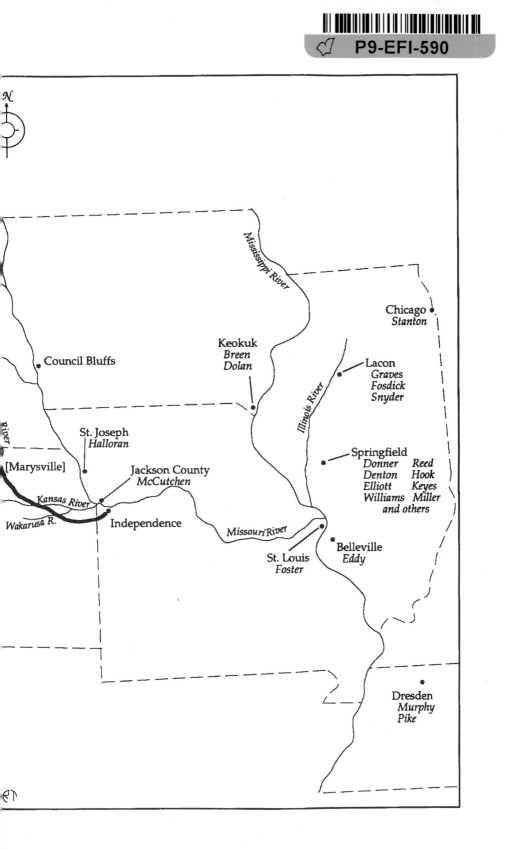

N

Mississippi River

Chicago •
Stanton

Keokuk
Breen
Dolan

• Council Bluffs

Lacon •
Graves
Fosdick
Snyder

Illinois River

St. Joseph
Halloran

Springfield •
Donner   Reed
Denton   Hook
Elliott   Keyes
Williams Miller
and others

[Marysville] •

Jackson County
McCutchen

Kansas River

Wakarusa R.

Independence

Missouri River

• Belleville
Eddy

St. Louis
Foster

Dresden •
Murphy
Pike

"Unfortunate Emigrants"

Narratives of the Donner Party

"Unfortunate Emigrants"

NARRATIVES OF THE DONNER PARTY

edited by
Kristin Johnson

Utah State University Press
Logan, Utah
1996

To My Parents

Utah State University Press
Logan, Utah 84322-7800

Typography by WolfPack
  Cover design by Michelle Sellers

  Library of Congress Cataloging-in-Publication Data

"Unfortunate emigrants" : narratives of the Donner Party / edited by Kristin
  Johnson.
      p. cm.
  Includes bibliographical references and index.
  ISBN 0-87421-204-9. – ISBN 0-87421-208-1 (paper : alk. paper)
  1. Donner Party. 2. Overland journeys to the Pacific. I. Johnson, Kristin, 1953- .
  F868.N5U54 1996
  978'.02--dc20   96-9996
                                                                     CIP

CONTENTS

ILLUSTRATIONS

Maps

Photos

ACKNOWLEDGMENTS

Many people and institutions have assisted the creation of this volume. I am very much indebted to Will Bagley for his help and encouragement at every stage along the way. Robert K. Hoshide kindly researched elusive biographical details. Particular thanks are due to Florence Johnson, who good-naturedly undertook some valuable long-distance research and helped in many ways with the project. Donna Woolsey's timely assistance sped the production of the manuscript, and my indefatigable typist, Jane Carpenter, saved my wrists, time, and temper. It was a pleasure to work with Rose Ann Tompkins, who created the maps.

Other individuals who provided much useful information and advice are David L. Bigler; Don Buck; Peter H. DeLafosse; Donna Diehl; Maxine Durney; Alan Feldhausen; Tanya K. Goodrich; Todd C. Grey, M.D.; Sarah F. Johnson, M.D.; Bill, Lucy, and Karl Kortum; Marilyn Kramer; Juanita Larimore; Al Mulder; and Jane Nelson.

The Marriott Library, University of Utah, provided a number of the texts, both from its own collections and through interlibrary loan. I particularly thank Walter Jones of Western Americana, Special Collections Department, for much assistance and many courtesies. Nancy Young went to a great deal of trouble to track down the W. C. Graves memoir. I would also like to thank the Markosian Library at Salt Lake Community College for providing the facilities for much of my work.

Other institutions providing documents, illustrations, or information include the Harold B. Lee Library, Brigham Young University; the Utah History Information Center, Salt Lake City; the Family History Library, Salt Lake City; the Bancroft Library, University of California, Berkeley; the California State Library, Sacramento; the Sutter's Fort State Historic Park, Sacramento; the Lake County Public Library, Lakeport, California; the Oregon State Library, Salem; the Marion County Historical Society, Salem; the Tennessee State Library and Archives, Nashville; and the Illinois State Historical Library, Springfield.

There are many people—family, friends, and co-workers—without whose encouragement, support, and, especially, forbearance this book would not have become a reality, and to whom I am very grateful. Not least do I thank John Alley of Utah State University Press for the insight, assistance, and advice which attended this anthology's creation.

INTRODUCTION

At the beginning of November 1846 a party of California-bound emigrants was trapped by early snow in the Sierra Nevada. Despite their
own efforts to escape and the efforts of others to rescue them, by the following April nearly half the company had died of cold and starvation.
Some of the emigrants had resorted to cannibalism to stay alive.

Though this last detail has become synonymous with the Donner party,
it was merely the culmination of a long series of events in which both
human weakness and the forces of nature played a role. The story has been
told many times and in many ways over the past 150 years but, interestingly, has never been treated at length by historians. Certainly historians
have written about the Donner party in brief articles or in longer works on
other topics, but to date none of the books devoted solely to the Donner
story has been written by a professional historian. Two important works in
the literature of the Donner party by well-known scholars, Dale L. Morgan's *Overland in 1846* and Bernard DeVoto's *Year of Decision: 1846,* place
the Donner party in the context of the westward movement. In the broader
historical perspective, the disaster itself is of minor significance—it had little
effect on subsequent events.

Yet, if the effect of the Donner party on history has been slight, its
impact on people has been profound. Since 1847 the ill-fated wagon train
has figured in hundreds of works, not only histories and articles but also
novels, short stories, juvenile literature, poems, plays, films, documentaries,
even an opera and a ballet. Though the lurid fact of cannibalism is the
Donner party's best-known aspect, the story's wide appeal cannot be attributed to mere prurience, for most of these works gloss over the horrors.
Instead, the motivating factor appears to lie in the human story: unlike
many epics of the American West, the Donner saga is not centered on the
exploits of a few exceptional men who sought adventure but on families,
on ordinary people caught up in an extraordinary situation. It is a dreadful
irony that hopes of prosperity, health, and a new life in California's fertile
valleys led many only to misery, hunger, and death on her stony threshold.

Since the public's interest in the Donner party has not been matched by
that of scholars, it has fallen to amateur historians to tell the tale. The first

1

comprehensive account appeared in 1849 with the publication of J. Quinn Thornton's *Oregon and California in 1848,* a two-volume work which included a lengthy section on the Donner party. Thornton, a lawyer, had traveled for two weeks with members of the Donner party. After the tragedy, in the fall of 1847, he interviewed survivors in San Francisco. His account, though much flawed by melodramatic flourishes, literary embellishments, and the author's tendency to favor sensationalism over factual reporting, has nevertheless been the basis for many subsequent writings.

In 1879 a Truckee, California, newspaper editor and lawyer, C. F. McGlashan, published his *History of the Donner Party: A Tragedy of the Sierra.* McGlashan, too, contacted survivors, but by his time most of those who had been adults in 1846 were dead; some of his informants had been young children at the time of the tragedy and could relate very little first-hand information. Using published accounts and his own voluminous correspondence with survivors and rescuers, McGlashan put together a classic work which has rarely if ever been out of print. McGlashan was a kindly man who became friends with his correspondents and, loathe to cause them pain, smoothed over the rough spots by adopting a notably sentimental approach. As a result, his account is weak in its balance, its organization, and its facts, particularly in the details of the events leading up to the final debacle in the Sierra Nevada.

One of McGlashan's correspondents was Eliza Donner Houghton, who had been three years old in 1846. In the 1880s she began collecting the materials used in her *The Expedition of the Donner Party and Its Tragic Fate,* eventually published in 1911. Despite its title, barely half of Houghton's account deals directly with the Donner party; the rest is her autobiography up to the time of her marriage. Houghton relied heavily on Thornton, but also used McGlashan and the recollections of her older sisters, along with other sources. Anecdotes and personal details add charm and pathos to her story, but in general her account is derivative and sometimes untrustworthy.

The most influential version of the Donner story has been *Ordeal by Hunger* by George R. Stewart. First published in 1936 and revised in 1960, this was the first attempt at a scholarly treatment of the Donner party and has come to be regarded as the definitive history. Though Stewart was undoubtedly a scholar, a professor of English at the University of California, Berkeley, he was not, strictly speaking, a historian. Much of his success can be attributed to his skill as a storyteller rather than to his historical expertise. *Ordeal by Hunger* is gripping, well-paced, and convincingly told; but the seamless construction which makes for good reading also obscures the many places where inference is presented as fact. A comparison of Stewart's book with his sources reveals that he often sacrificed accuracy for the sake of art.

Ordeal by Hunger is largely responsible for the popular perception of the Donner party; however, Stewart's vision was not universally accepted. Utah historian Dale L. Morgan in particular disputed Stewart's interpretations of several issues in his own writings on different aspects of Western history. *The Humboldt: Highway of the West* (1943); *The Great Salt Lake* (1947); with J. Roderic Korns, *West from Fort Bridger* (1951; rev. 1994); and *Overland in 1846* (1963) reveal Morgan's evolving perceptions of the tragedy. Dispersed as they were into these several works, however, Morgan's contributions to Donner scholarship did little to alter the public perception of the tragedy shaped by Stewart.

In the 1950s two minor works appeared, Walter M. Stookey's *Fatal Decision: The Tragic Story of the Donner Party* (1950) and Homer Croy's *Wheels West* (1955). Although both authors presented interesting original research, their books are inaccurate and amateurish; Croy's book is also heavily fictionalized. Neither contributes greatly to our understanding of the Donner story.

It was not until 1992 that Stewart's primacy in the field was directly challenged by Joseph A. King in *Winter of Entrapment: A New Look at the Donner Party,* a work which was more an attack upon Stewart than a history of the wagon train in question. King, with reason, criticizes many of Stewart's interpretations, asking important questions and making several good points. Nevertheless, King's objections are overstated and unbalanced, and though he accuses Stewart of prejudice, misinterpretation of sources, and poor research, King himself is guilty of precisely the same errors. The revised edition of 1994 corrected some problems and gave the work a badly needed reorganization, but *Winter of Entrapment* still leaves a great deal to be desired as a history of the Donner party.

Certainly professional status or graduate training do not guarantee a historian's competence, and just as certainly amateurs have written excellent histories. As it stands, however, none of the currently available histories of the Donner party was written by a trained historian, and each suffers from its author's lack of objectivity, unfamiliarity with standards of historical scholarship, literary inclinations, or a combination of these factors. These defects may not be apparent or important to some readers, but they pose grave problems for others. Perhap the 1996 sesquicentennial of the tragedy will inspire a competent history; but until a balanced, scholarly synthesis of the documentary evidence appears, those with a more than casual interest in the Donner party will have to read the source materials themselves.

Fortunately for students of the Donner party, most of the primary documents are available in print. A few of these–newspaper articles, letters, and diaries dating from 1846–47–are included in secondary histories, but the majority can be found in a single work, Dale Morgan's monumental *Overland in 1846: Diaries and Letters of the California-Oregon Trail* (1963). Its two volumes include most of the early sources and portions of later ones, along with Morgan's invaluable notes. This work was reprinted in 1993.

Another source of primary documents is *Donner Miscellany: 41 Diaries and Documents,* edited by Carroll D. Hall and published in 1947 in a limited edition by the Book Club of California. Since its major documents are included in *Overland in 1846,* the general unavailability of the *Miscellany* is not as serious as it might appear; its minor documents are nevertheless of interest, providing brief but intriguing glimpses of the emigrants.

In 1921 a few early documents dealing with the efforts to rescue the trapped emigrants were published with other items from the Edward M. Kern Papers by Edward Eberstadt as *A Transcript of the Fort Sutter Papers.* This privately printed volume was published in a limited edition of twenty copies and is consequently very difficult to find; however, although the documents it contains shed light on the relief parties, their contribution to the history of the Donner party is slight.

These three works contain virtually all the firsthand sources of the Donner story dating from 1846–47. In the 1870s and 1880s C. F. McGlashan and H. H. Bancroft collected a number of memoirs and letters dealing with the Donner party, which are now held by the Bancroft Library at the University of California, Berkeley. Other collections of Donner party materials are held by the California State Library, the Sutter's Fort Historical Museum, and the Huntington Library. Many of these documents have been used by secondary writers, but few have been published, except as excerpts.

There is, however, another body of important documents which are not readily available. Several accounts published in early books, newspapers, and magazines have been widely used by secondary writers, yet are all too often hard to find. They are held in the special collections of research libraries and do not circulate, or they are available as microforms, inconvenient to use and often issued in large and unindexed sets. Many of these documents have been excerpted in other works, but few are easily available in their entirety.

The present anthology grew out of my own frustration in trying to track down items in this latter category of sources. *"Unfortunate Emigrants": Narratives of the Donner Party* is not intended as a substitute for a scholarly history; rather it augments the available collections of documents, providing the complete texts of previously unanthologized documents in one convenient volume and with additional information in the form of annotations. I have taken a textual approach, attempting to identify themes recurring in the literature and to correlate the documents with one another.

The texts included here are of several types, widely divergent in date, form, and approach. The interplay among some of these accounts is fascinating: certain survivors contributed information to early writers, whose works in turn influenced the later recollections of other participants. The motivations of the informants are also different—to inform, to shock, to justify—but all are to a degree self-serving. The discrepancies among the accounts suggest that the Donner experience may best be viewed not as a public event but as a personal tragedy—an experience so complex and so traumatic that survivors were hard pressed to make sense of it. Because of the contradictions among the sources, a complete and accurate retelling of the Donner story may prove impossible, but its historiography and folklore are a fertile ground for further research.

The documents also vary widely in their publication history and availability. Two of the documents, J. Quinn Thornton's history and Virginia Reed Murphy's memoir, are well known but are currently available only in unannotated forms which leave important details unclear. On the other hand, the memoirs of James F. Reed and William C. Graves are well known but surprisingly hard to come by in their entirety, having remained out of print for more than a century. William McCutchen's brief account has been overshadowed by Reed's longer one. The two articles by Frances H. McDougall are not particularly valuable in themselves, but they provide the framework necessary for understanding the Reed and McCutchen memoirs. The lengthy accounts of Eliza W. Farnham and Jacob Wright Harlan are less difficult to find than some of the others but are not as familiar to researchers as they might be. Though both documents are confused and present many problems of interpretation, they illuminate many aspects of Donner history and folklore.

Two authors, H. A. Wise and J. Ross Browne, represent popular reactions to the Donner story. Although neither writer intended his work as history, some of their statements taken out of context have influenced other writers. The publication of the relevant passages in their entirety allows for a more balanced interpretation.

Also included here are three sources which have not influenced the Donner story due to the fact that they are almost unknown in the literature. These documents, letters written by Lilburn W. Boggs and Mary Ann Graves in 1847 and a late memoir of Lovina Graves Cyrus written down by her granddaughter Edna Maybelle Sherwood, are of minor significance but add detail to our knowledge of the Donner party.

The anthology opens with material from J. Quinn Thornton's *Oregon and California in 1848*. This rather lengthy document introduces the characters and tells the complete story of the Donner party, providing a frame of reference for the subsequent texts, which are presented in chronological order.

The intent in reproducing these texts has been to make them both accurate and readable. Obvious typographical errors and uncharacteristic misspellings have been silently corrected, but stylistic usages are unchanged. Brief corrections or clarifications are given in brackets within the text wherever possible, notes being reserved for more extensive comments.

J. QUINN THORNTON (1810–1888)

J essy Quinn Thornton was born August 24, 1810, near Point Pleasant in what is now West Virginia and grew up in Ohio. He studied law for several years, including nearly three years in London, England, and was admitted the Virginia bar in May 1833. In 1835 he began to practice law in Palmyra, Missouri; he married Nancy Logue three years later. An abolitionist, Thornton left Missouri because of the slavery controversy, moving to Quincy, Illinois, in 1841. There the Thorntons lived until their ill health prompted them to leave for Oregon in the spring of 1846.

On May 13 J. Quinn and Nancy Thornton became members of a wagon train camped about 100 miles west of the "jumping off point" of Independence, Missouri. William H. Russell had been elected captain of this company, which was joined on May 19 by the nine wagons of James F. Reed and George and Jacob Donner of Springfield, Illinois. These three families and their hired hands, thirty-one souls in all, formed the nucleus of what was to become the Donner party. Most of the other eventual members of the Donner party also traveled in the Russell train.

Thornton's diary records his journey with the Donners, Reeds, and others from May 19 until June 2, at which time the Oregon-bound wagons separated from those headed towards California. Thereafter his journal refers occasionally to the "California company," which his own party periodically "passed and repassed" on the road.

For the sake of clarity, some events unrecorded by Thornton should be mentioned here: on June 27 diarist Edwin Bryant exchanged his wagon and team for packmules at Fort Bernard in what is now eastern Wyoming, as he, Russell, and several others had become dissatisfied with the company's slow rate of travel. Hiram O. Miller, who had traveled with the Donner families as a teamster, was prevailed upon to join Bryant on July 2. This small party, consisting of nine single men, soon drew ahead of the others and became the first group of emigrants to take Hastings Cutoff.

Also, on or about July 12, at Independence Rock, the Donners and their companions met a solitary horseman, Wales B. Bonney, returning to the East from Oregon. He carried an open letter from Lansford W. Hastings, whose *Emigrants' Guide to Oregon and California* had inspired many of the travelers to head west. In this letter Hastings notified "all California emigrants now on the road" that he would wait for them at Fort Bridger to conduct them along a newly explored cutoff, which, passing south of the Great Salt Lake, would greatly reduce the time and distance to California.

Thornton records that by July 19 several emigrant companies had camped together at the Little Sandy River in what is now western Wyoming. There those emigrants who had decided to try Hastings Cutoff formed a new party and elected George Donner captain. On July 20 the companies separated, the Donner party taking the left-hand road towards Fort Bridger, the others the established route via Fort Hall, near present-day Pocatello, Idaho.

Thornton's travels with the Donner party had ended; the remainder of his diary details his journey to Oregon. He took the new Applegate Cutoff, suffering great hardship along the way. As a result, he became involved in a lengthy and acrimonious dispute with the trail's promoters, Jesse Applegate and David Goff, in the course of which he was challenged to a duel.

In early 1847 Thornton was appointed to the supreme court of Oregon's provisional government. At the end of that year he was sent to Washington, D.C., to present Oregon's petition for territorial status to Congress. He went by sea, arriving on November 10, 1847, in San Francisco. There he met survivors of the Donner party, his former traveling companions, who requested him to publish their version of events to offset the distorted and sensational accounts which had appeared in the press. Thornton had a relatively brief time in which to interview survivors, as he sailed from San Francisco on December 12. After arriving at Boston in May 1848, Thornton proceeded to Washington. The Oregon bill, which he had drafted, was passed in August.

During his travels Thornton wrote up his diary and notes, which were published in early 1849 by Harper and Brothers of New York in two volumes as *Oregon and California in 1848*. The first volume contains Thornton's overland diary and a description of Oregon; the information about Oregon continues in the second volume, which also contains a description of California, the Donner party narrative, and an appendix about the gold discovery. The Donner material constitutes roughly half of the second volume.

In addition to the demands on his time, Thornton's political duties also taxed his delicate health. He excuses his work in its preface, explaining that his notes had been "written out under circumstances of great embarrassment, and with many unavoidable interruptions." Receiving an urgent summons back to Oregon, he had to send his manuscript to the publishers without revision.

In May 1849 Thornton arrived once more in Oregon, where he spent the remainder of his life. He practiced law in various cities and was active in public affairs throughout his lifetime, taking a particular interest in educational issues. He died in Salem on February 5, 1888.

The Origins of the Text

In *Winter of Entrapment* (1994) Joseph A. King assails Thornton's credibility, charging that his claim to have interviewed more than one survivor of the Donner party is false. Since Thornton named only William H. Eddy as a source, King concludes that Eddy was Thornton's only informant. The rest of the narrative, King alleges, is derived from secondary sources, especially "wild accounts" which appeared in the press and circulated as hearsay. However, much of the material in Thornton's account is not sensational and many minor details are corroborated by contemporary sources. Some information can only have been derived from eyewitnesses, including both survivors and rescuers.

William H. Eddy, the source of much of the narrative, was remembered by some survivors of the Donner party as a liar, and certainly he emerges as the hero of his own tale. At times Eddy seems to have exaggerated his role, and occasionally to have represented himself as participating in events in which he was not involved. This does not mean that everything he says is necessarily false. For example, his account of killing a grizzly bear might sound boastful, but archaeological evidence confirms that a grizzly was killed, or at least eaten, by the emigrants at Donner Lake. As with any historical source, one must decide for oneself how much credence to accord Eddy on any given point.

James F. Reed must also have been one of Thornton's informants. The description of his unsuccessful attempt to take supplies to the snowbound emigrants could have come only from him or his companion, William McCutchen. The story of his next expedition, the Second Relief, was doubtless also from Reed, as he is the focus of this part of the narrative. Furthermore, on December 9, 1847, J. H. Merryman published an article about the disaster in the *Illinois Journal* based on information sent by Reed. While they are by no means identical, the similarities between Thornton's account and Merryman's strongly suggest that Reed was one of Thornton's informants.

The detailed account of the fundraising efforts in San Francisco may have come from Reed, from Thornton's friend William Clark, or from any of a number of people living in San Francisco at the time. It did not come from the *California Star*. Nor can the story of the First Relief have come from the newspaper, as Thornton gives many details not reported in its pages. For instance, on March 13, 1847, the *Star*, in an article titled "Later from the California Mountains" printed extracts from a journal provided by Aquilla Glover. This version mentions only that the relief party visited the Donner families' camp, some miles away from the other emigrants; the actual diary records that Tucker and two others went; but Thornton names Reason P. Tucker and his companions. He must therefore have spoken with a member of the relief party, perhaps Aquilla Glover, who was living in San Francisco in 1847. Many details of the First Relief's journey to the lake are verified by a later source, the 1873 memoir of rescuer Daniel Rhoads.

Thornton may well have had additional informants whose contributions are not easily discerned, but he obviously relied on newspaper accounts for some of his narrative. From January to June 1847 the *California Star* published several articles about the Donner party, some of which Thornton paraphrased and wove into his text. Others, ostensibly given verbatim, have been edited. Although many of his changes are minor, in some instances Thornton has "improved" his sources.

Regarding the genesis of his history, Thornton informed historian Hubert Howe Bancroft in 1878:

When I left here in the autumn of 1847 to go to Washington, I stopped at San Francisco—a little insignificant village—I there met with some of the survivors of the party; & knowing that I had been in the habit of keeping a journal on the way to this country several of them had kept journal notes, & they desired me to take up the story of their journey from the time we separated & until they got here. None of them kept their journals perfectly & clear through; there were intermissions, sometimes of a week, & sometimes even more. But where one omitted a week some other one would cover that time. I was enabled to get, in this way, the events of every day from the time we seperated until they were all gotten through, with a complete & perfect history of the relief parties that were fitted out in California & sent up to them, & their being brought out, one by one. I made a complete history of it.[1]

The passage of thirty years had clouded Thornton's memory, for this description is clearly at variance with his earlier statement mentioning only interviews. Perhaps he meant that his informants refreshed their memories with notes while they spoke with him; he may also have been thinking of Patrick Breen's diary, Glover's First Relief diary, and Fallon's Fourth Relief journal, versions of which had been published in the *California Star* and which he had used in his own text. The diary kept by Hiram Miller from May 12 to July 2 and continued by James Reed from July 3 to

---

1 Jessy Quinn Thornton, Oregon history: Salem Ore., and related materials, Bancroft MS P-A 70. Bancroft Library, University of California, Berkeley.

October 4—the Miller-Reed diary—was obviously not one of the journals to which Thornton alludes, for there are many discrepancies between it and his narrative.

Thornton seems to have compiled his account piecemeal, receiving the bulk of the story from Eddy, then filling in the gaps with information from other sources. Thornton clearly did not take a complete statement from Reed, for in that case several errors in the account would doubtless have been corrected. There is no personal testimony about events at the lake between Eddy's departure and the arrival of the First Relief, a break which Thornton bridges with Patrick Breen's diary.

In addition to the question of Thornton's informants is the problem of his style, the intent of which appears to be to impress the reader with the author's erudition and aesthetic sensibilities as much as it is to inform. This is not merely an annoying affectation, for Thornton's approach is sometimes so melodramatic or sentimental that it undermines his credibility.[2] This defect is particularly noticeable in the dialogues which Thornton invents. The scenes of the killing of a deer by William Eddy, much of the Curtis episode, Margaret Breen's tirade, and Tamsen Donner's tearful conversation with her dying husband are particularly suspect. Also, the negative remarks about Hastings which Thornton attributes to members of the Donner party very likely reflect his own rancor against Jesse Applegate rather than the actual opinions of survivors; certainly other early Donner sources make scant mention of the man whose shortcut led to disaster.

Since Thornton spent only a month in San Francisco and could interview but few of the participants, his narrative is necessarily unbalanced; comparatively little is said about the Murphy and Graves families, for instance. The circumstances of the book's creation also allowed considerable room for error between what Thornton was told, what he wrote down, and what he made of his notes months later. He had no opportunity to clarify points he may have questioned while he was writing, or to revise the manuscript after it was written.

Despite its flaws, Thornton's book was the only complete account of the Donner party for thirty years. When *Oregon and California in 1848* first came out in 1849 news of the gold discovery had created an enormous demand for information about California. The book sold well and Thornton's version of the Donner story was thus widely disseminated. The work was reprinted in 1855 and again in 1864.

Thornton's influence can be detected in many Donner party writings up to 1879, the year C. F. McGlashan published his *History of the Donner Party,*

---

2 For a discussion of the narrative voice in Donner party accounts see Richard C. Poulsen, "The Donner Party: History, Mythology, and the Existential Voice," in *Misbegotten Muses: History and Anti-History* (New York: Peter Lang, 1983), 103–16.

and beyond. McGlashan and Eliza Donner Houghton often relied on Thornton, as did George R. Stewart in his influential *Ordeal by Hunger*. While there are many difficulties with Thornton's account, his influence in shaping perceptions of the Donner tragedy cannot be denied.

The Text

Oregon and California in 1848 has been republished in several forms over the years. In addition to the Harper reprints of 1855 and 1864, a facsimile edition was published by Arno Press in 1973. The book has also appeared in microfilm and microfiche formats.

Another version of Thornton's account is *The California Tragedy,* which contains a few diary entries from Volume One and the Donner material from Volume Two, along with some passages from Edwin Bryant's *What I Saw in California* (1848). Published by Biobooks in 1945, this version is no longer in print. The well-illustrated *Camp of Death: The Donner Party Mountain Camp, 1846-47* (1986) is widely available but contains only the Donner chapters from Volume Two, omitting the passages describing the early stages of the journey. Although it includes a handful of corrections, *Camp of Death* has no detailed annotations.

The text published here consists of selected passages from Volume One of the 1849 edition in addition to the twelve chapters containing the Donner party narrative from Volume Two. The passages included from the first volume are Thornton's introduction and diary entries mentioning Donner party members or other individuals referred to later in this volume. Since Thornton is quite discursive, the passages from Volume One are not complete entries but only the portions of them relevant to the narrative.

The Problem of Itinerary

Thornton's work was the only detailed account of the Donner party's journey available until 1946, when the many items donated by a Reed descendant to the Sutter's Fort State Historic Park were cataloged. Among them was the Miller-Reed diary, published by the museum's curator, Carroll D. Hall, in *Donner Miscellany* the following year.

The Miller-Reed diary was a boon to historian Dale L. Morgan and his friends J. Roderic Korns and Charles Kelly, with whom he was avidly researching Hastings Cutoff. In 1951 Morgan published *West from Fort Bridger* as Volume 19 of the *Utah Historical Quarterly,* attributing the authorship to Korns, who had died in 1949. This work minutely analyzes source documents dealing with early emigrant trails across Utah. Among other texts, the Reed portion of the Miller-Reed diary is printed along with references to other sources, including Thornton's work. By studying mileages and landmarks given in the sources, examining maps, and traveling over much of the terrain, the compilers established the probable itineraries of several emigrant groups to and through Utah.[3]

The many discrepancies between Thornton's account and the Reed diary are intriguing and worthy of study; however, space cannot be devoted to studying them here. The itinerary reported by Thornton is obviously based on a reminiscence, as the details are often vague, events are sometimes given out of sequence, and the dating is faulty. While it is not without problems, Reed's contemporary journal presents a much clearer and more accurate picture of the journey. In the absence of an alternative and in light of Morgan's acknowledged mastery of the subject, *West from Fort Bridger*'s itinerary of the Donner party is generally regarded as definitive. Morgan's dates have been inserted into the text, using a bold typeface to distinguish them from corrections of errors in the original. In those instances where Thornton's account gains or loses time in relation to Reed's, the reader is referred to *West from Fort Bridger* for more detailed information.

Thornton's itinerary of the First Relief also differs slightly from that of another source, the diary begun by M. D. Ritchie and continued by Aquilla Glover. For the sake of comparison, the dates from the Ritchie-Glover diary have also been inserted into Thornton's account.[4]

---

3 A new edition of this classic, revised by Will Bagley and Harold Schindler according to Morgan's notes, was published in 1994 by Utah State University Press. Though he wished Korns to be given credit for *West From Fort Bridger,* I here refer to Morgan as the author.

4 The diary can be found in Morgan, *Overland in 1846: Diaries and Letters of the California-Oregon Trail* (Lincoln: University of Nebraska Press, 1993), 331–34.

J. Quinn Thornton (1810–1888). Marion County Historical
Society

From *Oregon and California in 1848*

VOLUME I.

Chapter I.

The Rendezvous.

The ill health of Mrs. Thornton and myself caused us to determine upon a residence in Oregon, with the hope that its pure and invigorating climate, would restore this inestimable blessing we had long lost. Having completed the necessary preparations, we departed from Quincy, Illinois, April 18, 1846. In due time we arrived at Independence, Missouri, the place of rendezvous.[5]

On the evening of the last Sabbath previous to leaving this place, we repaired to a house of worship, where we listened, with unusual attention and interest, to a sermon preached by a Methodist minister. We believed that it was probably the last time that we should hear preaching until after our arrival in Oregon. It is not wonderful, therefore, that we felt not only solemn but sad. Our hopes and fears had been greatly excited during several preceding weeks, while preparing for our long and arduous journey, and in bringing ourselves to submit to the severance of those endearing ties that bound us to the place and to the people; but the potent and sublime truths to which we then listened, nerved us for the effort, by tranquilizing our excited feelings. We were about, too, to enter upon scenes in which we were to endure great mental and physical suffering, and we therefore felt that it was especially necessary to go up to the house of God; for nothing so effectually as Christianity can assuage these, or prepare the mind and heart for encountering them. And in our subsequent experience upon the way, we realized that Christianity is adapted to the peculiar condition and wants of the emigrant in the wilderness, no less than to persons in an improved and settled

---

5 Now a suburb of Kansas City, Missouri, Independence was founded in 1827 as a center for the Santa Fe and other western trade. It became a last outpost or "jumping-off point" for westward bound travelers and in the spring of 1846 was jammed with emigrants making final preparations for their journey.

state of society; where the delicate sensibilities of refined and highly cultivated minds grow with the growth and expand with the expansion of the moral powers and affections.–(Mercury at sunrise, 53°; sunset, 76°.–Calm.)

This is the place where emigrants usually rendezvous for the purpose of completing their purchases for the journey, and making their final preparations. Most of the emigrants had already departed. Some were assembled at Indian Creek; a few were still in this place not yet prepared to depart. Among these, I became acquainted with Messrs. James F. Reed, George Donner, and Jacob Donner, together with their wives and families, all from the neighborhood of Springfield, Illinois, and all of whom proposed to go to California.

The town of Independence was at this time a great Babel upon the border of the wilderness. Here might be seen the African slave with this shining black face, driving his six-horse team of blood-red bays, and swaying from side to side as he sat upon the saddle and listened to the incessant tinkling of the bells. In one street, just driving out of town, was an emigrant, who, having completed all his preparations, was about entering upon the great prairie wilderness; whistling as though his mouth had been made for nothing else. The shrill notes seemed to come up from the bottom of a throat without "a stop."

Here might be seen the indolent dark-skinned Spaniard smoking a cigar as he leans against the sunny side of a house. He wears a sharp conical hat with a red band; a blue round-about, with little brass buttons; his duck pantaloons are open at the side as high as the knee, exhibiting his white cotton drawers between his knee and the top of his low half-boots.

Santa Fé wagons were coming in, having attached to them eight or ten mules, some driven by Spaniards, some by Americans resembling Indians, some by negroes, and others by persons of all possible crosses between these various races; each showing in his dress as well as in his face some distinctive characteristic of his blood and race–the dirty poncho always marking the Spaniard. The traders had been out to Santa Fé, and having sold their goods in exchange for gold dust, dollars, and droves of mules, were then daily coming in; the dilapidated and muddy condition of their wagons, and wagon-sheets, and the sore backs of their mules, all giving evidence of the length and toil of the journey they had performed and were now about to terminate.

Merchants were doing all in their power to effect the sale of supplies to emigrants. Some of the emigrants were hurrying to and fro, looking careworn, and many of them sad, as though the cloud had not yet passed away, that had come over their spirits, as they tore themselves from friends and scenes around which had clustered the memories of the heart. One was seen just starting, calling out to his oxen, and cracking his whip as though the world was at his control. Although some four or five children in the wagon were crying in all possible keys, he drove on, looking as cheerful and happy, as though he was perfectly sure that he was going to a country where the valleys flowed with milk and honey. Behind the wagon, with her nose almost over the end board, an old mare slowly and patiently stepped along, evincing as much care as though she knew that she was carrying "mother" and "the baby," and therefore must not stumble on any account.–(Mercury at sunrise, 56°; sunset, 69°.–Calm.)…

May 13.–…In the afternoon we overtook Ex-Governor Boggs[6] and some California emigrants.…

May 15.–…About the middle of the afternoon, Ex-Governor Boggs and myself with our wagons, teams, and those of some others, came up with the main body of the California emigrants, consisting of 63 wagons, under Col. W. H. Russell,[7] who were still considered as being at the rendezvous, having moved forward a little, but having halted again, for emigrants whom they expected to join them. We were immediately invited to attach ourselves to their party, and to remain with them until those of us who proposed to go to Oregon, should find ourselves in sufficient numbers, by new accessions, to form a company of our own.…

In the evening, an inquiry was instituted for the purpose of ascertaining the sufficiency of the wagons, teams, and provisions; the number of persons capable of bearing arms, and the number of all other persons of either sex. The notes of this enumeration, having been made in pencil, have become partially illegible. The following are believed to be the numbers:

Wagons, 72; men; 130; women, 65; children; 125; breadstuff, 69,420 lbs.; bacon, 40,200 lbs; powder, 1100 lbs.; lead, 2672 lbs.; guns, mostly rifles, 155; pistols, 104; cattle and horses, estimated at 710.

Chapter II.

Journey to the Great Blue-Earth River.[8]

. . . *May* 19.–An event occurred, which ought to be chronicled in due form in our journal of adventure. At 10 o'clock on the previous night, Mrs. Hall became the mother of twin boys. Dr. [Reuben P.] Rupert, the

---

6 Lilburn Williams Boggs had been governor of Missouri from 1836 to 1840. His letter about the Donner party appears in this volume.

7 William Henry Russell, a native of Kentucky but more recently from Missouri, was, like Thornton, a lawyer. Jacob Wright Harlan remembered Russell as "a large, portly gentleman. He was of rather dark complexion, and what hair he had was gray. He was a good talker."

8 The Big Blue River, rising in eastern Nebraska, is a tributary of the Kansas River.

attending physician, gave his own name to one of them, and the name of our worthy leader, Col. Wm. H. Russell, was given to the other. While we moved forward to a new encampment, Mrs. Hall and her husband, and a few friends remained behind to "hunt cattle," alleged to have strayed. Eleven wagons, belonging to James F. Reed, George Donner, Jacob Donner, and Mr. Hall, the latter containing the little fellows, came up to us where we had remained in camp on account of these interesting young strangers.[9]

A new census of our company was taken during the day, which resulted in showing that we had: Fighting men, 98; women, 50; wagons, 46; cattle, 350.–(Mercury at sunrise, 70°; sunset, 70°.–Calm)…

May 25.–We traveled until about the middle of the afternoon; but scarcely had we got our tents spread, when a tremendous storm of wind and rain came up, accompanied by vivid lightning and almost deafening thunder. The rain poured in torrents down the hill sides, and tumbled tumultuously into the streams below. The clouds at length passed away, the bright sun shone out again, and a remarkably beautiful rainbow appeared to complete a scene of unsurpassed loveliness.

After the storm had passed away, and the waters had left the hill side hard, and comparatively dry, I strolled along the road to enjoy the scene, when I came up with little Patty and her brother, children of one of our company. She was busied in calling the attention of little Tom to a variety of objects that seemed to please and delight him. At the moment I came up they were admiring a large butterfly, which, like us, had ventured out after the storm.

"You are a dear, sweet little girl," I said to Patty, as I approached them, and tenderly put my hand upon her cheek.

"Yes, and Tommy here is a dear, sweet little boy; so he is, isn't he? He is my dear little brother," she continued, affectionately, as she threw her arms around his neck and drew him nearer to her.

"Oh! you, Patty, you, do quit," said Tom, somewhat fretfully and impatiently, as he stumbled; "you almost threw me down. You are always a-huggin' me, so you are."

"May God bless the little girl," I exclaimed, "and bless both the children," I continued, as I remembered that in the greater interest which Patty's unselfishness had caused me to feel for her, I had for the moment lost sight of the boy.

---

9 Under the same date Edwin Bryant recorded, "We were joined to-day by nine wagons belonging to Mr. Reed and the Messrs. Donner, highly respectable and intelligent gentlemen, with interesting families. They were received into the company by a unanimous vote." *What I Saw in California* (1848; Lincoln: University of Nebraska Press, 1985), 46. According to Bryant, the twins were born the preceding morning, May 18.

What a simple yet touching instance was this of sisterly regard, and the absence of selfishness; and how eminently beautiful will be the piety of that interesting child, if in after years her heart should be given to the Saviour in a consecration of her life to his service. The words of the other, and the manner in which they were uttered, show the speaker to be a boy. He is a rough, boisterous little fellow, who loves Patty very much, but himself more. He evidently has no sort of objection to the affectionate caresses of his sister, but he does not like to be made to stub his toes. Patty's heart is so warm with love, and is so brimful of joy, that she does not stop to debate the question as to whether her brother may not possibly stumble a little; nor does she delay, until she has cleared the ground for her loving demonstration, and the bid him have a care to his feet, since she is about to be upon his neck. Tommy has not yet learned, in the language of one of the mottoes at the head of this chapter, that

> "They that do much themselves deny,
> Receive more blessings from the sky."

Nor indeed, has Patty. She has never made a nice calculation of how much she would receive in return for her love; and yet, if we may believe Tommy, she was "always a-huggin'" him, because "he is a dear, sweet little boy; so he is, isn't he?"...[10]

May 26.–In the evening, Ex-Governor Boggs, Mr. J. F. Reed, Mr. George Donner, and some others, including myself, convened in a tent, according to an appointment of a general meeting of the emigrants, with the design of preparing a system of laws for the purpose of preserving order, etc. We proposed a few laws, without, however, believing that they would possess much authority. Provision was made for the appointment of a court of arbitrators, to hear and decide disputes, and to try offenders against the peace and good order of the company.–(Mercury at sunrise 69°; sunset, 78°.)

Chapter III.

The Blue-Earth River Encampment.

. . . *May* 29.–Mrs. Keyes, the mother of Mrs. Reed, who had been for some time ill, died on the morning of this day. John Denton, an Englishman

---

10 These two children are almost certainly James F. Reed's daughter Martha Jane, called Patty, and son, Thomas Keyes, aged eight and three, respectively. Later events in the Sierra Nevada demonstrated Patty's devotion to her little brother.

from Sheffield, busied himself in preparing a decent slab of stone to put at her head, and in carving upon it a suitable inscription. A humble grave was dug under the spreading boughs of a venerable oak, about sixty or seventy yards from the wayside, and thither her remains were followed by a silent, thoughtful, and solemn company of emigrants, who were thus admonished that they were indeed pilgrims, hastening to a land "from whose bourne no traveler returns." After obtaining permission from Mrs. Reed, I requested the Rev. J. A. Cornwall to preach upon the occasion.[11] He delivered an impressive and eloquent sermon to us, as we sat around the grave, and under the green boughs of the spreading oak. The afflictive event was pointed out to us as one that should impress our minds and hearts with the fact, that is was a matter of the highest importance to us to seek for another and "better country," where there is no sickness or death.

I had no acquaintance with the deceased. She had been, indeed, confined to her bed, when her son-in-law, Mr. Reed, was making his arrangements for the journey. She could not, however, bear the thought of remaining behind.[12] A wagon had been arranged with reference to her comfort.[13] She had been carried to it in her bed, and had there remained until her spirit returned to God who gave it, and her body was laid in its silent grave in the wilderness. I was informed that her departure was peaceful and full of hope. The inscription upon the grave-stone, and upon the tree above it, is as follows: "MRS. SARAH KEYES, DIED MAY 29, 1846: *Aged* 70."[14]

---

11 Josephus Adamson Cornwall was a Cumberland Presbyterian minister, Margret Reed a devout Methodist.

12 According to Edwin Bryant, Sarah Keyes had intended to go no further than Fort Hall, where she hoped to meet her youngest son, Robert Cadden Keyes, who had left Springfield for Oregon in 1845. George McKinstry reported the same information in his diary; see Morgan, *Overland in 1846*, 208–9.

13 James F. Reed's family wagon, described much later as a "Pioneer palace car" by his daughter Virginia, has become a legend. Despite the popular perception that this wagon was enormous, contemporary sources refer only to the wagon's comforts and conveniences. Kristin Johnson, "The Pioneer Palace Car: Adventures in Western Mythmaking," *Crossroads* 5 (Summer 1994): 5–8.

14 This grave was noted by many later passersby. Decades after Sarah Keyes's death, family members attempted unsuccessfully to locate her grave. In the 1930s Utah historian Charles Kelly corresponded with John Ellenbecker of Marysville, Kansas, who believed he had identified the site. A gravestone thought to be that of Mrs. Keyes has been found near Marysville and the site where Ellenbecker located the grave rediscovered; Alan Feldhausen, personal communication.

Chapter IV.

Journey from the Blue-Earth River to Chimney Rock.

...*June 2.*–Twenty wagons, including mine–all for Oregon, except Mr. Clark's[15]–separated from the California wagons, and proceeded on in advance. The day was cool, and the way in many places very bad for short distances, being crossed by swails, the mud in which was so deep as to make it necessary to double teams. We traveled fifteen miles; and encamped about sundown upon a prairie, where we could not obtain wood for culinary purposes, nor any water, except from a shallow pond....

June 16.–...Road hunters do not hesitate to tell very many marvelous stories of their respective adventures–things they have actually seen; or, what is the same thing, they certainly will see.

Lansford W. Hastings, who, if an opinion may be formed of him from the many untruths contained in his "EMIGRANT'S GUIDE TO OREGON AND CALIFORNIA," is the Baron Munchausen of travelers in these countries,[16] says, at page 8 of his book, "Having been a few days among the buffalo" (they are not buffalo, but bison), "and their horses having become accustomed to these terrific scenes, even the *'green-horn'* is enabled not only to kill the buffalo with expertness, but he is also *frequently seen driving them to the encampment, with as much indifference as he used formerly to drive his domestic cattle about his own fields, in the land of his nativity.* Giving the buffalo rapid chase for a few minutes, they become so fatigued and completely exhausted that they are driven from place to place with as little difficulty as our common cattle. Both the grown buffalo and the calves are *very frequently* driven in this manner to the *encampment* and slaughtered."

It cannot be necessary to affirm that no respectable writer will make such an assertion, and that no man of truth will affirm that the statement is consistent with fact.[17]–(Mercury, at sunrise, 57°; sunset, 74°.)...

---

15 William Squire Clark became a noted early settler of San Francisco; Thornton interviewed Donner party survivors in his presence. Jacob Wright Harlan mentions Clark in his memoir, this volume.

16 Lansford Warren Hastings, a young lawyer from Mt. Vernon, Ohio, had traveled overland to Oregon in 1842. To encourage emigration to California, thus furthering his own political ambitions, Hastings painted the region's charms in glowing terms in his *Emigrants' Guide, to Oregon and California* (1845; Bedford, Mass.: Applewood Books, 1994). This work inspired many, including the Donners, Charles T. Stanton, and George W. Harlan, to head west in 1846. For Hastings's political maneuverings see Will Bagley's "Lansford Warren Hastings: Scoundrel or Visionary?" *Overland Journal* 12 (Spring 1994): 12–26.

17 James F. Reed did in fact perform the feat described. A fellow emigrant wrote, "Mr. Reid also shortly after came driving a fine buffalo bull, which he had

Chapter VI.

Journey from Fort Laramie to Independence Rock.

[*June* 28.]–...For the purpose of conciliating good-will, our party prepared a supper for all the Indians who then had lodges near the fort.
Among the chiefs, was one who showed us a certificate from L. W. Hastings, to the effect that this savage had saved his life at Independence Rock,
in 1842, by delivering him out of the hands of the Indians, who had there
seized him....[18]

June 30.–...Between 10 and 11 o'clock intelligence came to our little
camp that a large body of emigrants had arrived at Fort Laramie, after one
of their number, a Mr. Trimble, had been killed by the Pawnees; and that a
large number of Sioux Indians would probably arrive at our camp during
the day.[19] This determined us to break up camp without delay; and at 2
o'clock we were again *en route* among the Black Hills, which we had
entered soon after passing the large spring at 2 o'clock on the day
before....

July 19.–Sabbath.–...Near the close of a day of toil and discomfort, we
encamped on Little Sandy, which is a small stream of clear water, about
three feet deep, and forty or fifty feet wide, running with a swift current
over a sandy bottom, and finally discharging itself into the Colorado, or
Green River of the Gulf of California....

A large number of Oregon and California emigrants encamped at this
creek, among whom I may mention the following:–Messrs. West, Crab-
tree, Campbell, Boggs, Donners, and Dunbar. I had, at one time or
another, become acquainted with all of these persons in those companies,
and had traveled with them from Wokaruska [Wakarusa], and until subsequent divisions and subdivisions had separated us. We had often, since our
various separations, passed and repassed each other upon the road, and
had frequently encamped together by the same water and grass, as we did
now. In fact, the particular history of my own journey is the general history of theirs. This fact in mentioned now for reasons which will more
fully appear hereafter. I shall, after having noted the principal events of
our journey, again introduce the reader to some of these emigrants, for the

---

slightly wounded, as he would an ox, up to the wagons." Charles T. Stanton to
Sidney Stanton, July 12, 1846; in Morgan, *Overland in 1846,* 613.

18 Hastings described this incident in his *Emigrants' Guide,* 11–17.

19 Word of Trimble's death sent ripples of alarm through the emigrant trains and
was widely reported in western newspapers. Trimble had been member of the
company with which the Graves family traveled before they joined the Donner
party; see W. C. Graves, "Crossing the Plains in '46," in this volume.

purpose of enabling him to acquaint himself with the events connected with their journey from this place into Upper California. I shall, therefore, dismiss them here, with the remark, that the greater number of the Californians, and especially the companies in which George Donner, Jacob Donner, James F. Reed, and William H. Eddy, and their families traveled, here turned to the left, for the purpose of going by the way for Fort Bridges [Bridger], to meet L. W. Hastings, who had informed them, by a letter which he wrote, and forwarded from where the emigrant road leaves the Sweet Water, that he had explored a new route from California, which he had found to be much nearer and better that the old one, by the way of Fort Hall,[20] and the head waters of Ogden's [Humboldt] River, and that he would remain at Fort Bridges to give further information, and to conduct them through.

The Californians were generally much elated, and in fine spirits, with the prospect of a better and nearer road to the country of their destination. Mrs. George Donner was, however, an exception. She was gloomy, sad, and dispirited, in view of the fact, that her husband and others could think for a moment of leaving the old road, and confide in the statement of a man who of whom they knew nothing, but who was probably some selfish adventurer.[21]–(Mercury at sunrise, 46°; sunset, 52°.)

July 20.–The previous night having passed away cheerfully and pleasantly, we all resumed our journey; our California friends turning to the left, and we continuing along the right-hand road, over a country, the face of which was a brown sand–the granite detritus of the mountain in the vicinity–until 3 o'clock, when we encamped on an open, grassy plain, on the banks of Big Sandy, which is another tributary of the Green River. Blocks of granite, containing magnetic iron, were seen on both sides of our road. The escarpments along the creek showed a formation of party-colored sand. We had an abundance of good grass. Our fuel was drift-wood, *bois de vache* [buffalo chips], and artemisia [sagebrush]; the latter of which, burning with a quick and oily flame, made a very hot fire, and was always acceptable, when sufficiently abundant.–(Mercury at sunrise, 48°; sunset, 58°.)

---

20 Fort Hall, located on the Snake River about ten miles north of present-day Pocatello, Idaho, was established in 1834 to sell supplies to fur traders; like many other such forts, it became an important stop for overland emigrants.

21 This oft-cited presentiment of Tamsen Donner's may owe something to hindsight on Thornton's part.

VOLUME II....

Chapter VII.

Journey of a Party of California Emigrants in 1846 from Fort Bridger to the Sinks of Ogden's River.

Upon my arrival at the town of San Francisco [on November 10, 1847], I had the pleasure of receiving the friendly salutations and cordial greetings of many who had been my traveling companions in 1846. We had all commenced our journey together from the Wokaruska creek, west of the frontier settlements of Missouri, with my valued friend Col. Russell for our leader. In the divisions and subdivisions of the company which subsequently occurred, at the times and places noted in my journal, we were separated. Our respective companies, however, often traveled near to each other, and not unfrequently we encamped at the same grass and water. The reader, by turning back to my journal entries, under dates of July 21 and 22 [19 and 20], 1846, will see that these California emigrants, at that time, determined upon following Lansford W. Hastings, upon a "cut-off" into California. This man had left California, and proceeded as far as the eastern side of the Rocky Mountains, and encamped at a place where the Sweet Water breaks through a cañon, at the point where the emigrants leave that river to enter the South Pass. He had come out for the purpose of inducing the emigrants to follow him through a "cut-off" into California. After meeting some of the advanced companies, and sending forward a messenger with a letter to those in the rear, informing them that he had explored a new and much better road into California than the old one, he returned to Fort Bridger,[22] where he stated that he would remain until the California and Oregon emigrants should come up, when he would give a more particular description of his "cut-off."

The emigrants having all in time arrived at that place, Hastings assured them in the most solemn manner that the road over which he proposed to conduct them, was much nearer and better than the one via Fort Hall. He stated that there was an abundant supply of wood, water, and grass upon the whole line of the road, except one dry drive of thirty-five miles, or of

---

22 Located about 115 miles northeast of modern Salt Lake City, the fort had been established in 1843 by mountain man Jim Bridger. Stewart suggests that the fort's existence may have been threatened by the opening of the Greenwood (or Sublette) Cutoff, which bypassed the fort, in 1845.

forty at most; that they would have no difficult cañons to pass, and that the road was generally smooth, level, and hard.[23]

Upon meeting in California many of those who survived the dangers of that disastrous cut-off, some of them expressed a wish that I would embody the facts, and publish them to the world in connection with my own journal, as constituting an important part of the history of the journey of the emigration of that year to the Pacific coast.

The notes from which I write the history of the journey of that party, after our final separation at Sandy, were written in the presence of Mr. Clarke of San Francisco, as the facts were verbally communicated to me by survivors.

It is proper to state, likewise, that such was the character of many of the shocking and heart-sickening scenes of the journey, that the emigrants had at first determined that they would, as far as practicable, keep these occurrences from the gaze of the world. But those who went from the settlements of California to the relief of the emigrants, at the Mountain Camp, necessarily obtained a knowledge of many facts. These were published, on their return, in the California Star, and also others that were materially erroneous. The latter class of newspaper notices, together with a multitude of floating rumors, finally led to the opinion that a circumstantial and plain narrative of the events referred to should be given to the world.

The California Company, after parting, on the 22d August, 1840 [20th July, 1846], at Sandy, from the company in which I traveled, proceeded on their road to Bridger's trading post, where they arrived July 25th [27th]. They left that place on the 28th [31st], buoyant with hope, and filled with pleasing expectations of a speedy and happy termination of the toils and fatigues of travel. They continued traveling, without any circumstance of especial importance occurring, until August 3d [6th], at which time a letter from Lansford W. Hastings was found by them, at the first crossing of Weber river,[24] placed in the split of a stick, in such a situation as to call their attention to it. In this letter they were informed that the road down

---

23 Though Thornton states that all the emigrants had arrived at Fort Bridger, the Donner party—"those in the rear"—had not. They had received Hastings's message sent via Bonney, but arrived at the fort after Hastings had left. It was Bridger and his partner, Louis Vasquez, who passed on the false assurances about the cutoff, as it was to their advantage to encourage potential customers to take the route via their fort. On July 18 Edwin Bryant left letters at the fort warning friends coming along behind him against the cutoff, but his letters were never delivered; see Reed's "The Snowbound, Starved Emigrants of 1846," in this volume.

24 Near present-day Henefer, Utah.

the Weber river, over which the sixty-six[25] wagons led by Lansford W. Hastings had passed, had been found to be a very bad one, and expressing fears that their sixty-six wagons could not be gotten through the cañon leading into the valley of the Great Salt Lake, then in sight; and advising them to remain in camp until he could return to them, for the purpose of showing them a better road than that through the cañon of Weber river which here breaks through the mountains. The company, piloted by Hastings, did with great difficulty succeed in passing. In this letter, Hastings had indicated another road which he affirmed was much better; and by pursuing which they would avoid the cañon. Messrs. Reed, Stanton, and Pike then went forward, for the purpose of exploring the contemplated new route.[26] In eight **[four]** days, Mr. Reed returned, reporting the practicability of the way, and that Messrs. Stanton and Pike were lost. These eight days thus spent materially contributed in bringing upon them the disasters which ensued. Upon receiving this report, they dispatched a party in search of Messrs. Stanton and Pike, and resumed their journey.

The company at that time consisted of the following persons:–J. F. Reed, wife, and four children; George Donner, wife, and five children; Jacob Donner, wife, and seven children; Patrick Brinn [Breen], wife and seven children; William Pike, wife and two children; William Foster, wife and one child; Lewis Kiesburg [Keseberg], wife, and one child; Mrs. [Levinah W.] Murphy, a widow woman, and five children; William McCutcheon [McCutchen], wife, and one child; W[illiam]. H[enry]. Eddy, wife, and two children; Noah James; Patrick Dolan; Samuel Shoemaker, John Denton; C. F. [T.] Stanton; Milton [Milford, called Milt] Elliot[t]; —— [James] Smith; —— Hardcoop; Joseph Rianhard [Rheinhard]; Augustus Spitzer; John Baptiste [Trudeau]; —— Antoine [or Antonio]; —— Herring [Walter Herron]; —— Hallerin [Luke Halloran]; Charles Burger; and Baylis Williams.[27]

On the second day after resuming their journey they came to a grove of willows, and quaking asp, through which their way led. Here they were

---

25 Estimates of the number of wagons preceding the Donner party on Hastings Cutoff range from sixty to eighty.

26 The three went ahead to overtake Hastings and get his advice about an alternate route into the Salt Lake Valley. The identity of the third member of this party has been a matter of some confusion–Reed later stated that he went with Stanton and McCutchen, but a letter published in the *California Star* on February 13, 1847, confirms that it was Pike, not McCutchen, who went. Reed returned to the mountains with Hastings, who pointed out a likely route, and Reed blazed the trail back to the wagons. See Reed's memoir in this volume.

27 Thornton has omitted a Keseberg child, the Wolfingers, and Eliza Williams. See the Roster at the end of this volume.

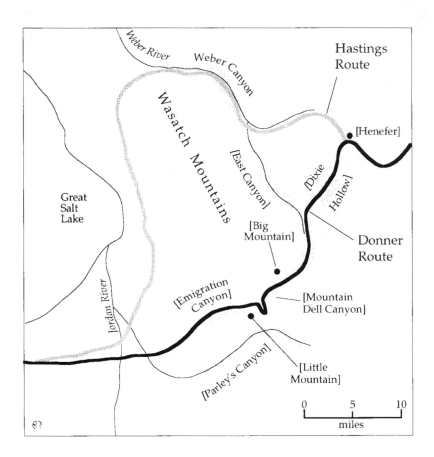

The Wasatch Mountains. Cartography by Rose Ann Tompkins

compelled to open a road, which occupied one day. They again continued their journey, and passing over some very difficult bluffs, entered a hollow leading into the Utah [Jordan] River valley, and through which they were under the necessity of cutting eight miles of very thick timber and close-tangled underbrush.[28] This difficult labor occupied eight days. On the sixth day of their being thus employed, Mr. [Franklin] W[ard]. Graves, wife, and eight children, and his son-in-law Jay Fosdick and wife, and John Snyder, came up with them.[29] On the ninth day they left their encampment, and traveled into an opening [Parleys Canyon] which they supposed led out into the Utah river valley. Here Messrs. Stanton and Pike, who had been lost from the time Mr. Reed had gone forward with them to explore, were found by the party they had sent to hunt for them. These men reported the impracticability of passing down the valley in which they then were;[30] and they advised their companions to pass over a low range of hills [Little Mountain] into a neighboring valley [Emigration Canyon]. This they did. Here they worked five days in cutting through the timber. On the seventh day they came out of the timber into a prairie, which led down to a cañon opening into the valley of the Utah.[31] The cañon being impracticable as a

---

28 Thornton's geography and chronology cannot be reconciled in this paragraph. The amount of time given suggests the party's entry into Dixie Hollow and the roadmaking up Big Mountain, but Dixie Hollow is not part of the Jordan River drainage. Thornton may possibly be describing the descent of Big Mountain ("very difficult bluffs") down Mountain Dell Canyon (the "hollow leading into the Utah River valley"), but the amount of time stated does not agree with the amount of terrain that the emigrants would have had to travel.

29 The "sixth day" would have been August 16, according to Morgan; in 1871 Reed recollected that the Graveses came up on the day he broke an axletree, an event which he recorded on August 18. According to three survivors of the Graves family, however, they overtook the Donner party while it was encamped on the Weber River waiting for Reed, who returned on August 10. See Eliza W. Farnham, "Narrative of the Emigration of the Donner Party to California, in 1846," an excerpt from *California, Indoors and Out;* W. C. Graves, "Crossing the Plains in '46"; and Edna Maybelle Sherwood, "Tragic Story of the Donner Party"; all in this volume.

30 If Reed had gone up Parleys Canyon with Hastings, as Morgan has suggested in *West from Fort Bridger,* he would not have needed Stanton's and Pike's report that the canyon was impassable; see Reed's memoir, this volume, note 9.

31 Thornton's terminology is confusing. He uses *valley* for *canyon*, while his *cañon* refers to a narrow, steep-sided passage. To translate, the Donner party traveled down Emigration Canyon to its mouth, which they found blocked by heavy timber where the stream curves around Donner Hill jutting into the canyon from the south. Rather than chop down any more trees, the party elected to double-team the wagons up the hill. John Breen describes this event in Farnham's account, as does Virginia Reed Murphy in her memoir, both in this volume. In

wagon way, they doubled teams and got their wagons to the top of the hill [Donner Hill], from which there was a gradual descent into the valley. They encamped in this; and resuming their journey on the next morning, struck the trail of the company in advance, at the crossing of the [Jordan] river which flows from the Utah Lake into the Great Salt Lake. They were thus occupied thirty days in traveling forty miles.[32] On September 3d [**August 24th**], they again resumed their journey, pursuing their way around the south side of the Salt Lake, and along the trail of the company in advance.

The valley of the Utah river is about thirty-five miles long. One of the emigrants expressed to me the opinion, that as a happy abode for man, it surpassed in beauty, fertility, and every thing that can render a spot of earth desirable, any country that he had seen or expected to see. It is well supplied with streams of clear water, filled with salmon-trout. The atmosphere is remarkably pure and healthful, and the whole face of the country is covered with a heavy coat of the most nutritious grass. It is surrounded by high and rugged mountains, in the bosom of which it reposes in a calm and quiet beauty, that invites the weary and worn traveler to stay his wanderings and to enjoy, in the seclusion and loveliness of the scene, the happiness which he has sought in vain amidst the crowded marts of commerce or the fashion and dissipation of cities. The peaceful stillness and loveliness of this most interesting valley, and the happiness to which it seemed to invite, strangely contrasted with the suffering of body and the anguish of spirit which that devoted party subsequently endured.

In listening to the description of this valley, as thus substantially given to me by the emigrants, I was strongly reminded of my own emotions and feelings when, after passing over a long and cheerless waste, I suddenly emerged from sands and artemisia into a beautiful little valley of bubbling springs, and verdure, and flowers. At such a time, it has appeared far more interesting and lovely, from the striking contrast, then it would have done, had I met with it in a country of general fertility. On these occasions I have often experienced a cloud of sadness to come over my spirit, as I reflected that the leaves around me must wither, and the flowers, that modestly turned up their beautiful faces to the sun, must fall silently and unobserved. The beauty of the place, the penciling of the leaves, the

---

July 1847 the Mormon pioneers followed the Donner party's route down the canyon and cleared the obstruction after only four hours' work. The Donner party's trailblazing is commemorated by a large bronze plaque on the This is the Place Monument near the mouth of Emigration Canyon in Salt Lake City.

32 According to James F. Reed, it took eighteen days to travel thirty miles; he recorded these figures in his diary and supplied them to J. H. Merryman, who repeated them in his *Illinois Journal* article. W. C. Graves remembered that it took much longer; see his memoir in this volume.

sparking of the fountains, the rippling of the streams, and the whole aspect of the surrounding scenery of nature rejoicing in her beauty, yet induced within my mind saddened emotions, as I reflected how evanescent were all these varied expressions of the beautiful and the real. The interest I have thus felt in all this, was but a tribute of grief and affection, eminently befitting and proper in one whom Nature had never deserted in adversity, but had a thousand times whispered in his ear the promise of a new and better condition of being, in a world not subjected to the decree of the fell destroyer, where the fields are ever fresh and verdant, and the flowers never fade.

It is in this valley that the Mormons have made a settlement and laid out a town, about four miles above the emigrant road.

The Mormons, upon being expelled from Nauvoo, in 1846, made a large settlement at Council Bluffs, upon the Missouri river. This is designed rather for a place of outfit and preparation for the journey across the Rocky Mountains, than as a permanent settlement. A party, consisting of about three hundred and fifty, left Council Bluffs very early in the year 1847, for the purpose of exploring the Salt Lake country. In June they were followed by about fifteen hundred souls, with provisions and supplies for eighteen months. They purpose to plant and sow crops for 1848; and if the climate and soil should be found favorable to the plan of making a permanent settlement at this place, they will establish one here, for the purpose of making it a half-way or stopping place for persons traveling from the Atlantic to the Pacific. Many thousands are expected, during each succeeding year, to settle at this point.

So soon as a settlement shall be established at this place, they propose to explore the mountains, for the purpose of obtaining minerals. They also contemplate opening a new road from the Salt Lake into California. They measured the distance from the Council Bluffs to the Salt Lake, and found it to be eleven hundred miles. The distance from the Salt Lake to San Francisco, now estimated at seven hundred miles, they believe can be diminished to five hundred.[33]

On the evening of September 3d [**August 24th**], the emigrants encamped on the southeast side of the Great Salt Lake. On the morning of the next day, they resumed their journey, and at about 9 o'clock commenced passing round the point of a mountain which here runs down to the beach of the lake. This occupied the entire day. Here Mr. Reed broke an axletree, and they had to go a distance of fifteen miles to obtain timber

---

33 Neither the Mormons nor anyone else have been able to reduce the distance; Salt Lake City remains 601 miles in a direct line from San Francisco and about 735 miles by road.

to repair it.[34] By working all night, Mr. Eddy and Samuel Shoemaker completed the repair for Mr. Reed. About 4 o'clock, P.M., Mr. Hallerin, from St. Joseph, died of consumption, in Mr. George Donner's wagon.[35] About 8 o'clock, this wagon (which had stopped) came up, with the dead body of their fellow-traveler. He died in the exercise of a humble trust and confidence in the ability and willingness of the blessed Redeemer to save his soul. The melancholy event filled all hearts with sadness, and with feelings of solemnity, they committed his body to its silent and lonely grave in the wilderness. Nor did they seek to disguise the tears that silently coursed down many a care-worn face, as they took their last adieu of the lost fellow-traveler. The day of the 5th was spent, with the exception of a change of camp, in committing the body of their friend to the dust. They buried him at the side of an emigrant who had died in the advance company.[36] The deceased gave his property, some $1500, to Mr. George Donner.

On September 6th [August 27th], they resumed their journey, and after dark encamped at the place to which they gave the name of the Twenty Wells. The name was suggested by the circumstance of there being at this place that number of natural wells, filled to the very surface of the earth with the purest cold water. They sounded some of them with lines of more than seventy feet, without finding bottom. They varied from six inches to nine feet in diameter. None of them overflowed; and, what is most extraordinary, the ground was dry and hard near the very edge of the water, and upon taking water out, the wells would instantly fill again.[37]

---

34 As mentioned in note 29 above, Reed broke an axletree on August 18, while the company was still in the mountains. This accident near the Great Salt Lake is not recorded in his diary, but the circumstantial detail of having to travel fifteen miles for wood lends credibility to Thornton's statement; apparently there were two accidents.

35 Luke Halloran, from County Galway, Ireland, opened a general store in St. Joseph in the fall of 1845. Only a few months later he was "very much indisposed, and desirous of going this Spring to the Rocky Mountains" to recover his health. Halloran was unable to sell his business and left his affairs in the hands of a friend, John Corby, who later administered his estate.

36 The emigrant near whom Halloran was buried was John Hargrave of the Harlan-Young party; see Jacob Wright Harlan's memoir in this volume. The exact location of their graves in Tooele Valley is uncertain. Halloran was given a Masonic funeral, conducted by James F. Reed.

37 These wells were located in present-day Grantsville, Utah. Nearly a century and a half of human activity has reduced them to seeps or obliterated them entirely. Grantsville is also the home of the Donner-Reed Memorial Museum, whose exhibits include artifacts brought in from the Salt Desert; there is no proof, however, that any of them are from the Donner party. The museum, located at 97 North Cooley Street, is open by appointment.

On the morning of the 7th **[August 28th]**, they left camp; and after making a long and hard drive, encamped in a large and beautiful meadow, abundantly supplied with the very best grass. Here they found a number of wells, differing in no respect from those just mentioned. Here they found a letter from Lansford W. Hastings, informing them that it would occupy two days and nights of hard driving to reach the next water and grass. They consequently remained in camp on the 8th **[August 29th]**, to rest and recruit their cattle. Having done this, and cut grass to carry on the way, they resumed their journey at daylight on the morning of September 9th **[August 30th]**, with many apprehensions, and at about ten o'clock A.M., of the 12th, Mr. Eddy and some others succeeded, after leaving his wagons twenty miles back, in getting his team across the Great Salt Plain, to a beautiful spring at the foot of a mountain on the west side of the plain,[38] and distant eighty miles from their camp of the 7th and 8th. On the evening of the 12th, just at dark, Mr. Reed came up to them, and informed them that his wagons and those of the Messrs. Donner had been left about forty miles in the rear, and that the drivers were trying to bring the cattle forward to the water. After remaining about an hour, he started back to meet the drivers with the cattle, and to get his family. Mr. Eddy accompanied him back five miles, with a bucket of water for an ox of his that had become exhausted, in consequence of thirst, and had lain down. Mr. Reed met the drivers ten miles from the spring, coming forward with the cattle. He continued on, and the drivers came into camp about midnight, having lost all of Mr. Reed's team after passing him. The Messrs. Donner got to water, with a part of their teams, at about 2 o'clock, A.M., of September 13th **[3rd]**. Mr. Eddy started back at daylight on the morning of the 13th, and at dawn of day on the 14th **[4th]**, he brought up Mrs. Reed and children, and his wagon.[39] On the afternoon of the 14th **[6th]**, they started back with Mr. Reed and Mr. Graves, for the wagons of the Messrs. Donner and Reed; and brought them up with horses and mules, on the evening of the 15th **[7th]**.[40]

---

38 Donner Spring, at the foot of Pilot Peak, is located on the privately owned TL Bar Ranch north of Wendover, Utah. In 1994 the Utah Crossroads Chapter of the Oregon-California Trails Association (OCTA) placed a fence around the spring and erected interpretive panels. The ranch can be reached by taking Exit 4 off Interstate 80, east of Wendover, and following a dirt road north about twenty-three miles.

39 Reed family members report, however, that it was Jacob Donner who brought them to the spring.

40 Accounts of the Great Salt Lake Desert crossing are understandably confused; see also the memoirs of James F. Reed and Virginia Reed Murphy in this volume.

It is impossible to describe the dismay and anguish with which that perilous and exhausting drive filled the stoutest hearts. Many families were completely ruined. They were yet in a country of hostile Indians, far from all succor, betrayed by one of their own countrymen. They could not tell what was the character of the road yet before them, since the man in whose veracity they reposed confidence, had proved himself so utterly unworthy of it. To retreat across the desert to Bridger was impossible. There was no way left to them, but to advance; and this they now regarded as perilous in the extreme. The cattle that survived were exhausted and broken down; but to remain there was to die. Feeble and dispirited, therefore, they slowly resumed their journey.

On this drive thirty-six head of working cattle were lost, and the oxen that survived were greatly injured. One of Mr. Reed's wagons was brought to camp; and two, with all they contained, were buried in the plain.[41] George Donner lost one wagon. Kiesburg also lost a wagon.[42] The atmosphere was so dry upon the plain, that the wood-work of all the wagons shrank to a degree that made it next to impossible to get any of them through.

The name of this place indicates its character to some respects, and I need not now detain the reader with a description of it; but I can not forbear mentioning an extraordinary optical illusion related to me by one of the emigrants. They saw themselves, their wagons, their teams, and the dogs with them, in very many places, while crossing this plain, repeated many times in all the distinctness and vividness of life. Mr. Eddy informed me that he was surprised to see twenty men all walking in the same direction in which he was traveling. They all stopped at the same time, and the motions of their bodies corresponded. At length he was astounded with the discovery that they were men whose features and dress were like his own, and that they were imitating his own motions. When he stood still, they stood still, and when he advanced, they did so also. In short, they were living and moving images of himself, and of his actions. Subsequently he saw the caravan repeated in the same extraordinary and startling manner.

---

41 It is unlikely that the exhausted emigrants would have taken the time for such a procedure, which would have been rendered difficult, if not impossible, by the deep, sticky mud under the desert's crust.

42 Over the years, several individuals have investigated the remains of five wagons abandoned in the Salt Desert; see Charles Kelly, *Salt Desert Trails* (1930, rev. 1996); Walter M. Stookey, *Fatal Decision* (1950); and Bruce R. Hawkins and David B. Madsen, *Excavation of the Donner-Reed Wagons* (1990). Researchers have often assumed that all these vehicles must have belonged to the Donner party, but later emigrant companies also reported leaving wagons behind in the desert; see Robert K. Hoshide, "Salt Desert Trails Revisited," *Crossroads* 5 (Spring 1994): 5–8.

Mr. Eddy having ascended the side of the mountain that commanded a view of the plain below, saw the morning spread out upon the hills, and, at length, beheld the sun arise above the plain, and cover it with splendor and glory. The mind can not conceive, much less the tongue express, the ravishing beauty of the scene that instantly kindled into a magnificence, grandeur, and loveliness unequaled–cloud-formed masses of purple ranges, bordered with the most brilliant gold, lay piled above the eastern mountains. Peaks were seen shooting up into narrow lines of crimson drapery, and festooning of greenish orange, the whole being covered with a blue sky of singular beauty and transparency. All the colors of the prism bordered the country before him, and ten thousand hues of heavenly radiance spread and diffused themselves over it, as the sun continued to ascend. The king of day seemed to rise from his throne, and cast upon his footstool his gorgeous robes of light, sparking with unnumbered gems. Here nature appeared to have collected all her glittering beauties together in one chosen place.

Having yoked some loose cows, as a team for Mr. Reed, they broke up their camp on the morning of September 16th [10th], and resumed their toilsome journey, with feelings which can be appreciated by those only who have traveled the road under somewhat similar circumstances. On this day they traveled six miles, encountering a very severe snow storm. About 3 o'clock, P.M., they met Milton Elliot and William Graves, returning from a fruitless effort to find some cattle that had got off. They informed them that they were then in the immediate vicinity of a spring [Hall Spring], at which commenced another dry drive of forty miles. They encamped for the night, and at dawn of day of September 17th [11th], they resumed their journey, and at 4 o'clock, A.M., of the 18th [12th] they arrived at water and grass,[43] some of their cattle having perished, and the teams which survived being in a very enfeebled condition. Here the most of the little property which Mr. Reed still had, was buried, or *cached,* together with that of others. As the term *cache* will frequently occur, I ought to remark that it is used for what is hidden. *Cacher,* the verb, is equivalent *to conceal.* Here, Mr. Eddy, proposed putting his team to Mr. Reed's wagon, and letting Mr. Pike have his wagon, so that the three families could be taken on. This was done. They remained in camp during the day of the 18th to complete these arrangements, and to recruit their exhausted cattle.

What is the cause of the sterility and aridness of this region, and also of much of the country between the Mississippi and Middle Oregon, is a question that will never, perhaps, be fully answered. It is a remarkable fact, however, that all such districts of country are destitute of timber. And Humboldt has almost demonstrated that the streams of a country fail in

---

43 Big Spring, on the Johnson Ranch in Elko County, Nevada.

proportion to the destruction of timber. If the streams fail the seasons will continue to be worse, because of their becoming each year more dry. It has been observed by the old settlers of a country, that water-courses have failed as the forest have been cleared away. Humboldt, in speaking of the valley of Aragu, in Venezuela says that the lake receded as agriculture advanced, until fine plantations were established on its banks. The desolating wars that swept over the country after the separation of the province from Spain, arrested the process of clearing. The trees again grew up, with a rapidity known only to the tropics, and the waters of the lake again rose, and inundated the low plantations.

Early on the morning of Sept. 19th [16th], the emigrants broke up their encampment, and passing over a low range of mountains [East Humboldt Range], came down into the head of a most beautiful and fertile valley [Ruby Valley], well supplied with water and grass. They encamped on the west side of this valley. They gave to it the name of the Valley of the Fifty Springs, the name being suggested by that number being here found. They encamped by one of them, situated in the centre of a cone about ten feet high.[44] The water rose to the top, but did not flow over. Many of the springs were hot, some warm, and many cool, and slightly acid. They saw hundreds of Indians, who were friendly, and seemed never before to have seen a white man. Here were great numbers of antelopes and Rocky Mountain sheep, which they had no difficulty in killing. This valley is destitute of timber, and is about fifteen miles wide.

Early on the morning of the 20th [17th], they continued their journey, and traveling about fifteen miles down the valley in a southerly direction, encamped at night near good grass and water. They proceeded down this valley three days, making about fifty miles of travel. The valley, however, still continued to extend south, beyond the reach of their vision, and presenting the same general appearance.

On the morning of Sept. 23d [21st], they left the valley of the Fifty Springs, and crossing over a low range of mountains [Ruby Mountains], came into a valley [Huntington Valley] of great beauty and fertility. Crossing this valley, which was here seven miles wide, and finding water, they again encamped. In all these valleys, there are no springs on their eastern sides. The water being uniformly found breaking out at the foot of the mountains, upon the western side.

They had been traveling in a southerly direction for many days but on the morning of the 24th [22nd], they commenced traveling due north. This they continued to do three days, following the tracks of the wagons in

---

44 This description suggests Mound Springs; if that is the case, however, Thornton's informant has transposed events—the springs are about twenty miles east of Ruby Valley.

advance. They then turned a little west of north, and traveled two days, so that in nine days' travel they made but about thirty miles westward.

On the night of the 28th [24th], they encamped at the head of a cañon [South Fork of the Humboldt] leading into the valley of Mary's or Ogden's [Humboldt] river. Here they saw large bodies of Indians in a state of perfect nudity. They hovered around in the vicinity, but did not come into camp.

On the morning of the 29th [25th], they entered the cañon, and traveling about eight miles, found, at 11 o'clock, P.M., a place sufficiently large to admit of an encampment out of the water.

On the 20th [30th] [26th], they pursued their way down the cañon, and after traveling eight miles, came out into the valley of Mary's river, at night, and encamped on the bank of the stream, having struck the road leading from Fort Hall.[45] Here some Indians came to camp, and informed them by signs, that they were yet distant about two hundred miles from the sinks of that river.

Chapter VIII.

Journey of the California Emigrants from Ogden's River to the East Side of the Sierra Nevada.

On the morning of October 1st [September 27th], they resumed their journey, and traveled along the usual route down Ogden's river, and encamped that evening at some hot springs [Emigrant Springs], at the foot of a high range of hills.

On the morning of the 2d [28th], they commenced passing over these hills. About 11 o'clock, an Indian, who spoke a little English, came to them, to whom they gave the name of Thursday, on account of their believing that to be the day; although at the time they were inclined to believe that they had lost one day in their calculation of time. About 4 o'clock, P.M., another came to them, who also spoke a little English. He frequently used the words, "jee," "who," and "huoy;" thereby showing that he had been with previous emigrants. They traveled all that day, and at dark encamped at a spring about half way down the side of the mountain. A fire broke out in the grass, soon after the camp fires had been kindled, which would have consumed three of the wagons, but for the assistance of these

---

45 As the crow flies, the distance from the head of the canyon to the Humboldt is only about half the length reported here, but the route is so rugged and tortuous that Thornton's informant may be excused the exaggeration; Reed described it as "a very rough Cannon a perfect Snake trail." Hastings Cutoff rejoined the California Trail about seven miles southwest of modern Elko, Nevada.

two Indians. The Indians were fed, and after the evening meal they lay down by one of the fires, but rose in the night, stealing a fine shirt and a yoke of oxen from Mr. Graves.

On the evening of October 5th [4th] [1st], the emigrants again encamped on Ogden's river, after a hard and exhausting drive. During the night the Indians stole a horse from Mr. Graves.[46]

On the morning of October 5th, they broke up their camp, and the caravan proceeded on its way. Mr. Eddy went out hunting antelope, and spent the forenoon in this manner, being frequently shot at by the Indians. At noon he came up with the company, which had stopped to take some refreshments, at the foot of a very high and long sand-hill, covered with rocks at the top. At length they commenced ascending the hill. All the wagons had been taken up but Mr. Reed's, Mr. Pike's, and one of Mr. Graves', the latter driven by John Snyder. Milton Elliot, who was Mr. Reed's driver, took Mr. Eddy's team, which was on Mr. Reed's wagon, and joined it to Mr. Pike's team. The cattle of this team, being unruly, became entangled with that of Mr. Graves', driven by Snyder; and a quarrel ensued between him and Elliot. Snyder at length commenced quarreling with Mr. Reed, and made some threats of whipping him, which threats he seemed about to attempt executing. Mr. Reed then drew a knife, without, however, attempting to use it, and told Snyder that he did not wish to have any difficulty with him. Snyder told him that he would whip him, "any how;" and turning the butt of his whip, gave Mr. Reed a severe blow upon the head, which cut it very much. As Reed was in the act of dodging the blow, he stabbed Snyder a little below the collar-bone, cutting off the first rib, and driving the knife through the left lung. Snyder after this struck Mrs. Reed a blow upon the head, and Mr. Reed two blows upon the head, the last one bringing him down upon his knees. Snyder expired in about fifteen minutes.[47] Mr. Reed, although the blood was running down over his face and shoulders from his own wounds, manifested the greatest anguish of spirit, and threw the knife away from him into the river.[48] Although Mr.

---

46 Graves's losses to the Indians are confirmed by two independent sources, the contemporary Miller-Reed diary and the later memoir of W. C. Graves, a striking concordance of minor details.

47 Not surprisingly, the fight was an issue of great controversy among the Donner party survivors who corresponded with McGlashan, and hostility between the Reed and Graves factions is evident in letters written thirty years later. McGlashan accepted the version essentially as told here. Despite having acted in self-defense, Reed was haunted by Snyder's death; for years he maintained, in public at least, the half-truth that he had merely gone ahead for supplies.

48 Researchers have long debated the fight's location. McGlashan wrote that it took place at Gravelly Ford, a few miles east of Beowawe, Nevada, but this is

Reed was thus compelled to do as he did, the occurrence produced much feeling against him; and in the evening Kiesburg proposed to hang him. To this, however, he was probably prompted by a feeling of resentment, produced by Mr. Reed having been mainly instrumental in his expulsion from one of the companies, while on the South Platte, for grossly improper conduct.[49] Mr. Eddy had two six-shooters, two double-barreled pistols, and a rifle; Milton Elliot had one rifle, and a double-barreled shot gun; and Mr. Reed had one six-shooter, and a brace of double-barreled pistols, and a rifle. Thus Mr. Reed's comrades were situated, and they determined that he should not die. Mr. Eddy, however, proposed that Mr. Reed should leave the camp. This was finally agreed to, and he accordingly left the next morning; not, however, before he had assisted in committing to the grave the body of the unhappy young man.

On the morning of October 6th, they quitted the wretched scene of mortal strife, and in the evening encamped on Ogden's river.

Leaving camp on the morning of the 7th, they proceeded on until about eleven o'clock, when they found a letter from Mr. Reed, informing them of a battle between one of the advanced companies and the Indians. On the

obviously based on a misreading of W. C. Graves's memoir. Several alternative sites have been suggested, but the most likely one is Iron Point near Golconda, about seventy-five miles west of Beowawe.

49 As a result of his Donner party experiences, Louis Keseberg earned an unenviable reputation. The exact nature of the impropriety referred to here is uncertain, but Keseberg was remembered by several Donner party survivors as a wifebeater.

George R. Stewart, however, gives another reason, based on the memoir of Antonio B. Rabbeson, who had known "Boonhelm the Cannibal among the Donner party" on the plains. "Boonhelm" and another German had stripped the buffalo robe from the deceased occupant of a Sioux burial scaffold, thereby leaving the entire company open to retaliation by the Indians. The culprits were forced to restore the robe, but Rabbeson does not mention that they were banished from the train. In 1858 "Boonhelm" visited Olympia, Washington, and boasted in a local saloon that "human liver was the best meat he ever ate." Rabbeson heard a rumor that "Boonhelm" had been killed in the 1860s in eastern Washington. Antonio B. Rabbeson, Growth of Towns, Bancroft MS P-B 17, Bancroft Library, University of California, Berkeley.

The identification of Keseberg as "Boonhelm" is fraught with difficulty. If Keseberg had been one of the Germans involved in the incident, Rabbeson may simply have confused the names, but Keseberg is not known to have visited Washington; then again, "Boonhelm" may have been mistaken for Keseberg and made the most of it by claiming to be the notorious maneater. Whatever the case, without confirmation Stewart's identification is open to question.

forenoon of this day, a number of arrows were shot at Mr. Eddy and Mr. Pike, while out hunting for game, which the reduced amount of their provisions had by this time made it necessary to seek. Upon arriving at their evening encampment, they found that Hardcoop, a Belgian, who had given out, and had been carried in Kiesburg's wagon for several days, was missing. Kiesburg professed not to know what had become of him, but suspecting that there was some wrong committed, a man was sent back upon a horse, for the old man. He was found about five miles in the rear. Hardcoop stated that Kiesburg had put him out of the wagon to perish.

On the morning of Oct. 8, they *cached* a part of Mr. Eddy's tools and clothing, and Mr. Reed's wagon, and procured a lighter wagon of Mr. Graves.[50] At about nine o'clock they started. In about half an hour Hardcoop came to Mr. Eddy, and informed him that Kiesburg had again put him out of the wagon—that he was an old man, being more than sixty years of age, and in addition to the infirmities usually attendant upon one of his advanced years, was sick and worn down by the toils and hardships of the way; and he concluded by requesting Mr. Eddy to carry him in his wagon, as it was utterly impossible for him to travel on foot. Mr. Eddy replied that they were then in the sand, and if he could in some way go forward until they got out, he would do what he could. He told me that he shuddered at the thought of seeing him left to perish by the way; and that he knew that the picture of his bones bleaching in the wilderness would haunt his memory to the latest day of his life. Hardcoop replied that he would make an effort. The emigrants traveled on until night. As soon as they got into camp, inquiry was make for Hardcoop. Some boys who had been driving cattle stated that they had seen him last sitting under a large bush of sage, or artemisia, exhausted and completely worn out. At this time his feet had swollen until they burst. Mr. Eddy, having the guard during the fore part of the night, built a large fire on the side of the hill, to guide Hardcoop to the camp, if it was possible for him to come up. Milton Elliot had the guard during the latter part of the night, and he kept up the fire for the same purpose. The night was very cold; but when morning dawned, the unhappy Hardcoop did not come up. Mrs. Reed, Milton Elliot, and Mr. Eddy then went to Kiesburg, and besought him to return for the old man. This, Kiesburg, in a very heartless and inhuman manner, refused to do. No other persons, excepting Patrick Brinn and Mr. Graves having horses, upon which he could be carried, they then applied to Patrick Brinn, who replied that it was impossible, and that he must perish. Application was then made to Graves, who said that he would not kill his horses to save the life of

---

50 A minor detail confirmed by Virginia Reed in a letter dated May 16, 1847: "in 2 or 3 days after pa left we had cash our wagon and take Mr graves wagon." Morgan, *Overland in 1846,* 282.

Hardcoop, and that he might die; and, in great anger, requested that he might not be troubled any more upon the subject. Milton Elliot, William Pike, and Mr. Eddy then proposed to go back on foot and carry him up, but the company refused to wait. Being in an Indian country, they were compelled to go forward with their traveling companions. They arrived at the place where Applegate's cut-off leaves the Ogden's river road,[51] about 11 o'clock, A.M., of this day (Oct 9); and having halted for the purpose of resting and taking a little refreshment, they again sought to induce Brinn and Graves to let them have horses to go back for the unfortunate Hardcoop: the proposal was again violently repulsed. Thus disappointed and defeated in every effort, they were, at last, under the dreadful necessity of relinquishing every hope, and of leaving their aged and exhausted fellow-traveler to die a most miserable death. He was from Antwerp, in Belgium—was a cutler by trade, and had a son and daughter in his native city. He had come to the United States for the purpose of seeing the country. He owned a farm near Cincinnati, Ohio, and intended, after visiting California, to go back to Ohio, sell his farm, and return to Antwerp, for the purpose of spending with his children the evening of his days.

Proceeding from their 11 o'clock halt, they arrived at a bed of deep, loose sand about 4 o'clock, P.M., and did not succeed in crossing it until 4 o'clock in the morning of Oct. 10, when they halted upon the place where Mr. Salle[e], who had been killed by the Indians, had been buried. His body had been dug up by the savages, and his bones, which had been picked by wolves, were bleaching in the sun.[52] Here they *cached* another wagon, and at this place all of Graves' horses were stolen. At 10 o'clock they drove on, and encamped at night on Ogden's river, with scarcely any grass for their cattle, the water being very bad.

On the morning of the 11th George Donner, Jacob Donner, and Wolfinger lost eighteen head of cattle. Graves, also, had a cow stolen by Indians. They encamped on the night of the 11th on a small spot of very poor grass. The water here, also was deficient in quantity and bad in quality. Brinn had a fine mare die in the mud. He asked Mr. Eddy to help him get her out. Mr. Eddy referred him to poor Hardcoop, and refused. Several cattle had arrows shot at them during the night, but none of them died in consequence.

On the morning of Oct. 12, the emigrants resumed their journey. One of Mr. Eddy's oxen gave out during the day, and they left him. At 12

---

51 The Applegate Cutoff left the California Trail in the vicinity of present-day Imlay, Nevada.

52 The Indians disinterred Sallee several times; Jacob Wright Harlan was one of those who reported having to rebury him.

o'clock at night they encamped at the sinks of Ogden's river.[53] At daylight on the morning of the 13th they drove their cattle to grass, and put them under a guard. The guard came in to breakfast, and in their absence the Indians killed twenty-one head, including the whole of Mr. Eddy's team, except one ox; and the whole of Wolfinger's except one. Wolfinger wished to *cache* his goods at the sinks, but the company refused to wait. Rianhard and Spitzer, who were traveling with him, remained behind to assist him. Three days afterward the two former came up to the company at Truckee river, and said that the Indians came down from the hills upon them, and after killing Wolfinger, drove them from the wagons, which they burned, after taking the goods out. Wolfinger had a considerable amount of money. I was informed by Mr. Eddy that George Donner, with whom Rianhard subsequently traveled, told him that Wolfinger had not died as stated—that this fact he learned from a confession made by Rianhard a short time previous to his death; and that he would make the facts public as soon as he arrived in the settlements. Donner having perished, nothing further was ever known of the matter.

In mentioning these facts I am aware that I am anticipating some of the events of this narrative, and I will only remark that Donner, Rianhard, and Spitzer having all been subsequently starved to death, it is probable the facts will never be revealed.[54]

Here Mr. Eddy *cached* every thing he had, except the clothing which he and his family had on. On this morning they partook of their last remaining mouthful of food. The Indians were upon the adjacent hills, looking down upon them, and absolutely laughing at their calamity. The lock of Mr. Eddy's rifle had been broken some days before, and the gun left. He could not obtain one, and had he been able to do so, it would have been worse than insanity for him to have encountered the Indians alone. Dejected and sullen, he took up about three pounds of loaf sugar, put some bullets in his pocket, and stringing his powderhorn upon his shoulders, took up his boy in his arms while his afflicted Eleanor carried their still more helpless infant, and in this most miserable and forlorn plight, they set

---

53 The Humboldt River has no apparent outlet; it dwindles away into an intermittent lake, the Humboldt Sink, a basin about twenty miles long and eight to ten miles across at its maximum width. The sink is about twenty miles southwest of Lovelock, Nevada.

54 In a letter penned by her daughter, Leanna Donner App informed C. F. McGlashan on April 29, 1879: "Joseph Rhinehart was taken sick in our tent, when death was approaching and he knew there was no escape, then he made a confession in the presence of Mrs. Wolfinger that he shot her husband; what the object was I do not know."

out once more on foot to make their way through the pitiless wilderness. Trackless, snowclad mountains intercepted their progress, and seemed to present an impassable barrier to all human succor:—mountains, the passage of which, with even the accessories of emigrant wagons, and in the most pleasant season, would have been a feat of no small difficulty. Without shoes—these having been worn out by jagged rocks—they had nothing to protect their feet but moccasins, which were also so much worn as to be of little service. Their painful and perilous way led over broken rocks, presenting acute angles, or prickly pears, which alike lacerated their feet in the most dreadful manner. Nature disputed their passage, and Heaven seemed to be offended. They struggled on, however, with their precious charge, without food or water, until 4 o'clock on the morning of the 14th, when they arrived at a spring that jetted up a column of boiling hot water, about twenty feet high.[55] It was situated in a region that had been rent into millions of fragments by volcanic fires. The desolation was such as to impress upon the mind the idea of expiring nature convulsed with the throes and agonies of the last great and terrible day, or of an angry Deity having taken vengeance upon a guilty world. Having obtained some coffee from Mrs. Donner, Mr. Eddy put it into a pot, and thus boiled it in the hot spring for the nourishment of his wife and children, refusing to partake of it himself. He told me that he should never forget the inexpressible emotions he felt on seeing them thus revive. Under such circumstances of extreme privation, how much more forcibly does the wasteful prodigality of the rich appear. Although he had suffered the loss of all he possessed, yet had it pleased Heaven to have spared him one blow, he might have still been comparatively happy. But God, who is ever wise and just in the allotments of his providence, had decreed otherwise.

About 9 o'clock the party left the Geyser Spring and traveled all that day until sunset, over a road in no respect different from that of the 13th. At this time Mr. Eddy's children were in great danger of perishing for the want of water. He applied to Patrick Brinn, who he knew had ten gallons, for a half pint to give to them. Brinn denied having any; but this Mr. Eddy knew to be untrue, for he had himself filled Brinn's cask at the sinks of Ogden's river; Brinn finally admitted that he had water, but said he did not know how far water was yet distant from them, and he feared that his own family would require it. Mr. Eddy told him, with an energy he never before felt, that he would have it or have Brinn's life. He immediately

---

55 Evidently Thornton refers to the boiling spring about half-way across the desert between the Humboldt Sink and the Truckee River, although the description of it as a geyser appears to be an exaggeration. Much later this spring was known as Brady's Hot Springs.

turned away from Brinn, and went in quest of the water, and gave some to his children.

At sunset they arrived at an exceedingly difficult sand-ridge of ten miles in width. They crossed it about 4 o'clock on the morning of the 15th, the company losing three yoke of cattle that died from fatigue.

Neither Mr. Eddy nor his wife had tasted food for two days and nights, nor had the children any thing except the sugar with which he left the sinks [of] Ogden's river. He applied to Mrs. Graves and Mrs. Brinn for a small piece of meat for his wife and children, who were very faint. They both refused. The emigrants remained in camp to rest the cattle. The Indians killed some of them during the day.

Mr. Eddy procured a gun in the morning, and started to kill some geese which he heard. In about two hours he returned with nine very fat ones. Mrs. Brinn and Mrs. Graves congratulated him, and expressed the opinion that they were very fine, and wondered what he would do with them. He invited them to help themselves, and each took two. He gave Kiesburg one.

Oct. 16th, early in the morning, they resumed their journey, and commenced driving up Truckee river. Nothing of importance occurred until Oct. 19th, about 10 o'clock, A.M., when they met Mr. C. F. Stanton and two Indian *vaqueros* (cow-herds) of Capt. Sutter, one named Lewis, and the other Salvadore.[56] Mr. Stanton had flour and a little dried meat, which he had procured for them. I omitted to state that on the day they broke up their encampment on the Salt Lake, they dispatched Messrs. Stanton and McCutcheon to go to Capt. Sutter's Fort for relief.[57] They drove on during the day, and Mr. Stanton and the *vaqueros* continued on to some of the families one day in the rear.

---

56 The date of Stanton's arrival with supplies is variously given, but Thornton is clearly in error: on October 20 Stanton wrote a note to John Sutter from the vicinity of Johnson's Ranch on the western side of the mountains. See Morgan's discussion in *Overland in 1846*, 444–45. McGlashan reported that the emigrants spent three or four days at Truckee Meadows (the site of present-day Reno, Nevada) resting their cattle for the hard pull up the mountains, but Thornton does not refer to this interlude.

57 Swiss-born John Augustus Sutter had come to California in 1839. The headquarters for his huge estate was his fort near the confluence of the Sacramento and American rivers where the city of Sacramento now stands. Sutter had become extremely wealthy from cattle raising and farming; he encouraged American immigration to California and many travelers besides the Donner party had reason to be grateful for his generosity. The gold rush swept away his prosperity, however, and Sutter ended his life in Washington D.C., petitioning the government for redress.

October 20–On this day Wm. Pike was killed by the accidental discharge of a six-shooter in the hand of Wm. Foster. He died in one hour: he was shot through in the back.[58]

On the evening of October 22d, they crossed the Truckee river, the forty-ninth and last time, in eighty miles. They encamped on the top of a hill. Here nineteen oxen were shot by an Indian, who put one arrow in each ox. The cattle did not die. Mr. Eddy caught him in the act, and fired upon him as he fled. The ball struck him between the shoulders, and came out at the breast. At the crack of the rifle he sprung up about three feet, and with a terrible yell fell down a bank into a bunch of willows.

On the morning of October 23d they resumed their journey, and continued traveling

without any thing of importance occurring until October 28th at dark, when they encamped upon Truckee [Donner] Lake, situated at the foot of Fremont's [Donner] Pass of the main chain of the Sierra Nevada. The Pass is here 9838 feet high.[59]

On the morning of Oct. 29th, they again continued their journey, and went on within three miles of the top of the Pass, where they found the snow about five feet deep. This compelled them to return to a cabin, which was situated one mile in advance of their camp of the previous night.[60] Here they remained in camp during the 30th. At dark their fellow-travelers, Stanton, Graves, the Donners, and some others, came up.

On the morning of Oct. 31st the whole body again started to cross the mountain. They succeeded in getting within three miles of the top of the Pass. The snow had deepened to about ten feet. The night was bitterly cold; the wind howled through the trees, and the snow and hail descended. Finding it utterly impossible to cross, they commenced retracing their steps

---

58 Mary Murphy wrote of her brother-in-law's death: "Mr Foster was going ahead and come back with provisions bt in loading the six shooter it went of and shot Mr Pike in the back he died in about one half hour and in that time he suffered more than tongue can tell it was on the last day of October we was then about 2 hundred miles from the settlements that evening it commenced snowing in three days we got to the dividing ridge of the sirenavada or snowy range of the California mountains." Letter to relatives, May 25, 1847, Tennessee State Library and Archives MS 72-29. Thornton's date for Pike's death is very different from Mary Murphy's but their dates for the emigrants' arrival at the lake are quite close. William M. Pike, said to be a relation of explorer Zebulon M. Pike, left a widow and two small children.

59 Donner Lake is 5,933 feet above sea level, Donner Pass 7,088 feet, and Donner Peak 8,019 feet.

60 The cabin had been erected by members of the Townsend-Stephens-Murphy party of 1844, one of whom, eighteen-year-old Moses Schallenberger, spent the winter there alone.

on the morning of November 1st, and arrived at the cabin about 4 o'clock.[61]

Chapter IX.

The Mountain Camp.

They now saw that it would be necessary to winter here. On the morning of November 2d, Mr. Eddy commenced building a cabin. When finished, the following day, he went into it, with Mrs. Murphy and family, and Wm. Foster and family, Nov 3d.[62] The snow at the place at which they were encamped, was about one foot deep. A single ox constituted the whole stock upon which the family were to winter.

Mr. Eddy commenced hunting on the 4th, and succeeded in killing a prairie wolf [coyote], of which supper was made in the evening for all in the cabin. On the 5th he succeeded in killing an owl, of which supper was made. The Messrs. Graves, Donner, Dolan, and Brinn commenced killing their cattle. Mr. Eddy also killed his ox. On the 6th, an ox belonging to Graves starved to death. He refused to save it for meat, but upon Mr. Eddy's applying to him for it, he would not let him have it for less than $25. This, Mr. Eddy told me, he had paid to the estate of the deceased Graves since getting into the settlement. Mr. Eddy spent the 7th in hunting, but returned at night with a sad and desponding heart, without any

---

61 Survivors gave a variety of dates for their arrival at the lake, but by November 4 they had given up trying to cross the Sierra and had resigned themselves to wintering in the mountains. The Breens occupied the existing cabin, against which Keseberg built a lean-to for his family; the large monument at Donner Memorial State Park was erected on the site. The Graves and Reed families lived in a double cabin about one-half mile northeast of the Breens; the location, across Interstate 80 from the park, is marked by a large white cross and a plaque on a nearby rock. Contrary to what Thornton says in the preceding paragraph, the Donner families lagged behind. They hastily erected crude shelters in Alder Creek Valley northeast of the lake, about seven miles away by road from the rest of the emigrants by the lake. Their camp was located near the present Donner Camp Picnic Area off Highway 89, about two and a half miles north of Interstate 80.

62 This, the Murphy cabin, was built against a boulder about 150 yards southwest of the old Schallenberger cabin occupied by the Breens. The boulder is marked by a large bronze plaque bearing the names of the members of the Donner party. In 1984–85 Donald L. Hardesty of the University of Nevada, Reno, excavated the site; see "The Archaeology of the Donner Party Tragedy," *Nevada Historical Quarterly* 30 (Winter 1987): 246–68.

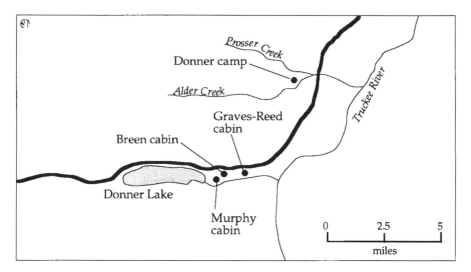

Donner Lake. Cartography by Rose Ann Tompkins

game. The three following days he assisted Graves in putting up a cabin for himself and family, and Mrs. Reed and her family. The day after, they cooked some of their poor beef.

On the 12th, Mr. Eddy, C. T. Stanton, Wm. [Franklin Ward] Graves, Sen., Jay Fosdick, James Smith, Charles Burger, Wm. Foster, Antoine (a Spaniard), John Baptiste, Lewis, Salvadore, Augustus Spitzer, Mary Graves, Sarah Fosdick, and Milton Elliot, being the strongest of the party, started to cross the mountains on foot. Mr. Eddy, in narrating the afflicting story, said to me, that he could never forget the parting scene between himself and family; but he hoped to get in and obtain relief, and return with the means for their rescue. They started with a small piece of beef each; but they had scarcely gone within three miles of the top of the Pass, when the snow, which was soft, and about ten feet deep, compelled them again to return to the cabins, which they reached about midnight.

Nov. 13th, Mr. Eddy succeeded in killing two ducks, but no one would let him have a gun without he gave them half he killed. The next day, very faint from want of food, he resumed his hunting, and at length came upon an enormously large grisly-bear track. Under other circumstances, he would have preferred seeing the tracks of one to seeing the animal itself. But now, weak and faint as he was, he was eager to come up with it. So fierce and powerful is this animal, and go great is its tenacity of life, that the Indians almost uniformly avoid it. Even the most daring and successful white hunters who are acquainted with its habits, usually decline shooting at it, unless they are in a position that enables them to spring up into a tree in the event of the first shot failing to bring it down. This very seldom happens, unless the shot takes effect in the brain. Lewis and Clarke give an account of a bear killed by their party, which was not brought down until it had received five wounds, any one of which would have immediately disabled any other animal. Even then, one of their number very narrowly escaped with his life by leaping down a precipice and plunging into the river. It invariably attacks all persons whom it suddenly finds near it. If it be distant, a noise will cause it to run away; but even in this case it uniformly makes battle if wounded. With a full knowledge of its real character, and although he had heard the stories of many exciting adventures, which were not the less interesting because some of them were unreasonable, and others even impossible, yet he now was exceedingly desirous of coming up with an animal he would otherwise have been most careful to shun. He was not long in finding the object of his search. At the distance of about ninety years he saw the bear, with its head to the ground, engaged in digging roots. The beast was in a small skirt of prairie, and Mr. Eddy, taking advantage of a large firtree near which he was at the moment, kept himself in concealment. Having put into his mouth the only bullet that was not in his gun, so that he might quickly reload in case of an emergency, he deliberately fired. The bear immediately reared upon its hind feet, and seeing the smoke from Mr. Eddy's gun, ran fiercely toward him, with open jaws. By the time the gun was reloaded, the bear had reached the tree, and, with a fierce growl, pursued Mr. Eddy round it, who, running swifter than the animal, came up with it in the rear, and disabled it by a shot in the shoulder, so that it was no longer able to pursue him. He then dispatched the bear by knocking it on the head with a club. Upon examination, he found that the first shot had pierced its heart. He then returned to the Mountain Camp for assistance to bring in his prize.

Graves and Eddy went out after the bear. On the way out Graves said that he believed he should perish in the mountain; that he feared that the judgment of God would come upon him, for not assisting Hardcoop up to the wagon, when Kiesburg put him out, and for driving Mr. Reed out of camp. They, however, finally contrived to get in the bear after dark. Mr. Eddy gave one half to Mr. Foster for the use of the gun. A part of it was likewise given to Mr. Graves and to Mrs. Reed. The bear weighed about 800 lbs.[63]

Nov. 15th, Mr. Eddy killed a duck and one gray squirrel. Nothing of importance occurred between this date and the 21st, beyond the fears of

---

63 Numerous fragments of grizzly bear bones were recovered during the excavation of the Murphy cabin site.

starvation, and the increasing weakness of the emigrants. On this day, six women and sixteen men, including Stanton and the two Indians, made another effort to cross the mountain on foot. The morning was fine; the wind from the northwest.[64] They crossed the pass on the crust of the snow. Mr. Eddy measured the snow here, and found it to be twenty-five feet deep. They encamped in a little valley on the west side of the mountain, in six feet snow. They experienced great difficulty in kindling a fire and in getting wood, in consequence of their extreme weakness. Here Mr. Stanton and the two Indian boys refused to go any further, in consequence of not being able to get along with seven mules belonging to Capt. Sutter. Fully aware of their peril, Mr. Eddy exhausted all his reasoning powers in a vain effort to induce them to proceed; urging the imminent danger of their all perishing from starvation, and offering to become responsible for the mules. He knew that Capt. Sutter would rather lose the animals, than know that his fellow-beings had perished in a foolish attempt to save them: but all persuasion was in vain. He then proposed that they should compel the Indians to go forward. This was objected to; and a good deal of angry feeling was exhibited by Mr. Eddy, and those against whose plans he vainly remonstrated. Accordingly, on the morning of the 22d, faint and dispirited, they again commenced their return to their unhappy companions in peril. They arrived, almost exhausted, at the cabins about midnight. The previous night had been most bitterly cold; but the weather of this day was clear, and the sun shone brightly upon the snow.

The subsequent day the weather was clear, and the wind westerly. Mrs. Eddy and her children were very weak, but exhibited great courage and fortitude.

The weather on the 25th was very cloudy, and there was every appearance of another snow-storm. The previous night had been intensely cold. They proposed to make another effort the next day, if the weather would admit of it; but the snow began to descend on the afternoon of the 25th, in great flakes, and so thick that it was impossible to see beyond a few feet. This continued with greater or less violence, and with but occasional intermissions, until the 29th, when it ceased for a few hours. The wind changed from northwest to west. By this time it was three feet deep in the valley, which made it very difficult, in their feeble condition, for the emigrants to get wood. On this day Patrick Brinn sold William Foster a yoke of oxen, taking a gold watch and some other property in security, and then killed the last ox he had. On the 30th it snowed very heavily, and there was

---

64 The weather and snow conditions in this and following chapters are taken from Patrick Breen's diary, published anonymously in the *California Star* on May 22, 1847. Many of the incidents Thornton reports are also from this diary.

every appearance of its continuing. It was next to impossible for any living thing without wings to get out.

December 1.–The snow continued to fall as when it first commenced, and upon being measured was found to be from six to six and a half feet deep. The wind blew in fearful and terrific blasts from the west. The cold was intense: the wretched sojourners were nearly naked, and almost with out food: the snow had now become so deep as to make it increasingly difficult to get wood for fuel. The were completely housed up, and were cut off from all the world, and sympathies of life. The few cattle that lived up to this time, and the horses, and Capt. Sutter's mules, were all supposed to be lost in the snow, and none now cherished the least hope of ever finding them.

The snow ceased falling on the 3d; and although the weather continued cloudy all day, the atmosphere was sufficiently warm to thaw the snow a little. They measured the snow on the 5th, and found it seven or eight feet deep. The sun shone again, clear and beautiful, causing every thing, after the long and terrific storm, to assume its wonted aspect. The cheering light once more rekindled hope in the hearts of the desolate travelers.

The morning of the 6th opened upon them fine and clear; and Messrs. Stanton and Graves spent the day in manufacturing snow-shoes, preparatory to making another effort to cross the mountains.[65] Nothing had been heard from the mules, and all, now, at last, saw that they ought to have been killed for food, as Mr. Eddy proposed at the camp on the 22d, after their return from the mountain. Then Graves and others objected, fearing that it might be necessary to pay for them. The morning of the 8th was fine and clear, although the previous night had been distressingly cold. They found it very difficult to obtain enough wood to cook their now nearly putrid beef, or even to keep them warm. The wind, during the day, was from the southwest.

About 1 o'clock, A.M., Dec. 9, the wind commenced blowing from the northwest, and their hearts almost died within them, as they again saw the snow beginning to descend. Mr. Stanton sought to obtain some food for himself and the two Indians, Lewis and Salvadore, but did not obtain much. Patrick Brinn, on the day before this, took Spitzer into his cabin in a state so weak from starvation, that he could not rise without help. The snow continued to fall on the 10th. On the 13th, it fell faster than on any previous day; and in a short time was eight feet on a level. The prospect became every moment more appalling. Death seemed inevitably to be awaiting them. Messrs. Eddy, Stanton, Graves, and others spent the day in preparing to make another attempt to cross the mountains. On the 14th Baylis Williams died of starvation. He was the first victim of this hapless

---

65 The oxbows were sawed lengthwise into strips and laced with rawhide.

company who thus expired, and their feelings and reflections may, perhaps, be imagined, but can not be described.

Chapter X.

Journey of a Party from the Mountain Camp into the Settlements of California.

On the 16th of December, the following persons started on snow-shoes to cross the mountains:—Sarah Fosdick, Mary Graves, William Foster, Sarah Foster, C. T. Stanton, William [Franklin] Graves, Jay Fosdick, Wm. Murphy, Charles Burger, Harriet Pike, Lemuel Murphy, Patrick Dolan, Antoine, Lewis, Salvadore, Mrs. McCutcheon, and William Eddy.[66]

The night previous to their departure was exceedingly cold. Their friends were in a state of extreme suffering and want. The hollow cheek, the wasted form, and the deep sunken eye of his wife, Mr. Eddy told me he should never forget. "Oh," said he, "the bitter anguish of my wrung and agonized spirit, when I turned away from her; and yet no tear would flow to relieve my suffering." The wind was from the southeast, and the weather comparatively fair and pleasant. William Murphy found it to be impossible to get along, and he finally turned back during the day. Ultimately, Charles Burger was missed, and it was supposed that he had gone back. They struggled on until night, and encamped at the head of Truckee lake, about four miles from the mountain. The day following they resumed their painful and distressing journey; and after traveling all day, encamped on the west side of the main chain of the Sierra Nevada, about six miles from their last camp. They were without tents. The wind, on this and the previous day, was from the southeast. On the 18th they traveled five miles, and encamped. Mr. Stanton became snow-blind during the day, and fell back, but came up after they had been in camp an hour.

As several instances of snow-blindness will be mentioned in the subsequent progress of this narrative, I will here observe that it is produced by the glare of the snow, combined with great fatigue. It may be prevented, or

---

66 This expedition is generally referred to in the Donner party literature as the "Forlorn Hope," a usage begun by C. F. McGlashan. Eddy gave three different versions of this journey: the one told here; another recorded by John Sinclair, dated "February 1847" and published in Bryant's *What I Saw In California;* and a third published in the Merryman article. In discussing the many discrepancies among these accounts, Stewart concludes that Thornton's is the least reliable; see *Ordeal by Hunger* (Lincoln: University of Nebraska, 1986), 305.

its effects obviated, by the use of either dark green glasses or black hand-kerchiefs. Of these they had none.

December 19.–Although the wind was from the northwest, yet the snow which had fallen on the previous night, thawed a little. Mr. Stanton again fell behind, in consequence of blindness. He came up about an hour after they were encamped. The wind on the 20th was from the northeast. In the morning they resumed their journey, and guided by the sun, as they had hitherto been, they traveled until night. Mr. Stanton again fell behind. The wind next day changed to southwest, and the snow fell all day. They encamped at sunset, and about dark Mr. Stanton came up. They resumed their journey on the 22d, Mr. Stanton came into camp in about an hour, as usual. That night they consumed the last of their little stock of provisions. They had limited themselves to one ounce at each meal, since leaving the mountain camp, and now the last was gone. They had one gun, but they had not seen a living creature. The weather was clear and pleasant during the day, and the wind northeast. The weather was always clear when the wind was east or northeast. A south and southwest wind always brought a snow-storm.

December 23.–During this day Mr. Eddy examined a little bag for the purpose of throwing out something, with a view to getting along with more ease. In doing this, he found about half a pound of bear's meat, to which was attached a paper upon which his wife had written in pencil, a note signed "Your own dear Eleanor," in which she requested him to save it for the last extremity, and expressed the opinion that it would be the means of saving his life. This was really the case, for without it, he must subsequently have perished. On the morning of this day Mr. Stanton remained at the camp-fire, smoking his pipe. He requested them to go on, saying that he would overtake them. The snow was about fifteen feet deep. Mr. Stanton did not come up with them. On the morning of the 24th, they resumed their melancholy journey, and after traveling about a mile, they encamped to wait for their companion. They had nothing to eat during the day. Mr. Stanton did not come up. The snow fell all night, and increased one foot in depth. They now gave up poor Stanton for dead. A party that subsequently returned from the settlement, headed by Mr. Fallen, found his remains at the place where they had left him. His pistols, pipe, and some other arti-cles, were found by him; but his body was in a great measure consumed by beasts of prey.

Mr. Stanton was from Syracuse, New York, and had been a merchant at that place. He was kind and benevolent in his feelings, and gentlemanly in his deportment and manners. He had, as has been stated in a previous part of this narrative, been sent on in company with Mr. McCutcheon from the Great Salt Lake, to obtain supplies from the settlements. He traveled sev-eral hundred miles through hostile Indians, across deserts and over lofty mountains. He arrived at Capt. Sutter's Fort about the first of October, and from this generous and noble man, obtained supplies for his suffering fellow-travelers. Furnished with seven mules loaded with provisions, and two Indian *vaqueros,* he returned, and met them at the crossing of Truckee river, about half way between Pyramid Lake and Truckee Lake—their route having led them within ten miles of the former. Had it not been for the disinterested sympathy of Mr. Stanton for the unfortunate emigrants, all must have perished before the first party sent out to their assistance reached them.

Before he left Capt. Sutter's Fort to return to their assistance, he left a vest in charge of that gentleman, in one of the pockets of which a small package was subsequently found, directed to Capt. Sutter, with a memorandum as follows: "Capt. Sutter will send the within, in the event of my death, to Sydney Stanton, Syracuse, N.Y."[67] Enclosed was a diamond breast-pin, with a note from his sister, addressed to him at Chicago, Illinois, from which the following is an extract: "Sidney has requested me to do up your breast-pin, and send it to you. As you perceive, I have done it up in a newspaper....May God bless you, my dear brother.

A. S."

The only entire article on the piece of newspaper, was the following translation from the True Sun, from the French:—

"The Withered Flower.
"O! dying flower, that droop'st alone,
Erewhile the valley's pride,
Thy withered leaves, disordered strown,
Rude winds sweep far and wide.

"The scythe of Time, whose stroke we mourn,
Our common doom shall bring.
From thee a faded leaf is torn
From us a joy takes wing.

"As life flies by, oh! who but feels
Some sense, some charm decay?
E'en every fleeting moment steals
Some treasured dream away.

---

67 More than thirty years later Sidney Stanton sent C. F. McGlashan letters which his brother Charles had written on the trail. McGlashan's excerpts enabled Dale Morgan to identify Stanton as the author of several other letters published in the New York *Herald* and signed "S. T. C." Stanton's letters are reproduced in *Overland in 1846.*

"Some secret blight each hope destroys,
Till at length we ask in grief,
If, than life's ephemeral joys,
The floweret's be more brief."[68]

Every one who understands a woman's heart, who has enjoyed a sister's love and confidence, and who observes the peculiar appropriateness of the poetry to the circumstances then surrounding this affectionate girl, will see in a moment that the paper was selected by her on that account.

On Christmas Day the painful journey was again continued, and after traveling two or three miles, the wind changed to the southwest. The snow beginning to fall, they all sat down to hold a council for the purpose of determining whether to proceed. All the men but Mr. Eddy refused to go forward. The women and Mr. Eddy declared they would go through or perish. Many reasons were urged for returning, and among others the fact that they had not tasted food for two days, and this after having been on an allowance of one ounce per meal. It was said that they must all perish for want of food. At length, Patrick Dolan proposed that they should cast lots to see who should die, to furnish food for those who survived. Mr. Eddy seconded the motion. William Foster opposed the measure. Mr. Eddy then proposed that two persons should take each a six-shooter, and fight until one or both was slain. This, too, was objected to. Mr. Eddy at length proposed that they should resume their journey, and travel on till some one died. This was finally agreed to, and they staggered on for about three miles, when they encamped. They had a small hatchet with them, and after a great deal of difficulty they succeeded in making a large fire. About 10 o'clock on Christmas night, a most dreadful storm of wind, snow, and hail, began to pour down upon their defenseless heads. While procuring wood for the fire, the hatchet, as if to add another drop of bitterness to a cup already overflowing, flew from the handle, and was lost in unfathomable snows. About 11 o'clock that memorable night, the storm increased to a perfect tornado, and in an instant blew away every spark of fire. Antoine perished a little before this from fatigue, frost, and hunger. The company, except Mr. Eddy and one or two others, were now engaged in alternatingly imploring God for mercy and relief. That night's bitter cries, anguish, and despair, never can be forgotten. Mr. Eddy besought his companions to get down upon blankets, and he would cover them up with other blankets; urging that the falling snow would soon cover them, and they could thus keep warm. In about two hours this was done. Before this, however, Mr. Graves was relieved by death from the horrors of that night. Mr. Eddy told him that he was dying. He replied that he did not care, and soon expired.

---

68 This passage about Stanton appeared in the *California Star* on May 22, 1847.

They remained under the blankets all that night, until about 10 o'clock, A.M., of the 26th, when Patrick Dolan, becoming deranged, broke away from them, and getting out into the snow, it was with great difficulty that Mr. Eddy again got him under. They held him there by force until about 4 o'clock, P.M., when he quietly and silently sunk into the arms of death. He was from Dublin, Ireland. Lemuel Murphy became deranged on the night of the 26th, and talked much about food. On the morning of the 27th, Mr. Eddy blew up a powder-horn, in an effort to strike fire under the blankets. His face and hands were much burned. Mrs. McCutcheon and Mrs. Foster were also burned, but not seriously. About 4 o'clock, P.M., the storm died away, and the angry clouds passed off. Mr. Eddy immediately got out from under the blankets, and in a short time succeeded in getting fire into a large pine tree. His unhappy companions then got out; and having broken off boughs, they put them down, and lay upon them before the fire. The flame ascended to the top of the tree, and burned off great numbers of dead limbs, some of them as large as a man's body; but such was their weakness and indifference, that they did not seek to avoid them at all. Although the limbs fell thick, they did not strike.

On the morning of December 28th, they found themselves too weak to walk. The sensation of hunger was not so urgent, but it was evident to all that some substantial nourishment was necessary to recruit their bodies. The horrible expedient of eating human flesh was now again proposed. This Mr. Eddy declined doing, but his miserable companions cut the flesh from the arms and legs of Patrick Dolan, and roasted and ate it, averting their faces from each other, and weeping.

They gave some of this horrible food to Lemuel Murphy, with the hope that he would revive; but he continued to grow weaker, until at length the lamp of life, which had been flickering so long, went out, and the darkness of death covered him forever.

They were all reduced to mere skeletons. The skin upon the face, particularly, was drawn tight over the bones; the eyes were sunken, and had a fierce and wild expression. Perhaps the eye of a famished tiger would have something of the same expression. But as death came on, the countenance became more settled and calm; the eyes retreated still farther back into the head, losing their fierceness; and the whole features assuming, in some cases, a sort of fixedness, while in others they exhibited a calm and gentle repose, illuminated by the expiring rays of departing reason; like the surface of a lake, no longer lashed by the tempest into foaming surges; but reflecting from its bosom the last rays of the setting sun, indicating that night will soon come on, and cover it with darkness. In other cases, however, some time after this, the expression of the countenance was horrid, ghastly, and restless. The eye was wild and fierce, up to the very moment when its fire was quenched in death forever.

To this place they gave the name of "The Camp of Death." The horrors of that awful scene exceed the power of language to describe, or of imagination to conceive. Besides starvation, they had to contend also with trackless mountains and almost unfathomable snows. The wind and hail had beaten upon them with a fury that seemed to indicate that the Almighty had let loose the elements upon their devoted heads. The deep stupor into which their calamities had plunged the most of them, often changed to despair. Each seemed to see inevitable destruction, and expressed in moans, sighs, and tears, the gloomy thoughts over which their minds were brooding. Mr. Eddy dissembled his own fears, and sought, by preferred consolations and an unmoved countenance, to inspire them with hope and courage. He found it impossible to dissipate the terror of the men. With his female companions there was less difficulty. Some of them, indeed, exhibited a want of fortitude; but the most of them manifested a constancy and courage, a coolness, presence of mind, and patience, which he had not, previous to entering upon this journey, suspected to form any part of female character. He had often occasion to remark the fortitude with which the most of the females sustained the sad reverses by which they were overwhelmed on the way. The difficulties, dangers, and misfortunes which frequently seemed to prostrate the men, called forth the energies of the gentler sex, and gave to them a sublime elevation of character, which enabled them to abide the most withering blasts of adversity with unshaken firmness. She who had been, while in prosperity, all weakness and dependence, clinging around her husband as the ivy does to the oak, now suddenly rose to be his comforter.[69]

On the morning of December 29th they resumed their journey from "The Camp of Death." They had been guided heretofore, partly by the sun, and partly by the two Indian *vaqueros,* Lewis and Salvadore, but now Lewis, who spoke a little English, informed them that they were lost, and that he was, therefore, unable to guide them. They proceeded on, however, in the best way they could, until night, when they encamped. Mr. Eddy had now been a long time without food. The half-pound of roasted bear meat, which his "own dear Eleanor" had, by stealth, put into the bottom of his sack, had preserved his life up to this moment. And even now he felt no hunger—that almost intolerable and maddening sensation had long since passed away. His feelings were peculiar, but altogether indescribable. His companions told him that he was dying. He did not, however, believe them; and so informed them. But he felt that he was sinking, and that there was a rapid breaking up of his energies, which, under God, had hitherto saved his own life and that of his companions. Although he

---

69 The surprising hardiness of the female emigrants is a recurrent theme in Donner party writings.

felt no hunger, his body imperiously demanded nourishment. Such were the circumstances under which he made his first cannibal meal. He experienced no loathing or disgust, but his reason, which he thought was never more unclouded, told him that it was a horrid repast. The hard hand of necessity was upon him, and he was compelled to eat or die.

The night passed away as tranquilly as could have been expected of persons situated as they were. Mr. Eddy talked with his unfortunate fellow-travelers of the means by which they would save themselves. He sought to reanimate them with courage, and to inspire them with hope, by speaking of their deliverance as certain. More than one vowed vengeance upon Hastings, for having decoyed them into his cut-off. Their feelings will perhaps be understood by those whom Jesse Applegate, in similar manner, decoyed into the "Applegate cut-off."

On the morning of December 30th they resumed their journey, their feet being so swollen that they had burst open, and, although they were wrapped in rags and pieces of blankets, yet it was with great pain and difficulty that they make any progress. They encamped, late in the afternoon, upon the high bank of a very deep cañon. From this point they could distinctly see a valley which they believed to be the valley of the Sacramento.

December 31st was spent in crossing the cañon, and although they toiled hard during the entire day, they affected no more than the crossing. Every foot of that day's struggle was marked with the blood from their feet. They encamped that night on the banks of the cañon. Here Mr. Eddy saw that poor Jay Fosdick would not survive much longer; and reminded him that his end was nigh, if he did not summon up all his energies.

On this night they ate the last flesh of their deceased companions. One of the company then proposed that they should kill the two Indian boys, Lewis and Salvadore, who, it will be remembered, met them with Mr. Stanton, with provisions for their relief; Mr. Eddy remonstrated, but finding that the deed was resolved upon, he determined to prevent it by whatever means God and nature might enable him to use. Desiring, however, to avoid extremities, if possible, he secretly informed Lewis of the fate that awaited him and his companion, and concluded by advising him to fly. The expression of the face of Lewis, never can be forgotten; he did not utter one word in reply, but stood in mute astonishment. In about two minutes his features settled into Indian sullenness, and he turned away to fly from the scene of danger. Their complicated sufferings were of a character that rendered it impossible for them to judge accurately, of the right or wrong of many actions. But this was a deed which nothing could justify or excuse. Had it been proposed to cast lost for the purpose of determining who should die, and the lot had fallen upon these Indians, or upon Mr. Eddy, he would have submitted to it without a murmur or complaint. But the thing proposed, he could not but regard with feeling of abhorrence. His very soul recoiled at the thought.

January 1, 1847.–They made their New Year's dinner of the strings of their snow-shoes. Mr. Eddy also ate an old pair of moccasins. They struggled on until night, and encamped in six feet snow. On the morning of the following day they resumed their journey, their feet being still greatly swollen and cracked, and encamped at night in three feet snow. That night they took some old boots and shoes, and having slightly crisped them in the fire, made an evening meal of them.

They staggered on during the 3d, and encamped at night on bare ground, the snow, however, being still in patches. The whole face of the country had gradually changed; the hills had become less and less rugged, and they were not encamped in an open oak grove. They had nothing to eat during this long and melancholy night. Mr. Eddy saw that death was beginning to grapple with poor Jay Fosdick. He had been sinking for some time; but now it was evident that he was drawing very near to the close of his sorrowful pilgrimage. He also saw that they would all very soon perish, if they did not obtain relief. He therefore determined secretly to leave the camp, and go on with a gun, hoping, now they had left the snows behind, that he would find some game. If successful, it was his purpose to return and share with his companions. If successful, he might save himself and them; if otherwise, he could but die. Finally, he determined to give the company some hint of his plans. They at once comprehended his purpose, and the women besought him not to leave them; assuring him that their only hope for life, was in his continuing with them.

On the morning of the 4th, Mary Graves, who had more strength than any of the other women, resolved that she would go with him or perish. Mrs. Pike threw her arms around his neck, imploring him, by every thing to which she could appeal, not to leave them. The other women added their tears and entreaties to those of Mrs. Pike. But to remain with them was to die. To go forward might possibly be the means of their preservation. Although they had seen no game nor a living thing since they had left the Mountain Camp, they were now in an open country, and this circumstance, although trifling in itself, was one that afforded him a hope. Those who have not been in situations in which they were exposed to extreme peril, can form no correct conception of the value which sometimes attaches to the simplest object. They can never know with what desperate eagerness and energy one seizes upon the slightest means capable of mitigating the rigor of a fate into which their circumstances seem about to plunge them.

Mary Graves and Mr. Eddy accordingly set forward. They had not proceeded above two miles, when they came to where a deer had lain the previous night. In an instant a feeling took possession of his heart to which it had been a stranger. He knew not what were all the elements of his emotions; but gratitude to God, and a hope in his providence were at least two. Tears immediately began to flow down his haggard cheeks. He turned round and saw Mary weeping like a child. As soon as his choked utterance would admit of his speaking, he said, "Mary, don't you feel like praying?" "Oh, yes," she replied with sobs and tears, "I do, but I never prayed in my life! Do you pray?" He replied that he knew not how to pray. But in an instant they were both upon their knees, and by a feeling natural to the unfortunate, their hearts were turned toward heaven. Surrounded by danger, and not having a prayer-book, they addressed themselves to the invisible Being in terms neither studied nor measured, but which were the spontaneous outburstings of hearts that felt that nothing but the God who maintains the order of the universe could afford them succor in this their last and most fearful extremity. They then rose from their knees, experiencing the cheering influence of hope. Their vows were solemn and their prayers fervent and impassioned. There was in that first prayer a luxury, the remembrance of which was delightful. In all Mr. Eddy's anguish of spirit upon this most disastrous road he had not shed a tear. Some had wept and prayed; others had wept and cursed Almighty God for their hard fate. He had never felt like cursing God, or blaming his Providence; but he had not wept. The fountains of his tears were as dry as many of the deserts over which they had passed, and upon which they had wrecked their little fortunes. Tears would have relieved the agony of a spirit which, although not disposing him to blaspheme his Maker, did not incline him to submit to the chastisement of his hand. But now he had wept and prayed, and rose from his knees, feeling an humble but not presumptuous trust, that God would fill his mouth with food, and his heart with gladness. They had not proceeded far before they saw a large buck, about eighty yards distant. Mr. Eddy raised his rifle, and for some time tried to bring it to bear upon the deer; but such was his extreme weakness that he could not. He breathed a little, changing his manner of holding the gun, and made another effort. Again his weakness prevented him from being able to hold upon it. He heard a low and suppressed sobbing behind him, and turning round saw Mary Graves weeping and in great agitation, her head bowed, and her hands upon her face. Alarmed lest she should cause to deer to run, Mr. Eddy begged her to be quiet, which she did, after exclaiming, "O, I am afraid you will not kill it!" He brought the gun up to his face the third time, and elevating the muzzle above the deer, let it descend, until he saw the animal through the sights, when the rifle cracked. The deer bounded up about three feet, then stood still. Mary immediately wept aloud, exclaiming, "O, merciful God, you have missed it!" Mr. Eddy assured her that he had not; that he knew the rifle was upon it the moment of firing; and that, in addition to this, the deer had dropped its tail between its legs, which this animal always does when wounded. They were at the moment standing upon a precipice of about thirty feet, a snow-bank being at the bottom. In a short time the deer ran. Mr. Eddy immediately sprang down the precipice, and in a moment Mary followed him. The deer ran about two hundred yards, and fell. Mr. Eddy got to it while it was yet alive, and taking it by the horns, cut its throat with a pen-knife. Before this was done, Mary was at his side, and they drank the blood together as it flowed from the expiring beast. This gave to them a little strength, and with their faces all covered with blood, they sat down to rest a little. In a short time they rolled the deer near by to a spot where they made a fire. That night they ate the entrails; and with their hearts glowing with the gratitude of the Giver of all good, they enjoyed a degree of refreshing slumber to which they had long been strangers.

Their dreams were wont to tantalize and mock them with rich and varied food, prepared in the most inviting manner. But this night they had made an abundant meal upon the entrails of the deer—a meal that they enjoyed more than any they had ever eaten; and their rest was not broken by dreams that insulted their misfortunes.

They rose on the morning of the 5th of January, filled with renewed hopes, and deeply impressed with the sublime idea of a Great and Good Being extending a protecting Ægis over the unfortunate.

Several times during the night of the 4th, Mr. Eddy had fired his rifle for the purpose of informing his companions where they were. Jay Fosdick, who, it will be remembered, was expected to die, was about a mile back. He had lain down, unable to proceed any further; and his wife was with him. Upon hearing Mr. Eddy's rifle crack, at the time of his killing the deer, he exclaimed, in a feeble voice—"There! Eddy has killed a deer. Now, if I can only get to him, I shall live." William Foster and wife, Mrs. Pike, and Mrs. McCutcheon, were encamped about half way between Mr. Eddy's camp, and the place at which Mr. Fosdick and his wife were. One of the emigrants, believing that Mr. and Mrs. Fosdick had died during the previous night, sent a person back to the place, with instructions to get Mrs. Fosdick's heart for breakfast; and to be sure to secure her jewelry, and her husband's watches and money. The person sent for this purpose met Mrs. Fosdick on the way to Mr. Eddy's camp. The individual thus sent turned about, and came on with her to Mr. Eddy's camp; who gave them some of the roasted liver of the deer, and upon their returning to the other camp, he requested that all should come to him, and partake of his venison.

Mrs. Fosdick had been with her husband during the previous night, which was bitterly cold; and after his death, she rolled his body in the only blanket they possessed, and laid herself down upon the ground, desiring to die, and hoping that she would freeze to death. The scenes surrounding her were rendered still more terrible by the horror inspired by the darkness of the night; and she prayed, and in a certain sense, struggled for death, during the whole of its heavily-passing hours. But the return of the morning's light brought with it an instinctive love of life, and she now proposed to go back to the body of her husband, and for the last time kiss his lips, then cold and silent in death. Two individuals accompanied her, and when they arrived at the body, they, notwithstanding the remonstrances, entreaties, and tears of the afflicted widow, cut out the heart and liver, and severed the arms and legs of her departed husband.[70]

Mrs. Fosdick took up a little bundle she had left, and returned with these two persons to one of the camps, where she saw an emigrant thrust the heart through with a stick, and hold it in the fire to roast. Unable to endure the horrible sight of seeing literally devoured a heart that had fondly and ardently loved her until it had ceased to throb, she turned away, and went to another camp, sick and almost blinded by the spectacle.

Mr. Eddy cut up the deer, dried it before his fire, and then divided it with his unhappy companions in misfortune and peril, of both camps.

The day having thus passed away, on the morning of the 6th of January they all started together. They went down to the north branch of the American fork of the Sacramento, and after crossing it, encamped for the night. They resumed their journey the next morning, and being unable to proceed down the river, the commenced climbing a very high and difficult mountain. The sides were very steep, and the pulled themselves up the rocks, by laying hold of shrubs growing in crevices. There were many places in which, had these given way, they would have been precipitated hundreds of feet below.

Their feet were greatly bruised, and so swollen that they had literally burst open, and were bleeding so much, that the fragments of blankets with which they were bound up, were saturated with blood. But a merciful God assisted them in a wonderful manner; and after struggling all day, they reached the top, where they encamped. The day was fine, and although the minds of the company were singularly altered by untold sufferings, yet the most perfect tranquillity reigned among them, as calms are said sometimes to precede the most desolating storms. Mr. Eddy lamented the loss of their unfortunate companions, but carefully avoided making any allusion to recent revolting events. They sat down upon the ground to their evening repast, and consumed the last of their venison.

Soon after, Eddy and Foster were apart from the company. Despondency had again seized upon the mind of the latter. He had all along

---

70 Thornton may be romanticizing here; other sources report that Sarah Fosdick acquiesced to the use of her husband's body. See Eliza Gregson, "Mrs. Gregson's 'Memory,'" *California Historical Quarterly* 19 (June 1940): 121–22; C. F. McGlashan, *History of the Donner Party* (Stanford: Stanford University Press, 1947), 87.

exhibited evidences of a partial and, perhaps, perfect insanity, caused by mental anxiety, hardships, and perils. He had also shown, as a consequence of this, a total want of energy, making no effort, rendering no assistance in making fires, and seeming to look to Mr. Eddy, and to depend upon him—as, indeed, did all the company—to guide and save the lives of the party. He doubted not that they were approaching the last critical hour of their fate. Suffering and danger had rendered him selfish to the last degree; and seeming firmly to believe that the sacrifice of the lives of some of their companions was necessary to the preservation of the others, he proposed to kill Mrs. McCutcheon, alleging that she was but a nuisance, and could not keep up. Mr. Eddy remonstrated, and told him that she was a wife and a mother, and was with them, helpless and without protection, unless she found it in them; and finally informed him, with much sternness in his manner, that she should not die. Foster then proposed that they should kill Mary Graves and Mrs. Fosdick, as they had no children. Mr. Eddy told him that he would inform them of his purpose. This he did in the presence of the company. Foster said he did not care, he could handle Mr. Eddy. Seeing that he was lost to all reason, and perfectly insane, and firmly believing that they would all fall a sacrifice to his insane appetite, unless the further development of this spirit of selfishness was checked, Mr. Eddy said, "Perhaps you intend to make a victim of me. If this is so, we will proceed to settle the question." Seizing a large club, and striking it across a log, to ascertain whether it would break, Mr. Eddy threw it to him, and bade him defend himself. At the same time he advanced upon him with a knife which had belonged to Jay Fosdick, as rapidly as he could in his weak and feeble condition, with the intention of taking his life. Having gotten almost within striking distance, with his arm raised to strike a fatal blow, he was seized by Mary Graves, Mrs. Pike, Mrs. McCutcheon, and Mrs. Fosdick, and thrown down. The knife was then taken away from him. He then told Foster, who stood apparently powerless, that he would kill him if he ever again manifested the slightest inclination to take the life of any of the party; and that if it should become necessary to take life, in order to the preservation of other lives, one of them should be the victim; and that this point should be determined by fighting, since Foster had shown a determination not to cast lots, which was the only just method of deciding upon the victim. Foster might easily, had he possessed the energy, have dispatched Eddy at the time when the females, whose lives he had saved, by resolutely resisting Mr. Foster's purpose, had thrown him down. But devoid of energy, and conscious, perhaps, although he could not have been sane, that he had meditated a wicked act, he cowered before Eddy's look.[71]

---

71   Eddy protests too much. By this point the mental equilibrium of all the snowshoers was precarious at best, and Eddy's own conduct was not beyond suspicion.

On the other hand, Mr. Eddy was conscious of doing right; and, in addition to this, his was a courage animated by desperation. He had left behind him in the Sierra Nevada a most beloved and affectionate wife, and two young children, whom he tenderly loved. He had been unable to take them out, and was now staggering into the settlements for the purpose of obtaining the means of rescuing them. He saw that Foster was evidently deranged, and therefore a dangerous man to be with, in the circumstances in which they were then placed; and while he was willing to share the risk of life incident to their situation, yet, the ghastly images of his famine-stricken wife and children appealed to every generous feeling of his nature, to require of others a similar and equal risk. He might have reached the settlements sooner, perhaps, by consenting to the death of his companions; but had he done this, and thereby have saved his wife and children, the remembrance of the price paid would have embittered every subsequent moment of his miserable being.

The morning of Jan. 8th they resumed their journey from the "Camp of Strife," order being re-established. They had not proceeded above two miles, when they cam into a small patch of snow, where they found the tracks of Lewis and Salvadore, for the first time since Mr. Eddy informed them of their danger. Foster immediately said that he would follow them, and kill them if he came up with them. They had not proceeded more than two miles when they came upon the Indians, lying upon the ground, in a totally helpless condition. They had been without food for eight or nine days, and had been four days without fire. They could not, probably, have lived more than two or three hours; nevertheless, Eddy remonstrated against their being killed. Foster affirmed that he was compelled to do it. Eddy refused to see the deed consummated, and went on about two hundred yards, and halted. Lewis was told that he must die; and was shot through the head. Salvadore was dispatched in the same manner immediately after.[72] Mr. Eddy did not see who fired the gun. The flesh was then

---

On March 30, 1879, W. C. Graves wrote to C. F. McGlashan that Sarah Fosdick and her sister, Mary Graves, had feared that Eddy was trying to lure Mary away to kill and eat her.

72 Several versions of the deaths of Luis and Salvador were reported, but this one is probably close to the truth. This is the only known instance of human beings being killed for food by Donner party members, but apparently Foster was not greatly blamed. Peter H. Burnett wrote, "Foster was a man of excellent common sense, and his intelligence had not been affected, like those of so many others. His statement was clear, consistent, and intelligible." *Recollections and Opinions of an Old Pioneer* (New York: Appleton, 1880), 275. Foster was prominent in the early history of Marysville, California, named for his sister-in-law Mary Murphy Covillaud. The Fosters moved to Minnesota in the mid-1850s

cut from their bones and dried. Mr. Foster and wife, and Mrs. Pike encamped at "The Place of Sacrifice." Mary Graves, Mrs. Fosdick, Mrs. McCutcheon, and Mr. Eddy encamped about two hundred yards in advance. They never encamped again with Foster; and some one of their number was always awake, to avoid being surprised.

Mr. Eddy make his supper upon grass. Although they saw deer in great numbers every day, and sometimes very near them, yet such was the extreme weakness to which Mr. Eddy was reduced, that it was impossible for him to take accurate aim at them. He staggered like a drunken man; and when he came to a fallen tree, though no more than a foot high, he had to stoop down, put his hands upon it, and get over it by a sort of rolling motion. They were under the necessity of sitting down to rest about every quarter of a mile. The slightest thing caused them to stumble and fall. They were almost reduced to the helplessness of little children in their first essays to walk. The women would fall and weep like infants, and then rise and totter along again.

January 9.–They proceeded during the day over a rocky country, and encamped at night, after a day of immense toil and suffering. Mr. Eddy gathered some grass near by, to sustain, in his wasted body, the almost extinguished spark of life.

On the following morning they staggered forward, and toward the close of the day, which seemed interminable, they arrived at an Indian village, which in this country is called a *rancheria*. The Indians seemed to be overwhelmed with the sight of their miseries. Proverbial as they are for their cruelty and thievish propensities, they now divided their own scanty supply with them. The wild and fierce savages who once visited their camps only for the purpose of hostility; who hovered around them upon the way; who shot their cattle, and murdered their companions; who actually stood upon the hills, laughing at their calamity, and mocking as their fear came, now seemed touched with the sight of their misfortunes; and their almost instinctive feeling of hostility to the white man, gave place to pity and commiseration.[73] The men looked as solemn as the grave; the women wrung their hands and wept aloud; the children united their plaintive cries to those of their sympathizing mothers. As soon as the first brief burst of feeling had subsided, all united in administering to their wants. One hurried here, and another there, all sobbing and weeping, to obtain their stores of acorns. The acorns grow upon a species of the live oak, and are from one to two inches in length. They are in appearance and taste very much like the chestnut.

---

but in the 1860s returned to San Francisco, where Foster died of cancer on February 25, 1874.

73 The Indians who had plagued the emigrants along the Humboldt were Paiutes; these California Indians were Miwoks, an unrelated people.

While they were eating these the Indian women began to prepare a sort of bread from the acorns, pulverized. As fast as they could bake them, they gave them to starving emigrants. It was a sort of food that made Mr. Eddy sick, producing constipation. It did not affect the others in this manner.

On the morning of January 11th, the chief, after sending on runners to the next village, informing them of the approach of the sufferers and to prepare food for them, accompanied them during the day with many of his tribe, an Indian being on either side of each of the sufferers, supporting them, and assisting them forward. They thus continued from day to day until the morning of the 17th, the chief from one village accompanied by some of his men, supporting them to the next, where they witnessed the same exhibition of feeling and sympathy. They received the best food the Indians had, which was acorns. But this, as I before remarked, made Mr. Eddy sick, and he could not eat them, but had lived upon grass only. On the morning of this day, the chief, with much difficulty and labor, procured for him about a gill of pine-nuts, which he ate, and found himself wonderfully refreshed.

They resumed their journey on the next morning, as usual, accompanied by a chief and a number of Indians, supporting and assisting them. Mr. Eddy felt a renewed strength, derived in part, as he supposed, from the pine-nuts, and in part, from the energy which a prospect of a speedy termination of his unhappy journey imparted. Nature seemed to have gathered up all her strength for the last effort; so that he was even able to proceed without assistance.

They had not gone more than a mile when the whole party, excepting Mr. Eddy, sunk under their complicated toils and sufferings, and all laid down to die. The Indians appeared to be greatly distressed. But the picture of his wife and children, perishing with hunger among the terrible snows of the Sierra Nevada, filled the spirit of Mr. Eddy with unspeakable anguish, and he resolved to get to where relief for them could be obtained, or to perish by the way. The old chief sent an Indian with him, instructing him, as well as Mr. E. could understand, to take him to the nearest settlement.

Mr. Eddy had suffered unutterably sorrows by the way. Fear and anguish had got hold upon him; and although he believed that his reason was never more unclouded, yet continued anxiety, the most cruel privations, and circumstances presenting the severest tests of principle, had changed his feelings and his nature in a considerable degree. Let it not therefore be imagined, that in all the dangers surrounding him he had preserved himself entire, if I may be permitted thus to express myself. Now he felt that he was escaping from a painful dream of combats, of famine and death; of cries of despair; of fathomless snows, and impassable mountains; dreams that tormented his soul and exhausted his body with fatigue. The scene was changed. The day was calm and beautiful, and the sun shone as bright as though no murder had ever been committed in its light. A ray of hope beamed to quiet his agitated and over-wrought spirit. He expected soon to be once more among the abodes of society and civilization, and to be able to send succor to his wife and children.

Thus situated, and thus feeling, he hastened on, as though famine and death were close upon the heels of himself and his family. They had not proceeded more than five miles, when they met another Indian, to whom Mr. Eddy promised some tobacco, if he would accompany them. At last it became necessary for them to assist him; and they hurried forward until they arrived at the house of Col. M. D. Richey [Matthew Dill Ritchie], about half an hour before sunset, having traveled eighteen miles. The last six miles of the way were marked by the blood from Mr. Eddy's feet. The first white woman he saw, was the daughter of the truly excellent Mr. Richey. Mr. Eddy asked her for bread. She looked at him, and without replying, burst into tears, and took hold of him to assist him into the house. He was immediately placed in bed, in which, during four days, he was not able to turn his body. In a very short time he had food brought to him by Mrs. Richey, who sobbed as she fed the miserable and frightful being before her. In a brief period Harriet, the daughter, had carried the news from house to house in the little neighborhood;[74] and horses were seen running at full speed from place to place, until all the necessary preparations were made for taking out relief to those Mr. Eddy had left in the morning. William Johnson, John Howell, John Rhodes [Rhoads], Mr. Kiser [Sebastian Keyser], Mr. Segur [Pierre Sicard], Daniel [Reason P.] Tucker, and Joseph Varro [Verrot], assembled at Mr. Richey's immediately. The females collected all the bread they had, with tea, sugar, and coffee; amounting in the whole to as much as four men could conveniently carry. Howell, Rhodes, Segur, and Tucker, immediately started on foot, with the Indians for guides, and arrived at the company, eighteen miles distant, about midnight. One man was employed all night in cooking food, and although Mr. Eddy had cautioned these gentlemen not to give the sufferers as much as they desired, yet the provisions were all consumed that

---

74 The location was Johnson's Ranch, the American settlement closest to the mountains. Howell, Keyser, Sicard, and Verrot were Johnson's neighbors; the Ritchies, Tuckers, and Rhoadses were emigrants of 1846 who, arriving too late in the season to find permanent homes, had erected cabins at or near the ranch in which to spend the winter. The ranch's owner, William Johnson, contributed supplies to the rescue parties, for which the ranch was the starting and ending point. Johnson later married and was divorced by Donner party survivor Mary Murphy. Over time his ranch faded into oblivion, until diligent research enabled Jack and Richard Steed to locate the site a few miles east of Wheatland, California; see Jack Steed, *The Donner Party Rescue Site: Johnson's Ranch on Bear River* (Santa Ana: Graphic, 1993).

night. They wept and begged for food continually, until it was exhausted. It is needless to say that they were all sick; none, however, died.

On the morning of Jan. 18th, Mr. Richey, William Johnson, Joseph Varro, and Mr. Kiser, proceeded on horseback, with more provisions for the emigrants, and to bring them in. About 10 o'clock at night they returned, surprised at the distance Mr. Eddy had traveled, which they said they could not have believed, had they not passed over it. Mr. Richey remarked when he returned, that he had followed Mr. Eddy's track six miles by the blood from his feet.

The 19th was a beautiful day, and although Mr. Eddy felt great solicitude for his family, his soul was in harmony with the aspect of the heavens, which seemed to shed upon him a new ray of hope. Filled with gratitude for his own deliverance, he sought to obtain immediate relief for those who yet remained in the Sierra Nevada. For this purpose he dictated a letter to John Sinclair, Alcalde of the Upper District,[75] residing near Sutter's Fort, about forty miles distant, informing him of the condition and peril of the emigrants, and urging him to adopt measures for their immediate rescue from famine, cannibalism, and death. An Indian courier was sent with it. Mrs. Sinclair sent back by the Indian a considerable amount of underclothing for the females of Mr. Eddy's party, who had arrived almost in a state of nudity.

Mr. Sinclair immediately dispatched a courier to San Francisco with a letter containing the intelligence.[76] The letter was taken up to the City Hotel, and read at the tea-table. The scene that followed will never be forgotten by those present. The ladies immediately left the table, sobbing and in tears. The men, overwhelmed with the picture of distress it presented, rose in haste; and many an eye unused to tears, expressed how much was felt by the burthened and sickened heart.

Chapter XI.

Preparations for Relieving the Sufferers.

The insurrection, which had entirely occupied the attention of the United States officers, and of all classes of citizens in the northern district of California, of which San Francisco was the "head-quarters"–having been

---

75 Sinclair, a Scot, had arrived in California in 1839. He served as alcalde, or judicial and administrative officer, of the San Francisco district from 1846 to 1849.

76 A letter by Sinclair describing the plight of the Forlorn Hope survivors appears in Bryant, *What I Saw in California,* 251–55.

entirely suppressed, and order restored by the middle of January, 1847, Mr. Reed, who, in consequence of that insurrection, had not been able to obtain any assistance which would aid him in making another effort to recross the mountains, now hoped to effect something, at the earliest moment that experienced mountaineers, acquainted with the Sierra Nevada, believed that sufficient intervals would elapse between the storms in that elevated region, and the settling of the snows, to warrant such an undertaking. Experienced men supposed this might occur by the last of February or first of March; although such an attempt must ever be attended with much risk and no little suffering to the party who should undertake it before the melting of the snows.

At this time Mr. Reed was at the Pueblo de San Jose, on the southeast side of San Francisco Bay, about one hundred and twenty miles from Sutter's Fort. His situation, and that of his suffering companions in misfortune, soon became known to the whole people. Among the people in the town and immediate vicinity, particularly the Mission of Santa Clara, were many immigrants of the last season, who had got in safely and in good time by the old Fort Hall road; and also some who had been caught on and near the summit of the Sierra, in the month of December, 1844, but had got through the snows themselves with great difficulty, leaving behind them all their property, most of which was destroyed by the Indians, in the spring of 1845, before they could recross the mountains to recover it.

Great sympathy was expressed for Mr. Reed and the sufferers, by all parties, as they feared that the company must soon be in a starving condition. Nothing, however, was done.

Mr. Reed, perceiving that nothing could be done at San Jose, proceeded to San Francisco, to bring the condition of the sufferers to the knowledge of the Governor, by personal representation; and with that view called upon the Alcalde of the town and district of San Francisco, Washington A. Bartlett, Lieutenant U. S. Navy, who at once took a lively interest in all his statements, and assured him that assistance should certainly be afforded him, and that immediately. Lieut. Bartlett waited upon the Governor, and introduced Mr. Reed, who told his painful story; when Capt. Hull stated that he had that morning received a petition from the Pueblo de San Jose; but as he had neither the men nor means to fit out such an expedition as the petition called for, he would consult with the Alcalde, and see what could be done. He remarked, that he thought petitions would do but little toward affording relief, if that was all the people were disposed to do. Lieut. Bartlett informed him that, from what he had already learned in conversation with the principal citizens of the town, a very liberal subscription could be obtained, and a relief company started in a very short time, if the Governor would give it his countenance and support. Governor Hull stated that he would do all in his power, both officially and as a private citizen, and that relief must be sent.

Lieut. Bartlett then informed the Governor that he would issue a call for a public meeting that evening, when the Governor authorized him to subscribe fifty dollars on his account. Capt. Mervine, U. S. Navy, and Mr. Richardson, U. S. Collector, subscribed the same amount.

The meeting was at once called; and at 7, P.M., February 3d, nearly every male citizen of San Francisco, and the officers of the United States forces, assembled in the saloon of the principal hotel, to consider what should be done.

His Honor the Alcalde called the meeting to order, by reading his call upon them to assemble; and then, after stating that Governor Hull designed to do all he could in the matter, read to the meeting the petition from San Jose, and expressed his belief that, although the citizens of San Francisco had never before been called upon to exercise a collective charity, this call would result in something more than petition; but that, as he did not wish to forestall their action by his suggestions, he hoped they would organize the meeting independently of the magistracy, and thus afford him an opportunity of acting in his private capacity with his fellow-citizens and brother officers. Frank Ward, Esq., was then called to the chair, and William Pettet, Esq., was appointed secretary.

Mr. Reed having come into the room, the people desired him to state to them his opinion of what would be required to make an expedition successful in its results. But Mr. Reed begged to decline, alleging that his feelings were such, that he could not command himself sufficiently to express himself publicly, with the conviction ever on his mind that, in all probability, his wife and children were then starving. Overpowered with emotion by the delivery of a few remarks, he sat down with tears streaming from his eyes, and showing how severe was his suffering.

Mr. Dunleary, with whom Mr. Reed lodged (himself an immigrant),[77] now rose, and stated that, in conversation with Mr. Reed at his house, he had gathered his views, and that he himself had traveled the road, and supposed he could estimate pretty closely where the company then must be; he should, with the indulgence of the meeting, give the views of Mr. Reed and himself as to what was best to be done.

Those who heard that thrilling address of Mr. Dunleary will never forget the effect upon his attentive audience, while he related the trials of their journey and the probably fate of the starving company, unless relief was soon carried to them—perhaps already too late; but it was hoped that, if prudent, they could hold out till the first of March. (It must be remembered

---

77 James Dunleary, a Methodist minister, is frequently mentioned in accounts of the 1846 migration.

that nearly the entire population of San Francisco, then resident there, were immigrants by sea, and entirely unacquainted with life on the road or in the mountains.) It is worthy of notice, that the sufferers encamped on the very spot (Truckee Lake) where Mr. Dunleary supposed they must have arrived the day the first snow fell, which was only thirty miles beyond the point reached by Reed and McCutcheon when they failed their first effort.

The speaker had scarcely taken his seat, when the people rushed up to the chairman's table, from all parts of the hall, with their hands full of dollars. But the chairman begged they would stay their hands for a moment, and organize a little; when two committees were elected—one to solicit subscriptions (scarcely necessary), and also a treasurer, and a committee of purchases of supplies. These were instructed to consult with the Alcalde, who was requested to act with both committees. The subscription was then opened, and $700 subscribed before the meeting adjourned.

Messrs. Ward and Smith, in addition to a generous subscription, offered their fine launch, *"Dice mi Nana,"* free of charge, to transport the expedition to Feather river. Mr. John Fuller volunteered to pilot the launch, and Passed-midshipman [Selim E.] Woodworth, U. S. N., volunteered to take charge of the expedition, under instructions from the committee and Governor, and carry out the wishes of the people in aiding Mr. Reed to save the sufferers.

The committee at once dispatched a courier to the Redwood, forty miles south, for Mr. Dennis Martin, as it was not known that any other person could be had who could pilot in the mountains, when covered with snow. A pilot was all-important to prevent the loss of the party going out— at least to take the very shortest route to Truckee's lake.

The next day was employed in adding to the subscription, and purchasing any thing in the market which the best judgement could suggest as necessary. Howard Oakley volunteered to go with Mr. Woodworth, and men were obtained to work the launch up the river. The utmost expedition was used to get Messrs. Woodworth and Reed started. The courier returned from the Redwood, stating that Mr. Martin could not possibly go, in consequence of his engagements.

On the 5th all was ready for a start with the evening tide, when Captain Sutter's launch, "Sacramento," appeared off the town, and on anchoring, the Alcalde received from Justice Sinclair a letter, which, while it filled the hearts of all with horror by its terrible details; and incited to additional efforts of relief, was softened by the pleasing reflection that they had not waited for such an appeal to move them to action.

That letter, honorable to the writer and Captain Sutter, and well calculated to rouse to exertion, was at once laid before Governor Hull, and read at the tables of the principal hotels, by the committees and citizens generally; and, as it contained the information so much needed, enabled the committees of relief to act more understandingly. It being now known that a relief-party were actually on the route, and would probably succeed in bringing out of the snows a considerable number of the sufferers, it was determined to make every provision necessary to relieve both the sufferers and those who had gone to their aid, and to have a relief-camp established at the most eligible point on the route, and also to provide liberally for the wants of the emigrants, in food and clothing, should any party succeed in getting them out. It was, therefore, determined to increase the funds during the next day, and thus increase the supplies, in all that could be considered useful.

The same evening, February 5th, Mr. [Caleb] Greenwood,[78] an old mountaineer, also appeared at San Francisco to ask for assistance in fitting out a party to go out with himself and McCutcheon, to which end the citizens of Sonoma and Nappa [Napa], headed by Lieutenant William L. Maury, U. S. N., Commandant of the port, and Don Mariaño G. Vallejo, Ex-Commandant-general of California, had subscribed over $500 for the party, besides large donations of horses and mules, which $500 was to be paid Greenwood and company, *if they succeeded* in raising a party and going out; but as warm clothing and ready money were absolutely necessary to start an expedition, they went to San Francisco for them. Greenwood thought he would succeed, if he could secure ten or twelve men he could depend upon in the snow. He believed he could secure such men by having ready money. His horses and provisions were already in his camp, at the head of the Nappa valley.

Governor Hull now desired Lieutenant Bartlett to lay before him a statement of what was proposed to be done, as a basis for his action, on the part of the government; trusting to its generosity and humanity in sustaining him in an extraordinary expense which his position as Governor and Military Commandant of the Northern Department called upon him not to hesitate in incurring, even at the risk of its not being allowed by the government; and, on receiving from Lieutenant Bartlett a communication setting forth the facts already stated, and the appeal of Greenwood for aid to start his expedition, Captain Hull determined to appropriate $400 on government account to organize that party. Greenwood stated to Captain Hull, that he could easily get men, if he had this ready money to make advances and purchase clothing; and, as he had crossed the Sierra Nevada, while the snow lay on the summit, in April, 1846, he thought he could do it again, as soon as he could reach the mountain; and possibly, he might succeed in driving over some of his

---

78 "Old Greenwood," in his eighties, helped organize the rescue efforts. He did not himself accompany the relief parties to the camps, though his son Britton did.

horses, which he would kill in the Mountain Camp for provision for the sufferers. At any rate he and his sons, with Turner and others, could reach them on snow shoes.

As it was believed that Mr. Reed could get to the mountains quicker, by going via Sonoma and Nappa valleys, he determined to leave the next day with Mr. Greenwood, and get animals and packs prepared to meet Mr. Woodworth, at Feather river. Fifty dollars in money was given to Mr. Reed, by the committee, to pay contingencies, and an order, signed by Capt. Hull, to enable him to get the horses, and secure some men if possible. Greenwood was also to start on his independent expedition, at the earliest possible moment. Messrs. Reed and McCutcheon were supplied gratis by the committee, with every thing they required for the journey; and to Mr. Reed was also given a supply of clothing and goods, necessary for the women, who had already reached Johnson's. Mr. Reed was further directed, that in case he should have to waste any time at Feather river, for Mr. Woodworth's arrival, he was not to do so, but push on, and, if possible, drive some cattle to the edge of the snow, to relieve the party now known to be out; in which case, Mr. Woodworth had orders to get his horses, packs, and men, from Sutter's Fort; and if he could not take all on at once, Capt. Sutter was charged with the forwarding of the supplies, which he should leave behind. And Mr. Woodworth was to unload the launch at the Fort, if he should think he could get on faster by so doing.

During the 6th, the crews of the U. S. frigate Savannah, sloop of war Warren, and the marines, in garrison, on shore, carried the subscription up to $1300, which enabled the committee to get other necessaries; and, besides, to place in Mr. Woodworth's hands $100, with which to purchase cattle to drive as far as the snow, and then kill them for food for the relief-parties and sufferers. Capt. Hull, also, sent orders to Capts. Kern and Sutter, to do all in their power, by assisting with men and horses, to hurry forward the supplies.

On an application to Capt. Mervine, commanding the U. S. frigate Savannah, by Lieut. Bartlett, on the part of the committee of supplies, he furnished from the provisions of the ship twenty days' full rations for ten men or two hundred rations; that there should not be any expenditure of the supplies by the persons who should work the launch up and back.

Mr. Greenwood, with the $400 supplied to him by Capt. Hull, purchased the clothing necessary for his party, retaining the balance to make advances, and purchase provisions. All parties being thus supplied, so far as their necessities could be foreseen, set out on their errands of mercy. Messrs. Mellus and Howard tendered the gratuitous use of their launch to transport Messrs. Reed, Greenwood, McCutcheon, and others to Sonoma.

Chapter XII.

Mr. Glover's Two Expeditions for the Relief of the Sufferers.

It will be seen from the foregoing chapter, that an expedition was fitted out at San Francisco, for the relief of the emigrants at the Mountain Camp. But as another was organized a little before that, I will take it up as being the first in point of time.

In about a week after Mr. Sinclair received the letter, which has been mentioned as having been dictated by Mr. Eddy, he came to the place at which Mr. Eddy was temporarily abiding. Capt. E. [Edward M.] Kern had made an unsuccessful effort to induce men to go with relief to the immigrants, offering three dollars per day. Aquilla Glover, R. S. Mootrey, and Joseph Sel[s], were all that would consent to go;[79] and they were willing to enter upon the hazardous enterprise, without any other reward than the satisfaction derived from a consciousness of the fact that they might be instrumental, in the hands of God, in rescuing from the jaws of a miserable death a multitude of men, women, and children.

John Sinclair, Esq., and Mr. George McKinstry, Jr., returned from San Francisco about the time of the failure of the effort made by Capt. Kern. Capt. Sutter and Mr. Sinclair then proposed that they would become responsible for three dollars per day, which they would pay, if the Government of the United States would not. This induced Daniel Rhodes, John Rhodes, Daniel Tucker, and Edward Coffeymier, to join the three above mentioned. William Koon, and a man for whom I have never known any other name than that of "Greasy Jim," [probably Adolph Brueheim] also joined the expedition; but as these did not go through, no other notice will be taken of them. Capt. Sutter and John Sinclair furnished supplies and horses.

On the last day of January, the party set out, and after traveling fourteen miles, encamped on Dry Creek.

February 1.–Immediately after sunrise, Mr. Glover, who had command of the party, set out, and after traveling all day, encamped about three miles below Mr. Johnson's on Bear river. The party proceeded, the next day, on to Mr. Johnson's, where the company was occupied during the 3d and 4th, in making pack-saddles, drying beef, and in completing the preparations for the journey. Mr. Eddy had greatly improved in strength, and fancying that he could be serviceable, he here determined to accompany the expedition.

On the 5th, the party set forward; and after being helped upon a horse, Mr. Eddy proceeded on with it. They continued traveling, with some

---

79 This party, led by Glover, has come to be known as the First Relief.

delays, till February 9 **[10th]**, when they arrived at the Mule Springs. Here they found the snow so deep that it became necessary to leave the horses. And such was Mr. Eddy's weak and feeble condition, that the party refused to permit him to go any further. The 10th **[11th]** was occupied in making preparations for carrying provisions over on foot.

The following day Mr. Eddy started back for the settlements, intending to procure fresh supplies, and to return with two men to meet Mr. Glover on his way in. The party set out early in the morning, sinking at each step knee-deep in the snow. That night they encamped on Bear river. They had believed that they would be able to follow it up, and in this manner avoid the hills. But upon examination, this route was found to be impracticable, in consequence of the river breaking through cañons.

On the 12th, the party resumed their journey, and after traveling about two miles, in snow waist-deep, found it impossible to proceed, and encamped for the purpose of making snow-shoes. The following day, they traveled until noon when they encamped, and spent the afternoon in removing the snow from a *cache* of provisions made by Mr. Reed in the autumn. After digging and melting away thirteen feet of snow, the wagon was found torn in pieces by the grisly bears. The party remained in camp during the 14th, preparing packs and provisions.

On the 15th, they left Bear River valley, in consequence of the immense show-drifts upon the sides of the ridge, over which the emigrant road passes, from Yuva [Yuba] river to this valley. After traveling fifteen miles, they encamped on the wake of Yuva river. The river was entirely concealed by snow of unknown depth.

The next day, the company proceeded on three miles, when it became necessary to stop and make snow-shoes. On the 17th, after traveling five miles, they encamped on Yuva river, in dry and soft snow fifteen feet deep. They traveled eight miles, on the 18th, and encamped at the head of Yuva river, where the snow was so deep that all the low trees, and of course all the undergrowth, were covered.

February 19.–On the morning of this day, the party resumed its journey. Mr. Glover and Daniel Rhodes became so much exhausted in crossing the Sierra Nevada, that their companions were under the necessity of carrying their packs. After traveling about nine miles, they arrived at The Mountain Camp as the last rays of the setting sun were departing from the tops of the mountains. Every thing was as silent as the grave. A painful stillness pervaded the scene. Upon some of the party raising a shout, for the purpose of finding the cabins, by attracting the attention of the living–if, indeed, any did live–the sufferers were seen coming up out of their snow-holes, from the cabins, which were completely covered, the snow presenting one unbroken level. They tottered toward their deliverers, manifesting a delirium of joy, and acting in the wildest and most extravagant manner. Some wept; some laughed. All inquired, "Have you brought any thing for me?" Many of them had a peculiarly wild expression of the eye; all looked haggard, ghastly, and horrible. The flesh was wasted from their bodies, and the skin seemed to have dried upon their bones. Their voices were weak and sepulchral; and the whole scene conveyed to the mind the idea of that shout having awaked the dead from the snows. Fourteen of their number, principally men, had already died from starvation, and many more were so reduced, that it was almost certain they would never rise from the miserable beds upon which they had lain down. The unhappy survivors were, in short, in a condition the most deplorable, and beyond the power of language to describe, or of the imagination to conceive. The annals of human suffering nowhere present a more appalling spectacle, than that which blasted the eyes and sickened the hearts of those brave men, whose indomitable courage and perseverance, in the face of so many dangers, hardships, and privations, snatched some of these miserable survivors from the jaws of death, and who, for having done so much, merit the lasting gratitude and respect of every man who has a heart to feel for human woe, or a hand to afford relief.

Many of the sufferers had been living for weeks upon bullock hides, and even this sort of food was so nearly exhausted with some, that they were about to dig up from the snow the bodies of their companions, for the purpose of prolonging their wretched lives. Mrs. Reed, who lived in Brinn's cabin,[80] had, during a considerable length of time, supported herself and four children, by cracking and boiling again the bones from which Brinn's family had carefully scraped all the flesh. These bones she had often taken, and boiled again and again, for the purpose of extracting the least remaining portion of nutriment.

Some of the emigrants had been making preparations for death, and at morning and evening the incense of prayer and thanksgiving ascended from their cheerless and comfortless dwellings. Others there were, who cursed God, cursed the snow, and cursed the mountain, and in the wildest frenzy deplored their miserable and hard fate. Some poured bitter imprecations upon the head of L. W. Hastings, for having deceived them as to the road upon which he had conducted them; and all united in common fears of a common and inevitable death. Many of them had, in a great measure, lost all self-respect. Untold sufferings had broken their spirits, and prostrated every thing like an honorable and commendable pride. Misfortune had dried up the fountains of the heart; and the dead, whom their weakness make it impossible to carry out, were dragged from their cabins by means of ropes, with an apathy that afforded a faint indication of the extent of the change which a few weeks of dire suffering had produced, in hearts that

---

80 The Reeds had moved into the Breen cabin about the middle of January.

once sympathized with the distressed, and mourned the departed. With many of them, all principle, too, had been swept away from this tremendous torrent of accumulated and accumulating calamities. It became necessary to place a guard over the little store of provisions brought to their relief; and they stole and devoured the raw-hide strings from the snowshoes of those who had come to deliver them. But some there were, whom no temptation could seduce, no suffering move; who were

"Among the faithless, faithful still."

Upon going down into the cabins of this mountain camp, the party were presented with sights of woe, and scenes of horror, the full tale of which never will be told, and never ought; sights which, although the emigrants had not yet commenced eating the dead, were so revolting, that they were compelled to withdraw, and make a fire where they would not be under the necessity of looking upon the painful spectacle.

On the morning of February 20th, John Rhodes, Daniel Tucker, and R. S. Mootrey, went to the camp of George Donner, eight miles distant, taking with them a little beef. These sufferers were found with but one hide remaining. They had determined, that, upon consuming this, they would dig up from the snow the bodies of those who had died from starvation. Mr. Donner was helpless. Mrs. Donner was weak, but in good health, and might have come into the settlements with Mr. Glover's party, yet she solemnly but calmly declared that her determination to remain with her husband, and perform for him the last sad offices of affection and humanity. And this she did, in full view of the fact, that she must necessarily perish by remaining behind.

On the evening of the 20th, the party that had gone down to Mr. Donner's camp in the morning returned, bringing seven persons with them.

The next day, at noon, the party, after leaving all the provisions they could spare, commenced their return from the Mountain Camp to the settlement, with twenty-three persons, principally women and children. The results of the disastrous and horrible journey of Eddy and Foster were carefully concealed from these poor sufferers. To have acted otherwise would have been to overwhelm them with fear and despondency, and this in their condition would have proved fatal.

Mrs. Pike's child and Mrs. Kiesburg's were carried by the party. After proceeding about two miles, two of Mrs. Reed's children gave out; the one a little girl of eight years old, and the other a little boy of four. It became absolutely necessary, therefore, to return them to the Mountain Camp, or to abandon them to die upon the way. The mother was informed by Mr. Glover, that it was necessary to take them back. And now ensued that which it is hoped none may ever be called upon to witness again. She was a wife, and affection for her husband, then in the settlement, no doubt suggested her going on. But she was a mother, also and maternal love–that strongest of all feelings, that most powerful of all instincts–determined her, immediately, to send forward the two children who could walk, while she would go back with the two youngest, and die with them. It was impossible for Mr. Glover to shake this resolution, although he promised, that when he arrived at Bear River valley, he would go back for them. At length she asked, "Are you, a mason?" Upon receiving an answer in the affirmative she said, "Do you promise me, upon the word of a mason, that when you arrive at Bear River valley, you will return and bring out my children, if we shall not, in the mean time, meet their father going for them?" Mr. Glover replied, "I do thus promise." She then consented to go on. When the mother and children were about to separate, Patty, a little girl eight years of age, took her mother by the hand, and said–"Well, mamma, kiss me. Good-by! I shall never see you again. I am willing to go back to our mountain camp and die; but I can not consent to your going back. I shall die willingly, if I can believe that you will live to see papa. Tell him, good-by, for his poor Patty." The mother and little children lingered in a long embrace. Being separated, Patty turned from her mother to go back to camp. As Mr. Glover and Mr. Mootrey were taking the children back, she told them, that she was willing to go back and take care of her little brother, but that she "should never see mother again." I have given an imperfect sketch of that parting scene; but to do it justice is as impossible as to paint the rainbow, or to throw the sun upon the canvas.

While Mr. Glover and Mr. Mootrey were taking the children back to the Mountain Camp, the company continued to advance, and after proceeding about a mile, encamped at the upper end of Truckee's Lake. This lake, and the river flowing from it, derive their names from an Indian who piloted Mr. Child's company from the sinks of Mary's river to this lake. His name was Truckee, and the emigrants gave his name to the lake and the river. Fremont calls it Snow Lake or Lake Wood. The river is the west fork of Salmon-Trout river; the east fork heads in Salmon-Trout Lake; and the two unite and flow into Pyramid Lake. There are others in the neighborhood, of great beauty.

Messrs. Glover and Mootrey returned after the party had encamped; but they carefully concealed from Mrs. Reed the fact, that Brinn and wife absolutely refused to permit the children to come into the cabin, until many promises of immediate relief and succor were made. They were even then reluctantly, and with an ill grace, received.[81]

---

81 When Patty and Tommy were brought back to the cabin, the Breens were airing meat from bags which Mrs. Breen had previously assured Mrs. Reed contained only Dolan's clothes; this may account for some of the Breens' dismay.

The party were upon an allowance of one ounce of beef and a spoonful of flour, twice per day. The emigrants were almost famished, and some of them that night stole and ate the strings from Mr. Coffeymier's snow-shoes. This circumstance led to an amusing scene, which I would here present, did it not seem to be out of place in a narrative, every page of which presents scenes of horror and sights of woe.

February 22.–The company left camp in the morning, crossed the Sierra Nevada, and camped that night at the head of Yuva river. John Denton being missing at the camp, John Rhodes and one other went back and found him in a profound sleep upon the snow. They labored near an hour before they succeeded in rousing him. He was with great difficulty brought up to camp. Here a new misfortune awaited the party. Mr. Glover, upon his going out to the Mountain Camp, had made a cache of provisions at this place; but, upon examination, it was found to have been nearly all destroyed by a cougar. This circumstance rendered necessary a further reduction in the daily allowance of food. The effect and consequence of this discovery can not be fully comprehended by persons sitting in comfort, around their firesides, and in the enjoyment of an abundance of the provisions of God's mercy. The poor emigrants wept bitterly, and the stoutest and bravest hearts of those who had gone to rescue them, were not free from fear and despondency.

On the morning of the 23d, Aquilla Glover, R.S. Mootrey, and Edward Coffeymier, hastened forward in advance of the company, for the purpose of obtaining supplies at another *cache,* which had been made at Bear River valley. From this, it was proposed to obtain supplies with which to return to the sufferers. After the company had traveled about one mile, Mr. John Denton became so much exhausted, as to be unable to proceed. He informed his companions, that it was utterly impossible for him to go any further, and stated that they could be of no service to him, and that to remain with him would involve the lives of all. He therefore requested them to leave him, expressing the hope, however, that relief would be sent to him, if possible. They made a fire for him, and after gathering a pile of wood, and leaving with him nearly all the food they had, they left him by the wayside in the wilderness. It will be seen, that Mr. Reed, after this, hurried forward with the hope of rescuing him; but the vital spark had been extinguished in his weary and worn-out body. After Mr. Reed had passed on, Mr. Eddy found him with the provisions still in his pocket.

Farnham's account, derived from Mrs. Breen, does not allude to the children's chilly reception, but Patty Reed Lewis may have had it in mind when she wrote, "...if Mr. Mootry is living, & you can hear from him, he can, & will tell you, all the rest that is to be told, I close my chapter just here, Mr. McGlashan." Letter to C. F. McGlashan, April 11, 1879.

He was an intelligent and amiable young man about thirty years of age. He was a gunsmith by trade, and was a native of Sheffield, England, where he had a mother living at the time of his last hearing from home. The four years preceding his entering upon this journey, he had resided in Springfield, Illinois, where he left many warmly attached friends. Mr. Eddy had gone back into the mountains for the purpose of taking relief to the emigrants, and found him in a sitting posture, with his body slightly leaning against a snow-bank, and with his head bowed upon his breast. He had evidently fallen into a profound slumber, during the continuance of which the circulation had gradually diminished, until he ceased at once to live and suffer, and the transition of his spirit from time into eternity was unperceived.

Mr. Eddy found at his side a small piece of India rubber, a pocket pencil, and a little journal, containing a brief notice of some of the most prominent incidents of the journey, and among others of his Christmas dinner. On a slip of paper was a piece of poetry, which he had written, making some corrections by rubbing out with his India rubber, and rewriting. It was handed over to Mr. Woodworth, who published it in the "California Star." It was written in pencil, and there can be no doubt of his having composed it a little before the coming on of that heavy slumber, from which he will never awake, until the angel Gabriel shall rouse earth's sleeping millions from the grave. When the circumstances are considered in connection with the calamities in which the unhappy Denton was involved, the whole compass of English and American poetry may be challenged to furnish a more exquisitely beautiful—a more touching and pathetic piece. Simple and inornate to the last degree, yet coming from the heart, it goes to the heart. Its lines are the last plaintive notes, which wintry winds have waked from the äolian harp, the strings of which rude hands have sundered. Bring before your mind the picture of an amiable young man, who has wandered far from the paternal roof, is stricken by famine, and left by his almost equally unhappy companions to perish among the terrible snows of the great Sierra Nevada. He knows that the last most solemn hour is near. Reason still maintains her empire, and memory, faithful to the last, performs its functions. On every side extends a boundless waste of faithless snow. He reclines against a bank of it, to rise no more; and busy memory brings before him a thousand images of past beauty and pleasure, and of scenes he will never revisit. A mother's image presents itself to his mind; tender recollections crowd upon his heart, and the scenes of his boyhood and youth pass in review before him with an unwonted vividness; the hymns of praise and thanksgiving that in harmony swelled from the domestic circle around the family altar are remembered, and soothe the sorrows of the dying man; and finally, just before he expires, he writes—

"O! after many roving years,
How sweet it is to come
Back to the dwelling-place of youth–
Our first and dearest home:–
To turn away our wearied eyes
From proud Ambition's towers,
And wander in those summer-fields–
The scene of boyhood's hours.

"But I am changed since last I gazed
Upon that tranquil scene,
And sat beneath the old witch-elm,
That shades the village green;
And watched by boat upon the brook–
It was a regal galley,
And sighed not for a joy on earth,
Beyond the happy valley.

"I wish I could once more recall
That bright and blissful joy,
And summon to my weary heart
The feelings of a boy,
But now on scenes of past delight
I look, and feel no pleasure,
As misers on the bed of death
Gaze coldly on their treasure."[82]

The party, after providing as far as it was possible for the wants of Mr. Denton, resumed its journey, and after traveling about eight miles in advance, encamped. On that night a child of Mrs. Kiesburg died.

On the morning of February 24th the party resumed its journey, in great weakness, and after traveling within about eight miles of Bear River valley, encamped, and were met by R. S. Mootrey and Edward Coffeymier, with a little beef.

February 25 [27th].–The company again set out, and after traveling a short distance, met Mr. Reed. Mrs. Reed instantly rushed into her husband's arms. The affecting scene which followed the meeting of the husband and wife, the father and children, it is impossible to describe. The most generous and amiable sentiments of nature and humanity were testified in the joy this unfortunate couple exhibited, when they had sufficiently

---

82 Thornton's text of the poem differs somewhat from that which appeared in the *California Star* on April 10, 1847. The fate of Denton's journal is not known.

recovered their senses to realize that they were indeed restored to each other, after so many torturing anxieties, so many cruel misfortunes; and after encountering from their companions a madness so insensate, sustained by a courage the most heroic. They felt and expressed so vividly the happiness they enjoyed in that moment of unsurpassed rapture, that it would have drawn tears from the most obdurate heart.

But other duties and obligations made it necessary for them to separate. There yet remained in this Mountain Camp many who must die, without assistance. Patty was there; and her little brother, a pet of the whole family, was there. These aside from the peril of other sufferers, appealed to the father's heart to hasten to their rescue.

Mr. Glover's party encamped that night in Bear river valley, where they found their *cache* of provisions undisturbed. Having now a tolerable supply, young Donner [William Hook] ate too much, and was in consequence very sick. Some tobacco juice being given to him to make him vomit, he was well before morning. At breakfast, however, he again ate too much, and died before 10 o'clock.[83]

The company traveled six miles on the 26th, and encamped near the crossing of Bear river.

February 27 [March 2].–Mr. Glover's party resumed its journey early in the morning, and encamped that night at the Mule Springs, where Mr. Woodworth was encamped on bare ground, the snow being in patches. Horses had been sent from the settlements for the use of the emigrants. After resting over night, such of the sufferers as could ride, were put upon horses; and the party resuming its journey, traveled on to Cache Creek, where it encamped. On the second day of March the sufferers arrived at Johnson's, and finally terminated their laborious, exhausting and fatiguing journey, at Sutters Fort (Fort Sacramento), on the 4th of March, grateful to Almighty God for His delivering mercy, and to those whom he had honored by making them the instruments of that deliverance.

On the day of the arrival of Mr. Glover's party at Fort Sacramento, he started back with two of Capt. Sutter's Indians, having ten or twelve horses and six mules loaded with provisions.

They proceeded on to Capt. Kern's camp, about sixty miles from the fort. Here Mr. Glover sent a man (for whom, after inquiring of a number of persons in San Francisco, I could learn no other name than that of "Greasy Jim") forward to Mr. Woodworth, who was in camp at the Mule Spring, about thirty miles distant. Mr. Woodworth sent back the messenger with a

---

83 Hook, about twelve years old, was the younger of Jacob Donner's stepsons. McGlashan gives a slightly different version of his death based on the description of William G. Murphy; see *History of the Donner Party,* rev. ed. (Stanford: Stanford University Press, 1947), 155–56.

note, requesting that the horses should be brought up. Mr. Glover, upon arriving at Mr. Woodworth's camp, met Mr. Reed with Solomon Hook, Patty, and little Tommy.

Mr. Woodworth informed Mr. Glover that Eddy, Foster, and others had gone on, for the purpose of assisting the emigrants, and that it was with difficulty that a party had been obtained. He stated also that he had promised to meet the party of Messrs. Eddy and Foster, with supplies of food; but that his men were not able to go. Messrs. Mootrey and Coffeymier proposed to go, if Mr. Glover would accompany them. These three gentlemen then started, with packs of provisions upon their backs, Mr. Woodworth accompanying them. They traveled eight miles, and halted, about 3 o'clock, P.M., and made a bark shelter for Mr. Woodworth. The next morning, the party again set out, and after traveling six miles encamped at the head of Bear River valley, where a shelter had previously been prepared for Mr. Woodworth. On the following morning, the party resumed its journey, and after traveling twelve miles, encamped at the last Yuva river cañon upon the emigrant road. On the following morning, Messrs. Woodworth, Glover, and Coffeymier set out, and after traveling until about 2 o'clock, halted to make a fire and cook dinner. While thus employed, Mr. Eddy and party met them. Messrs. Woodworth, Glover, Coffeymier, and Mootrey, after dinner, commenced their return toward the settlements, and encamped at the last crossing of Yuva river, at a place where the emigrant road leaves the river. Some time after the fire had been made, Messrs. Foster, Miller, Thompson, and Eddy came up, and encamped. On the following morning, Mr. Woodworth proceeded on, with the gentlemen who where with him.

Here terminated the events connected with Mr. Glover's second expedition. The occurrences from this point properly refer themselves to the account of the expedition of Messrs. Foster and Eddy, whose story will be found.

Chapter XIII.

The First Expedition of Messrs. Reed and McCutcheon.

...... Farrago libelli.

JUVENAL.

"The miscellaneous subjects of my book."

Mr. James F. Reed, it will be remembered, had been compelled to leave his company, far back on Ogden's river, on the morning after the unhappy contest with young Snyder. Such was the hostility of the company, with the exception of Milton Elliot and William H. Eddy, to him, that he was not permitted to take a gun, or any other arms, with which to procure game, or to defend himself from savages. After he left camp, Mr. Eddy resolved that he should not be turned upon the road, under circumstances in which he must necessarily perish; and at the hazard of a quarrel with his companions in travel, he followed Mr. Reed, with a gun and some ammunition.[84]

Those who are only conversant with the modes of thought of well-regulated society, will find it difficult to understand the nature and elements of a feeling of hostility, of which the very best men upon the road often become objects. Far removed from the salutary restraining influence which law and the tribunals of justice exert upon even the most profligate and wicked; there being no public opinion in this vast wilderness, a man may have escaped from the gallows, or be a fugitive from the penitentiary, and yet exert an influence, which will finally result in producing a prejudice, and, perhaps, even a positive hostility against men of virtue and intelligence. But there were in Mr. Reed's case some elements of ill-feeling, in addition to those alluded to, which all persons can appreciate. Snyder was one of Mr. Graves' ox-drivers, a daughter of whom he was to marry.[85] This was in itself sufficient to array Mr. Graves with his family, together with all his dependents, and those over whom he could exert an influence, against Mr. Reed. Kiesburg had been required to leave another company, far back on the way, for a great impropriety, often repeated. Mr. Reed was mainly instrumental in that ejection. The divisions and subdivisions of companies, which subsequently took place, had again brought them together in the same company. And now the killing of Snyder, although clearly justifiable, seemed to present an opportunity to for gratifying a deep-seated purpose to be revenged. Accordingly we find that this man, whose character will be more fully exhibited before the curtain falls upon the scenes of this most shocking and revolting tragedy, was the first to propose hanging Mr. Reed, after the arrival of the company, at the evening encampment. This was prevented by the firmness and resolution of Messrs. Eddy and Elliott. Mr. Reed, it will be remembered, left camp on the next morning, leaving his

---

84 This according to Eddy; Virginia Reed Murphy, however, tells us it was she and Milt Elliott who took ammunition and food to the banished Reed; see her memoir, in this volume.

85 This is the earliest reference in print to the alleged romance between Mary Graves and John Snyder, which McGlashan mentioned in the first (1879) edition of his history. In a letter dated July 18, 1879, Mary Graves, by then Mrs. J. T. Clarke, denounced the tale as "trash, false trash" and requested the historian to remove it; the offending passage was revised in subsequent editions. Mary Graves has also been linked romantically with Charles T. Stanton, for little apparent reason.

family behind him, to make his way, alone and without food, through a hostile country into the settlements.[86] The history of that journey would, if carefully written, make a volume, every page of which would be replete with instruction and interest. After a thousand hairbreadth escapes, passing through the most terrible scenes, enduring the most cruel sufferings from famine and thirst, struggling with almost inevitable death, and passing days and nights of inexpressible anguish, he finally succeeded, in the good providence of God, in arriving at the settlements.

After recruiting his wasted energies, Mr. Reed obtained provisions and horses, for the purpose of going back to the relief of his family, and the other emigrants. Having passed over the road, after being thrust out by his traveling companions, he knew that they would require assistance, in order to get through. In this enterprise he was assisted by William McCutcheon, who, it will be remembered, had been sent forward with Mr. Stanton from the Salt Lake, to obtain supplies, with which to meet the emigrants. Worn down and exhausted by the journey into the settlements, Mr. McCutcheon did not accompany Mr. Stanton, on his return with two of Captain Sutter's *vaqueros*.

Messrs. Reed and McCutcheon, after obtaining twenty-six horses and mules, with the necessary provisions, and two Indians, from Captain Sutter, set out upon their expedition to cross the mountains. On the second day after leaving Mr. Johnson's, they encountered the snow. On the third day they reached the head of Bear River valley, in two feet snow, with their flour, beef, and beans, in good condition. At this place they found a man, named Jotham Curtis, who had become greatly grieved and vexed with the evil deeds of the uncircumcised Philistines, who had been the companions of his travel. He had fixed upon this spot, as an abiding place, a sort of lodge in the "vast wilderness," in which he might cease to hear of wrong and oppression. But his late companions fully reciprocated the feeling— though, perhaps, even unjustly—which prompted him to desire a separate abode, and, without asking for even a lock of his hair, had hurried forward into the settlement, leaving their afflicted and sorrowing companion to the undisputed possession of his dominions.

He had built a sort of pen, over which he had stretched his tent for a roof. This, in two feet of snow, very imperfectly answered the purpose of a palace for the mountain monarch. Not having any one as yet connected with his establishment to perform the functions of purveyor, he had been reduced to the vulgar necessity of killing and eating his old dog. Upon the whole, Jotham's opinions, like some fruits, had been matured and ripened by frost and snow. In short, his views upon the subject of the blessings of solitude had undergone a most marvelous change, which caused him to

---

86 Reed was actually accompanied by Walter Herron, one of his teamsters.

determine upon abdicating his sovereignty, on the first suitable occasion. Frost, and hail, and sleet, and snow, had conducted him through a somewhat painful process, to the conclusion that, although a "boundless contiguity of shade" would do well enough for the summer, it was not quite the thing for winter. He was therefore profuse in his thanks to Messrs. Reed and McCutcheon for having come to carry him and his "household" into the settlements. He was informed, however, that they were on their way to their friends and traveling companions, on the eastern side of the mountain; but he was assured that, upon returning, every practicable assistance would be rendered.

Messrs. Reed and McCutcheon resumed their journey the following morning, leaving one Indian and nine head of horses at Jotham's camp, to remain until they returned.

They pursued their way over a difficult mountain, along the emigrant road. Those who subsequently went to the relief of the emigrants avoided this mountain, by continuing up Bear River valley, until they entered the valley of Yuva river. The traveling was so heavy that they were unable to proceed more than three miles, when the encamped in Dry Valley, in three feet of snow. The snow was soft, day, and very light, and the horses were, in consequence, almost exhausted. The Indian who had accompanied them, became so much discouraged that he secretly left camp to return. His departure being soon discovered, Mr. Reed went back to the camp of Jotham Curtis, who stated that the Indians, after whispering together, suddenly left, about half an hour before; and that they had taken with them three of the horses, which he did not attempt to prevent, because he believed that any effort of that sort would have been useless. The fact was, that Curtis had persuaded them to leave, believing that this would make it necessary for Messrs. Reed and McCutcheon to return, when, he flattered himself, he would be taken out of the snow. Mr. Reed, finding that a further pursuit would be unavailing, returned to this camp in Dry Valley, where he arrived before daylight.

After finishing a hasty breakfast, they resumed their journey for the eastern side of the mountain, along the still ascending ridge between Bear and Yuva rivers. They proceeded, with almost incredible toil, about three miles, when they found the snow four feet deep. They at length arrived at the summit of the ridge, along which they traveled about one mile and a half to a point where they found the snow four and a half feet deep. There some of the horses becoming exhausted, lay down greatly distressed, with their noses just out of the snow. The saddle-horses were then rode about one mile further, and left; when Messrs. Reed and McCutcheon proceeded on foot for the purpose of ascertaining whether it would be possible to advance. After toiling onward about one mile, the snow was up to their arm-pits. This brought them to the ground which descends towards Yuva river. They now halted to consult. Neither had ever seen snow-shoes. After a few minutes of most anxious and painful deliberation, they resolved to go back. Upon returning to their pack-horses, they found them completely exhausted, and some of them almost smothered in snow. The heads of some were only partially visible; the packs of others were seen a little above the snow, while the head was below. Being at length extricated and taken back into the trail, they were driven to the camp of Jotham Curtis, where Messrs. Reed and McCutcheon arrived at night, suffering greatly from fatigue, and with feelings of the deepest dejection and despondency.

After a very brief rest, Mr. McCutcheon commenced cooking their supper in silence. Mrs. Curtis was unwell and weary. Her husband was dispirited, worn down, and cross as the grisly bear in the forest in which he had made his camp. At length, upon some trifling pretense, he commenced pouring upon Mr. McCutcheon abuse without measure or stint. To all this, however, Mr. McCutcheon gave no attention. His hands were busy with the preparations for the evening meal, and his mind was beyond the mountain. Curtis, however, was rather encouraged by this silence, and his whole conduct was calculated to remind one of a little dog barking at a mastiff. A close observer might indeed have observed, at intervals, the color coming into Mr. McCutcheon's face, and an occasional curl of the brow, which seemed to indicate that it was possible for the little fellow, sitting upon the ground with his toes in the ashes, to get a snap after a while. Mrs. Curtis ventured indeed, once or twice, to hint that neither of the gentlemen were doing any thing wrong, and that herself and husband ought to be very grateful for the deliverance thus brought to them. This, however, only served to increase his wrath, and he made some remarks, amounting to something more than a hint, of his intention to revive in practice an old common-law right, which, although now obsolete, yet was once connected with the marital relation. Mr. McCutcheon, who was a great stalwart Kentuckian, full six feet six inches in height, with a habit of quoting hard names from Shakespeare, as will hereafter be seen, seemed now to be roused into something like a sudden sharp growl, which indicated that he was not in the habit of showing his teeth for nothing; and that he would probable give some little dog a most terrible bite before long.

"Harkee, here, you little mister," said McCutcheon, straightening himself up from over the fire where he had been cooking meat. "Lookee here, I say; if I hear you, you little pictur, saying another word upon the subject, I'll put you on the fire there, and I'll broil you to a cracklin' in two seconds."

Curtis cowered in an instant before the fire of the eyes that flashed upon him; and his wife said, with a trembling voice, that "Jotham meant no harm; he did not intend to do such a thing for any thing in the world—he was only tired, unwell, and a little fretful; but he didn't mean what he said."

84

"He'd better not," said McCutcheon, as he stooped down again to resume his cooking, "if he don't want me to tear off his arms, and beat him with the bloody ends."

In a short time supper was ready; and McCutcheon said to Mr. Reed, in a whisper, "Reed, ask that starveling, eelskin, snapper, and his wife, to eat of our supper. I don't want to do it; but I know they must be as hungry as wolves. Poor thing, she looks as though she needed food. He's cross, to be sure; but I'd feed Beelzebub, if he was hungry, rather then have him go away and report that a Kentuckian ever turned any one away empty."

"Well, for my part," replied Mr. Reed, with a laugh, "I would not like to have the devil for a guest; but I'll do as you desire."

Mr. Reed then kindly and cordially invited Mrs. Curtis and her husband to partake of the evening meal which had been prepared. The poor woman was hungry, and of course did not decline; but her husband looked sullen, and sat like a spoiled boy in the pouts.

"Why," said McCutcheon at length, as he ran his fingers backward through his long, bushy hair, and looked with well-affected fierceness upon Curtis, "why don't you come to your supper?"

"I–I–I ca–can–can't eat."

"I know better," bellowed McCutcheon, in a voice of thunder. "You're not sick; you can eat; you shall eat. You are as hungry as a wolf. What's the use of being a fool here in the woods. If you don't get right up now, and come here and sit down by your wife, and take hold of your supper, sick or well, I'll take hold of you, and I'll shake you right out of your trowsers in two seconds, you ugly little pictur, you."

This eloquent harangue evidently impressed the mind of Curtis, with the conviction that at least seven evil ones had taken possession of McCutcheon; and deeming it imprudent, at the time, to contend against such odds he acquiesced, and contrived to do most ample justice to the supper.

During the night, when Messrs. Reed and McCutcheon were supposed to be asleep, Curtis commenced bestowing the most abusive epithets upon his wife for having eaten so readily of the supper. She seemed to be half frightened out of her wits, and replied, in a faltering voice, that he knew very well, that at that time, they had not a mouthful remaining of the old dog.

"Reed, Reed!" said McCutcheon, in a low whisper, accompanied with a smart nudge of the elbow in the ribs, "listen to that villainous compound of all that is cowardly, that woman-fighter, that thing, who is so fierce and pugnacious just now. Listen, Reed, she's crying. Shall I get up, and beat him to death? Tell me, quickly!"

"No, no!" replied Mr. Reed. "What will you beat him to death for? Let them alone. It is not probable he will offer any personal violence to his wife?!"

"Yes, yes, I know that," said McCutcheon, "but then he's making her cry. It's almost breaking my heart," he continued, as he seemed to be gulping down a sob. "I never could bear to hear a woman cry. And I won't bear it," added he, with an emphatic expletive, and in a voice which had gradually risen from a whisper to a shout.

His actions corresponded with his words; and Curtis, before he expected it, found himself performing sundry feats of ground and lofty tumbling, which finally ended by his finding himself, by some process of legerdemain, in a deep snow-drift, where he was told to remain until it had cooled his wrath.

Curtis at length gathered himself up, and upon coming to the fire, said something about his having fallen among thieves. McCutcheon replied that he had just before fallen into a snow-drift, but that he had previously fallen among the frost and snows of the Sierra Nevada, where he had been found by a couple of good Samaritans, who were not willing to be called hard names, while they were taking him to an inn. Nor would they permit him to abuse one whom he was under obligation to cherish and protect.

Day at length dawned; the morning meal was prepared, and eaten. Reed and McCutcheon then set about *cacheing* their beef, etc., up in the trees, and the flour in Curtis' wagon, reserving only enough for present use. They then resumed their journey, with all the animals, except a mule that had frozen to death during the night.

After traveling about four miles, they encamped at the foot of the valley. During the night Curtis again became very abusive. No one, however, seemed inclined to notice him, except McCutcheon, who said to Reed, in a whisper, "Reed, Reed! do you hear that fellow again, that starveling, piti-ful-hearted Titan, that plague of all cowards, that—"

"Stop, stop," said Reed, amused at his quotations from Shakespeare, and following the example, continued—

> "'breathe, awhile,
> You tire yourself in base comparisons.'"

"Well, well, I have no patience with him," said McCutcheon. "I have a mind to get up and maul him, until nothing is left of him."

Curtis hearing a whisper, and having a very sensible recollection of the snow drift, observed during the remainder of the night a very becoming silence, and his conduct was otherwise unexceptionable. In the morning, however, he was observed before breakfast to take a firebrand to a place some distance from the camp, as though he was about to make a separate fire. This did not escape the keen eye of the rough and resolute McCutch-eon, who immediately went to him, and thundered out a series of his favor-ite Shakespearian epithets—"You villainous coward! You panderly rascal! You Phrygian Turk! You knave! You—You—"

Here he seemed to have reached the end of his breath, and of his vocab-ulary at the same moment. But Curtis, anticipating what he would have said, replied, that he was "afeard" of being killed, and that he had gone out there to make a fire.

"Now march right back," said McCutcheon, "and sit down by the fire, and behave yourself, and don't let me know you to make a Judy of yourself any more, or I'll whip you half to death. If it was not for your wife, we would leave you, and trouble ourselves no more with you. But prudence requires us to take you both in together. But you will, I expect, provoke me to give you a most terrible thrashing."

After breakfast, the horses and mules were caught and packed. They resumed their journey, and Curtis pushed forward for the purpose of avoiding the labor of assisting to drive. McCutcheon observed it, and suggested to Reed the propriety of calling back "that unconfinable baseness," as he denominated Curtis. He was permitted to go forward, however; he seemed to hurry on as though he knew that McCutcheon or the pestilence was at his heels. About 10 o'clock, A.M., a pack of goods, owned by Curtis, became loosened, and fell under the mule. This brought McCutcheon's stentorian lungs into full play, calling Curtis to return. The hills and valleys echoed back the Shakespearian epithets by which he sought to arrest the onward progress of the fugitive. Curtis was driving through the snow at full speed. McCutcheon was behind gaining upon him, and bellowing like "a bull of Bashan." Curtis was in the mean time "booming it," as McCutcheon phrased it, as though he every moment expected to feel the horns. At length, McCutcheon game up with him, and suddenly restored him to hearing, by making some half a dozen very professional applications, not to the organs affected, but to another part, upon the principle of counter-irritation; repeating the application some two or three times on their way back to the mules. As they came with hearing distance McCutcheon called out, "I tell you Reed, he was booming it! The Flemish drunkard—the book of riddles—the mechanical salt-butter rascal—the Banbury cheese—the base Gangorian wight, was going as fast as a race-horse, and was as deaf as an adder, though I bellowed at him like a mad bull, when no more than twenty feet from him."

This little incident having passed off, the party continued on until night, when they encamped. The evening wore away without any thing of much interest occurring. In the morning, after breakfast, they resumed their journey.

After getting out of the snow, Messrs. Reed and McCutcheon gave to Mrs. Curtis and her husband all the food that remained, and then pushed on to Mr. Johnson's, where they arrived in the evening.[87]

---

87 In 1871 Mrs. Curtis related a very different version of these events to Frances H. McDougall. The latter's article, "The Donner Tragedy: A Thrilling Chapter in Our Pioneer History," prompted rebuttals from Reed and McCutchen, which Mrs. McDougall rebutted in turn. The exchange is printed in this volume.

Chapter XIV.

Second Expedition of Messrs. Reed and McCutcheon.

About the 22d of February, 1847, Mr. Reed again started from William Johnson's house, with nine men on foot, loaded with provisions.[88] Mr. Eddy wished to accompany him, but such was his weak and feeble condition, that it was not thought safe for him to attempt it. About the 27th February, this party met that of Mr. Glover in Bear River valley, coming out of the snow, at a place where the parties passed in one hour from naked ground to ten feet of snow. Here Mr. Glover informed him that, on the day previous, he had left John Denton at the head of the wake of Yuva river, twenty-five miles distant. That they had gathered for him a pile of wood, and left him with but a very scanty supply of provisions, because they had not more themselves; and that if Mr. Reed would hasten forward he might find him alive. Mr. Reed pressed on; but he was too late; the vital spark had fled. He had died like a lamp which ceases to burn for want of aliment. Without remaining to observe any thing beyond the fact of his decease, a quilt was hastily thrown over him, and the party pursued their journey. About 11 o'clock, A.M., of each day, the snow would become so soft as not to sustain their weight, and this made it necessary for them to remain in camp until midnight, at which time each day's journey was commenced. They thus continued to toil on until March 1st, when they arrived at the Mountain Camp, where they found the emigrants in a most distressing condition.

When Mr. Reed found them, they were in circumstances the most desperate and shocking. He had in the morning sent forward three of his strongest and most active young men, Charles Cady, Charles Stone, and Mr. [Nicholas] Clark, with provisions to the Mountain Camp, with directions to distribute the food among those most requiring it, and to remain by them until he came up, for the purpose of preventing them from eating so much as to injure them. The first camp which he reached was that of Mr. Brinn, whom he found with a sufficient supply of provisions, consisting of beef which he had killed when he first made this camp. He had

---

88 There is some uncertainty as to the membership of this group. Reed's diary of the Second Relief names William McCutchen, Charles Cady, Nicholas Clark, Charles Stone, Joseph Gendreau, Matthew Dofar, and John Turner. Hiram Miller is known from other sources to have been present. A document in *Donner Miscellany* (pp. 80–81) dated March 2, lists items from the estate of Jacob Donner which Miller sold to Dofar, Stone, Clark, Cady, and "Jaundro." Henry Dunn and Joseph Verrot, who are not mentioned elsewhere as having taken part in this relief party, are also listed as purchasers. The items may have been bought for them rather than by them, for Keseberg is listed as a purchaser even though he was not present; see below, note 93.

previously consumed all, or nearly all, of his hides. He had, in fact, been more provident in this respect than any of the other emigrants.

At this camp Mr. Reed saw his daughter Patty sitting on the top of the snow with which the cabin was covered. Patty saw her father at some distance, and immediately started to run and meet him. But such was her weakness, that she fell. Her father took her up, and the affectionate girl, bathed in tears, embraced and kissed him, exclaiming, "Oh! papa, I never expected to see you again, when the cruel people drove you out of the camp. But I knew that God was good, and would do what was best. Is dear mamma living? Is Mr. Glover living? Did you know that he was a mason? Oh! my dear papa, I am so happy to see you. Masons must be good men. Is Mr. Glover the same sort of mason we had in Springfield? He promised mamma, upon the word of a mason, that he would bring me and Tommy out of the mountain.* Mr. Reed told Patty that masons were every where the same, and that he had met her mother and Mr. Glover, and had relieved him from his pledge, and that he had himself come to her and little Tommy to redeem that pledge, and to take out all that were able to travel. Mr. Reed, not seeing little Tommy, feared that he was dead. But Patty informed him, as well as her sobs would permit, that he was sleeping. He immediately descended through the snow-hole that led down into the cabin, and found his little boy asleep, and reduced to a mere skeleton. The feelings of the father upon seeing his child in a situation which may not here be described, may be imagined. He woke him up, but the little boy did not recognize him, and would frequently ask Patty, to whom he looked as a sort of mother, if that really was his father. At length he became assured and happy, and seemed to feel that he once more had a protector and friend.

After giving some bread to his own and Mr. Brinn's children, he went to Kiesburg's cabin, about two hundred yards distant, where he found Mr. Stone, who had given to them some refreshments, and was washing the children's clothes. He found them in a most deplorable condition. Mr. Foster's child and Mr. Reed's [Eddy's] were in bed, crying incessantly for something to eat. They would stretch out their arms and beg, in the most moving terms and accents, for food. Mr. Stone had already given the children all that he prudently could. But such was the force of the affecting appeal made by these poor, helpless, and unprotected sufferers, that Mr. Reed could not restrain the prompting of his Irish heart,[89] or refrain from

---

* It may be proper to mention that the author is not himself a mason. [Thornton's note]

89 Reed had been born in northern Ireland and came to the United States in his youth. He may have retained an accent, for Mary Graves also refers to him as an Irishman in her letter to Levi Fosdick, this volume.

giving heed to their cries, and he gave them more, perhaps, than was prudent. Mrs. Murphy, an amiable woman, and the grandmother of Mr. Foster's children, informed Mr. Reed that these children had been in that bed fourteen days. The imagination must fill up the picture.

Messrs. Reed and McCutcheon warmed water, and then divested themselves of their clothing, and left it out upon the snow, in order to avoid becoming polluted with vermin, thoroughly washed the children in soap suds, oiled them, and wrapped them in flannel, and put them in bed in comparative comfort. It is due to Mrs. Murphy to say, that she could not prevent this condition in which Mr. Foster's child and Mr. Reed's were found, for she was herself so reduced by famine, that she was helpless. Mr. Reed was now under the necessity of helping her up. She would sometimes weep, and then again laugh. She was, in short, reduced to childishness.[90] Such, indeed, was the condition of the greatest number.

After the children were thus washed, and their wants supplied, Mr. Reed took a kettle of warm water to Kiesburg, and proposed, with the aid of Mr. McCutcheon, to perform the same offices for him. Kiesburg seemed to be greatly moved, and exclaimed in broken English, "Oh, Mr. Reed! is it possible that you have come to wash the feet and body of a poor miserable wretch who once sought to have you hung upon the end of his wagon-tongue? I have so wronged you—have so mistaken your whole character that I can not permit you to do it. Any one but you may do it. This is too much." Mr. Reed said to him that it was an office of humanity, which he was called upon to perform, irrespective of the past; and that oblivion should cover the unhappy scenes and circumstances that had occurred by the way. The men had now, for the first time, a little leisure to observe. The mutilated body of a friend, having nearly all the flesh torn away, was seen at the door—the head and face remaining entire. Half consumed limbs were seen concealed in trunks.[91] Bones were scattered about. Human hair of different colors was seen in tufts about the fire-place. The sight was overwhelming; and outraged nature sought relief by one spontaneous outcry of agony, and grief, and tears. The air was rent by the wails of sorrow and distress that ascended at once, and, as if by previous concert, from that charnel house of death beneath the snow.

---

90 No doubt all the emigrants had become mentally unstable to some degree. Describing the survivors she saw at Sutter's Fort, Eliza Gregson reported, "the most part of them were crazey & their eyes danced & sparkled in their heads like stars"; "Mrs. Gregson's 'Memory,'" 121. Although characterized as "old Mrs. Murphy" in the Donner literature—W. C. Graves estimated her age as fifty—Levinah Murphy was only thirty-seven years old when she died in March 1847.

91 The reference to body parts concealed in trunks became part of Donner party folklore; see note 114, below.

Messrs. Reed, Joseph Jaundro, Matthew Dofar, and Hiram Miller then proceeded some eight miles to the camp of Messrs. Donner; Messrs. Turner, Wm. McCutcheon, and Britton Greenwood, being left with Mrs. Graves, for the purpose of *cacheing* her few effects, and to have the sufferers in readiness to return with the party to the settlements. When Mr. Reed arrived there he found Messrs. Cady and Stone, who had been sent in advance with provisions to this camp. They informed him that when they arrived at the camp, Baptiste had just left the camp of the widow of the late Jacob Donner, with the leg and thigh of Jacob Donner, for which he had been sent by George Donner, the brother of the deceased. That was given, but the boy was informed that no more could be given, Jacob Donner's body being the last they had. They had consumed four bodies, and the children were sitting upon a log, with their faces stained with blood, devouring the half-roasted liver and heart of the father, unconscious of the approach of the men, of whom they took not the slightest notice even after they came up. Mrs. Jacob Donner was in a helpless condition, without any thing whatever to eat except the body of her husband, and she declared that she would die before she would eat of this. Around the fire were hair, bones, skulls, and the fragments of half-consumed limbs. Mr. Reed and party, after removing the tent to another place, and making Mrs. Donner as comfortable as possible, retired for the purpose of being relieved for a brief period from sights so terrible and revolting. They had not gone far when they came to the snow-grave of Jacob Donner. His head was cut off, and was lying with the face up, the snow and cold having preserved all the features unaltered. His limbs and arms had been severed from the body which was cut open—the heart and liver being taken out. The leg and thigh which the boy, John Baptiste, had obtained, had been thrown back, upon the party coming up with relief. Other graves were seen, but nothing remained in them but a few fragments.[92]

The party then proceeded to the tent of George Donner, who was in a weak and helpless condition. Mrs. Donner appeared to be strong and healthy. She would not consent to go, leaving her husband; and she declined letting her children go, because she said that she hoped, from what she had learned, that Mr. Woodworth, would be in camp in a few days, at most, when she thought they would all be able to go into the settle-ment. Mr. Cady was in the mean time sent back to the upper camp with instructions to return that night with seven days' provisions. After leaving a man to take care of the sufferers, and to give them their food, Mr. Reed and party returned to the upper camp, taking two of Jacob Donner's children,

---

92 The harrowing scene at the Donner camp is also reported, but without the names, in the Merryman article.

and bringing up a pair of new boots for Kiesburg.[93] After leaving Mr. Stone to take care of those at this camp, and to give to them, in proper quantities and at proper intervals, seven days' provisions, the party set out to cross the mountain.

The following are, in substance, extracts from a journal kept by one of the emigrants, and are introduced here for the purpose of presenting at least an imperfect account of the sufferers in their Mountain Camp.[94] Although it possesses great interest, as showing some of the dire sufferings of the miserable survivors who passed through an ordeal more horrible and terrific than that of either fire or water, yet it must not be regarded as perfect. A multitude of the most shocking and revolting circumstances are designedly suppressed, as being unfit for the sober pages of history. Notwithstanding the unspeakable distress which is known by the world to have existed, and the thrilling scenes which the narrative of this lamentable affair presents, the *full* story will never be told, and the half of that which is known by the people of California will never appear in print; and indeed ought not.

"*Dec.* 17.–Pleasant. William Murphy returned from the mountain last evening. Milton and Noah started for Donner's eight days ago, and not having returned, it is probable that they are lost in the snow."

"*Dec.* 19.–Snowed last night, but is thawing today, although the wind is northwest."

"*Dec.* 20.–Clear and pleasant. Mrs. Reed is here. We have yet received no account from Milton. Charles Burger set out for Donner's, but was unable to proceed, and turned back. These are tough times, but we are not discouraged for our hope is in God."

"*Dec.* 21.–Milton got back last night from Donner's camp, and brings with him the sad news of the death of Jacob Donner, Samuel Shoemaker, Rianhard, and Smith. The others are in a low situation. The snow fell during the whole of the last night, with a strong southwest wind."

---

93 These boots, priced at $4.00, are listed as Keseberg's purchase in the document referred to in note 88 above.

94 Patrick Breen kept a diary from November 1846 to March 1847, which he gave after his rescue to George McKinstry. McKinstry submitted it to the *California Star,* which published a much edited version of it on May 22, 1847. The diary appeared in this form in many newspapers across the United States, sometimes attributed to McKinstry, since no other name appeared in connection with it. Thornton changes the *Star*'s version in many particulars: entries have been omitted, names inserted, and punctuation altered. The *Star*'s text and its derivatives were the only versions available until 1910, when Francis J. Teggart published an accurate transcription based on the original manuscript in *Publications of the Academy of Pacific Coast History.* Another version of this diary appears in W. C. Graves's memoir, in this volume.

"*Dec.* 23.–Clear to-day. Milton took some of his meat away. All well at their camp. Began this day to read the 'Thirty days' prayers.' Almighty God, grant the request of unworthy sinners."

"*Dec.* 24.–Rained all night, and still continues. Poor prospect for any kind of comfort, spiritual or temporal."

"*Dec.* 25.–Began to snow yesterday. Snowed all night, and it continues to fall rapidly. Extremely difficult to get wood. Offered our prayers to God this Christmas morning. The prospect is appalling, but we trust in Him."

"*Dec.* 27.–Cleared off yesterday, and continues clear. Wood growing scarcer. A tree when felled sinks into the snow, and is hard to get at."

"*Dec.* 30.–Fine, clear morning. Froze hard last night, about ten o'clock."

"*Dec.* 31.–Last of the year. May we spend the coming year better than we have the past. This we purpose to do, if it is the will of the Almighty to deliver us from our present dreadful situation. Amen. Morning pleasant, but cloudy. Wind east by south. Looks like another snow-storm. Snowstorms are dreadful to us. It is very deep."

"*Jan.* 1, 1847.–We prayed the God of mercy to deliver us from our present calamity, if it be His holy will. Commenced snowing last night, and snows a little yet. Provisions getting very scarce. dug up a hide from under the snow yesterday, but have not commenced on it yet."

"*Jan.* 3.–Fair during the day. Froze during the night. Mrs. Reed talks of crossing the mountain with her children."

"*Jan.* 4.–Fine morning. Looks like spring. Mrs. Reed and Virginia, Milton Elliott, and Eliza Williams, started a short time ago, with the hope of crossing the mountains. Left their three children here. It was hard for Mrs. Reed to part with them."

"*Jan.* 6.–Eliza came back yesterday, being unable to proceed. The others kept ahead."

"*Jan.* 8.–Very cold this morning. Mrs. Reed and the others came back, not being able to find the way on the other side of the mountain. They have nothing to live on but hides."

"*Jan* 10.–Began to snow last night, and it still continues. Wind north-northwest."

"*Jan.* 13.–Snowing fast; snow higher than the shanty. It must be thirteen feet deep. Can not get wood this morning. It is a dreadful sight for us to look upon."

"*Jan* 14.–Cleared off yesterday. The sun shining brilliantly renovates our spirits. Praise the God of Heaven!"

"*Jan* 15.–Clear day again. Wind northwest. Mrs. Murphy snow-blind. Lanthron not able to get wood. Has but one ax between him and Kiesburg. Looks like another storm. Expecting some account from Sutter's soon."

"*Jan* 17.–Eliza Williams came here this morning. Lanthron crazy last night. Provisions scarce. Hides our main subsistence. May the Almighty send us help."

"*Jan.* 21.–Fine morning. John Baptiste and Mr. Denton came this morning with Eliza, who will not eat hides. Mrs. —— sent her back to live or die on them."

"*Jan.* 22.–Began to snow after sunrise. Likely to continue. Wind west."

"*Jan.* 23.–Blew hard, and snowed all night. The most severe storm we have experienced this winter. Wind west."

"*Jan.* 26.–Cleared off yesterday. To-day fine and pleasant. Wind southwest. In hopes we are done with snow-storms. Those who went to Sutter's Fort not yet returned. Provisions getting scant, and the people growing weak, living on a small allowance of hides."

"*Jan.* 27.–Commenced snowing yesterday, and continues today. Lewis S. Kiesburg died three days ago.[95] Wood growing so scarce, that we don't have fire enough to cook our hides."

"*Jan.*30.–Fair and pleasant. Wind west. Thawing in the sun. John and Edward Brinn went to Mr. Graves' this morning. Mr. —— seized upon Mrs. ——'s goods, to hold them until paid for a little food which she bought. The hides which herself and family subsisted upon were also taken away from her. An opinion may be formed from these facts of the fare in camp. Nothing is to be had by hunting; yet, perhaps, there will soon be."

"*Jan.* 31.–The sun does not shine out brilliantly this morning. Froze hard last night. Wind northwest. Lanthron Murphy died last night, about 10 o'clock. Mrs. Reed went to Graves' this morning, to look after her goods."

"*Feb.* 5.–Snowed hard until 12 o'clock last night. Many uneasy for fear we shall perish with hunger. We have but a little meat left, and only three hides. Mrs. Reed has nothing but one hide, and that is in Graves' house. Milton lives there, and likely to keep that. Eddy's child [Margaret] died last night."

"*Feb.* 8.–It snowed faster last night and to-day than it has done this winter before. Still continues. Wind southwest. Murphy's folks and Kiesburg's say they can not eat hides. I wish we had enough of them. Mrs. Eddy died on the night of the 7th."

"*Feb.* 9.–Mrs. Pike's child all but dead. Milton is at Murphy's not able to get out of bed. Kiesburg never gets up. Says he is not able. Mrs. Eddy and child were buried in the snow to-day. Wind southeast."

---

95 This is the infant son of Louis Keseberg, apparently born on the journey. On June 3, Bryant wrote, "A wagon belonging to a German emigrant named Keyesburgh, whose wife carried in her arms a small child, and was in a delicate situation [i.e., pregnant], was upset." The child was Ada Keseberg, aged about three, who died after leaving the camps with the First Relief.

"*Feb.* 10.–Beautiful morning. Thawing in the sun. Milton Elliot died last night at Murphy's shanty. Mrs. Reed went to see after his effects this morning. J. Denton trying to borrow meat from Graves. Had none to give. They had nothing but hides. All are entirely out of meal, but a little we have. Our hides are nearly all eaten up; but, with God's help, spring will soon smile upon us."

"*Feb.* 12.–Warm, thawy morning."

"*Feb.* 14.–Fine morning, but cold. Buried Milton Elliot in the snow. John Denton not well."

"*Feb.* 15.–Morning cloudy until 9 o'clock, then cleared off warm. Mrs. Graves refused to give Mrs. Reed her hides, and to prevent her from getting Sutter's pack-hides to eat, put them upon her shanty."

"*Feb.* 16.–Commenced raining last evening, and then turned to snow in the night, which continued to fall until morning. Weather changeable; sunshine, then light showers of hail, accompanied by strong winds. We all feel very unwell, and the snow is not getting much less at present."

"*Feb.* 19.–Froze hard last night. Aquila Glover, R. S. Mootrey, Joseph Sell, Daniel Rhodes, John Rhodes, Daniel Tucker, and Edward Coffeymier, arrived from California with provisions, but left the greater part on the way. To-day is clear and warm for this region."

"*Feb.* 20.–John Rhodes, Daniel Tucker, and R. S. Mootrey went to Donner's Camp this morning, and returned this evening, bringing seven persons to go into the settlements. They start tomorrow."

"*Feb.* 21.–To-day, at noon, the party set out with twenty-three of our number, some of them being in a very weak state. Two of Mr. Reed's children brought back."

"*Feb.* 22.–Mrs. Kiesburg started with the Californians yesterday, and left her husband here unable to go. Pike's child [Catherine] died two days ago, and was buried in the snow this morning."

"*Feb.* 23.–Froze hard last night. To-day pleasant and thawy; has the appearance of spring, all but the deep snow. Wind south-southeast. Shot a dog to-day, and dressed his flesh."

"*Feb.* 25.–To-day, Mrs. Murphy says, the wolves are about to dig up the dead bodies around her shanty. The nights are too cold to watch, but they hear them howl."

"*Feb.* 26.–Hungry times. Mrs. Murphy said here yesterday, that she thought she would commence on Milton and eat him. I do not think she has done so yet. It is distressing. The Donners told the California folks six days ago, that they would commence on the dead people, if they did not succeed that day or the next in finding their cattle, then ten or twelve feet under the snow. They did not know the spot or near it. They have done it ere this."

"*Feb.* 28.–One solitary Indian passed by yesterday, coming from the lake. He had a heavy pack on his back, and gave me five or six roots resembling onions in shape, have tough fibers, and tasting something like a sweet potato."

"*March* 1.—Mr. J. F. Reed and nine men arrived this morning from Bear Valley with provisions. They are to start in two or three days, and *cache* our goods here. They say that the snow will remain until June."

The foregoing extracts from a journal kept during the winter, will present some imperfect view of the scenes and events which occurred in the Mountain Camp during the long and dreary winter. But this journal affords only indistinct glimpses of scenes as they passed. The full and complete record of even those circumstances which were entered in that journal were never read by above three persons. They preserve a silence as unbroken as the grave. But many things occurred in that Mountain Camp previous to the first of March, which were not written, except by the recording angel; and which will never be fully known until God shall bring every secret work into judgement, whether it be good or evil.

After leaving about seven days' provisions with them to sustain them until Mr. Woodworth could come to them with relief, Mr. Reed's party commenced their return to the settlements, with seventeen of the unhappy beings, whose condition during the winter is in part shown by the foregoing journal. These persons were Patrick Brinn, wife, and five children; Mrs. Graves and four children; Mary and Isaac Donner, children of Jacob Donner; Solomon Hook, a step-son of Jacob Donner, and two of his [Reed's] children. He had met his wife with two of his children in the Bear River valley.

On the first day they traveled but three miles, although greatly urged by Mr. Reed to go faster and further. They encamped that night on the side of Truckee's [Donner] Lake. It will scarcely be credited that on this night this company of emigrants, although surrounded by the circumstances of extreme peril, amidst the most terrible scenes, and still struggling with death, were in fine spirits, and some of them uttered pleasantries which made their companions smile, notwithstanding the horrors of their condition. Patrick Brinn played about two hours upon a violin, which had been owned by Jay Fosdick, and which Mrs. Graves was taking into the settlement for him, she supposing him to be still living.

On the day that Mr. Reed's party left the camp in Bear River valley, he instructed the men with him not to let the sufferers know any thing in reference to the disasters which befell the party that came in with Mr. Eddy. This was necessary, because of the effects which might, and probably would, have resulted from the depression the communication of the intelligence would have produced.

The night passed away, and in the morning a young man who was carrying $500 in specie for Mrs. Graves, said to one of his companions in a vein of pleasantry, such as that in which they had indulged during the previous night, "I think that we had better play *euchre,* for the purpose of determining who shall have this money." Although nothing was seriously meditated, yet the remark alarmed Mrs. Graves, who, when the company set forward, remained behind for the purpose of concealing the money. Mrs. Graves having perished a few days after this, a knowledge of her secret perished with her.[96] The party traveled about five miles to the foot of the mountain and encamped, Mr. Reed finding it impossible to induce them to go further. The music of the violin again beguiled the heavily-passing hours. It could not, however, dispel the anxiety which Mr. Reed felt, upon observing a heavy and portentous cloud that hung, with a threatening vengeful aspect, about the top of the mountain. Fearing the effects which might result from communicating his apprehensions to any one, he looked in silence upon the gathering storm, which was to sweep with desolating fury and a fearful energy over the sides of the mountains; the pines, standing upon which, seemed even then, as they swayed to and fro in the wind, to be moaning for the dead. After the evening meal, there remained only provisions sufficient to last them one day and a half. On the following morning Mr. Reed sent Joseph Jaundro, Matthew Dofar, and Mr. Turner forward, with instructions to get supplies at a *cache* that had been made about fifteen miles from that place, and to return. If, however, that should be found robbed, they were to go still further on to a second *cache,* unless, in the mean time, they should meet Mr. Woodworth coming to the relief of the sufferers; in which event, they were instructed to return with him as soon as possible. Upon these being sent forward, the party resumed their journey, expecting to meet the supplies thus sent on the next day. They crossed the Sierra Nevada, and after traveling about ten miles, encamped on a bleak point on the north side of a little valley, near the head of Yuva river. During the night a most terrible snow-storm came down upon them, accompanied by a fierce wind, which increased to a tremendous gale before morning. The altitude of the mountain at the pass is 9838 feet. The camp was situated about 1500 feet below, and upon about 40 feet of snow—the snow above being from 60 to 100 feet deep. The storm continued, without

---

96 In 1891, near the shore of Donner Lake, two prospectors found a hoard of coins, none dated later than 1845. The money was claimed by W. C. Graves, who, according to family tradition, identified one coin by marks caused by the teething of various Graves babies. The money was divided between the finders and the claimant; some of the coins are still being passed down as heirlooms among descendants of the Graves family. See the Lovina Graves Cyrus memoir written by Edna Maybelle Sherwood, this volume. Mrs. Graves's attempt to carry out the coins may have contributed to the story that the emigrants clung to their property at the cost of their lives; see the accounts by H. A. Wise, Eliza W. Farnham, and Frances H. McDougall, in this volume.

the slightest intermission, for two days and three nights. On the morning of the third day the dark and angry clouds gradually passed off, and the air became, if possible, more intensely cold. The sufferings of the party, and especially of the unhappy and emaciated famine stricken emigrants, can never be portrayed with that vividness of coloring which is necessary to convey to the mind an adequate conception of what they endured. It is not possible to present upon the cold, and necessarily imperfect pages of a narrative, the true picture of the distress and anguish of spirit with which this terrible storm overwhelmed them. Individuals who have been so unfortunate as to have been at some times similarly situated, can sympathize, to some extent, with those upon whom it descended with resistless fury. But the more inexperienced reader, sitting in a comfortable parlor, by a cheerful fire, surrounded by happy faces, can never know the suffering of body and tortures of mind, endured by those who felt that they were abandoned by those whose duty it was to come to their relief.

The bleak point upon which they encamped was selected, not from choice, but necessity. Mr. Glover had encamped here on his way to the Mountain Camp, and the snow had in consequence been partially trodden down. It was an object to encamp there, in order to enable the sufferers to keep their feet dry. They had, moreover, traveled ten miles, which, if the feeble condition of the emigrants be considered, will at once be seen to be a hard day's travel, especially so when it is remembered that the party had crossed the mountains. Mr. Glover's party had also left at it some logs; and this, too, was an object with men who, in addition to assisting forward the sufferers during the day, were under the necessity of performing the severest camp duty at night.

The manner in which the fires upon these terrible snows were made by those who were engaged in these expeditions was as follows:—two green logs were cut and laid down at a distance corresponding with the length of the fire necessary to be made. Large green logs of pine or fir were then cut and placed transversely upon the first two. These served as a foundation upon which to build the fire up out of the snow, and upon these the fire was made by piling dry wood. Boughs were cut down and laid upon the snow around the fire, and upon these the emigrants lay, with their feet to the fire. If the green logs burnt through, the fire fell upon the snow below, and was of course extinguished. Unless, therefore, this could be prevented by putting in other green logs, there was the greatest danger of all perishing with the cold. The heat of the fire above would also sometimes melt the snow below; and if this melting was greater at one end, or upon one side than another, the logs would become displaced, and the fire rolling down into the snow would become extinguished. If the process of melting was uniform, a hole in the snow would thus be made, varying from ten to thirty feet deep.

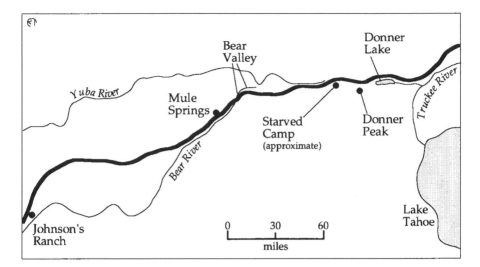

Donner Lake to Johnson's Ranch. Cartography by Rose Ann Tompkins

Such were some of the dangers to which they were exposed during the continuance of this dreadful storm, especially on the third night. Boughs had been set down around the fire. The snow was then thrown from the inside against the boughs, and upon the outside, so as to form a bank to break off the force of the wind and driving snow, which fell so thick as to make it impossible to see beyond a few feet. The cold was so intense as to make it impracticable to chop more than a few minutes without returning to the fire to warm. the party had all lain down, and were seeking to shelter themselves beneath their blankets. The driving snow soon covered them up. Upon some of them rising, the logs were found displaced, and the fire almost extinguished. The men, women, and children, were all so cold as to be in great danger of freezing. Mr. Reed had become snow-blind during the evening, and it was impossible for him to do any thing. The men, with the exception of Hiram Miller, and Wm. McCutcheon, were worn down and disheartened. All became greatly alarmed. The children were all crying. One of the women was weeping–another praying. A portion of Mr. Reed's men were also praying. The two above named were alternately struggling to save the expiring coals, and swearing at the others, urging them to leave off praying and to work for the purpose of saving the fire; assuring them that all would inevitably perish before morning. Mrs. Brinn's voice was heard above the roaring of the storm, the weeping of the women and children, the prayers of some of the men and the swearing of others. She screamed, "Mr. Rade! Mr. Rade! Do in the name of the

blessed Vargin make yer min get up and make a fire. We're all frazin'—
every sowl of us! In the name of Saint Patrick and the Vargin, make them
get up. They are all gettin' three dollars a day to take us out of the snow,
and here they are a-lettin' us all fraze. The Vargin save us! Oh! you've
brought us here to murther us! You brought us away from our comfortable camp to fraze us! Oh! Johnny's fell down in the pit and is kilt
entirely. Patrick's froze to death. Little Jammy's legs are burnt off by the
knees; and Patsy's heart has sased to bate for the space of faftane minutes!" Here Mr. McCutcheon, no longer able to bear this torrent of words,
with a multitude of adjectives and expletives, informed her, in a voice he
contrived to raise above hers, that if she did not "sase" this abuse and
invective, he would, in less time than "faftane minutes," make her heart
"sase to bate." The whole scene, though one of distress and the most
imminent peril, was one in which the comic and tragical, the terrible and
the ludicrous were strangely mingled. At length, however, a fire was
made, and it was soon found that Johnny had not been "kilt," nor Patrick
froze to death, nor little Jammy "burnt off by the knees," and that Patsy's
heart was still "bating," and that Mrs. Brinn's tongue was running with an
increased velocity.

Morning came at length, and the storm passed away. The whole party
had then been two days without any sort of food. Mr. Reed urged them to
resume the journey. None of the party, however, were able to travel except
Solomon Hook and Patrick Brinn and family. The latter affirmed that they
could remain in camp better without food than travel without it. Mary
Donner had burned her foot very much during the previous night, and,
although she made an effort, she soon fell, and was assisted back to camp.
Mr. Reed and party, after leaving wood for three days, then set out, taking
his two children and Solomon Hook, Mr. Miller carried Tom, Solomon
Hook also walked. Patty refused to let her father carry her, and continued
to travel in the newly fallen snow, into which they all sunk about two feet.
Her father frequently asked her if she was not tired or cold, but such was
her energy and courage, that she continued to travel on foot, refusing to be
carried. At length she called out to her father that she saw the stars and a
multitude of angels. He immediately saw that she was freezing, and having
wrapped her in a blanket, carried her upon his back. The child derived
warmth from the body of her father. The party were all without food, and
Mr. Reed had no hope of obtaining assistance from Mr. Woodworth. In
fact, he informed the eleven, he had been under the necessity of leaving,
that Mr. Woodworth ought to have met them long before, and that to rely
upon him any more, was leaning upon a broken stick.[97] The men were

---

97 Donner party survivors were not impressed by Woodworth's efforts on their
   behalf; see W. C. Graves's memoir, this volume, note 31.

very much reduced, from want of food, and worn down by toil. They were, in consequence, greatly discouraged, and expressed their fears that they would all perish; but Patty, who was herself, as has been seen, so near perishing in the morning, said, "No! no! God has not brought us so far to let us perish now." The remark of the child so filled the heart of the rough and resolute McCutcheon, that his eyes immediately felled with tears, that froze as they fell, and he exclaimed, with an oath, "Boys, if there is an angel on earth, Patty is that angel. Just listen to the child." No apology can be made for swearing; and yet the first wish of the heart is, that the tears of the recording angel may have blotted out the oath forever.

Soon after arriving at the encampment, Mr. Stone and Mr. Cady, who had been left at the Mountain Camp, came up. All the men, excepting Mr. Miller and Mr. Stone, found, upon coming to the fire, that their feet were without sensation. Mr. Reed, suspecting that they were frozen, thrust his into the snow, and advised the others to do so. Some of them did it. Mr. Cady, Mr. Dunn, and Mr. Greenwood lost more or less of their toes. Some of them were crippled for life.

The next morning, the party resumed their journey, this being the fourth day they had all been without food. Lake in the afternoon, they found a little that had been left in a tree by Mr. Dofar, who had at length, with Mr. Jaundro and Mr. Turner, got forward to a small *cache*. It will be remembered that these men had been sent forward for provisions, when the party arrived at the Starved Camp, where Brinn and his family had been left. The storm, however, had caught these, and they were themselves near perishing. Mr. Turner had been so much frozen, that he was with great difficulty taken forward. They had come to the first *cache,* which they found robbed by wild animals. After the storm abated, they had proceeded on to the second *cache.* A part of this was found, and with it Mr. Dofar had returned, and after depositing it in such a manner as to enable Mr. Reed's party to find it, pursued his way toward Mr. Woodworth's camp.

A little strengthened by this timely supply, the party continued on until night, and encamped. Mr. Cady and Mr. Greenwood had, however, pushed on with the hope of finding Mr. Woodworth. They arrived at his camp after night, I believe, and informed him of the condition of the party. After dark, Woodworth came to Mr. Reed's camp, with Mr. John Starks and Mr. Oakley, the two latter carrying provisions.

This party, finally, after immense toil and extreme peril, arrived in the settlement, without further disaster, or loss of life.[98]

---

98 For firsthand accounts of this relief party, see the memoirs by Reed and Mc-Cutchen in this volume and Reed's Second Relief diary in Morgan, *Overland in 1846,* 342–50.

Chapter XV.

Expedition of Messrs. Foster and Eddy from the
California Settlements to the Mountain Camp.

The chapter which I have devoted to showing what were the nature and
extent of the preparations made by the people of California for the relief of
the sufferers of the Mountain Camp, present the facts which show the manner in which Passed-midshipman S. E. Woodworth became connected
with the expeditions for the relief of the emigrants.

Furnished with the most ample supplies, Mr. Woodworth set forward
with instructions from Captain J. B. Hull, U. S. Navy, and at that time
commander of the northern district of California, to use every possible
exertion to rescue the unhappy sufferers, agreeing, on the part of the
United States, to pay whatever might be necessary to prevent this countrymen from perishing.

Four days after Mr. Woodworth's party left Johnson's ranche, Messrs.
Foster and Eddy obtained horses which had been purchased under the
order of Captain Hull. With these they set out to meet Mr. Reed and his
party.

Mr. Eddy had heard that his wife and one of his children had perished,
but he cherished a feeble hope that he was not left to mourn the loss of all;
and that he would find one of his children with Mr. Reed; and in any event
he felt it to be a duty which he owed to suffering humanity, to do all in his
power to rescue others, although his wife and children might be no more.
Mr. Foster believed that his child yet survived. He hoped also to find his
mother-in-law, Mrs. Murphy, and his brother-in-law, Simon Murphy, alive.

On the second day after they left, they arrived at Bear River valley,
where they found Passed-midshipman Woodworth remaining in camp
with one man to bring water, make fires, and cook for him. There were
also other men in other ways to assist him. Messrs. Eddy and Foster
believed that at that time he was over the mountain, and upon inquiring of
him why he was not, he replied that he could not go without a guide. Mr.
Eddy replied that he had the best guide in the snow trail of those who had
preceded him. Mr. Woodworth promised that he would set forward on the
following morning, but he advised Messrs. Foster and Eddy not to attempt
the passage of the mountain. They informed him that they had passed over
under vastly more difficult circumstances, and that they would certainly
attempt it again.

They according set out, eight in number, on the following morning. Having crossed a ridge, they arrived at Yuva river, where Passed-midshipman
Woodworth, who had become tired from carrying his blanket, proposed, at
about 3 o'clock, P.M., to encamp. That night two of Mr. Reed's men came to

Mr. Woodworth's camp, and informed him that Mr. Reed's party were encamped about one mile in advance (in the direction of the mountains). Mr. Woodworth then went to Mr. Reed's camp, and after conversing with him, returned. Mr. Reed had informed him that some miles from that place he had left fourteen of the sufferers. Mr. Woodworth asked the men with him, if they would go to the relief of these emigrants, and received a reply in the negative.**[99] Messrs. Foster and Eddy proposed to make themselves responsible for almost any sum to persons who would go with them. To this it was replied that they, having lost all their property and money, were irresponsible. J. F. Reed and Hiram Miller said that they would be responsible for any amount, for which Messrs. Eddy and Foster would engage. But these it was said were in the condition of the first. Mr. John Starks [Stark] offered to go out without any reward beyond that derived from the consciousness of doing a good act. But the snow made it prudent to have only light men for the service. It was necessary for each man to carry fifty pounds of provisions; and this, added to Mr. Starks' own weight, of two hundred and twenty-four pounds, made it imprudent for him to go.

Being unable to induce any of them to consent to go, Messrs. Eddy and Foster were about to set out alone. Mr. Reed, however, remonstrated against this, and at length induced them to consent to return to Bear River valley, where he said he would use his utmost efforts to prevail upon Mr. Woodworth and his party to enter upon the enterprise. Upon returning to Bear River valley, Mr. Woodworth finally said that he would engage, under the authority he had received from Capt. Hull to pay three dollars per day to every man who would go, and fifty dollars in addition to every man who would bring out a child not his own. Mr. Eddy hired Hiram Miller, formerly of Springfield, Illinois, engaging to pay him fifty dollars.*** Mr. Foster hired a Mr. Thompson for the same sum. Howard Oakley, John Starks, and Mr. Stone looked to Capt. Hull for their wages.

The company thus organized, through the instrumentality of Messrs. Eddy and Foster set out for the Mountain Camp, on the following morning.[100] They encamped that night about half way up Yuva river, in fifteen

---

** I ought to say here, that in this chapter I omit several facts communicated to me by the emigrants, because I do not wish unnecessarily to involve myself in a newspaper controversy with others, and because their omission does not affect the fidelity of a narrative, having for its object the showing of how and in what numbers the sufferers were rescued. [Thornton's note]

*** During my sojourn in California I saw this debt paid. [Thornton's note]

99 Woodworth may have had good reasons for refusing to go back for the refugees at Starved Camp, but he did not manage to convey them to his contemporaries, who were convinced that he was either shirking or a coward.

100 This party is known in the Donner literature as the Third Relief.

feet of snow. The next day, at 4 o'clock, they arrived at the camp of those whom Mr. Reed had been compelled to leave. The fire at the Starved Camp had melted the snow down to the ground, and the hole thus made was about twelve or fifteen feet in diameter, and twenty-four feet deep. As the snow had continued to melt, they made steps by which they ascended and descended.

The picture of distress which was here presented, was shocking indeed. And yet Patrick Brinn and his wife seemed not in any degree to realize the extent of their peril, or that they were in peril at all. They were found lying down sunning themselves, and evincing no concern for the future. They had consumed the two children of Jacob Donner.[101] Mrs. Graves' body was lying there with almost all the flesh cut away from her arms and limbs. Her breasts were cut off, and her heart, and liver taken out, and were all being boiled in a pot then on the fire. Her little child, about thirteen months old, sat at her side, with one arm upon the body of its mangled mother sobbing bitterly, cried, Ma! ma! ma! It was a helpless and innocent lamb among the wolves of the wilderness. Mr. Eddy took up its wasted form in his arms, and touched even to tears with the sight he witnessed, he kissed its wan and pale cheeks again and again; and wept even more bitterly in the anguish of his spirit as he thought of his own dear ones, and the departed companion of his perils and sorrows. The child looked up imploringly into his face, and with a silent but expressive eloquence, besought him to be its protector. In a few minutes it nestled in his bosom, and seemed to feel assured that it once more had a friend. As soon as possible, he made some thin soup for the infant, which revived it, and, with the exception of an occasional short convulsive sob or sigh, it again appeared quiet and happy. It was brought safely into the settlements, where its very misfortunes made friends for it. But it drooped and withered away like a flower severed from the parent stem. It now blooms in the paradise of God, in a better and happier clime, where the storms and disasters of life will affect it no more.[102]

After supplying these emigrants with food, Messrs. Oakley, Starks, and Stone were left to lead them on to Bear River valley, and to carry out Mrs. Graves' babe and two other children. Messrs. Eddy, Foster, Thompson,

---

101 Only one of the children was Jacob Donner's, his son Isaac; the other was Franklin Ward Graves, Jr.

102 Starved Camp was undoubtedly a place of horror, but the scene reported by Thornton is suspect. Comparing it with Farnham's account (in this volume), Joseph A. King points out that the corpses had been left on the surface of the snow when the refugees clambered down into the pit; the infant Elizabeth Graves would not have been in the vicinity of her mother's remains. Joseph A. King, *Winter of Entrapment* (Walnut Creek: K & K, 1994), 109.

and Miller, started at about 4 o'clock, on the following morning, for the Mountain Camp, where they arrived at about 10 o'clock, A.M.

A more shocking picture of distress and misfortune, can not be imagined, than the scene they witnessed upon their arrival. Many of those who had been detained by the snows had starved to death. Their bodies had been devoured by the wretched survivors; and their bones were lying in and around the camps. A body with half the flesh torn from it, was lying near the door. Upon turning over a head which was severed from the body, Mr. Eddy instantly recognized the familiar face of an old friend and traveling companion. A dead child lay near. The wild, fiery, and fierce look of the eyes, and the emaciated and ghastly appearance of the survivors added tenfold horror to this scene of the Mountain Camp.

It is impossible for human language to describe the change wrought in the feelings of those who, but a few weeks before, would have preferred a thousand deaths to eating human flesh. The change which their unspeakable sufferings had produced seemed to affect the very texture of their nature and being. In the solitude and horror of the Mountain Camp, long nights of physical suffering and mental anguish had succeeded each other, in a manner of which it is impossible to have an adequate idea. Days had followed each other in a long succession; but no sun of hope had arisen to dispel the darkness of their misery; and as the long nights came on, the yet driving snow was heaped in impenetrable drifts above them, and extinguished even the dim rays which had sometimes shone fitfully through the dark clouds of disaster, which seemed to be fast thickening, and settling down upon them in a night of death. Surmisings had often been indulged, as to their probably fate; and questions had ben asked for the thousandth time, as to the probabilities of relief. They had made calculations for the next and succeeding meals, as they sat gloomily around the fires of their miserable camps. Some had added the last little fuel to the dim and flickering flame, and had given themselves up to the ravings of despair and madness, as they felt the crush of their reliance for aid from the settlements. Others had bowed their heads in moody silence upon the palms of their hands, and given themselves up to the tortures of thought. Here and there one was found, in whose face meekness and resignation were visible, and they seemed to say, "Father, not my will, but thine be done."

Day after day had passed away, and the scanty store of food, miserable and loathsome as it was, had rapidly diminished, until the last hide had been consumed. Then hunger, keen, gnawing, and maddening, preyed upon them, until it might have been said of those who unlike some of their more miserable companions, had up to that time refrained from eating human flesh, "In their gloomy looks you might see the longings of the cannibal." Many expedients had been discussed, for the purpose of avoiding the dreadful alternative of dying themselves, or of killing their companions, by lot or otherwise, to preserve their own lives. But at that juncture a greater number of persons perished from famine, than was necessary to supply, for a time, all the miserable survivors with this horrible food.

It is said that, immediately previous to this, a sacrifice had been agreed upon, and that an individual, who was supposed to have less claims to life than the others, had been selected as the victim. But Providence interposed, and some of them sank into the arms of death, whispering praise for unmerited mercies; while others expired, cursing their miserable fate. And now those who, but a short time before, would have shuddered at the thought of devouring the dead bodies of their companions, rejoiced at their decease, and regarded it as a providential interference in their behalf.

In a very brief period, all the fountains of the heart's purest, noblest, and best affections were dried up, and in some instances every tie was sundered by the one great absorbing thought of individual self-preservation, which led them to escape, if possible, and without regard to others, from the calamities surrounding them.

Something was absolutely necessary to be done to sustain their miserable existence; yet all of them, except Kiesburg, had refrained from this most monstrous food as long as any thing else could be had. Once, when the snows had partially melted away, and the emigrants were enabled to find four hides and a dead bullock, upon which this man, as did the other emigrants, might have subsisted for a time, he took a child of Mr. Foster's, aged about four years, and devoured it before morning. What adds, if possible, to the horror of this horrible meal, is the fact that the child was alive when it was taken to bed; leading to the suspicion that he strangled it, although he denies this charge. This man also devoured Mr. Eddy's child, before noon on the next day, and was among the first to communicate the fact to him.[103] When asked by the outraged father why he did not eat the hides and bullock, he coolly replied, that he preferred human flesh, as being more palatable, and containing more nutriment.

Such was the horrible and emaciated appearance of this man that Mr. Eddy, as he informed me, could not shed his blood there; but he resolved to kill him upon his landing at San Francisco, if he ever came to the place. Mr. Eddy subsequently armed himself for that purpose, but was prevented

---

103 Stories similar to these were published in the *California Star* of April 10, 1847. This single article, beginning "A more shocking scene cannot be imagined...," was the source of many of the sensational untruths about the Donner party which plagued survivors for decades; see the Wise and McDougall accounts, in this volume, and Eliza Donner Houghton's *The Expedition of the Donner Party,* (Chicago: McClurg, 1911), 229–31, 335–44. This article was widely disseminated in Edwin Bryant's best-selling *What I Saw in California.*

by Mr. J. F. Reed and Edwin Bryant, Esq., the author of "What I saw in California."

I would without hesitancy express the opinion, that Kiesburg was at the time insane, had he not, long after his subsequent arrival in the settlements of California, shown himself to be a wild beast, by declaring with a profane expletive, that "A man is a fool who prefers poor California beef to human flesh." But the closing scenes of the Mountain Camp will more fully show that this man is perhaps without a parallel in history.

Whatever may be our feelings toward Kiesburg, we should not censure others who were already overwhelmed with misfortunes, but pity their condition, rather than cherish indignation against them for doing that which they could not avoid. We should rather shed tears of sorrow and sympathy for those who were reduced to such dreadful extremities, that their own lives could only be preserved by devouring the bodies of their companions. It will be impossible to prevent some share of our indignation from being directed against those who, by inducing the emigrants to leave the usual route, were the causes of their misfortunes.

The party of Messrs. Eddy and Foster, upon their arrival at the Mountain Camp, found five living children, to wit: three of George Donner's, one of Jacob Donner's and one of Mrs. Murphy's. They also found a man whose name is Clarke. He was a shoemaker. He had been a sailor also, and I believe he ran away from the ship. I mention these particulars that he many not be confounded with a worthy gentleman of the same name [i.e., William Squire Clark] in San Francisco, with whom I traveled upon a part of my journey to Oregon.

Clarke had gone out with Mr. Reed, I believe, under the pretense of assisting the emigrants. He was found with a pack of goods upon his back, weighing about forty pounds, and also two guns, about to set off with his booty. This man actually carried away this property, which weighed more than did a child he left behind to perish.[104] But this is not the only instance of the property of emigrants in distress being appropriated under some pretense, or directly stolen by thieves who prowled about the camp.

In addition to these, there were in camp, Mrs. Murphy, Mr. and Mrs. George Donner, and Kiesburg—the latter, it was believed, having far more strength to travel than others who had arrived in the settlements. But he would not travel, for the reason, as was suspected, that he wished to

---

104 McGlashan spoke with Clark in 1879 and wrote of him, "I think Eddy did him an injustice in Thornton, and yet I do not consider him a saint." Letter to Eliza Donner Houghton, December 5, 1879, in *From the Desk of Truckee's C. F. McGlashan,* ed. by M. Nona McGlashan and Betty H. McGlashan (Fresno, Ca.: Truckee-Donner Historical Society, 1986), 67–68. The *Truckee Republican* published an account of Clark's life on October 24, 1885.

remain behind for the purpose of obtaining the property and money of the dead.

Mrs. George Donner was in good health, was somewhat corpulent, and certainly able to travel. But her husband was in a helpless condition, and she would not consent to leave him while he survived. She expressed her solemn and unalterable purpose, which no danger and peril could change, to remain, and perform for him the last sad offices of duty and affection. She manifested, however, the greatest solicitude for her children; and informed Mr. Eddy that she had fifteen hundred dollars in silver, all of which she would give to him, if he would save the lives of the children. He informed her that he would not carry out one hundred dollars for all that she had, but that he would save the children, or perish in the effort.

The party had no provisions to leave for the sustenance of these unhappy and unfortunate beings. After remaining about two hours, Mr. Eddy informed Mrs. Donner that he was constrained by the force of circumstances to depart. It was certain that George Donner would never rise from the miserable bed upon which he had lain down, worn out by toil, and wasted by famine. It was next to absolutely certain, if Mrs. Donner did not leave her husband, and avail herself of the opportunity then presented for being conducted into the settlement, that she would perish by famine, or die a violent death at the hands of a cannibal. The instinct of a mother strongly urged her to accompany her children, that she might be able to contribute her own personal efforts and attention to save the lives of her offspring. The natural love of life, too, was without doubt then felt, urging her to fly from a scene of so many horrors and dangers. Her reason, many have asked the question, "Why remain in the midst of so much peril, and encounter an inevitable death—a death of all others the most terrible—since it is certain that nothing can rescue your husband from the jaws of the all-devouring grave? and when you can not hope to do more than beguile, with your society, presence, and converse the solitude of the few hours that remain of a life, the flame of which is already flickering, and must in a very brief period be extinguished in the darkness and gloom of death?"

A woman was probably never before placed in circumstances of greater or more peculiar trial; but her duty and affection as a wife triumphed over all her instinct and her reason. And when her husband entreated her to save her life and leave him to die alone, assuring her that she could be of no service to him, since he probably would not survive, under any circumstances, until the next morning, she bent over him, and with streaming eyes kissed his pale, emaciated, haggard, and even then death-stricken cheeks, and said:—

"No! no! dear husband, I will remain with you and here perish, rather than leave you to die alone, with no one to soothe your dying sorrows, and to close your eyes when dead. Entreat me not to leave you. Life, accompanied with the reflection that I had thus left you, would possess for me more than the bitterness of death; and death would be sweet with the thought, in my last moments, that I had assuaged one pang of yours in your passage into eternity. No! no! this once, dear husband, I will disobey you! No! no! no!" she continued, sobbing convulsively.

The parting scene between parents and children is represented as being one that will never be forgotten, as long as reason remains, or memory performs its functions. My own emotions will not permit me to attempt a description, which language, indeed, has not the power to delineate. It is sufficient to say that it was affecting beyond measure; and that the last words uttered by Mrs. Donner, in tears and sobs, to Mr. Eddy, were, "O, save! save my children!"

Mr. Eddy carried Georgiana Donner, who was about six years old; Hiram Miller carried Eliza Donner, about four years old; Mr. Thompson carried Frances Ann Donner, about eight years old; William Foster carried Simon Murphy, eight years old; and Clarke carried his booty, and left a child of one of the Donners to perish.[105]

The first night after leaving the Mountain Camp, the party encamped at the foot of the pass, on the eastern declivity of the mountain. On the next day they crossed the pass, where Mr. Eddy found an aperture in the snow which had been kept open by a spring, where, by letting down a cord, he ascertained the depth of the snow to be sixty-five feet. That night they encamped half way down Yuva river. The next morning, they resumed their journey, and came up with Mr. Starks, with Patrick Brinn and family, and others, who were the eleven persons that remained alive of the fourteen whom Mr. Reed had been constrained to leave. They at the same time met Messrs. Glover, Coffeymier, Mootrey, and Woodworth, who had halted to prepare dinner. After the meal was taken, these gentlemen set out for the Mule Spring.

Toward the close of the afternoon, Mr. Woodworth's party encamped at the last crossing of Yuva river. At night Messrs. Eddy, Foster, Thompson, and Miller came up, bringing with them the children with whom they had left the Mountain Camp. John Baptiste and Clarke were also with them. Here they encamped in the snow.

On the following morning, Mr. Woodworth gave to the party a little food. He was informed that there were persons yet remaining at the Mountain Camp, for whose rescue an effort ought to be made. He replied, that

---

105 This child is evidently Jacob Donner's son Samuel. Houghton reports that he had died before the Third Relief left, but her account is late and often suspect; a letter by Selim Woodworth published in the *California Star* on April 3, 1847, states that one Donner child was still alive when the Third Relief left the camps. See also Lilburn W. Boggs's letter, "Immigrants to California," in this volume.

he could not remain any longer, and after giving his blankets to Mr. Mootrey to carry, he said he would go forward and prepare horses for proceeding immediately on into the settlements. Messrs. Woodworth, Glover, Mootrey, and Coffeymier than proceeded forward to the Mule Spring, where they encamped.

Messrs. Foster, Eddy, Miller, and Thompson resumed their journey, and at 10 o'clock, A.M., arrived at the Mule Spring. Here they came up with Messrs. Oakley and Stone, who, having left Mr. Starks, had passed Messrs. Foster, Eddy, Miller, and Thompson.

On the evening of the second day after their arrival at this camp, Mr. Starks came up, with Patrick Brinn, his wife, and children. Mr. Starks carried Jonathan Graves, a boy twelve [seven] years of age.

Mr. Stone had carried the deceased Mrs. Graves' babe. Mr. Oakley carried Mary Donner, a girl thirteen [seven] years old, one of whose feet had been severely burnt at the Starved Camp, previous to Mr. Reed leaving at that place the fourteen, as previously mentioned.

The morning following the day upon which Mr. Starks came up, the whole number of persons thus brought together set out for the settlements; and in three days arrived at Fort Sacramento, the residence of Capt. Sutter.

Chapter XVI.

Expedition of Messrs. Stark and Others.

It will be remembered that Messrs. Starks, Stone, Oakley, Thompson, Miller, Foster, and Eddy, when on their way from the Mountain Camp, with a company of sufferers, met Messrs. Woodworth, Glover, Mootrey, and Coffeymier, and that Mr. Woodworth was informed that here yet remained several persons at the Mountain Camp, for whose rescue an effort ought to be made.

From the point at which this information had been communicated, Mr. Glover proceeded on to Fort Sacramento, where he saw Mr. McKinstry, and informed him that Mr. Woodworth had declined making any further efforts to have the emigrants rescued. Mr. McKinstry promised to send a letter to Mr. Woodworth, urging him to send a party out. Mr. Woodworth received this letter March 23d. He then organized a party, consisting of John Rhodes, John Starks, E. Coffeymier, John Sel, Daniel Tucker, William Foster, and the son [William C.] of Mrs. Graves; who were dispatched with provisions and horses.

This party proceeded no further than Bear River valley, or the foot of the mountain, from which point they returned, in consequence of the snow upon the mountain having become so soft, as to make the traveling impracticable.[106]

Chapter XVII.

Mr. Fellun's Expedition.

Mr. Fellun[107] set out from the settlements in April, with six others, for the relief of such persons as might be found to survive at the Mountain Camp; and also to collect and, as far as practicable, secure the scattered property of both the living and the dead.

Upon arriving at the Mountain Camp, he found that all had perished except Kiesburg. A perusal of the following extract from Mr. Fellun's journal, as published in the California Star upon his return, is well calculated to create a painful suspicion, that this man remained at the Mountain Camp, to appropriate the property and money of the dead, and that he killed Mrs. Donner, Mrs. Murphy, and the child which the man Clark left there to perish. But this is not the only instance of the property of emigrants in distress being appropriated. Almost all which the perils and dangers of my own journey had left to me, in going into Oregon, was taken by a needy adventurer, who had come from the settlements, and had united with another, distinguished for even less principle than himself.

Mr. Fellun says:–[108]

"Left Johnson's on the evening of April 13th, and arrived at the lower end of the Bear River valley on the 15th. Hung our saddles upon the trees, and sent the horses back, to be returned again in ten days, to bring us in again. Started on foot, with provisions for ten days, and traveled to the head of the valley, and encamped for the night; snow from two to three feet deep. Started early in the morning of the 15th, and traveled twenty-three miles; snow ten feet deep.

"*April* 17.–Reached the cabins between 12 and 1 o'clock. Expected to find some of the sufferers alive, Mrs. Donner and Kiesburg, in particular.

---

106 Lilburn Boggs refers to this mission in his letter.

107 William O. Fallon or O'Fallon was "a very large stout rough" mountain man, according to Reason Tucker's son, who assisted with the relief efforts. George W. Tucker to C. F. McGlashan, April 5, 1879.

108 Fallon's account of the Fourth (and last) Relief was published in the *California Star* on June 5, 1847. The style of the text is too literary to be entirely his own, but to what degree this affects its accuracy is debatable; Edwin Bryant records a similar statement which he implies he got directly from Fallon in *What I Saw in California,* 261–63.

Entered the cabins, and a horrible scene presented itself—human bodies terribly mutilated, legs, arms, and skulls, scattered in every direction. One body, supposed to be that of Mrs. Eddy, lay near the entrance, the limbs severed off, and a frightful gash in the skull.[109] The flesh was nearly consumed from the bones, and a painful stillness pervaded the place. The supposition was, that all were dead, when a sudden shout revived our hopes, and we flew in the direction of the sound. Three Indians, who had been hitherto concealed, started from the ground and fled at our approach, leaving their bows and arrows. We delayed two hours in searching the cabins, during which we were obliged to witness sights from which we would have fain turned away, and which are too dreadful to put on record. We next started for Donners' camp, eight miles distant over the mountains. After traveling about half way, we came upon a track in the snow which excited our suspicion, and we determined to pursue it. It brought us to the camp of Jacob Donner, where it had evidently left that morning. There we found property of every description, books, calicoes, tea, coffee, shoes, percussion caps, household and kitchen furniture, scattered in every direction, and mostly in the water. At the mouth of the tent stood a large iron kettle, filled with human flesh, cut up. It was from the body of George Donner. The head had been split open, and the brains extracted therefrom, and, to the appearance, he had not been long dead—not over three or four days, at the most.[110] Near by the kettle stood a chair, and thereupon three legs of a bullock that had been shot down in the early part of the winter, and snowed upon before it could be dressed. The meat was found sound and good, and, with the exception of a small piece out of the shoulder, wholly untouched. We gathered up some property, and camped for the night.

"*April* 18.–Commenced gathering the most valuable property, suitable for our packs, the greater portion requiring to be dried. We then make them up, and camped for the night.

"*April* 19.–This morning, Foster, Rhodes, and J. Foster, started, with small packs, for the first cabins, intending from thence to follow the trail of the person that had left the morning previous. The other three remained behind to *cache* and secure the goods necessarily left there. Knowing the Donners had a considerable sum of money, we searched diligently, but were unsuccessful. The party from the cabins were unable to keep the trail of the mysterious personage, owing to the rapid melting of the snow; they, therefore, went direct to the cabins, and, upon entering,

---

109 On June 12, 1847, the *California Star* retracted this statement identifying the body.

110 Edwin Bryant, who passed the camp on his journey east in June 1847, reported that George Donner's body was found wrapped in a sheet; he made no mention of any mutilation.

discovered Kiesburg lying down amidst the human bones, and beside him a large pan full of fresh liver and lights. They asked him what had become of his companions; whether they were alive; and what had become of Mrs. Donner. He answered them by stating that they were all dead. Mrs. Donner, he said, had, in attempting to cross from one cabin to another, missed the trail, and slept out one night; that she came to his camp the next night, very much fatigued; he made her a cup of coffee, placed her in bed, and rolled her well in the blankets; but the next morning found her dead.[111] He ate her body, and found her flesh the best he had ever tasted.[112] He further stated, that he obtained from her body at least four pounds of fat. No traces of her person could be found, nor the body of Mrs. Murphy either. When the last company left camp, three weeks previous, Mrs. Donner was in perfect health, though unwilling to come and leave her husband there, and offered $500 to any person or persons who would come out and bring them in—saying this in the presence of Kiesburg—and that she had plenty of tea and coffee. We suspected that it was she who had taken the piece from the shoulder of beef in the chair before mentioned. In the cabin with Kiesburg were found two kettles of human blood, in all supposed to be over one gallon. Rhodes [John Rhoads] asked him where he had got the blood. He answered, "There is blood in dead bodies."[113] They asked him numerous questions, but he appeared embarrassed, and equivocated a great deal; and in reply to their asking him

---

111 This account of Tamsen Donner's end is consistent with death from hypothermia, according to Sarah F. Johnson, M.D. (personal communication). It does not differ materially from what Keseberg told McGlashan more than thirty years later.

112 Keseberg did not deny having eaten Tamsen Donner's body: "Believe me, Mr. McGlashan, no portion of Mrs. Donner's body remained when the Relief came." As quoted by C. F. McGlashan to Eliza Donner Houghton, April 23, 1879; in *From the Desk of Truckee's C. F. McGlashan*, 29.

113 The Fourth Relief took the "buckets of blood" as evidence of murder, believing that blood could be drained only from a newly dead corpse before coagulation had set in. However, the extent to which cadaveric blood coagulates is highly variable and even when there is significant clotting a fair amount of the blood remains liquid. In addition, the clotted blood eventually reliquifies, the length of time required for reliquefaction (lysis) depending on a variety of factors, according to Todd C. Grey, M.D. (personal communication). In other words, Keseberg was right.

"Buckets of blood" is a problematic description, in that blood collected into a vessel would separate into two layers—an upper yellowish layer of serum and a lower layer composed of red blood cells and clots—and would not much resemble blood. The presence of blood in buckets is by no means evidence of murder (though it might suggest orderly butchering), according to Sarah F. Johnson, M.D. (personal communication).

where Mrs. Donner's money was, he evinced confusion, and answered, that he knew nothing about it—that she must have *cached* it before she died. 'I hav'n't it,' said he, 'nor the money, nor the property of any person, living or dead!' They then examined his bundle, and found silks and jewelry, which had been taken from the camp of the Donners, amounting in value to about $200. On his person they discovered a brace of pistols, recognized to be those of George Donner, and, while taking them from him, discovered something concealed in his waistcoat, which on being opened was found to be $225, in gold.

"Before leaving the settlements, the wife of Kiesburg had told us that we would find but little money about him; the men, therefore, said to him, that they knew he was lying to them, and that he was well aware of the place of concealment of the Donner's money. He declared, before heaven, he knew nothing concerning it, and that he had not the property of any one in his possession. They told him, that to lie to them would effect nothing; that there were others back at the cabins, who, unless informed of the spot where the treasure was hidden, would not hesitate to hang him upon the first tree. Their threats were of no avail; he still affirmed his ignorance and innocence. Rhodes took him aside and talked to him kindly, telling him, that if he would give the information desired, he should receive from their hands the best of treatment, and be in every way assisted; otherwise, the party back at Donners' camp would, upon its arrival, and his refusal to discover to them the place where he had deposited this money, immediately put him to death. It was all to no purpose, however, and they prepared to return to us, leaving him in charge of the packs, and assuring him of their determination to visit him in the morning; and that he must make up his mind during the night. They then started back and joined us at the Donners' camp.

"*April* 20.—We all started for Bear River valley, with packs of one hundred pounds each; our provisions being nearly consumed, we were obliged to make haste away. Came within a few hundred yards of the cabin which Kiesburg occupied, and halted to prepare breakfast, after which we proceeded to the cabin. I now asked Kiesburg if he was willing to disclose to me where he had concealed that money. He turned somewhat pale, and again protested his ignorance. I said to him, 'Kiesburg, you know well where Donner's money is, and d—n you, you shall tell me! I am not going to multiply words with you, or say but little about it; bring me that rope!' He then arose from his pot of soup and human flesh and begged me not to harm him; he had not the money nor the goods; the silk clothing and money which were found upon him the previous day, and which he then declared belonged to his wife, he now said were the property of others in California. I then told him I did not wish to hear more from him, unless he at once informed us where he had concealed the money of those orphan children; then producing the rope, I approached him. He became frightened; but I bent the rope about his neck, and threw him, after a struggle, upon the ground, and as I tightened the cord, and choked him, he cried out that he would confess all upon release. I then permitted him to arise. He still seemed inclined to be obstinate, and made much delay in talking; finally, but with evident reluctance, he led the way back to Donners' camp, about ten miles distant, accompanied by Rhodes and Tucker. While they were absent, we moved all our packs over to the lower end of the lake, and made all ready for a start when they should return. Mr. Foster went down to the cabin of Mrs. Murphy, his mother-in-law, to see if any property remained there worth collecting and securing; he found the body of young [Landrum] Murphy, who had been dead about three months, with the breast and skull cut open, and the brains, liver, and lights taken out; and this accounted for the contents of the pan which stood beside Kiesburg, when he was found. It appears that he had left at the other camp the dead bullock and horse, and on visiting this camp and finding the body thawed out, took therefrom the brains, liver, and lights.

"Tucker and Rhodes came back the next morning, bringing $273, that had been cached by Kiesburg, who after disclosing to them the spot, returned to the cabin. The money had been hidden directly underneath the projecting limb of a large tree, the end of which seemed to point precisely to the treasure buried in the earth. On their return, and passing the cabin, they saw the unfortunate man within, devouring the remaining brains and liver, left from his morning repast. They hurried him away, but before leaving, he gathered together the bones and heaped them all in a box he used for the purpose,[114] blessed them and the cabin, and said, 'I hope God will forgive me what I have done; I couldn't help it! and I hope I may get to heaven yet!' We asked Kiesburg why he did not use the meat

---

114 In addition to the "buckets of blood" motif, the members of the Fourth Relief spread the story of Keseberg's "boxful of bones," mentioned above in note 91. Levi Hancock heard that Keseberg "had a man and women boxed up"; "Sooter's Fort to Salt Lake Valley," transcribed and ed. by Robert K. Hoshide and Will Bagley, *Crossroads* 4 (Winter 1993): 4. Henry Bigler reported that Keseberg had "a box full of arms and legs that he had to live on, and it was thought at the Fort that he had killed a woman and boxed her up to eat"; Henry W. Bigler, *Bigler's Chronicle of the West,* ed. by Edwin G. Gudde (Berkeley: University of California Press, 1962), 79. Eliza Gregson heard that there were "boxes filled with human flesh all cut and packed in butcherly style"; "Mrs. Gregson's 'Memory,'" 122. See also Farnham's account, note 38, below. Probably related to this motif is William A. Trubody's memory that Keseberg was accused of "killin' people at Truckee Lake and saltin' 'em down"; Charles L. Camp, ed., "William Allen Trubody and the Overland Pioneers," *California Historical Society Quarterly* 16 (June 1937): 143.

of the bullock and horse instead of human flesh. He replied, he had not seen them. We then told him we knew better, and asked him why the meat in the chair had not been consumed. He said, 'Oh, it's too dry eating! the liver the lights were a great deal better, and the brains made good soup!' We then moved on, and camped on the lake for the night.

"*April* 21.–Started for Bear River valley this morning; found the snow from six to eight feet deep; camped on Yuva river for the night. On the 22d, traveled down Yuva about eighteen miles, and camped at the head of Bear River valley. On the 25th, moved down to the lower end of the valley; met our horses, and came in."

The last of the survivors of the Mountain Camp had now been brought in. The following list presents the names of the party. Those who perished were:–C. T. Stanton; Mr. Graves; Mrs. Graves; Franklin Graves; Jay Fosdick; John Denton; George Donner; Mrs. Donner, his wife; Jacob Donner; Betsy Donner; Isaac Donner; Lewis Donner; Samuel Donner; Charles Burger; Joseph Rianhard; Augustus Spitzer; Samuel Shoemaker; James Smith; Baylis Williams; Bertha [Ada] Kiesburg; Lewis S. Kiesburg; Mrs. Murphy; Lemuel Murphy; Lanthron Murphy; George Foster; Catharine Pike; William Pike; Eleanor Eddy; Margaret Eddy; James Eddy; Patrick Dolan; Milton Elliott; Lewis and Salvadore, Capt. Sutter's vaqueros.–In all (including two who died before reaching the Mountain Camp) 36.

The following survived:–William Graves; Mary Graves; Ellen [Eleanor] Graves; Viney [Lovina] Graves; Nancy Graves; Jonathan Graves; Elizabeth Graves; Sarah Fosdick; Loithy [Elitha] Donner; Leon [Leanna] Donner; Frances Donner; Georgiana Donner; Eliza Donner; George Donner, Jun.; Mary Donner; John Baptiste; Solomon Hook; Mrs. Wolfinger; Lewis Kiesburg; Mrs. Kiesburg; William Foster; Sarah Foster; Simon Murphy; Mary Murphy; Harriet Pike; Miriam [Naomi] Pike; Patrick Brinn; Margaret Brinn; John Brinn; Edward Brinn; Patrick Brinn, Jun.; Simon Brinn; James Brinn; Peter Brinn; Isabella Brinn; Eliza Williams; Noah James; James F. Reed; Mrs. Reed; Virginia Reed; Patty Reed; James Reed; Thomas Reed; William H. Eddy.–In all, 44.

The following Table exhibits the sex of those who were lost, and those who were saved:–[115]

---

115 Thornton's table represents the first rudimentary analysis of Donner party mortality rates, an issue that has interested recent researchers. Anthropologist Donald K. Grayson published his statistical analysis in the *Journal of Anthropological Research* in 1990; Stephen A. McCurdy, M.D., reported his conclusions in *The Western Journal of Medicine* in 1994. Despite some differences in their methodology and approach, both determined that age was the greatest risk factor affecting mortality rates, followed by gender and the size of kinship group.

	Males.	Females.	Total.
Number who perished	28	8	36
" " survived	20	24	44
Total	48	32	80
Number who perished	28	8	
Had the rate of mortality in the sexes been equal there would have died. . . .	$21^3/_5$	$14^2/_5$	
Dif. against males, and in favor of females	$6^2/_5$	$6^2/_5$	

Chapter XVIII.

The Sensations and Mental Conditions of the Sufferers.

I will now make some remarks, in addition to those already made, respecting the sensations of the sufferers, and their mental condition, as far as I have been able to obtain information from the survivors, or to infer it from the events narrated.

Some of the unfortunate sufferers entirely lost their reason. Of this number was Patrick Dolan, at the Camp of Death. His words were vague and unconnected. He struggled until he got out from under the blankets. He called to Mr. Eddy, saying that he was the only person of their number who could be depended upon. He then pulled off his boots, and divesting himself of nearly all his clothing, he bade Mr. Eddy follow him, and said that they would be in the settlements in a few hours. He was with great difficulty brought under the blankets, and held there until at length he became as quiet and submissive as a child; when he soon expired, as though he was in a calm and pleasant sleep.

Lanthron Murphy was of this number also.

Mr. Foster was likewise insane; but his was an insanity which, though complete, was of a totally different character. He, in a considerable degree, realized his situation, and in some respects was capable of reasoning from cause to effect. Nevertheless, his mental condition was one which rendered him irresponsible for his actions. His conduct as exhibited in the account of the journey of the sixteen from the Mountain Camp, is not in any degree in keeping with his general character, both before he entered upon this journey, and since his arrival in San Francisco, where he now resides, and is esteemed a reputable and worthy man.

Mr. Eddy was probably the only really sane one of that party of sixteen.

With but few exceptions, all the sufferers, both those who perished and those who survived, manifested the same species of insanity as did Mr. Foster.

Objects delightful to the senses often flitted across the imagination; and a thousand phantasies filled and disturbed the disordered brain. Of this number I may mention the unhappy Denton, who, however, was sometimes perfectly sane; and was undoubtedly so when he finally perished. But the whole number, with very few exceptions, might be individually named as examples.

Their deluded fancies often represented to them during the day, beautiful farm-houses and extensive fields and gardens in the distance. Toward these they pressed forward with all the energy with which alternate hope and despair could inspire them. During the night they often heard men talking, dogs barking, cocks crowing, and bells tinkling. These cruel mockings were probably the effects of fever. Many believed that they were surrounded by familiar faces and old friends; and that they saw objects associated with scenes of other years and places. Some saw persons coming to their relief, and called to them to hasten. Many fancied, although in the midst of winter, that they were traveling through highly cultivated regions in the midst of harvest. There were instances of persons suspecting at times that the circumstances with which they were surrounded were not real; and that they would rub their eyes and put their hand upon the head for the purpose of assuring themselves, if possible, that all was not the result of a dreadful vision or nightmare. One was doubtful whether he had not in some way, unperceived, passed from time into eternity, in which the circumstances of his condition were a part of his new mode of being.

The following extract from the journal of the intrepid and enterprising Col. Fremont, will be interesting and appropriate in this connection:–

"We began," he says, "to be uneasy at Derosier's absence, fearing he might have been bewildered in the woods. Charles Towns, who had not yet recovered his mind, went to swim in the river, as if it were summer, and the stream placid, when it was a cold mountain torrent foaming among rocks. We were happy to see Derosier appear in the evening. He came in, and sitting down by the fire, began to tell us where he had been. He imagined he had been gone several days, and thought we were still at the camp where he had left us; and we were pained to see that his mind was deranged. It appeared that he had been lost in the mountain, and hunger and fatigue, joined to weakness of body, and fear of perishing in the mountains, had crazed him. The times were severe, when stout men lost their minds from extremity of suffering—when horses died—and when mules and horses, ready to die of starvation, were killed for food."

Some of the party, though sometimes, during brief intervals, perfectly sane, when awake, yet suffered from the most painful and terrifying dreams, in which they saw combats and heard cries of despair and anguish. Dreams of famine and death, of floundering in fathomless snows, frequently made them afraid to sleep; for when they did, they often started up from their miserable beds in horror and affright. These not only tormented the mind, but the body also was exhausted and fatigued, through the sympathy which exists between the mortal and immortal part of man's nature.

Some of these unhappy emigrants felt a general sinking of all the energies of the mind, and a total prostration of the body, without, however, experiencing any gnawing of hunger. The unfortunate Denton was probably an example of this. It will be recollected that he was found at one time asleep upon the snow. He was with great difficulty aroused, but was afterward left with a little food; and when found dead, the food left with him was in his pocket. It is probable that, after writing the piece of poetry which I have mentioned in a former part of this volume as having been discovered at his side, he did not experience a sensation of hunger; and a drowsiness overcoming him, he never awoke.

This absence of the sensation of hunger was generally followed by an irresistible desire to sleep. If great efforts were not made to arouse them from the torpor into which they were sinking, an unnatural and difficult manner of breathing was usually observed in about half an hour; and this was followed by a rattling of the throat in about three-fourths of an hour. This continued from one to four hours; when death closed the scene; the individual appearing to be in a profound slumber, until life was wholly extinct, and the spirit was released from its suffering body. Sometimes they were permitted thus to die, in order that the miserable survivors might in this manner obtain food, without resorting to a more horrid alternative. There were examples of no efforts being able to awaken persons from this dreadful slumber. On one occasion, a person in this sleep threw his arm out in such a manner that his hand fell into the fire. Mr. Eddy, who was awake, and observed it, hoped that it would awaken the miserable sleeper, and he permitted it to remain there until it was doubled and shriveled. He then threw the hand back upon the body; but the sleeper soon extended it again, and it fell into the fire, where it was consumed to a coal, without the slightest movement of a single muscle, or a perceptible change of the features, indicative of pain.

If the effort to arouse the sleeper was successful, as it frequently was, the poor sufferer often spoke of the most delightful visions, in which his imagination had present to his view, beautiful plantations of luxuriantly growing crops, and tables groaning with a weight of food, prepared in the most inviting manner.

Such was the condition, both mental, and physical, into which Mr. Eddy felt himself sinking, at the time of his making his first meal of human flesh. He had ceased to experience the sensation of hunger, although at other times this had almost maddened him. But he felt a general prostration of body and mind, and a heaviness and lethargy almost imperceptible stealing upon him. Those who were with him, told him that he was dying. This, however, he did not believe, but he, nevertheless, had witnessed enough to convince him that these were primary symptoms, which, if he did not resist them, would certainly terminate in his death in a few hours. He reasoned clearly concerning his condition, and he knew perfectly well that nothing but courage could rescue him from that state of stupor and mental imbecility into which he was falling.

A few became furious, and died without sinking into this slumber. Others died calm and peaceful, taking an affectionate leave of their friends, and expressing a confident hope in the mercy of the blessed Redeemer; and in the fullness of the provision made by His death for even the most wicked; and in His power and willingness to save them in His kingdom.

LILBURN W. BOGGS (1796–1860)

O ne of the most eminent of the overland emigrants of 1846 was former Missouri governor Lilburn Williams Boggs. Born in Kentucky on December 14, 1796,[1] Boggs emigrated to Missouri as a young man and engaged in trade before entering into politics, serving first as a state senator (1826–32), lieutenant governor (1832–36), governor (1836–40), and again as state senator (1842–46). Boggs is chiefly remembered for his role in the Mormon War of 1836–38, which culminated in the expulsion of the Latter-day Saints from Missouri.

Two years after he stepped down as governor, an unknown assailant–always assumed but never proven to have been the Mormon avenger Orrin Porter Rockwell–shot Boggs in the head as he sat reading after dinner. Miraculously Boggs survived, though he carried some of the shot for the rest of his life.

"Governor" Boggs is mentioned frequently in the annals of the 1846 migration. His immediate entourage included his married son, William M. Boggs, and his brother-in-law Alphonso Boone. Boggs campaigned for the captaincy of the large wagon train which included most of the families in the Donner party, but lost to William H. Russell.

Though he had started out with the intention of settling in California, Boggs grew alarmed at rumors of large companies of armed Mormons heading for the same place and decided to go to Oregon instead. He had intended to take the Applegate Cutoff, but after traveling to its junction with the California Trail he once again changed his mind–the main route had been so arduous and the distance so much at variance with what he had been led to believe that he decided Applegate was untrustworthy as a guide and continued to California as he had originally planned.

Boggs settled near Sonoma after arriving in California and quickly became a prominent citizen, serving as alcade of the Northern District of California until the state government was established. He again entered

---

1 Boggs's year of birth varies from source to source, but 1796 appears most likely to be correct.

Lilburn W. Boggs (1796–1860). © Utah State Historical Society, all rights reserved, used by permission

trade and profited greatly from the gold rush. Boggs retired to a farm in the Napa Valley, where he died on March 19, 1860.

The Text

The following extract from a letter Boggs wrote to Alphonso Boone appeared in the *Oregon Spectator* on July 8, 1847. The letter as printed is undated, but internal evidence indicates that it was written in early April of that year. At the end of March 1847 an abortive relief mission had been organized but, hampered by soft snow, the rescuers came back about the first of April. Boggs wrote after the return of this party but before he heard of the departure of the fourth and last relief later that month. Though the information he relates about the emigrants remaining to be saved echoes that in a letter by Selim E. Woodworth in the *California Star* on April 3, other details had not been published. Whatever its source, Boggs's information is accurate. He writes familiarly of the members of the Donner party, evidently expecting Boone to remember them.

This letter is virtually unknown in the literature of the Donner party. While not a major source of information, it provides several interesting details about the emigrants. The present transcription is from a photocopy provided by the Oregon State Library. It was reprinted in *Crossroads* 6 (Winter 1995). I thank Will Bagley for bringing this letter to my notice.

IMMIGRANTS TO CALIFORNIA.

—We publish the following extract of a letter from Gov. Boggs, one of the recent immigrants to California, addressed to his brother-in-law, Col. A. Boone, of this territory, giving a succinct account of the sufferings of the recent immigration to that country:

"You have heard, no doubt, something of the misfortune and suffering of Reed and Donna's[2] companies in the mountains. They went, you know, Hasting's Cut-off—nearly half of them perished in the California mountains. Those that lived had to use the bodies of their friends who died for food. The following are the names of those who perished as far as I can learn: Jacob Donna and wife and some of his children—three of his children got in. Pike was accidentally shot by Foster with a revolving pistol, and died. Wolfinger and all the Dutch, (except Wolfinger's wife and Mrs. Keesburg,) Dolan, Antonio the Spaniard that started with us,[3] Milt. Elliott, Stanton, Denton, Shoemaker, Mrs. Eddy and her two children, the foolish fellow that was with Reed,[4] a Mr. Elliott [Graves] and his wife, and a Mr. Fosdick, son-in-law of Mr. Elliott [Graves],[5] a little chunky Dutchman by the name of Charly that drove one of Geo. Donna's wagons.[6] George

---

2 It is not clear whether the phonetic spelling "Donna" reflects the Donner brothers' pronunciation of their name or Boggs's own dialect.

3 Very little is known about Antonio. According to Eliza W. Farnham, he joined the Donner party at Fort Laramie; that may have been because Boggs, with whom he was traveling, had changed his destination to Oregon.

4 Three of Reed's hired men perished. Since Boggs names Smith and Elliott, the third can only be Baylis Williams. Patty Reed Lewis much later described Williams as an albino who slept in a wagon by day and did odd jobs by the campfire at night. Evelyn Wells, "The Tragedy of Donner Lake," *San Francisco Call,* June 14, 1919.

5 Boggs's confusion about the Graves family can be attributed to the fact that he had not known them on the trail; they had joined the Donner party after the companies broke up at the Little Sandy.

6 "Dutch Charley" Burger is usually reported to have been a teamster for Keseberg, but other sources support Boggs.

Donna and wife, and Keesburg, and Mrs Murphy, and a young child of
Geo. Donna's[7] were left in the mountains by those who went out to their
relief, they not being able to travel, and we suppose they have all perished;
a child also of McCutcheon's; Smith, one of Reed's drivers, also perished.
Those that got in were Mr. Reed and wife and all his children; Brinn, the
Irishman,[8] and all his children and wife; Eddy and Foster; Mrs. Foster and
Mrs. Pike, and a single daughter of Mrs. Murphy; one [two] of Mrs. Murphy's little boys; three of Geo. Donna's girls; three of Jacob Donna's children; McCutcheon and wife and Mrs. Fosdick; Mrs. Wolfinger and Mrs.
Keesburg. There were about eighty souls in the company; about forty got
in, some of them badly frozen and entirely destitute. Mr. Reed lost every
thing but a little clothing. The snow was from 5 to 30 feet deep. Mr. Reed
had come in to Sutter's ahead of his company after provisions &c., and
returned, but couldn't get to them on account of the snow until he came
back again, raised a party of men and returned.–Lieut Woodworth and old
Greenwood, with parties, also went out to their relief. There were two
camps of the sufferers in the mountains, and the camps were eight miles
apart. Geo. Donna, wife and child were left at the farthest camp, and Mrs.
Murphy and Keesburg at the other camp unable to travel. A party has
since gone out to save these five, but returned, being unable to get to them,
so they must have perished."

---

7 The child left behind, evidently Jacob Donner's son Samuel, is mentioned in
  Selim E. Woodworth's letter in the *California Star* of April 3, 1847.
8 "Brinn" or "Brin" for "Breen" occurs in Thornton's account and several other
  early documents.

MARY ANN GRAVES (1826–1891)

Mary Ann Graves was born November 1, 1826, in Putnam County, Illinois, the second surviving child of Franklin Ward and Elizabeth Cooper Graves. The family moved to Marshall County about 1830, where they lived across the Illinois River from the town of Lacon.

Nineteen years old when her family left for California, Mary Graves has been depicted as the belle of the wagon train. According to one story, a smitten Indian attempted to purchase her, and she has been linked romantically with both John Snyder and Charles T. Stanton. Mary figures prominently in accounts of Forlorn Hope.

On May 16, 1847, only a few months after her escape from the mountains, she married Edward Gantt Pyle, Jr., who had been a member of one of the parties guided by Lansford W. Hastings across the cutoff ahead of the Donner party. He had also participated in the Donner relief efforts, transporting provisions to the relief parties.[1] The couple settled in Santa Clara County but their marriage was short lived, for in May 1848, Pyle disappeared. Foul play was suspected and his anxious wife walked along New Almaden Creek looking for a trace of his body, but it was not found until almost a year later. One Antonio Valencia had dragged Pyle to death behind a horse and hidden the corpse. Valencia was hanged on May 10, 1849; Mary Pyle is said to have cooked his food for him while he was awaiting execution, to ensure that he would not cheat the hangman.[2] This

---

1 While escorting the refugees with the First Relief to safety, "a young man" proposed to half-starved, thirteen-year-old Virgina Reed. She was still amused by the incident when she wrote of it to C. F. McGlashan more than thirty years later, on May 14, 1879. In a following letter she stated that her suitor was Mary Graves's first husband, but Stewart apparently missed the reference and incorrectly identified him as Perry McCoon. This confusion is understandable, since both McCoon and Pyle married Donner party survivors and were dragged to death by horses.

2 Nugget Editions Club, C. K. McClatchy Senior High School, *Early Day Romances: Sutter's Fort 1847–1848* (Sacramento: Nugget Press, 1943), 23; Karl Kortum, personal communication.

murder created a stir in the small Anglo community which was long remembered. The story passed into local folklore and several variants appear in later histories of San Jose and of Santa Clara County.[3]

Mary Pyle taught school in San Jose for a time. In 1853 she married Joseph Thomas Clarke; they moved to Visalia, Tulare County, about 1860. Despite the distance, Mrs. Clarke sometimes visited her sisters in northern California. Their children remembered her as a woman of decided opinions; they recalled that she was good-looking, had corkscrew curls, and smoked a pipe.[4] According to her grandchildren, she was a very serious person. She once said, "I wish I could cry but I cannot. If I could forget the tragedy, perhaps I would know how to cry again."[5]

The Clarkes had seven children, only two of whom survived their mother. Mary nursed her son Alexander through his last illness. He died on March 5, 1891; she died at the age of sixty-four only four days later.

The Text

Mary Graves's contributions to the literature of the Donner party are varied. She was one of the informants for the account published by Eliza Farnham in 1856 and in 1879 began a correspondence with C. F. McGlashan, who was gathering materials for his history. By that time she was having trouble with her eyes ("She don't even write to me," her brother William warned the historian) and some of her letters had to be written on her behalf by family members.

The following letter is the first of Mary's contributions. Shortly after she married Edward Pyle, Mary wrote a letter to Levi Fosdick, father-in-law of her widowed sister Sarah. The letter was printed at Lacon, the Graves family's home town, in the *Illinois Gazette* on September 9, 1847. It deals mostly with events in the Sierra and leaves out many details; nevertheless, it contains several points of interest. Although an early first-person account, the letter is little known and has been reprinted only once, as "Stay at Home," in *Crossroads* 5 (Summer 1994). This transcription is made from a photocopy provided by the Illinois State Historical Library.

---

3 The San Francisco *Alta California* of May 10, 1849, provided the dates given here.

4 Karl Kortum, comp., The McDonnell Ranch; unpublished family history.

5 Doris Foley, "Mary Graves, A Heroine of the Donner Party," *Nevada County Historical Society* 8 (July 1954).

Mary Ann Graves (1826–1891); date of photo, 1879. California Department of Parks & Recreation, Sutter's Fort State Historic Park

LETTER FROM CALIFORNIA.

The following letter, written by Miss Mary Ann Graves, who was one of the sufferers in the California mountains, to Levi Fosdick, of this county, father of Jay Fosdick, one of the party that perished, will we are sure be read with interest. She is a daughter of Mr. and Mrs. Graves who also perished in attempting to reach the settlements through the deep snows. Mr. Graves resided about one mile from this village, and had a good farm and a comfortable home. He left with $800 in money and a good out-fit for his long and perilous journey. What become of his money does not appear: we presume it was lost with the general wreck of the party.[6] Miss Graves writes that she has changed her name, having married a Mr. Pyle. The name of her residence does not appear in the date, but we suppose it to be at or near the Sacramento river. The letter is dated

"May 22d, 1847

Dear Friends: I take this opportunity of relating to you our sad fate. Our travels and sufferings are too horrible to relate. The number of our family now living is only eight.[7] We are all orphan children in a strange land without friends or relatives.

We were caught in the California mountains, in the snow, the 4th of November, where we remained until the 16th of December. During this period we subsisted on our few remaining cattle, which were very poor. The number of our company was 81. There were 25 or 30 men, and but 4 survived to reach the settlement.[8]

---

6 See Thornton, note 96, above, for the fate of the Graves money.

7 Two of Mary's siblings, Jonathan and Elizabeth, died not long after this letter was written.

8 Mary is somewhat mistaken here; presumably she is counting the four men who were rescued from the camps (Noah James, Baptiste, Patrick Breen, and Louis Keseberg) and does not include Eddy and Foster, who snowshoed out with the

On the 16th of December 15 of us had snow shoes prepared; and we started with 8 pounds poor beef each,[9] to endeavor to cross the mountains, reach the settlement, and procure assistance. The distance was 150 miles. We made good progress until the 8th day, when we got lost. It commenced raining and continued until the next day at night—then commenced snowing and continued three days and nights. Father died on Christmas night at 11 o'clock in the commencement of the snow storm. During that storm we had neither fire nor food. When it was over we started, (leaving 4 of our number there,) and travelled on until the 5th of January, subsisting on human flesh. Jay died, the idol of his loving wife. Sarah and myself were now the only members of our family [in this party of 15][10] left. Two Indians were killed,[11] whose flesh lasted until we got out of the snow and came where Indians lived. Thence we subsisted nine days on acorns when we obtained relief from the settlements, being the 18th of January. 7 out of 15—2 men and 5 women—reached the settlements.

We related the situation of those remaining at the camp, & 10 men went to their relief. On reaching the camp many were found dead from starvation. Mother and the 7 children were alive. The men could not bring the small children—they took only those that could walk. Mother and the small children remained behind. On returning they met another company pushing over the snow as fast as possible, to save those that were yet behind—(the snow was 30 to 40 feet deep.) Mother and children were found yet alive. They took them, and travelled 15 miles, when a snow storm came on and they had to stop. They run out of provisions; and the men were obliged in order to save their own lives, to leave the company and make their way thro' with frozen feet—some of them have lost their feet. Mother and Franklin died before relief could reach them.

On Mary's river a quarrel took place between John Snyder and an overbearing Irishman, in which the latter stabbed the former.[12]

I have told the bad news, and bad as it is I have told the best. No tongue can exceed in description the reality.

Forlorn Hope. William McCutchen, James F. Reed, and Walter Herron had left the company before it was trapped in the snow.

9 This amount indicates that the Forlorn Hope was better provided for than has been described in other sources.

10 Original editor's comment.

11 This appears to be the earliest published reference to the killing of Luis and Salvador for food.

12 Mary Graves was not alone in calling Reed "overbearing"; see Frances H. McDougall, "The Donner Tragedy Once More: Reply to Mr. Reed," in this volume.

I will now give you some good and friendly advice. Stay at home,—you are in a good place, where, if sick, you are not in danger of starving to death. It is a healthy country here, and when that is said all is said. Horses and cattle running wild on the commons are abundant. You can live without work if you are a complete rascal; for a rascal you must be to stand any chance at all. In the number of rogues this country exceeds I believe any other.

There is no timber here. All kinds of fruit are cultivated. Oats and clover grow wild from 1 to 6 ft. high. Wheat is raised in abundance—corn not much raised. Onions grow that measure 8 inches in diameter. It is a good climate.[13]

I have said enough in favor of the country—as much and perhaps more than I ought.

Mary Ann Graves."

---

13 Here one of Hastings's victims vindicates at least some of the claims with which he had enticed emigrants to California.

H. A. WISE (1819–1869)

A descendant of an old Virginia family, Henry Augustus Wise was born at Brooklyn, New York, on May 24, 1819. His naval career was launched in 1834 when an influential relative, Henry Alexander Wise—later governor of Virginia—had him appointed midshipman. Wise was promoted through the ranks and commissioned a lieutenant in 1847. He served in Mexico and California during the Mexican War on the razee *Independent.* Wise later served in France, the Mediterranean, and Japan. He also became a recognized authority on ordnance.

Because of his Southern origins, Wise was in a difficult position when the Civil War broke out, but he remained with the Union navy. During the early part of the war he saw action in Virginia; he was promoted to the rank of commander in 1862. That year he began to work in the Ordnance Bureau and was eventually appointed its head. Overwork caused him to resign the position in 1868 and he obtained a leave of absence for reasons of health. He died in Naples on April 2, 1869, leaving a widow and four children.

The Text

In addition to his naval career, Wise also found time for writing. Under his own name he published nautical reminiscences and scientific articles; as "Harry Gringo" he wrote fiction. In 1849 he published a lighthearted account of his Mexican War experiences as *Los Gringos, or, An Inside View of Mexico and California, with Wanderings in Peru, Chili, and Polynesia.* During his tour of duty Wise had visited Monterey and San Francisco, but his narrative does not make clear where he met Selim E. Woodworth and Jean Baptiste Trudeau.

In telling about the Donner party, Wise repeated a number of exaggerated tales; these included that the emigrants' stupidity and laziness brought about their destruction, that in the mountains they refused to leave their property even at the cost of their lives, and that intrafamilial cannibalism was common. Versions of some of these stories appeared in Thornton's account, while others resemble *California Star* articles which appeared on February 13, March 13, and April 10. Woodworth was the apparent source for similar stories that were published in the Monterey *Californian* on April 24.[1]

Wise's other informant, Jean Baptiste Trudeau, had hired on with the Donners at Fort Bridger and for several weeks was the only able-bodied male at the Alder Creek camp. Like Eddy, Baptiste was the hero of his own tale; unlike Eddy, he boasted of his cannibalism. Many years later, however, he tearfully told Eliza Donner Houghton that no cannibalism had occurred at the Donner camp.

This hypocrisy disgusted George R. Stewart and adversely affected "the Spanish boy's" characterization in *Ordeal by Hunger*. Baptiste's statements are indeed grisly, but Stewart seems to have reacted to the content without appreciating the context. Baptiste had just undergone a traumatic experience and, like other survivors, no doubt felt a great need to talk about his ordeal. In addition, Baptiste was only about sixteen years old, not twenty-three, as Stewart believed, and his statements to Wise probably reflect the common adolescent desires to be the center of attention and to shock one's elders. Thirty-five years later a more mature Baptiste did not wish to upset Mrs. Houghton, of whom he was fond, hence his contradictory statement to her.

That Wise took these stories seriously is not greatly to his credit, but considering the wild rumors in circulation he should not be blamed too harshly. His reminiscence was not intended as history and should not be taken as such; rather, it is an example of the folklore which had sprung up about the Donner party and with which its survivors had to contend. In 1871 James F. Reed broke his public silence on the Donner party in response to such stories as these told by Wise.

Los Gringos was first published by Baker & Scribner in 1849 and was subsequently reprinted several times. The present text is from Chapter XI of Baker & Scribner's 1850 edition.

---

1 These newspaper articles are reprinted in Morgan, *Overland in 1846.*

FROM *LOS GRINGOS*

Previous to our arrival in the waters of Francisco, a frightful incident transpired amidst the Californian mountains, which goes far to surpass any event of the kind heard or seen, from the black hole of Calcutta, to smoking the Arabs in Algeria.[2] It relates to a party of emigrants, whose shocking inhuman cannibalisms and sufferings exceeded all belief. The news first reached us in Monterey, and also that a party had been despatched to succor them. From an officer of the navy in charge of the expedition [Woodworth], and from one of the survivors, a Spanish boy, named Baptiste,[3] I learned the following particulars: The number of emigrants were originally eighty; through a culpable combination of ignorance and folly, they loitered many weeks on the route, when, upon gaining the sierra, the snows set in, the trails became blocked up and impassable, and they were obliged to encamp for the winter; their provisions were shortly exhausted, their cattle were devoured to the last horse's hide, hunger came upon them, gaunt and terrible, starvation at last—men, women and children starved to death, and were eaten by their fellows—insanity followed. When relief

---

2   The infamous Black Hole was a chamber measuring about 18 x 14 feet in the fortress of Calcutta. It was said that some 146 captured British defenders were crammed into the room the evening the fort fell, June 20, 1756; only twenty-three of them survived the night. This version of the tale is largely discounted as a gross exaggeration: one estimate puts the figures at about sixty-four soldiers and twenty-one survivors, another at twenty soldiers and three deaths.

"Smoking the Arabs" refers to an incident which occurred in June 1845 when French soldiers built up a large fire at the mouth of a cave in which a tribe of Algerians they were pursuing had sought refuge. The next day the fire was allowed to die down, the smoke cleared, and it was discovered that some 700 men, women, and children had suffocated.

3   Based on W. C. Graves's estimate, Jean Baptiste Trudeau, variously known as Trubode, Truvido, and Trauvico, has been described as twenty-three years old at the time of the Donner party. "Trubode" told Eliza Donner Houghton many years later, however, that he had been only about sixteen; the ages he reported in various censuses are consistent with that statement. That Wise and others refer to him as "the Spanish boy" supports the belief that he was younger than the age usually reported.

arrived, the survivors were found rolling in filth, parents eating their own offspring, denizens of different cabins exchanging limbs and meat—little children tearing and devouring the livers and hearts of the dead, and a general apathy and mania pervaded all alike, so as to make the scout the idea of leaving their property in the mountains before the spring, even to save their miserable lives; and on separating those who were able to bear the fatigue of traveling, the cursings and ravings of the remainder were monstrous. One Dutchman actually ate a full-grown body in thirty-six hours! another boiled and devoured a girl nine years old, in a single night. The women held on to life with greater tenacity than the men—in fact, the first intelligence was brought to Sutter's fort, on the Sacramento, by two young girls. One of them feasted on her good papa, but on making soup of her lover's head, she confessed to some inward qualms of conscience. The young Spaniard, Baptiste, was hero of the party, performing all labor and drudgery in getting fuel and water, until his strength became exhausted; he told me that he ate Jake Donner and the baby, "eat baby raw, stewed some of Jake, and roasted his head, not good meat, taste like sheep with the rot; but, sir, very hungry, eat anything."—these were his very words. There were thirty survivors, and a number of them without feet, either frozen or burnt off, who were placed under the care of our surgeons on shore.[4] Although nothing has ever happened more truly dreadful, and in many respects ludicrously so, yet what was surprising, the emigrants themselves perceived nothing very extraordinary in all these cannibalisms, but seemed to regard it as an every day occurrence—surely they were deranged. The party who went to their relief deserved all praise, for they, too, endured every hardship, and many were badly frostbitten. The cause of all this suffering was mainly attributable to the unmeaning delay and indolence attending their early progress on the route, but with every advantage in favor of emigration, the journey in itself must be attended with immense privation and toil. The mere fact, that by the upper route there is one vast desert to be travelled over, many hundred miles in width, affording very little vegetation or sustenance, and to crown the difficulty, terminated by the rugged chain of Californian mountains, is almost sufficient in itself to deter many a good man and strong, from exposing his life and property, for an unknown home on the shores of the Pacific.

---

4 Many of the survivors and rescuers suffered from frostbite and several lost toes. Mary Donner was the worst off, having lost four toes on her left foot, but reports of her injuries were greatly exaggerated in the memoirs of W. C. Graves (in this volume) and Eliza Gregson, among others.

Eliza W. Farnham (1815–1864)

Eliza Woodson Burhans was born November 17, 1815 in Rensselaerville, New York. As a result of her unhappy childhood she resolved to dedicate her life to reducing misery in the world. Throughout her life she took an active interest in various social causes, writing and lecturing on such subjects as prison reform, phrenology, and the role of women. She maintained that the latter are morally and biologically superior to men and urged women to develop intellectual interests to further their high calling, motherhood. Her feminism was sincere but limited: she also believed that mundane physical tasks and public affairs (including voting) should be left to men. She served as the matron of several institutions where her advocacy of enlightened reforms sometimes led to conflict. She also labored as a nurse during the Civil War. In the midst of her many activities she found time to write five books and edit a sixth.

In 1836 Eliza Burhans married Thomas Jefferson Farnham, a lawyer who later became known for his writings on Oregon and California. Thomas Farnham died in California in 1848 and his widow traveled west the following year to see to his estate, taking her two sons with her. A firm believer in the civilizing influence of females, Eliza Farnham had advertised for young women to accompany her to the wilds of California, where their presence would be "the surest check upon many of the evils that are apprehended there." Only three "migrating ladies" accompanied her, however.

Once in California, Farnham settled her husband's affairs and farmed in the Santa Cruz Valley on a ranch she named La Libertad, tackling the many unaccustomed chores of frontier life with energy and courage, though not always with good sense. She married William Fitzpatrick in 1852 but divorced him four years later, after which she went back to New York. She traveled to California again in 1859 but after three years returned once more to New York, where she died of tuberculosis on December 15, 1864.

The Text

In 1851 Farnham began a book about her California experiences which was published five years later as *California, In-Doors and Out*. It contains a 108-page appendix about the Donner party, based on interviews with survivors. It is not certain when the interviews took place—some may have been as early as 1849—or when the narrative was actually written. Farnham names as informants John and Margaret Breen; her "Miss G." can only have been Mary Ann Graves. There was at least one other, another member of the Forlorn Hope, whose contribution seems to have been minor.

True to her ideals, Farnham stresses an aspect of the Donner tragedy which continues to intrigue readers—the role of women. From 1847 to the present writers have noted that the women of the Donner party held up better than the men, a fact which Farnham attributes to women's moral superiority and self-sacrificing love of others. She uses the Donner disaster to demonstrate her thesis.

Like Thornton, Farnham is overly emotional and relies on a limited number of informants; like Wise, she repeats rumors as facts. The single greatest problem with her account, however, is its lack of precision. The dearth of such hard data as names, dates, and places leads to the garbling of some incidents. In her defense, however, it should be remembered that Farnham was a social reformer, not a historian, and gave only as much information as she needed to support her argument. Unfortunately, Farnham seems to have accepted that information uncritically; there is no evidence that she attempted to verify it.

Despite its faults, Farnham's account becomes comprehensible and useful, once one identifies the principals. Her narrative differs significantly in tone from Thornton's. She omits the invented conversations and much of the melodrama so evident in the earlier account, and she only mentions in passing scenes upon which Thornton dwells. These differences reflect not only the personalities, agendas, and interviewing styles of the two writers but also the passage of time: by the 1850s the details of the disaster were not as fresh in the survivors' minds and they did not have as much need to talk about it as had Thornton's informants some years earlier.

California, In-doors and Out also contains information not found elsewhere: particulars of the Graves family's journey before they joined the Donner party, a description of events at Starved Camp after the Second Relief had to abandon most of their charges there, an early account by John Breen which differs somewhat from one he wrote for H. H. Bancroft decades later, and the only statement we have by Margaret Breen. Like Eddy's statement to Thornton and Trudeau's to Wise, Mrs. Breen's statement to Farnham is self-serving. She emerges as a heroine—generous, resourceful, pious, resolute—a perfect demonstration of Farnham's thesis.

Thornton had portrayed the Breens unsympathetically, which probably accounts for Margaret Breen's exaggerations to Farnham. Whether or to what extent Farnham may have been responsible for the overstatement is impossible to prove.

In addition to the first edition of 1856, lengthy extracts of Farnham's narrative appeared in McGlashan's *History of the Donner Party,* parts of which were then reprinted in *History of San Benito County, California* (1881). A facsimile edition of Farnham's book was published by B. de Graaf in 1972; it also contains a biography of the author. The present text omits the first eight pages of the appendix in which Farnham expounds her philosophy.

FROM *CALIFORNIA, IN-DOORS AND OUT*

Narrative of the Emigration of the Donner Party
to California, in 1846.

The self-sacrifice to which women, in all conditions, are called, presupposes the better nature which would prompt them to make it; and California is an exemplification of this on a scale to which the history of ages offers no parallel. There was no salvation for the country but from her presence in it, and the necessity to come was in very, very many instances, the cruelest she could be called on to obey. Thousands have reached the land through incredible hardships and scenes shocking to every sensibility; and thousands more, without these trials, have landed on our shores, unconscious that in doing so they were literally laying themselves upon a rack.

And if the weakness which has been cultivated and nurtured at home, failed to become strength and self-reliance in the new and fearful trials that awaited them, who should exercise harsh and unrelenting judgment toward them? Shame and ruin have been not only the precursors, but the consequents of anguish to many a wretched woman among us; but truth, which compels this acknowledgement, glories also in placing side by side with it the noblest proofs of all that we claim for our sex—illustrations of sublime self-sacrifice, of heroic fortitude, of calm endurance such as may have been equaled but never surpassed in its history. The annals of the overland emigration are especially rich in these histories, kindling, despite the detestable demonstrations about us, a love and reverence for humanity, which refreshes and strengthens the soul.

One of these is related in the following pages. I have gathered its material from several individuals of both sexes, who were members of the unfortunate party; and I believe that in almost every particular it is deserving of entire credit. This party emigrated before the discovery of the gold, and consisted chiefly of persons led by the love of adventure and confidence in the charms of the clime they sought.

They set out from St. Joseph's, Missouri, in May of the year 1846.

California was then in a state bordering on revolution; and among the male members of this party were several persons who, doubtless, believed that among its half-civilized population, positions and advantages might be won, which they could never hope to enjoy at home. In any case, they were destined to a land unequaled in beauty, and in its magnificent generosity of soil and climate. And, though a long journey lay before them, they were confident, at the worst they could foresee, of a result that would satisfy, in a large measure, the hopes they entertained, and they were fearless of dangers by the way. They numbered from eighty to ninety, and comprised many families, with children of all ages, from a few months upward. They set out in spirits corresponding with the sunshine and breezes which accompanied them. The men were earnest—the young people gay—the mothers only, a little doubtful, when they considered the precious lives they had in charge, and the possible dangers that might have to be encountered before they should see them all safely housed in the distant land of their destination. Their journey was uninterrupted by any but the occurrences common to such travel—the delays to rest weary cattle or recover lost ones—the necessity to repair a broken wagon, or adjust some of the many affairs that on such a journey constantly lack adjustment.

There was then no thoroughfare on the great plains that lay stretched between them and the setting sun. Their solitude was rarely broken by the passage of a trading or trapping party, or a band of Indian hunters, moving to and fro, in search of game, or bearing homeward the trophies of the chase already past. But the emigrant fires burned at evening, and their light shone cheerfully into the silent darkness that walled them in. When supper was over, the young people gathered around one of the fires, and there were music and dancing, or social, cheerful chats, after the adventures of the day.

There was a family consisting of twelve members: a father, mother, nine children, and a son-in-law, husband of the eldest daughter.[1] The father was a man in middle life; healthy, hopeful, adventurous; with strong affections, that were generous enough to receive a powerful stimulus from the presence of his large, active, and promising family. They had been born in one of the most beautiful regions of Illinois. The youngest, at the time of starting, was a babe, of four or six months. The eldest unmarried, a daughter of eighteen. The young women rode on horseback, or in the wagons, as suited their convenience or fancy. They were excited by the novel features of the country over which they passed, and the anticipations with which they looked forward to that region which had, in their minds, but a vague, half-real existence; and seemed, to the more imaginative of them, more like the happy hunting-ground, of which the Indian dreams in his untutored reveries, than a part of the commonplace, work-a-day world.

---

1 The Graves family, from Marshall County, Illinois. Farnham has omitted their teamster, John Snyder.

140

They crossed the Missouri on the 20th of May, and, on the 3rd of July, reached Fort Laramie.[2] Here they found a party of Sioux Indians; warriors going out to give battle to their old enemies, the Snakes. The Sioux were then the most powerful race of the great prairies; and our emigrants, partly, I suppose, from a desire to conciliate them, partly, because of their abundance, gave them a dinner at the Fort, on the 4th. They were grand looking men, the warriors, well-made, powerful, and lithe, grave and courteous, dignified, solemn, and majestic. The hospitalities over, they parted, with friendly remembrances on one side, and wishes on the other. The emigrants moved on, and were overtaken by the same party on the afternoon of the 6th. The recollection of bread and salt did not restrain the commoner sort from attempting to steal various articles that seemed desirable to them. They heeded no remonstrance from the whites, nor even from their chief, till the latter personage, with a majestic determination to rule, shot down two of the robber's horses. They wished to buy one of the young ladies, who was riding a little in the rear of the company, with her brother, and made two or three handsome offers for her, which, being declined by the brother, one laid hold of her horse's bridle, and attempted to lead her off a prize, but he dropped the rein when her protector leveled his gun, and rejoined his company.[3] Such little incidents, happening rarely, served to enliven their travel, which now began to grow a little tedious.

They reached Fort Bridger in the latter part of August [July], and there heard much commendation bestowed upon the new route, via Salt Lake, by which Mr. Hastings had preceded them a few weeks. It was said to be shorter than the old one, by Fort Hall, and quite practicable. They debated, and delayed, and finally divided. A small company had proceeded, on the new route, from the fort, a few days before them, whom

---

2 Fur traders had established Fort Laramie in 1834 near the junction of the Laramie and North Platte rivers, about eighty miles northeast of present-day Cheyenne, Wyoming. W. C. Graves mentions the Independence Day celebration at Fort Laramie in his memoir, in this volume. At this point the other members of the Donner party were a week ahead of the Graves family, having reached the fort on June 27.

3 The young lady is Mary Graves, the brother, W. C. Graves. The latter does not allude to these events in his own memoir, but they appear in McGlashan's history. Indians also attempted to purchase Virginia Reed Murphy and her pony; see her memoir in this volume. These incidents may represent folklore rather than history: according to Francis Haines, Sr., stories about the attempted purchase of a white child or young girl by Indians are common in late reminiscences of the overland journey but are not recorded in contemporary diaries and letters written on the trail. "Goldilocks on the Oregon Trail," *Idaho Yesterdays* 9 (Winter 1965–66): 26–30. My thanks to John Alley for bringing this reference to my attention.

they overtook, and joined on the sixth day. Their whole number was now eighty-three, or, as some say, eighty-five; and this was the company fated to those appalling trials, under which so many perished, and so many more failed in all human senses. Terrors and sufferings, so great and protracted, seldom try the nature of men and women; but, rarely as they come, they find few among those whom they visit furnished to the occasion. In the trials of this kind, of which we have narratives, women have rarely been participators. Here the numbers were nearly equal; and the result is one of which every woman who reverences her sex may be justly proud.

At the time when they joined the advance company, it was lying still, awaiting the return of a small party that had been sent out to improve the road, and, if possible, overtake Hastings, who was supposed to be but a few days before them.[4] They hoped to secure his guidance into the valley of Bear [Jordan] river. They were disappointed in this, and, after the loss of many days, finally journeyed on. Could the fearful consequences of this delay have been apprehended, it would not have been submitted to. But the disposition of common characters to be controlled by anything but their own intelligent determination, prevailed over the dread of the women, and the impatience of the men. Days went by, till they amounted to weeks. The fair summer had drawn to a close, and autumn had tinted with matchless pencil the herbage and foliage of the great mountain barrier that divided them from their land of promise, before their feet, now growing weary and slow, touched its eastern base. I extract from a narrative furnished me by the kindness of Mr. John Breen, who was of the party, and, at that time about fourteen.[5]

He says: "We traveled several days, without much difficulty, till we left Weaver [Weber] river. Here our work commenced, for we had a new road to make through a heavily-timbered country, with no other guide than the sun. One day's travel from the river, the road became so bad that it was necessary to let the wagons lie still for two or three days at a time to prepare a way for them. Over much of the ground it was impossible to pass with the wagons till a great deal of labor had been done. In one place all the men in the company worked hard for two weeks, and only advanced

---

4 Though imprecise, this is the earliest report that the Graves family overtook the Donner party while Reed was away seeking Hastings. Farnham's source for this statement was almost certainly Mary Graves.

5 John Breen wrote a memoir for H. H. Bancroft in 1877, which generally agrees with what he had told Farnham years before, but the two accounts do not overlap at many points. The memoir appeared in the *Pony Express Courier* in January 1941 and in Stookey's *Fatal Decision;* King publishes most of it in *Winter of Entrapment* (1994).

thirty miles.[6] We, at last, came within one mile of Salt Lake Valley, when we were compelled to pass over a hill [Donner Hill] so steep that from ten to twelve yoke of oxen were necessary to draw each wagon to the summit. From this height we beheld the Great Salt Lake, and the extensive plains by which it is surrounded. It gave us great courage; for we thought we were going to have good roads through a fertile country; but the saline atmosphere, and the long drives, without water, rendered our route through that valley particularly harassing. When we reached what was called the desert, we had a drive of seventy or eighty miles, without grass, or water over a plain covered with salt. Here our real hardships commenced; cattle giving out, or straying away, mad with thirst. One man (Mr. R.) lost all his oxen but one yoke, and was, consequently, compelled to leave all his wagons but one; into which he put a large family and their provisions, which, of course, made traveling very tedious.[7] Several people came very near perishing on this desert for water; but, it was very remarkable that the women stood it better than the men. After we got across, we laid by one or two days to recruit; but, when we were ready to start, Mr. R.'s last yoke of cattle were missing; so, all hands turned out, and made a general search for six days, but we found no trace of them. In fact, it was impossible to find cattle on those plains, as the mirage, when the sun shone, would make every object the size of a man's hat look as large as an ox, at the distance of a mile or more; so one could ramble all day from one of these delusions to another, till he became almost heart-broken from disappointment, and famished from thirst. While we laid here, two men [Stanton and McCutchen] were sent on, on horseback, to California, to get provisions, and return to meet us on the Humboldt."

Thus their provisions were getting low. This, the loss of their cattle, and the reduced condition of those that were left, weighed upon their spirits, and impeded their progress. There had been no death in the party until they reached Salt Lake Valley.[8] They had a consumptive invalid [Luke Halloran], who had been steadily declining through all their rough experience, and one afternoon, the wagon in which he was carried was observed to fall behind the others. Inquiry was made. He was not much worse, it was

---

6 This is not far off Reed's statement in his memoir (this volume) that it took eighteen days to travel thirty miles.

7 Writers have inferred that Reed's allegedly huge family wagon had slowed the company's progress across the prairies, contributing to the animosity that erupted against him after Snyder's death. Breen is the only survivor who states that the Reeds impeded the company's progress, but only after the crossing of the Salt Desert, not previously.

8 Farnham started her account with the Graves family, who were not with the company when Sarah Keyes died.

said, but after the party had encamped at evening the wagon came up bringing his corpse. He had neither wife, nor child, nor near friend. He had set out an invalid in search of health, and happily had expired before the terrible days came that were now drawing fast on. Next morning a rude coffin was constructed of boards taken from one of the wagons, and the body committed to the earth, according to the rites and ceremonies of that mysterious, and world-wide brotherhood to which he belonged.[9]

Those who had before been comparatively indifferent to their delays, began, by this time, to be earnest. "The more so," Mr. Breen says, "that on the morning of their leaving the long encampment at the desert, there appeared a considerable fall of snow on the neighboring hills. The apprehension of delay from this cause, and of scarcity, made the mothers tremble. But they knew that to give way was to make unavoidable that which they dreaded, and they put the best possible face on to meet their discouragements. The men were irritable and impatient. A dispute arose one day after dinner, between two of them, respecting the driving of a wagon up a very difficult hill.[10] Hot words were followed, almost instantly, by blows—one with a knife, or dagger, which proved fatal in about twenty minutes. The man was buried next morning. Feeling respecting the affair ran high, and the survivor very soon left the company, alone, his family being constrained to remain in it, by the previous loss of their cattle, on the desert. How keen must have been that parting—from a wife and four or five children!

"They reached Truckee river without any incident of an extraordinary character except the disappearance of a German [Wolfinger] whose immediate party lagged behind awhile, and when they at length came up, could, or would give, but a vague account of him. It was said that he had strayed away in search of cattle and they supposed he might have been killed or lost. The press of care had now become too great, from the necessity to get forward, to permit the loss of any time, or even the manifestation of any interest in the fate of one who was a stranger, by blood and tongue, to most of his fellow travelers. At the last encampment on Truckee river, another life was lost, by the accidental discharge of a pistol. Two men, brothers-in-law [Foster and Pike], had been handling their arms by the camp fire in the morning. Wood to replenish it was called for, when one said to the other, 'hold my pistol while I go for some.' In the transfer, by some means it went off, and the contents lodged in the body of the unfortunate man [Pike], who lived only two hours. Death did not startle them now. They were too

---

9 This is the earliest reference to Halloran's Masonic burial.

10 In his 1877 memoir Breen recalled that the teams had stalled "on a sandbank on the Humboldt river," a description which suggests a different scenario than his statement here.

much engrossed by their own necessities to heed his presence, further than naked decency required. They had buried their first dead in a coffin and shroud, with masonic ceremonies, their second with only a shroud and a board beneath and above him. The last man was buried literally dust to dust, nothing to separate his clay from that of the great parent who opened her bosom to receive him."

They journeyed on, hoping that at the worst they should be met by relief, but as the mothers have told me, with inexpressible anxieties at heart already.[11] "On Truckee river," says Mr. Breen, "the weather was already very cold, and the heavy clouds hanging over the mountains to the west were strong indications of an approaching winter. This of course alarmed several people, while others paid no attention to it. My father's family, among the former, used every effort to cross the mountains if possible before the snow should become too deep. We traveled up the river a few days, when we met the excellent Stanton, returning with five or six mules, packed with flour and meat. Capt. John A. Sutter had given him the mules and provisions, for the mere promise of compensation, an act for which he deserves the love of every soul of that suffering company. He will always be remembered by me, with gratitude and reverence, for that generous act. And Mr. Stanton, who sacrificed his life to assist his companions—for he had no family or relations in the company—should be held in honored remembrance by every one who can appreciate a noble act. The clouds on the mountains looked very threatening, but he naturally looked at the bright side of things, and assured us there was no danger,[12] little thinking that the next summer's sun would bleach his unburied bones, not far from that spot."

It had snowed at the last burial on this river, and they traveled up its banks amid wintry desolation, made a hundredfold more desolate by the frowning presence of the stern gigantic mountains, by the feeble condition of their cattle, which the snow deprived of sustenance, by their scanty stores and already overtasked powers of endurance. They reached Truckee Lake on the fourth of November. It was cold, and on its banks the snow already lay to the depth of a few inches. They encamped for the night, availing themselves of a couple of huts which had been erected there the winter previous by a few belated emigrants or trappers.[13] They hoped to push on in the morning. Their exhausted and starving animals were

---

11 The word "mothers" is puzzling; it is not clear with what other mother or mothers besides Margaret Breen Farnham spoke. See note 19, below.

12 W. C. Graves also refers to Stanton's assurances, but gives a different impression; see his memoir, this volume.

13 When the emigrants arrived there was only the cabin which Moses Schallenberger had inhabited during the winter of 1844–45, which the Breens occupied.

offered some boughs. By this time their wagons were nearly empty of their burdens, but they were, even thus light, an overmatch for the feeble cattle.

Mr. Breen says of this day's work and that which followed it: "In the morning it was very cold, with about an inch of snow on the ground. This made us hurry our cattle still more, if possible, than before. We traveled on, and, at last, the clouds cleared, leaving the towering peaks in full view, covered as far as the eye could reach with snow. This sight made us almost despair of ever entering the long-sought valley of the Sacramento; but we pushed on as fast as our failing cattle could haul our almost empty wagons. At last we reached the foot of the main ridge, near Truckee Lake. It was sundown. The weather was clear in the early part of the night; but a large circle around the moon indicated, as we rightly supposed, an approaching storm. Daylight came only to confirm our worst fears. The snow was falling fast on that terrible summit over which we yet had to make our way. Notwithstanding, we set out early to make an effort to cross. We traveled one or two miles–the snow increasing in depth all the way. At last, it was up to the axle of the wagons. We now concluded to leave them, pack some blankets on the oxen, and push forward; but by the time we got the oxen packed, it was impossible to advance; first, because of the depth of the snow, and next, because we could not find the road; so we hitched to the wagons and returned to the valley again, where we found it raining in torrents. We took possession of a cabin and built a fire in it, but the pine boughs were a poor shelter from the rain, so we turned our cattle at large, and laid down under our wagon covers to pass the night. It cleared off in the night, and this gave us hopes; we were so little acquainted with the country as to believe that the rain in the valley was rain on the mountain also, and that it would beat down the snow so that we might possibly go over. In this we were fatally mistaken. We set out next morning to make a last struggle, but did not advance more than two miles before the road became so completely blocked that we were compelled to retrace our steps in despair. When we reached the valley, we commenced repairing the house; we killed our cattle and covered it with their hides."

The courage to make such great exertion was not evinced by the whole party. Many remained in the valley awaiting almost with indifference its result. One of the leading spirits in these efforts was the mother of our narrator, who had, indeed, a world to struggle for–a sick husband and seven children, the youngest a nursing babe, the oldest but fourteen years.

They were an Irish family, who had been well-to-do before leaving their last home in Iowa, and they had still a large number of cattle, and as many other resources as any other in the company.[14] The father, in these terrible

---

14 Patrick and Margaret Breen, natives of County Carlow, Ireland, had a farm near
    Keokuk, Iowa, before they and a neighbor, Patrick Dolan, left for California.

days, was nearly or quite disabled, from an attack of a distressing ailment which he had suffered for several days before reaching their encampment,[15] so that the responsibility of saving the family devolved chiefly on the mother. And the unshrinking firmness, resolution and self-devotion with which she served them, in that fearful season, deserve commemoration beside the noblest deeds of humanity. Conceive with what palpitating anxiety she watched every struggle of the faithful beasts; with what heart sinking she saw them utterly fail, thus dooming her tender babe, and young children, and feeble husband to trials of which human fear could not depict the appalling character and duration.

They sat down at the huts helpless—compelled to abide the issues that might await them. Their stores were nearly exhausted. Bread had quite disappeared—a little tea, coffee, and sugar were all they had left, except the flesh of their miserable beasts. The relief stores were very soon consumed by a community of seventy or seventy-five cold and hungry people, and as removal was impossible to any but the ablest, it was soon decided that the most hardy and capable should at once set off on foot, to complete their journey, taking with them only enough to support life for six days, by the end of which period, if ever, they thought they should reach Bear Valley. They set out, reached the tops of the mountain with infinite difficulty, and then, finding it impossible to ascertain what precise direction to take, waited on the snow two days and nights, for the man Stanton who had come out with the stores, and was to go in with them. His mules had strayed away, and he was reluctant to set off to go to their owner [Sutter] without them. So the foot party was obliged to return to camp, where, for the time, they might all be considered as settled. Trees had been felled for the walls of cabins, which were covered with the hides of their oxen and horses. There were three camps in the space of about three quarters of a mile, and another seven miles away further down the shores of the lake.[16] In these the whole party were in some manner sheltered from the rigor and storms of that unfriendly region, and they had need be well sheltered, for on the night after the return of the party last spoken of from the summit, a snow-storm set in which continued almost without intermission for ten days.

Whose hand will ever adequately record the discouragements of those days? the sickening apprehensions, the yearnings over the helpless and

---

King's *Winter of Entrapment* contains a great deal of information about the Breen family.

15 Patrick Breen records that he suffered from "the gravel"—kidney stones—in his diary entry for December 22.

16 There were three cabins near the eastern end of the lake—the Murphy, Breen, and Graves-Reed cabins. The Donner families and their dependents were seven miles away, as Farnham states, but their camp was not on the shore of the lake.

unconscious ones, the destroying fluctuations between hopes that only dawned upon the crushed spirit to be succeeded by fears of palpable midnight blackness! At length the storm was over. The dreary gray clouds, which had lowered so mercilessly upon the devoted party, trooped away, and the blue sky smiled coldly and finely down upon them, as a haughty spirit triumphant does upon its subdued victim. The adventurers made ready and started again on snow-shoes, it being impossible now to move in any other manner.

Every day of the storm had reduced the provisions fearfully, and now no relief could be relied on till fresh tidings of their dreadful situation were taken into the settlements. They set out on the 16th of December. They had been forty-two days at the cabins—an age of terror, anxiety, and dread—but up to the time of their departure, actual starvation had not taken place. They numbered fifteen—ten males and five females. The faithful Stanton, and the two Indians who had been sent with him by Gen. Sutter, were of the party. Under their guidance, hope was entertained that they might reach Bear Valley in five or six days, and they took with them enough of the poor dried beef to allow each person, thrice a day, a bit of the size of two fingers. There was the father, before spoken of [Franklin Ward Graves], and his two eldest daughters—the married one accompanied by her husband [Mary Graves, Sarah and Jay Fosdick];—an unfortunate young mother [Amanda McCutchen], who had been obliged to leave an infant behind her, and two other females [Sarah Foster, Harriet Pike]. A Mexican [Antonio], who had joined the emigrants at Fort Laramie, was of the number; the remainder were all men who had come through from the states. They took each upon his or her own person all on which the preservation of life depended in the fearful journey before them—coffee, a kettle to boil it in; beef, of their poor sort, barely enough to nourish their emaciated bodies sufficiently to support life; matches; a flint-gun; a small axe, and a blanket each. Their snow-shoes were made of their ox-bows and green hide interlaced. They were about two feet in length, by one in breadth. Thus they were equipped. There were but two or three who did not leave behind them father, mother, wife or child, or brother or sister. The country before them was a dreary waste of cold white. Frequently, only the tops of the trees were visible above the snow, its depth varying from a few feet to sixty.

All the long day—and it was long to them, though the sun was warming the southern tropic—they urged their fainting, wasted bodies onward, and, at nightfall, gathering a few boughs, they lighted a fire, boiled their morsel of coffee, and drank it with the little scrap of beef they could afford for the evening meal. They then wrapped their blankets about them and slept upon the snow till the morning light recalled them to their weary travel. On the morning of their fifth day out, poor Stanton sat late by the camp-fire.

The party had set off, all but Miss G., and as she turned to follow her father and sister, she asked him if he would soon come. He replied that he should, and she left him smoking. He never left the desolate fireside. His remains were found there by the next party who passed.

They pressed on. There was too little of life in them to wonder or fear at anything. They were alone with starvation, and would have been roused and even cheered by the sight of any living being ferocious or docile. Their helplessness and despair were fearfully increased by the loss of their guide. The Indians did not know the country when undisguised, and its chilling mantle would have deceived eyes the most familiar with it. They were now making the small allowance of one day serve for two; but even this could avail them nothing. Their whole store would not have satisfied the moderate appetite of one person for a meal. So, on the evening of the seventh day, when they had given up all expectation of seeing their guide, and would scarcely have lifted a hand or foot to escape from death, a violent rain set in. There was then no possibility of kindling a fire to warm their shivering frames. The pitiless flood drenched, in a short time, their tattered garments. They laid their aching bones upon the oozing snow, and wore away a night which inflicted the agonies of a hundred deaths upon them. The morning came, and still the flood fell. They roused themselves to move on a little, if it were possible, despite the storm; but they had lost their course, and the sun no longer befriended them. It was proposed to return to the cabins, following their own tracks, but the Indians would not consent, and Miss G. resolutely determined to follow them. There was nothing possible, there, but starvation. The fate before them could not be worse, and might be better. Miss G.'s resolution encouraged her companions. They went on all day without a morsel of food, the rain pouring continuously. At night it ceased. Some were confused in their perceptions, some delirious, some raving. Those who were still strong enough to realize their condition, might well now despair. The women bore up better than the men. One of them had about her a cape or mantle stuffed with raw cotton, and, upon a minute examination of it, she found, between the shoulders, about an inch square of the inner surface dry. The lining was cut, and enough taken out to catch the spark from the flint. They had lost or left their axe, but were able to make a fire, after much difficulty, of a few gathered boughs. They sat down around it. There was nothing else to be done. Preparing, distributing, or eating even the wretched morsel that had kept them alive to this time no longer occupied them. They had no speech but the ravings of their delirious companions, no hope but that of death.

Scarcely had they begun to feel the warmth which faintly revived their decaying sensibilities, when the angry clouds began to descend upon them in snow. It fell with a silent, blinding, merciless steadiness. It came as the messenger of that power whom they no longer dreaded—death. The father, whose two daughters were of the company, was the first released. The chilling rain had pierced his emaciated frame, and subdued the energy which had resisted courageously all that had gone before. He had much to struggle for. His wife and seven children were at the cabins, and he had pressed forward, feeling in that effort the only hope of saving them. But now, all power to serve them was gone, and, perfectly conscious of their own and his condition, he laid down under the relentless storm to die. In that desolate hour of death, he called his youngest daughter to his side, and bade her cherish and husband every chance of life, in the fearful days which he knew awaited them. They were still far from habitation or help, except such as God gave them, and their own courageous hearts. She must revolt at nothing that would keep life in her till she could reach some help for those whom they both loved. He clearly foreshadowed the terrible necessity to which, within a few hours, he saw they must come, and died, leaving his injunction upon her, to yield to it as resolutely as she had done everything else that had been required of her, since their sufferings began.[17]

His death scarcely moved those to whom it was most important. To the others, it, perhaps, furnished a hope–a fearful and terrible one certainly, yet still a hope. But another victim was fast preparing; and scarcely had the white mantle of the storm been softly and silently spread over the stiffening limbs that had just ceased to struggle, when another soul took its flight–the poor Mexican lad who had joined them at the fort. They had been forty-eight hours without tasting food. The storm increased. They were in imminent danger of perishing of cold, and the weight of the accumulating snow upon their persons. They wisely took the only measure of defense that was left them against the storm. They spread a blanket, and seating themselves upon it in a circle, stretched another over their heads, thus raising a community of warmth, which greatly assisted their slow vitality. Occasionally they had to raise the blanket, pushing up from beneath, to throw off the accumulating snow.

Under its shelter what horrors were endured and apprehended! Some, who raved, seized upon the persons of those near them–a hand or arm–mistaking it for food, which they were eager to devour. Others sat in the stupor of despair, the idiocy of inanition, or silent, sullen rebellion against the fate which clasped them as in the arms of iron. During the night they ate of the flesh of those who had died. That first dreadful repast! The heavens frowning above; the earth glaring beneath; the night air moaning over the great waste, whose silence seemed to snap and rend the very chords of sensation and life in the lightened brains of those who partook. It roused

---

17 McGlashan and Harlan also report that Graves told his daughters to save themselves by using his body for food.

them more effectually than anything had for days. It stirred their utmost remaining capacities for appreciating the horrors of their situation. But the voracious digestive function was more faithful to their need than the revolted will, which, though conquered, stood aloof. The sustenance they took assimilated rapidly and healthfully. They were better and stronger in a few hours.

The storm continued two days. At the end of that time they moved on. But two more died before they set out from the "camp of death."[18] While there, the Indians heard words which, though spoken in a language unknown to them, alarmed them. They left the party by stealth—ran away.

They now went forward without any guide but the setting sun. They took with them what they hoped would subsist them till they should reach human habitation; but when the last morsel was consumed, there was still the same white waste about them. Then the first providential relief came. A skeleton deer came in their way and was shot—for they had clung to their gun when every other implement had been cast away in weariness or despair. The wretched animal was starved, like themselves, upon the desert of snow, and its slight carcass was consumed to the last inch of hide—every atom that could be eaten. They descended till they reached bare ground. Their snow-shoes were no longer necessary, and the strings and bits of hide were eaten. And yet there were no indications that they were approaching relief. Suddenly they came, one day, upon the two fugitive Indians, resting. Poor fellows! They had had nothing to eat since they had fled from the camp of death on that terrible night. They had traveled on, feeble and hungry, but hopeful; for they knew that abundance was before them, and that it was really not far off, could they but struggle forward.

They never saw their bountiful home again. The starving emigrants, who could not slay each other, thought with less scruple of the fate of these. They had left the wintry mountains so far behind, that it seemed quite certain before the sustenance should be exhausted, which was thus providentially thrown in their way, relief would come from some source.

It was expected that parties would be out to meet them from the nearest settlement; and so, indeed, there were—but they did not fall in with the wanderers, and the first indication of human neighborhood to them was a rancherie, of Digger Indians, who gave them of their stores—acorns, seeds, etc. They sent them forward, when they had a little refreshed themselves, with a guide, to the next rancherie, whence another conducted them to the next, and so on, till they reached Bear Valley. In it an emigrant had settled the year previous, and there were shelter and food for them. They were then within a day's travel of the rancho, where they arrived after nightfall.

---

18 This melodramatic name was first published by Thornton, but Farnham's account shows little other sign of his influence.

Miss G. and one of her companions assured me[19] that the cheer of a royal palace could never so satisfy them as did that of this rude home. The friendly light shining, not, as they afterward observed, from a window, but through gaps in the walls, far into the dreary darkness that had walled them in so long, seemed to promise them, while yet afar off, princely comfort and abundance.

They entered it on the evening of the thirty-second day from the cabins! They had set out, fifteen in number; they were now seven—haggard, tattered, with naked feet, frozen and bleeding, emaciated, wild countenances, unnatural voices, and incoherent speech, they entered the hospitable dwelling where they had been expected and prepared for—two men and five women!!

No more starvation, no more horror before them! Did they consider it then? No; they sat down, housed and fed, and simply rejoiced in the blessed sense of warmth and plenty and repose. Few experiences can be richer in satisfaction than theirs of the first few hours, before memory began her painful work—before the stunned sensibilities revived to feel their own wounds—before the subdued intellect reasserted itself—before, indeed, the life which was not animal reclaimed its power. How perfect the rest to the exhausted nature.

The party whose sufferings I have attempted to record, left at the cabins in the mountains about sixty souls. Nearly half of them were children, from a few months old, upward. When this party left, there were no provisions in their camps but the poor beef of the wasted cattle they had slaughtered, and this was so scarce that it was very sparingly used—the question with the thoughtful and faithful minds of that unfortunate community being, How little is it possible for me to support life on? The relief party had made them fully aware of the almost impossibility of transporting provision to them over the deep snow. Animal strength was out of the question, and men could bear but little beyond what was necessary for their own support in the journey to and fro. There could no others leave the cabins without a guide; the feeble and the young it was thought impossible to start with till the snow that lay in their way should have, at least partially, disappeared. Thus they were to husband every atom of sustenance. A few inches of hide supported a family an entire day. Nursing mothers could no longer nourish their infants. Some were happily released before the days of sorest hunger came.

---

19 The phrasing indicates that another member of the Forlorn Hope spoke with Farnham. William Eddy is a possibility (see note 39, below); however, if this person was one of the mothers referred to in note 11 above, Amanda McCutchen is the most likely candidate: of the three mothers in the Forlorn Hope, she lived nearest Farnham.

Their cabins were deep down in the snow after the heavy storms came, and it had to be shoveled from the roof, and cut in stairs from the doorways, to afford communication with the upper world. In each of the three cabins that were near each other, as, indeed, in all, there were women and children, and kindly offices and sympathies were exchanged, as their needs varied.

There was little visiting, except when death entered one or more of those memorable homes. He was never preceded by disease; gaunter and feebler grew his victims daily, the strongest and ablest first. Men who loved none that were near—who felt themselves doing battle alone with the terrible foes that hemmed them in, were the first to surrender.[20] Some half-grown youths and children perished, but no women—especially no mothers—for a considerable period.[21] These went, where the deepest misery was, ministers of mercy and tenderness to the suffering—too earnest to mitigate the pains of others to be altogether consumed by their own;

"Love's divine self-abnegation"

raised them above the naked animal necessities which destroyed those not thus supported. With the true instinct which such a tremendous situation would unclothe of all conventional or false leanings, they were, in being always sought, acknowledged as the most merciful, the most tender, the most efficient. Starving men appealed to them. Women who had children perishing, called for help on women who also had children to suffer. In the middle cabin of the three I have described as being near together, lived the Irish family I have spoken of. They had reached that place with all their animals, and consequently were among those best prepared to meet the terrible emergencies before them. Their store of beef was piled in a corner of their little apartment, and upon the other side of a partition, which did not quite divide the house, there was a profane, coarse, blasphemous German, or Dutchman [Louis Keseberg]. His revolting language had terrified and shocked the good Catholic mother often, before they reached this spot, and now it made her tremble to hear his imprecations. He was entirely destitute, with a wife and two children, one of whom [Louis, Jr.], fortunately, died early in the days of starvation. He had wisely established himself near the largest stores and liberal hearts—his unblushing selfishness

---

20 When the Donner party was trapped it included ten men between the ages of eighteen and thirty-five (whose ages are known) traveling without family members; only one of them survived.

21 Of the fifteen women over the age of eighteen trapped in the mountains, only five perished. The first to die was Eleanor Eddy on February 7; seven men had predeceased her.

having proved, before that time, that he would not lack what was essential to support life while his neighbors had it.

There the indefatigable, self-denying mother and wife watched over her family, nursed, tended, fed, clothed, and kept them alive from the sixth or seventh of November till about the middle of February. What a record would the history of those three months make! One feature of it, not to be forgotten, was the constant expectation of relief. They lived, as it were, a subterranean life. The people who came would first be heard above; and the silence that surrounded them, no living thing approaching, was seldom broken without. Those who were of their community, came silently and went silently; and their ears had soon become so familiar to the accustomed noises, that they knew each one. But the painful tension of the organs, to catch a tone that should foretell release from their dreadful lot! A shifting of the wind, so that it brought from the angles of their snow embankment an unfamiliar tone, would make their hearts beat more quickly. They went to sleep with this hope, and woke with it. It attended them in the preparation and taking of every miserable meal, and in all the weary hours between those events; and though they talked many times as if it had utterly forsaken them, yet it never did for a moment. But for it few of those who survived to better days would have outlived those dreadful ones.

Mr. Breen says: "About this time an incident occurred which greatly surprised us all. One evening, as I was gazing around, I saw an Indian coming from the mountain. He came to the house and said something which we could not understand. He had a small pack on his back, consisting of a fur blanket, and about two dozen of what is called California soap-root, which, by some means, could be made good to eat. He appeared very friendly, gave us two or three of the roots, and went on his way. When he was going I could never imagine. He walked upon snow-shoes, the strings of which were made of bark. He went east; and as the snow was very deep for many miles on all sides, I do not know how he passed the nights."[22] One can believe that he would do as well in this respect as the poor starved men and women who had left the cabins.

One day a man [Augustus Spitzer] came down the snow-steps of Mrs. Breen's cabin, and fell at full length within the doorway. He was quickly raised, and some broth, made of beef and hide, without salt (that necessary article having been forgotten in the wagons at the top of the mountains, which were now entirely buried in snow), put into his lifeless lips. It revived him so that he spoke. He was a hired driver. His life was of value to no one. Those who would have divided their morsel with him, were in a land of plenty. She said that when a new call was made upon her slender

---

22 Patrick Breen recorded this incident on February 28.

store, and she thought of her children, she felt she could not withhold what she had. God had given and preserved it to her, and she trusted firmly in Him to save them when all should be gone.[23]

Thus she fed the fellow, her next neighbor, whose wickedness made her tremble lest it should provoke the judgment of God, and whose dreadful conduct afterwards showed a nature not human but altogether monstrous and fearful; and thus she shared with perishing women and children the store that had been spared to them. Her pious faith, her warm heart, and her energetic nature fitted her for her lot. In her the sublime promise, "As thy day, so shall thy strength be," was literally fulfilled. Her husband had been ill on their arrival, and he had barely recovered strength to move; but, seconding her humane purposes, he dispensed their meat to those who had none; and the houseless and starving never went from them altogether unfed. Their hut became the resort of the utterly destitute–those who had no share either in heart or hearth.[24] Eleven of the wretched ones expired in it, and more who fed there live to this day.[25]

"O! dear Mrs. Breen," said one of her neighbors, coming quickly in one morning, "my dear boy is dying. Will you not give me some food for him?"

"Indeed then I will, dear," was the ready answer. "Take some of the beef."

The poor mother had often had some before. She took it, and, fast as her wasted limbs would carry her, hurried back to her cabin. She first tasted a few morsels raw, to give her *heart;* but this time her speed was vain. The poor emaciated boy, though he tasted what she brought, was too far gone to revive; and in a short time she sent a messenger up to ask her good neighbor to come down with one of her sons, and assist in burying him in the snow![26] What a burial was that! Performed by two starving women, and a lad scarcely more alive than the one he was assisting to bury!

---

23 The Breens were in a difficult position: they had larger stores of meat than did their neighbors, but they also had a large family to feed. No doubt they were as generous as they dared be under the circumstances, but claims of their generosity to all and sundry are not confirmed by other sources.

24 On the contrary, the Breens permitted only Spitzer and the Reeds to live with them; the Reeds' hired help, Eliza Williams and Milt Elliott, had to fend for themselves. Patrick Breen became uneasy when the latter came to the cabin one day in early February and dozed off. Fearing that Milt would die and his death demoralize the children, Breen made the teamster leave. Mrs. Reed helped Milt drag himself to the Murphys', where he died a few days later. Patty Reed Lewis to C. F. McGlashan, bound letters, 47.

25 Only one person, Augustus Spitzer, died in the Breens' cabin before they left.

26 This particular incident is corroborated. William G. Murphy described his brother Landrum's death in a speech given at Donner Lake in 1896, which Houghton quotes in *The Expedition of the Donner Party,* 347–48.

The man who had fallen in their door, died with them.[27] Children, whose parents were gone before them, either to the grave or on the journey, were taken in and fed, and tended.[28] It was wonderful how, with her nursing babe, with the care that was necessary in preparing and dividing the little food she dared to give them each day, with the constant calls upon her humanity and strength to attend to those whose lot was more deplorable than her own, she bore up under all—encouraged everybody, and constantly gave out, as it were, life to the sinking, hope to the despairing, courage and faith to the doubting. They needed it all and more, for the long-hoped relief came not. Day after day went past, and they wasted, and death crept closer and closer to them.

Mr. Breen says: "About this time, Mrs. Reed put afoot, a brave an undertaking as was ever recorded of woman. It was to travel with a man [Milt Elliott] and another woman [Eliza Williams] across the mountains and send relief to her family (her husband was gone before, and she had four children in the camp).[29] But her heroic undertaking failed. After traveling several days she was obliged to return, and the greatest wonder is how they were ever able to retrace their steps, as the snow fell several feet while they were gone. The man who accompanied her died a few days after their return, then another man, then a child, and, in a few days, a woman, the mother of several children.[30] Death had become so common an event, that it was looked upon as a matter of course, and we all expected to go soon."

With what joy and hope a relief party was hailed that arrived about the last of January [February 18]. It brought but slender supplies, and the individuals composing it were to return immediately with as many of the sufferers as could set out with them. This party had been sent out chiefly, or in part, through Mr. Reed's effort, and his family were among twenty-one who left the cabins to travel over the snow, on the first of February. The

---

27   "Spitzer died... imploring, Mrs. Breen, to just put a little meat in his mouth, so he could just know, it was there, & he could die easy, & in peace. I do not think, the meat was given him, but he gave up the ghost, & was no more." Patty Reed Lewis to C. F. McGlashan, March (or April) 1879.

28   At this point in the narrative the Breens were not looking after any children whose parents had "gone before." Catherine Pike and George Foster were cared for by their grandmother, Levinah Murphy, who also tended James Eddy after his mother died; the Graves family took care of Harriet McCutchen. It was not until later that the Breens took in Patty and Tommy Reed and looked after the Graves and Donner children left with them at Starved Camp.

29   Patrick Breen records the departure of this group, which also included Virginia Reed, on January 4; they returned four days later.

30   These are the deaths of Milt Elliott, Charles Burger, Margaret Eddy, and Eleanor Eddy.

children were to be assisted forward by the strong men; but after a mile or more up the mountain, the difficulty proved too great in the case of the two younger, and they were taken back to Mrs. Breen's cabin to await their further chances there.[31] The rest of the party pressed on.

I know but little of that transit; some perished by the way, and all were reduced to the utmost extremity before they reached the settlements. Mr. Reed's wife and children reached him after a separation of four months. What a meeting must that have been! The wasted persons, the haggard countenances, the tattered clothing, and, then, the painful thought of those who were yet behind. Could they also be saved? Two of Mrs. Breen's sons [Edward and Simon] were in this party, the ablest and eldest. She received the little ones who were returned to her, and fed and cared for them with her own, and she told me that in giving them their scanty meals, she could never divide a larger portion to her own than to the strangers.[32] Their constant nourishment was the dry hide boiled without salt (she had a little pepper) and a very little beef with it. The hide was burned to remove the hair, scraped, and, when boiled, made a gelatinous broth, far more nutritious than the poor beef would have made without it. But this could not last them much longer. Already one cabin had been unroofed and thus rendered untenantable.[33]

Among those who perished was not the wretch who lived under the same roof with the Breen family. He yet lived to consume the sustenance that would have sustained a worthier life. His wife and surviving child had come in with the last party, and there is a sort of satisfaction in knowing that base and brutal as the man-cannibal was, the wife was not altogether lacking in traits that allied her to him. For the only act told of a woman in this whole dreadful history, that was unworthy of her sex, was of this one. It is said that on their way in, after they were a day or two from the cabins, her child appeared to be dying, and she herself seemed unable to travel. She was advised to return. It was much easier traveling back than advancing, because the road was well beaten, and she was in no danger of encountering anything, for the waste of snow was an utter solitude.

---

31 Farnham or her informant neglects to mention the Breens' unwillingness to take Patty and Tommy Reed back, as reported by Thornton.

32 Patty Reed Lewis does not confirm this statement in her letters to McGlashan. Further, according to a late account based her testimony, Glover left seven teaspoons of flour and seven strips of beef with the Reed children, which was to last them ten days. Patty cooked it herself over the fire in Keseberg's lean-to. She does not say that the Breens augmented this ration. Wells, "The Tragedy of Donner Lake," *San Francisco Call,* July 2, 1919.

33 The Reeds were reduced to eating the hides that roofed their side of the double cabin they shared with the Graveses. It was at this point that they attempted unsuccessfully to cross the mountains and afterwards took refuge with the Breens.

She refused; and with the word, tossed her helpless, sinking babe from her, saying: "Why should she go back with a half dead child!" The development of her husband's atrocity, which afterwards took place, would have made it painful to think of her as linked to him had she been altogether so noble and self-sacrificing as those of her sex who shared her lot.[34]

About the thirteenth of February [March 1], a relief party arrived. Mr. Reed conducted it. They had *cached* provisions on the road, and reached the cabins with only a small quantity of wheaten meal, made at Sutter's Fort. They left a morsel at each of the camps, and went below to the solitary one where death had been busy, indeed, and hunger had driven humanity to its last resort–preying upon the dead.

They left at this camp only a mother and her three children. Everybody else had perished, and the distraught mother refused to leave her wretched habitation because of the treasure of money and goods it contained, insisting that government should find means of transporting her family and effects safely to the country whither she was bound.[35]

There was no time to be lost. Every day imperiled lives. So the second day after the arrival of Mr. Reed's party, twenty-one souls set out; many of them were children, and two infants who had been nursing till the maternal fountain had been dried. The wheaten-meal had been baked into biscuit for the journey, and the provident Mrs. Breen had reserved through all, a few strips of their poor beef dried, four pounds of coffee, and a small paper of tea. The latter article, with a lump of loaf sugar, weighing about a pound, she carried at her waist.

When they set out they left at the cabins a father near to death, a mother and three children; at the lone cabin two children, two and four years, and

---

34 This anecdote is unique to Farnham; generally survivors were sympathetic to Philippine Keseberg, whom they regarded as a battered wife. W. C. Graves, also rescued by the First Relief, remembered that Mrs. Keseberg offered twenty-five dollars and a gold watch to anyone who would carry Ada for her.

35 This is a variation of Wise's tale that the emigrants refused to abandon their property at the risk of their lives. The story was told of Tamsen Donner in McDougall's 1871 *Pacific Rural Press* article (in this volume); apparently the emigrants believed that George Donner was dead and they could conceive no reason other than avarice or insanity to explain why his wife would refuse to leave her camp, as she was in good health. Her sister-in-law Elizabeth, Jacob Donner's widow, was too weak to travel. Farnham confuses the two Donner families; her later statements point to Elizabeth Donner as the "insane mother." See notes 36 and 43.

the grandmother of one of them, and the dreadful German at the upper cabins.[36]

The man was alone in the hut, he occupied; the woman and the two children in a neighboring one.

The moving party camped the first night at the top of the mountain, a place bleak and cold enough to bodies well fed and clothed, but dreadfully chilling and wretched to the feeble starving creatures who had, with difficulty, reached it from the comparative shelter and warmth of their habitation below. Here a very scanty supper was made of the biscuit; a few spoonfuls of meal, thrown into some snow-water, made a little gruel for the infants, and after a night of aching wretchedness which can well be imagined, they rose early, and taking a few morsels, each, of the bread, journeyed on. Mrs. B. was not fortunate enough to taste her beef or coffee, which she had, at starting, committed to the keeping of one of the men. Sometimes, when she sat in the long nights watching her perishing family by the camp-fire, she saw those on the opposite side of the logs preparing and drinking the latter; but with that feeling which will be readily understood by many natures, and those not of the worst, she could not ask for a drop of it.

On the third day out, they met a party going to the cabins—the fathers of the two children, to bring them on.[37] And I may as well state here, that when these men arrived, they found their two young children dead; also the grandmother who was with them, and the husband at the lower camp.[38] Evidences of the most atrocious conduct on the part of the German were too palpable to be mistaken; and on entering his hut, the father

36 Farnham has just said that everyone was dead at the farthest camp except the insane mother and her three children, but suddenly they have acquired a dying father. The individuals mentioned are evidently George and Tamsen Donner and their daughters, Frances, Georgia, and Eliza; George Foster, James Eddy, and Levinah Murphy; and Louis Keseberg. Farnham has overlooked Simon Murphy; Elizabeth, Lewis, and Samuel Donner, left at the Alder Creek camp; and Mary and Isaac Donner and Solomon Hook, rescued by the Second Relief.

37 After the Second Relief reached the emigrants, some of the rescuers stayed at the lake while Reed and others went to the Donner camp. When they returned to the lake they brought three children from Jacob Donner's camp: Isaac and Mary Donner and Solomon Hook. Farnham has confused Reed's small party with the Third Relief led by Eddy and Foster.

38 Eddy and Foster found that their sons James and George had died; Levinah Murphy and George Donner were still alive. Keseberg had resorted to cannibalism; there is no proof that he killed anyone for food, but there are several reports that he threatened to do so. Eddy and Foster rescued Simon Murphy and George Donner's three girls.

of one of the murdered children seized an axe with the purpose of cleaving him to the earth; but in the act of upraising it, he said he suddenly remembered to what dreadful straits they had all been reduced, and it fell at his side.[39] They left this wretch,* who was well able to travel, and the insane mother, at the lower camp (taking with them the three children), the only living beings in those homes of desolation and death, and journeying as rapidly as possible, overtook the party they had passed, before they were far on the way.[40]

On the afternoon of the day they joined them, a snow-storm set in very violently, and increased to blinding thickness before the evening was far advanced. They encamped early, and the men of the relief party gathered and set brush in the snow, and threw up a bank against it, to break the storm off the fire and those who surrounded it. Mrs. B. told me that she had her husband and five children together, lying with their feet to the fire, and their heads under shelter of the snow breast-work; and she sat by them, with only moccasins on her feet, and a blanket drawn over her shoulders and head, within which, and a shawl she constantly wore, she nursed her poor baby on her knees. Her milk had been gone many days, and the child was so emaciated and lifeless, that she scarcely expected at any time, on opening the covering, to find it alive. The other [Mrs. Graves] lay with her babe and three or four older children, at the other side of the fire, where were, also, most of the rest of the party. The storm was very violent all night; and she watched through it, dozing occasionally for a few moments, and then rousing herself, to brush the snow and flying sparks from the covering of the sleepers.

Toward morning, she heard one of the young girls opposite call to her mother to cover her. The call was repeated several times impatiently, when she spoke to the child, reminding her of the exhaustion and fatigue her mother suffered in nursing and carrying the baby; and bidding her cover herself and let her mother rest. Presently she heard the mother

---

* Not to have to return to this monster again, I may as well state, that the next party who went out in the spring, found him still there alone, and in a box in his cabin, the body of the unfortunate woman who had been left in the camp below, chopped up! When accused of her murder, he denied it stoutly, and said she had died; but a pailful of blood, found beneath his bed, gave the lie to his words. He had murdered the woman, plundered her cabin, and was at last compelled, after reaching California, to give up a part of his stolen treasure. [Farnham's note. Here again we encounter the "boxful of bones" and "bucket of blood" motifs; see Thornton, notes 113 and 114.]

39 Thornton also mentions Eddy's temptation to kill Keseberg; the phrase "he said" suggests that Eddy may have been one of Farnham's sources.

40 Eddy and Foster overtook the Breens after the events at Starved Camp; see note 37, above.

speak, in a quite unnatural tone, and she called to one of the men near her to go and speak to her. He arose after a few minutes, and found the poor sufferer almost past speaking. He took her infant; and after shaking the snow from her blanket, covered her as well as might be, and left her. Shortly after, Mrs. B. observed her to turn herself slightly, and throw one arm feebly up, as if to go asleep. She waited a little while, and seeing her remain quite still, she walked around to her. She was already cold in death. Her poor, starving child wailed and moaned piteously in the arms of its young sister; but the mother's heart could no more warm or nourish it.

This was the first death in this party.[41] The storm continued through two days and great part of two nights, and the whole party were obliged to lie awaiting its close. As the third morning advanced, it abated; and the men, feeling how nearly impossible it would be for the young and feeble to move on over the deep fresh-fallen snow, and the certainty of death to all, if they remained waiting, proposed going on rapidly, taking Mr. Reed's two children, and hurrying out help to those who were obliged to stay behind. The provisions that had been brought out to this point had been consumed; so that those who remained, remained to certain death, unless relief came speedily. They departed, promising, in this respect, everything that was possible,[42] and leaving poor Mrs. B., the only active, responsible adult, beside her feeble husband, to care for those ten starving children. A higher trust sustained her, or she had sunk in that appalling hour. The sky was yet draped in sad-colored clouds, which hung over them most of the day. They had no food—nothing to eat, save a few seeds, tied in bits of cloth, that had been brought along by some one, and a part of the precious lump of sugar. There were also a very few spoonfuls of the tea remaining in the bottle. They sat and lay by the fire most of the day, with what heavy hearts who shall ever know? The husband, the wife, their five children—the three just left motherless, and two or three others—the remnants of families that had perished.

They were upon about thirty feet of snow, beside a fire made by falling several trees together from opposite directions. The stark mother lay there before them—a ghastlier sight in the sunshine that succeeded the storm, than when the dark clouds overhung them. They had no words of cheer to speak to each other—no courage or hope to share, but those which pointed to a life where hunger and cold could never come, and their benumbed faculties were scarcely able to seize upon a consolation so remote from the thoughts and wants that absorbed their whole being.

---

41 J. H. Merryman's more nearly contemporary article, based on information from Reed, states that Isaac Donner was the first to die at Starved Camp.

42 Reed has been criticized for abandoning his charges at Starved Camp, but under the circumstances he could hardly have done otherwise.

A situation like this, will not awaken in common natures religious trust. Under such protracted suffering, the animal outgrows the spiritual in frightful disproportion; yet the mother's sublime faith, which had brought her thus far through her agonies with a heart still warm toward those who shared them, did not fail her now. She spoke gently to one and another—asked her husband to repeat the litany and the children to join her in the responses, and endeavored to fix their minds upon the time when relief would probably come. For nature taught her as unerringly and more simply than philosophy could have done, that the only hope of sustaining them was to set before them a termination to their sufferings.

What days and nights were those which went by while they waited. Life waning visibly in those about her; not a morsel of food to offer them; her own infant, and that little one that had been cherished and saved through all by the mother now lying dead; wasting hourly into the more perfect image of death; her husband, worn to a skeleton, indifferent to his own fate or any one's else. It needed the fullest measure of exalted faith, of womanly tenderness and self-sacrifice, to sustain one through such a season. She watched by night as well as by day. She gathered wood to keep them warm. She boiled her handful of tea and dispensed it to them; and when she found one sunken and speechless, she broke with her teeth a morsel of the precious sugar and put it in his lips. She fed her babe freely on snow-water, and, scanty as was the wardrobe she had, she managed to get fresh clothing next its skin two or three times a week.

Where, one asks in wonder and reverence, did she find strength and courage for all this? She sat all night by her family, her elbows on her knees, brooding the meek little victim that lay there; watching those who slept, and occasionally dozing, with a fearful consciousness of their terrible condition always upon her. The sense of peril never slumbered. Many times during the night she went to the sleepers to ascertain if they all still breathed. She put her hand under their blankets and held it before the mouth. In this way she assured herself that they were yet alive; but once her blood curdled to find, on approaching her hand to the lips of one of her own children, there was no warm breath upon it. She tried to open the mouth, and found the jaws set. She roused her husband.

"O, Patrick, man, rise and help me; James is dying!"

"Let him die," said the miserable father; "he will be better off than any of us."

She was terribly shocked by this reply. In her own expressive language, her heart stood still when she heard it. She was bewildered, and knew not where to set her weary hands to work; but she recovered in a few moments, and began to chafe the chest and hands of the perishing boy. She broke a bit of sugar, and with considerable effort forced it between his teeth with a few drops of snow-water. She saw him swallow; then a slight convulsive motion stirred his features; he stretched his limbs feebly, and in a moment more opened his eyes and looked upon her. How fervent were her thanks to the great Father, whom she forgot not, night nor day.

Thus she went on. The tea-leaves were eaten, the seeds were chewed, the sugar all dispensed. One child [Franklin Ward Graves, Jr.] of the mother, who lay upon the snow, perished—not the youngest. An older sister [Nancy] had that in charge, and it still lived, though not a particle of anything but snow-water had passed its clammy lips for near a week.

The days were bright, and, compared with the nights, comfortable. Occasionally, when the sun shone, their voices were heard, though generally they sat or laid in a kind of stupor, from which she often found it alarmingly difficult to rouse them; but when the gray evening twilight drew its deepening curtain over the cold, glittering heavens and the icy waste, and when the famishing bodies had been covered from the frost that pinched them with but little less keenness than the unrelenting hunger, the solitude seemed to rend her very brain. Her own powers faltered—her head seemed to distend enormously, and grow to a vast cavern, in which a thunderous silence reverberated—ceasing at intervals, when it appeared to have gone out into the borders of that great ringing space.

But she said her prayers many times over in the darkness as well as the light, and always with renewed trust in Him who had not yet forsaken her, and thus sat out her weary watch. After the turning of the night, she always sat watching for the morning-star, which seemed, every time she saw it rise clear in the cold eastern sky, to renew to her the promise, "As thy day is, so shall thy strength be."

Their fire had melted the snow to a considerable depth, and they were lying upon the bank above it. Thus they had less of its heat than they needed, and found some difficulty in getting the fuel she gathered, placed so that it could burn. One morning, after she had hailed her messenger of promise, and the light had increased so as to render objects visible in the distance, she looked, as usual, over the white expanse that lay to the southwest, to see if any dark moving specks were visible upon its surface. Only the tree-tops, which she had scanned so often as to be quite familiar with their appearances, were to be seen, and with a heavy heart she brought herself back from that distant hope, to consider what was immediately about her.

The fire had sunk so far away, that they had felt but little of its warmth the last two nights, and casting her eyes down into the snow-pit, where it sent forth only a dull glow, she thought she saw the welcome face of beloved mother earth. It was such a reviving sight, after their long freezing separation from it! She immediately roused her eldest son, and with a great deal of difficulty, and repeated words of cheering and encouragement, brought him to understand, that she wished him to descend by one of the tree-tops which had fallen in, so as to make a sort of ladder, and see if they could reach the naked earth and if it were possible for them all to go down. She trembled with fear at the vacant silence in which he at first gazed at her, but at length, after she had told him a great many times, he said, "yes, mother," and went.

He reached the bottom safely, and presently spoke to her. There was naked dry earth under his feet; it was warm, and he wished her to come down. She laid her baby beside some of the sleepers and descended. Immediately she determined upon taking them all down.

How good, so she thought, as she ascended the boughs, was God whom she trusted!

By persuasion, by entreaty, by encouragement, and with her own aid, she got them all into this snug shelter. At this removal another child was found dead. He was one of the three that had been brought from his mother in the lower cabin.[43] He had a young sister [Mary] who had set out in comparatively good condition, but was not emaciated and stupefied. The warmth of the fire revived and enlivened her, and when she missed her brother and learned that he was dead, she begged Mr. B. to go up cut a piece off him, for her to eat.

"O child," exclaimed the horror-stricken woman, "sure you would not eat your own brother."

"O yes, I will. Do, Mr. Breen, I am so hungry, and we ate father and uncle at the cabin!"[44]

The man dared not resist her entreaty; for he thought, If she should die when her life might be saved by it, the responsibility would be on me! He ascended to the terrible task. His wife, frozen with horror, hid her face in her hands and could not look up. She was conscious of his return, and of something going on about the fire; but she could not bring herself to uncover her eyes till all had subsided again into silence. Her husband remarked, that perhaps they were wrong in rejecting a means of sustaining life, of which others had availed themselves; but she put away the suggestion so fearfully, that it was never renewed nor acted upon by any of her family.[45]

---

43 Farnham intends Isaac Donner, though, as noted above, she has apparently confused the order of the deaths. Since Isaac was the son of Elizabeth Donner, she must be Farnham's "insane mother."

44 The reference to eating "father and uncle"–Jacob and George Donner–is evidence that some of Farnham's informants thought George Donner dead before the Second Relief left.

45 It is simply not credible that the Breens abstained from human flesh, a fact conceded by Joseph A. King, though he accuses Farnham of manufacturing the falsehood; see *Winter of Entrapment* (1994), 104.

But they were now, indeed, reaching the out most verge of life. A little more battle with the grim enemies that had pursued them so relentlessly, twenty-four or at most forty-eight hours of such warfare and all would be ended. They wished it was over; those who were capable of wishing anything. The infants still breathed, but were so wasted that they could only be moved by raising them bodily on the hands. It seemed as if even their light weight would have dragged the limbs from their bodies. Occasionally through the day, she ascended the tree to look out. It was an incident now, and seemed to kindle more life than when it only required a turn of the head or a glance of the eye to tell that there was no living thing near them. She could no longer walk on the snow, but she had still strength enough to crawl from tree to tree, and gather a few boughs, which she threw along before her to the pit and then tumbled in to renew the fire.

The children, who had refreshed their failing powers with the food that others refused, were soon in a better condition, and so her burden was somewhat lightened, and her fear lessened. But those, whose life was her life, were yet failing. The eighth day was past. She watched for the star of mercy. On the ninth morning,[46] clear and bright it stood over against her beseeching gaze, set in the light liquid blue that overflows the pathway of the springing day. She prayed earnestly as she gazed; for she knew there were but few hours of life in those dearest to her. If human aid came not that day, some eyes, that would soon look imploringly into hers, would be closed in death, before that star should rise again. Would she herself, with all her endurance and resisting love, live to see it? Were they at length to perish? Great God, should it be permitted that they, who had been preserved through so much, should die at last so miserably?

Her eyes were dim, and her sight wavering from inanition. She could not distinguish trees from men on the snow; but, had they been near, she could have heard them; for her ear had grown so sensitive, that the slightest unaccustomed noise arrested her attention.

She went below with a heavier heart than ever before. She had not a word of hope to answer to the languid inquiring countenances that were turned to her face, and she was conscious that it told the story of her despair, yet she strove with some half insane words to suggest, that somebody would surely come to them that day. Another would be too late, and the pity of men's hearts and the mercy of God would surely bring them.

The pallor of death seemed already to be stealing over the sunken countenances that surrounded her, and weak as she was, she could remain below but a few minutes together. She felt she could have died, had she let go her resolution at any time within the last forty-eight hours. They

---

46 The refugees had been at Starved Camp only five days; Farnham means the ninth morning since they left the cabins.

repeated the litany—the responses came so feebly that they were scarcely audible, and the protracted utterance seemed wearisome; but at last it was over, and they rested in silence.

The sun mounted high and higher in the heavens, and when the day was three or four hours old, she placed her trembling feet again upon the ladder to look out once more. The corpses of the dead lay always before her as she reached the top—the mother and her son, and the little boy, whose remains she could not even glance at, since they had been muti- lated. The blanket that covered him could not shut out the horror of the sight! The rays of the sun fell on her with a friendly warmth; but she could not look into the light that flooded the white expanse. Her eyes lacked strength and steadiness. She rested herself against a tree, and endeavored to gather her wandering faculties. In vain. The enfeebled will could no longer hold rule over them. She had broken, perceptious fragments of visions, contradictory and mixed, former with the latter times. Recollec- tions of plenty, and rural peace, came up from her clear, tranquil child- hood which seemed to have been another state of existence; flashes of her latter life—its comfort and abundance—gleams of maternal pride in her chil- dren, who had been growing up about her, to ease and independence.

She lived through all the phases which her simple life had ever worn, in the few moments of repose after the dizzy effort of ascending. As the thin blood left her whirling brain, and returned to its shrunken channels, she grew more clearly conscious of the terrible present, and remembered the weary quest upon which she came. It was not the memory of thought, it was that of love—the old tugging at the heart that had never relaxed long enough to say, "Now I am done; I can bear no more." The miserable ones, down there: for them her warring life came back; at thought of them, she turned her face listlessly the way it had so often gazed, but this time some- thing caused it to flush as if the blood, thin and cold a it was, would burst its vessels. What was it? Nothing that she saw; for her eyes were quite dimmed by the sudden access of excitement. It was the sound of voices. By a superhuman effort she kept herself from falling. Was it reality or delu- sion? She must, at least, live to know the truth. It came again and again. She grew calmer a she became more assured, and the first distinct words she heard uttered were, "there is Mrs. Breen, alive yet, anyhow!"

There were three men advancing toward her. She knew that now there would be no more starving. Death was repelled for this time from the pre- cious little flock he had so long threatened, and she might offer up thanks- giving unchecked by the dreads and fears that had so long frozen her.

A little food was soon dispensed, and shortly after a little more, and soon a third meal. It was astonishing to see the almost instantaneous revivifica- tion that took place. Some had voracious appetites, and had to be impera- tively restrained. In the other parties, lives had been lost by overeating at first. Here, that danger was carefully guarded against, and by morning they were all, except the poor infants, so much refreshed and strengthened, that it seemed possible to set out: indeed, it was an imperative necessity to move, as the supplies that had been brought were very slender, and were already materially reduced. They had snow-shoes, and sank deep–almost to the body at every step. O, it was weary traveling! but hope and fear both urged them forward, despite their extreme feebleness. The poor mother bore her baby, and the little orphan was taken by turns.

One source of exquisite suffering, was the dreadful condition of their feet. They had been so often frosted, that, in several cases, every trace of the integuments had disappeared, and the unsheathed, lacerated flesh left its bloody mark at every step on the snow. This was torture to the poor mother's heart. But she had to urge her little ones onward, painful though it was to them and herself. Their road often lay along the slopes of hills, where a single false step would have precipitated them fifty or a hundred feet; but feeble as they were, they went on without accident, sometimes two, sometimes five miles, a day, till they reached Mule Springs, whither government supplies had been sent, and were then awaiting them, together with animals, and whatever was necessary for the further safe transport of the disabled. There Mrs. B. learned of the safe arrival of her sons who had preceded her, and of the fate that had befallen others, and there she found new cause of thanksgiving for the unspeakable love that had sustained them through all the sufferings and perils which it froze her very heart to look back upon after they had escaped them.

Conclusion.

The sublime endurance which I have here attempted to portray, as well as that discovered by females in innumerable other instances where hardships and danger have had to be borne, are now confessed by all acquainted with these movements. And one is surprised to hear, even among intelligent persons, all causes but the true one assigned for so significant a fact. It is said that men perish first because they have all the care, but the same argument would prove that women–mothers, have none at all, or the least of any class for they are the last to perish, or they survive all. This is too absurd to deserve a moment's notice.[47]

---

47 The question of why there were more female survivors of the Donner party has intrigued many. Farnham's interpretation is in contrast to that of some (male) commentators who are inclined to attribute the difference to "male chivalry." There are no clear answers, and a combination of factors–physiological, psychological, and cultural–must be taken into account. See Donald K. Grayson's

It is not negative circumstances of qualities of character, that can confer the power of which I speak. It springs from the noblest human attributes—it is their highest exercise. It is love—the most devoted and self-oblivious—love, such as only woman's heart is capable of—love, that is nowise allied to intellect—neither limited nor expanded by it—love, such as outlived Gethsemane and triumphed over Calvary. Give to a nature, largely endowed with this divine quality, a motive, and it will prove itself possessed of fortitude as noble as its love. Thus have many delicate women, who at home were invalids, exhibited on these dreadful journey such powers, such miraculous endurance, such indifference to personal suffering, such fertility of resource, in serving others, as have seemed incredible when related. The littleness, the petty weaknesses, and querulous selfishness which women often show under the ordinary fatigues and annoyances of travel, are, in all characters of real worth, replaced, when times of danger and suffering come, by the nobles courage and self-sacrifice. Sensible, honest, and brave men, who have crossed the plains, agree that they would greatly prefer, for courage and resolution, a company of women to one of men, unless the latter were picked and proved beforehand.

I must be permitted to a single remark on the condition of my sex in this anomalous country before closing my last page. It is to express my full persuasion, that the distrust shown towards women here, is in a far greater degree a consequence of the corruptness of the other sex, than of ours. Men whose consciousness accuses them, if not of crime, at least of fearful proclivity to it, believe that they are not alone in experiencing this. They go further and judge others, whom they see tried in similar ways, to be worse than themselves; for if they have, perchance, resisted temptation a little, they are apt to believe that their neighbor, under the same circumstances, has yielded—it is so comforting to many persons, to think worse of the condition of those about them than of their own. And men of common intelligence and perception of character, often think women weak in the very directions wherein those whom they judge know themselves to be strongest, and thus it happens that in chaotic communities, the harshest judgments may be exercised toward large numbers who are least deserving of it. Every thoughtful observer of a new society can testify to this truth; and painful as it is, to think on the ruin that has overtaken such numbers in this land, there is strength in the knowledge that human nature never, in any other age or clime, resisted more potent of pervading temptations. Honor and love to the souls that have proved their integrity here! They should never more be doubted.

---

comments in Shipman, "Life and Death on the Wagon Trail," *New Scientist* 131 (27 July 1991): 40–42.

J. Ross Browne (1821–1875)

Born February 11, 1821, in Dublin, Ireland, John Ross Browne came to the United States with his family about 1832. They settled in Louisville, Kentucky, where Browne grew up. Although he did not attend college, he acquired a fair education, showing an early aptitude for writing and sketching.

In July 1842 Browne began his career as a professional traveler when he shipped out of New Bedford on a whaler. This experience provided the material for *Etchings of a Whaling Cruise* (1846), the first of several books Browne wrote about his adventures.

Browne did not remain a sailor long. During his travels around the world he held various positions, often in government service and including a brief stint as minister to China. Many of his humorous accounts, generally accompanied by his own drawings, were published as magazine articles before being collected into book form. In 1870 Browne and his family settled in Oakland, California, where he engaged in the real estate business. He died there on December 8, 1875.

The Text

Browne's brief connection with the Donner party came during the course of a journey he took to California to take up a commission as postal inspector. En route to San Luis Obispo, he spent a night in San Juan Bautista at an inn kept by Patrick and Margaret Breen. Though Browne does not actually name them, the Breens owned the inn at that time. Browne recounted the incident in a sketch, "A Dangerous Journey," first published in *Harper's New Monthly Magazine* in two installments in May and June 1862.

Browne's account was intended not as history but as an entertaining description of such perils of travel in early California as cattle stampedes and gangs of desperadoes; his stay with the Breens is a minor episode in his account. Together with Thornton and Farnham, however, Browne influenced the characterizations of the Breens in George R. Stewart's *Ordeal by Hunger*.

The picture that Browne paints of the couple is not flattering, but by far the most striking feature of his tale is its focus: Browne is actually describing his own emotions. The couple do nothing out of the ordinary, but the mere proximity of a known cannibal makes Browne so uncomfortable that he can neither eat nor rest. A similar theme appears in anecdotes told about Louis Keseberg by William Allen Trubody and Theodore T. Johnson, in which the legendary cannibal's mere proximity, actual or anticipated, causes anxiety.[1] Browne admits that his unease is uncalled for, but confesses that he cannot help himself. His reaction is one that many Donner party survivors encountered and had to endure—their trials did not end with their rescue.

The text is from *Harper's New Monthly Magazine,* May 1862, 742–43. "A Dangerous Journey" was also published as part of *Crusoe's Island: A Ramble in the Footsteps of Alexander Selkirk* (1864) and as a monograph by Arthur Lites in 1950. Ralph Herbert Cross quotes the Breen material in *Inns of Early California, 1844–1869* (1954).

---

1 Charles L. Camp, ed., "William Allen Trubody and the Overland Pioneers," 129; Theodore T. Johnson, *Sights in the Gold Region* (New York: Baker and Scribner, 1850), 125.

FROM "A DANGEROUS JOURNEY"

I stopped a night at San Jose, where I was most hospitably received by the Alcalde, an American gentleman of intelligence, to whom I had a letter of introduction. Next day, after a pleasant ride of forty-five miles, I reached the Mission of San Juan [Bautista]—one of the most eligibly located of all the old missionary establishments. It was now in a state of decay. The vineyards were but partially cultivated, and the secos, or ditches for the irrigation of the land, were entirely dry. I got some very good pears from the old Spaniard in charge of the Mission—a rare luxury after a long sea-voyage. The only tavern in the place was the "United States," kept by an American and his wife in an old adobe house, originally a part of the missionary establishment. Having secured accommodations for my mule, I took up my quarters for the night at the "United States." The woman seemed to be the principal manager. Perhaps I might have noticed her a little closely, since she was the only white woman I had enjoyed the opportunity of conversing with for some time. It was very certain, however, that she struck me as an uncommon person—tall, raw-boned, sharp, and masculine—with a wild and piercing expression of eye, and a smile singularly startling and unfeminine. I even fancied that her teeth were long and pointed, and that she resembled a picture of an Ogress I had seen when a child. The man was a subdued and melancholy-looking person, presenting no particular trait of character in his appearance save that of general abandonment to the influence of misfortune. His dress and expression impressed me with the idea that he had experienced much trouble, without possessing that strong power of recuperation so common among American adventurers in California.

It would scarcely be worth while noticing these casual acquaintances of a night, since they have nothing to do with my narrative, but for the remarkable illustration they afford of the hardships that were encountered at that time on the emigrant routes to California. In the course of conversation with the man, I found that he and his wife were among the few survivors of a party whose terrible sufferings in the mountains during the past winter had been the theme of much comment in the newspapers. He did not state—what I already knew from the published narrative of their adventures—that the woman had subsisted for some time of the dead body of a

171

child belonging to one of the party. It was said that the man had held out to the last, and refused to participate in the horrible feast of human flesh.[2]

So strangely impressive was it to be brought in direct contact with a fellow-being, especially of the gentler sex, who had absolutely eaten of human flesh, that I could not but look upon this woman with a shudder. Her sufferings had been intense; that was evident form her marked and weather-beaten features. Doubtless she had struggled against the cravings of hunger as long as reason lasted. But still the one terrible act, whether the result of necessity or insanity, invested here with a repellant atmosphere of horror. Her very smile struck me as the gloating expression of a cannibal over human blood. In vain I struggled against this unchristian feeling. Was it right to judge a poor creature whose great misfortune was perhaps no offense against the laws of nature? She might be the tenderest and best of women—I knew nothing of her history. It was a pitiable case. But, after all, she had eaten of human flesh; there was not getting over that.

When I sat down to supper this woman was obliging enough to hand me a plate of meat. I was hungry, and tried to eat it. Every morsel seemed to stick in my throat. I could not feel quite sure that it was what it seemed to be. The odor even disgusted me. Nor could I partake of the bread she passed to me with any more relish. It was probably made by her hands— the same hands that had torn the flesh from a corpse and passed the reeking shreds to her mouth. The taint of an imaginary corruption was upon it.

The room allotted to me for the night was roughly furnished, as might reasonably be expected; but, apart form this, the bedding was filthy; and in common with every thing about the house, the slatternly appearance of the furniture did not tend to remove the unpleasant impression I had formed of my hostess. Whether owing to the vermin, or an unfounded suspicion that she might become hungry during the night, I slept but little. The picture of the terrible Ogress that I had seen when a child, and the story of the little children which she had devoured, assumed a fearful reality, and became strangely mingled in my dreams with this woman's face. I was glad when daylight afforded me an excuse to get up and take a stroll in the fresh air.

---

2 The peculiar tale which Browne relates is otherwise unrecorded and reverses what Farnham reports, that Patrick Breen suggested cannibalism but Margaret demurred so strongly that he did not broach the subject again. If such stories had been circulating about Mrs. Breen, it would help explain the exaggerations in her statement to Farnham.

Frances H. McDougall (1805–1878)

On January 21, 1871, a San Francisco weekly, the *Pacific Rural Press,* published an article entitled "The Donner Tragedy" and signed "F. H. McD." It was based on the reminiscences of Mrs. Jotham Curtis, whom James F. Reed and William McCutchen had met on their first relief attempt, recounted by Thornton. The article's errors provoked the two men to pen rebuttals. Reed's lengthy response appeared in two installments on March 25 and April 1, with McCutchen's brief statement appended to the second installment. On April 21 the *Pacific Rural Press* printed a response to the rebuttals, this time signed "Frances H. McDougal."

The author was almost certainly Frances Harriet McDougall, a native of Rhode Island with a long record of published works. Born Frances Harriet Whipple in 1805, she married Charles C. Green in 1842 but divorced him five years later. Her early writings appeared under both surnames, Whipple and Green. She contributed poetry and articles to various publications, edited three papers, wrote novels, and coauthored a botany manual. Like Eliza Farnham, Frances Green was active in social causes, including temperance, abolition, suffrage, labor reform, and female education. She also became interested in spiritualism. She moved to California about 1860 and married William C. McDougall in 1861. She appears to have written relatively little in her later years; her last literary effort, *Beyond the Veil,* was published in 1878, the year she died.

McDougall's contribution to Donner history is not so in much what she wrote as it is in the effect her writing had: it stung Reed and McCutchen into responding, thus providing historians with Reed's detailed, though late, first-person account and McCutchen's statement. McDougall's "The Donner Tragedy" is included here to provide the context for Reed and McCutchen's rebuttals; it also serves as an example of the accretion of folklore around historical events and of the vagaries of human memory.

The article contains so many errors that little attempt is made to correct them. A comparison with Thornton's account reveals that Mrs. Curtis misunderstood a number of circumstances, which led her to condemn Reed and McCutchen; they address the major issues in their statements that follow.

THE DONNER TRAGEDY.
A THRILLING CHAPTER IN OUR PIONEER HISTORY

(WRITTEN FOR THE PRESS.)

The sufferings of the Donner party, who were snowed in, and detained on the mountains more than three months, in the winter of 1846-7, has been much talked about, and some garbled stories have been published; but from the very nature of the case, anything like a true history was difficult to come at. My informant, who was one of the general company to which the Donner party originally belonged, says that she has never seen anything like a true or competent history of that most horrible period in the lives of those unfortunates. The following she is ready to vouch for, as truth; and if anyone desires further information, or confirmation of what is already given, her name and address will be at their service.[1]

By retracing, though but in idea, the difficult and dangerous steps of the early emigrants, we are enabled more fully to appreciate the homes of comfort, competence and beauty, to which they have led us.

In the year 1846, about the 1st of May, 500 emigrants, under the guidance of Wm. Fowler, left Independence, Missouri, bound for California and Oregon. They all continued in one company until they reached Big Blue River, when the decline of pasturage made it necessary to separate into small companies, that of Mrs. C–being piloted by Wm. Fowler.[2] They were all in advance of the Donner party, but after crossing the Salt Lake Desert the latter nearly caught up with them.

On going over the mountains, the Read and Donner Company, when they came to the Devil's Canyon, known as Hasting's Cut-off, sent some men forward to examine the route. On their return, they represented the

---

1 It is unfortunate that McDougall did not provide more information about her informant, as virtually nothing is known about Mrs. Curtis.

2 William Fowler, Jr., together with his father and brother, had gone to Oregon in 1843, then to California the following year. They settled in the Napa Valley, where they became prominent landowners. Fowler went east in 1845 to bring out the rest of the family, returning in 1846. He is mentioned in Harlan's account, in this volume.

pass impracticable; and leaving the old road, they attempted to vent their way around the high peak, felling, or removing such timber as impeded their progress. In this toilsome work they spent eighteen days, thus exhausting their time, strength and provisions. This detention was one of the chief causes of their being caught in the snow, and of all their subsequent sufferings.

Read and McCutchins [Herron] came to their [the Curtises'] camps nearly starved, having made a meal of wheel-grease and mustard, taken from Mr. C–'s wagon, which he had left on the mountain, intending to go back for it.

A Night in the Snow.

At night, Mr. C–, finding that his cattle had gone off, set out in pursuit of them, leaving his wife alone in that wild and horrible place.[3] But the brave heart of the heroic woman was not easily to be dismayed. Patiently, hopeful, resolutely she watched the night through, with a kind of latent faith that her husband would be preserved, though he was exposed and unsheltered to the pitiless snow storm, which, soon after he left, began raging with great fury; and the dismal howling of their faithful dog, heightened the horrors of the scene. But the brave heart fainted not; and every little precaution the occasion prompted or required, was patiently and quietly taken. She trimmed the fire; she watched and adjusted the warming and drying garments; she heated and replenished the evaporating tea; and several times during the night she went out with a long-handled iron scraper to scrape the snow from the tented roof, lest it should be broken down by the weight, and leave her without shelter.

Morning came; for the most protracted periods of anxiety and anguish must some time have an end; and aided by the earliest light, the straining eyes of the lonely watcher went out over the wild, for sight or sign of the wanderer; but no track appeared on the mountain road, that lay, still and solemn as death, draped in a winding sheet of spotless snow. Still she hoped–still she believed–that her husband would yet come; and once more, and again and again, she went to the place of lookout; but over all the ghastly whiteness of the scene no form of life appeared.

Book look yonder, up the mountain road, to the remotest point of sight! Is that a man? a horse? Do they move? At first sight the motion was slow, so faint as to be nearly imperceptible. Ah, yes! her faith is rewarded at last. He is living! He comes! She flew to meet him, with whatever speed she could make through the depths of snow, and found him greatly exhausted

---

3 According to Thornton, at the head of Bear Valley.

and nearly insensible. He was soon put to bed, and by help of warm blankets, heated stones and hot drink, he partially revived and was able to give a coherent account of himself.

He had followed the cattle about twelve miles, and brought them to the brow of the long hill that overlooked their encampment; but in his weak and exhausted state he could not get them over the brink, from which they drew back in terror. Finally he became bewildered and lost in the storm. He had stood all night, hugging his horse to keep up animal life; and it was with the greatest difficulty that he was able to regain his seat in the saddle, and keep it until he reached the camp.

Mrs. C., being informed where the cattle were, put on snow-shoes and a pair of pantaloons and after a hard walk up the mountain side, found the cattle, and drove them down without any difficulty.

A Strange Proceeding.

That afternoon, for fear of being snowed in they killed an ox; and while they were preparing some of the meat for supper, Reed and McCutchins came to the camp with two Indians and 30 horses, sent by Gen. Sutter for the relief of the suffering party. During the night the Indians took two of the best horses and decamped; and in the morning Mr. Reed, with his companion, set off for the snow-bound company following the trail of the cattle about 12 miles. After traveling as far as the oxtrail reached, they concluded it was not safe to proceed further, and returning to the camp of Mr. C., staid all night. But instead of hastening forward to the relief of the sufferers, who were but a short days travel back, Mr. Reed left his provisions at the wagon of Mr. C., and returned to Sutter's Fort, Mr. and Mrs. C. accompanying them. Here was another great and terrible mistake, to say the least. This was about the middle of November; and had Mr. Reed pushed forward to the rescue of the sufferers, including his own wife and children more than 80 persons might have been spared three months of suffering, so horrible as to defy description. We cannot conceive of them. There were, doubtless sufficient reasons for this strange behavior but at the time the whole proceeding was draped in impenetrable mystery.[4]

---

4 Mrs. Curtis's greatest criticism deserves some discussion. When Reed and McCutchen discovered that they could take their packhorses no farther than Bear Valley, they turned back. Mrs. Curtis faults them for not pushing ahead on foot, as the First Relief did later; but the First Relief had more manpower, more provisions, and were equipped with snowshoes. In addition, the lake was farther away that Mrs. Curtis believed.

Snowed In.

Do any of you imagine what these two simple words may mean? Go with me then, to the Donner camp; and we shall see. Is this a company of ghastly spectres that haunt the snowy wilderness with the writhing memories of inconceivable, inscrutable suffering? Their wild eyes burn in the sockets; and the dilating pupil nearly covers the iris. They are dying of starvation; and even on the wan and wasted features of the dead, the biting expression of the horrible hunger still remains.

They are now taking their morning meal and yonder gentle matron–Mrs. Reed–ever more thoughtful for others than herself, is cutting off strips of raw hide, and dividing them into small pieces; and the children come around her with their little tin cups, to receive the precious morsel that may sustain life a little longer. O God! that *little longer* will lay many of them to rest in the sheltering snows!

They had killed all their animals; and their skins had been providentially saved. Hence the supply of raw hides. But at length even this became scarce, and, compared with what followed, was a luxury. Old boot and shoes, bits of saddles or harness, and fragments of leather in every form, were now gathered and rigidly economised. One of the company, who was a child at the time, but afterwards married and lived at San Jose, gave quite an account of the interior of the camp at this period. She said that she and a sister had a quarrel, and almost a fight, for the possession of a little shoe that one of them had found. She declared, too, that she, herself, had eaten a piece of her mother![5] It is believed, that, driven to the last extremity they devoured the bodies of their dead. But enough is known to show that their sufferings were drawn out to the most terrible strain that human anguish could support, or human strength endure. Let us then, leave these awful secrets undisturbed and gently draw a curtain over the revolting scene.

Mr. and Mrs. Brene [Breen], with their nine [seven] children, had encamped eight or ten miles behind the Donner party; and between the two camps there was kept up such an interchange of neighborly kindness, as the circumstances would allow. By this means the dreadful condition of the Donner camp became known to Mr. & Mrs. Brene. By a careful and wise economy, they had made their provisions hold out; and thus they were able, not only to sustain themselves, but to assist others. They took Mrs. Reed with her four children, and one adopted child, home to their

---

5 This may be a reference to Nancy Graves, who attended school in San Jose. She was severely traumatized by being told, after the fact, that she had partaken of her mother's body at Starved Camp; Eliza Donner Houghton to C. F. McGlashan, August 8, 1879.

camp, and kept them until relief arrived.[6] Let no one say that economy is an ignoble virtue, remembering that by its help, six precious lives were saved. The woman who could look upon her own nine children and give to others what would shorten their allowance—possibly bring them to starvation—must have a great heart indeed. It has been said, that there is no greater love than this, that a man should die for his friends; but this is by far a nobler action and a diviner love. Mrs. Brene was, indeed, a noble woman; and her name should be inscribed in golden lettering on the page of history. By such high examples, the world is made happier and better; for she who could give to another what her own children might soon suffer for, deserves and must soon receive; the *crown of virtue.*

Relief Itself Horrible To Behold.

About the middle of February, seven men and women, finding their condition intolerable, left the Donner Camp, hoping to reach the valley in safety; and out of the fourteen, only five women and two men, came into Mr. Johnson's ranch, then the first house on this side of the mountains, one-half of the whole number having perished by the way.

Mr. Johnson, on hearing the great distress of the snow-bound company, sent a messenger to Sutter's Fort, with an account of their terrible sufferings. When the news came in, the citizens volunteered for the rescue of the sufferers. Gen. Sutter, with his well-known promptness and liberality, offered them horses and provisions; and without delay seven men were despatched, Messrs. [Aquilla] Glover, O'Brien, Montgomery, Curtis and three others, whose names are not remembered.[7]

These seven brave men set off on their difficult and perilous undertaking, and pursued their journey as far as Bear valley, with their horses and packs. But finding their route thence impassible for horses, they resolved to take as much a each man could carry and proceed on foot. Leaving the horses and the remainder of the provisions with one of their number, the six men, each with a heavy load on his back, boldly set foot on the trackless mountain, and on the second day reached the Donner camp, when the desperate fate of the unfortunates was discovered. No description can give any

---

6 The Reeds moved in with the Breens in mid-January. The reference to the "adopted child" is puzzling—the Reeds took in the orphaned cousins Mary and Frances Donner afterwards in California, but neither girl stayed in the Breen cabin.

7 The identity of Mrs. Curtis's "O'Brien" is a mystery; Montgomery may be Moutrey; but, although Jotham Curtis assisted for a time in the relief efforts, he never reached the camps, nor was he paid for his labor.

competent idea of this horrible scene. Some were snow blind, others insane, others dying, others dead; while the wasted forms and ghastly looks of all presented a most shocking sight.

Language cannot describe the features of the living when they saw that relief had actually come. Some became nearly insensible or delirious from excess of joy; others were still as death in the intense strain of another moment's waiting; while many faces were distorted by a crazy, foolish, almost demoniac laugh, horrible to behold. They swallowed the small pittance allowed, almost without mastication, and held out their trembling hands for more. Great caution was necessary in order to avoid the ill effects of a giving them too much at a time, but the madness of their hunger soon began to subside.

Fortunately the news spread rapidly over all the then inhabited parts of the state. At San Jose another expedition was fitted out; and, with Mr. Reed at their head, they set off with sufficient food to bring the sufferers in. By the time this new supply arrived their former stock of provisions was exhausted, and now comes the task of getting the sufferers, all weak and emaciated, into some settlement.

Three were left behind to their fate; a Dutchman by the name of Reesburgh [Keseberg], old Mrs. Donner, and a child that Mrs. McCutchins, one of the fourteen who went out, had left behind. The child died the next day; and Mrs. Donner was probably murdered by the Dutchman. She had about her several thousand dollars in specie, and, not being permitted to take it with her, she preferred to stay with it, and with a true miser-feeling, loving her money better than life, she surrendered herself, hugging her purse to the last.[8]

A party of men who afterwards visited the camp, found the old lady with her throat cut, and a bucket near by which had been used to catch her blood. Part of the body was sliced into steaks to sustain the life of the murderer. This Resburgh was afterwards tried for the murder; but on the discovery of gold he came up from the Bay, where he had been sojourning since his acquittal, and opened an eating house at Fort Sutter, which was well known as *Cannibal Tent*.[9]

A touching little incident is related of these times. On the passage from the camp to Fort Sutter, Mr. Brene and one of his little daughters became very faint, and it was feared that they would die. It was proposed to Mr. Read that they should stop and light fires, and try to restore them. He treated the matter coolly, not to say gruffly, saying he didn't think it worth

---

8 This is another version of Wise's story that the emigrants cared more for their property than their lives, which Farnham also told of Elizabeth Donner.

9 Keseberg did in fact open a restaurant in Sacramento, but "Cannibal Tent" is not recorded elsewhere as its nickname.

while to take much trouble about it. On hearing his, his little girl took him by the hand, saying in the sweet earnestness of a grateful child, "Papa, if it hadn't been for Mr. Read [Breen] we should all have been dead!" The sight of the sweet pleader brought the lesson home to his heart. He instantly ordered a halt; when they kindled fires on each side of them, administered remedies, and the sufferers were saved.

F. H. MCD.

JAMES F. REED (1800–1874)

James Frazier Reed was born November 14, 1800, in County Armagh, Northern Ireland. While he was still a child his widowed mother brought him to Virginia. In the 1820s Reed moved to northern Illinois, where he became involved in lead mining.

In 1831 Reed moved to Sangamon County, Illinois. After serving in the Black Hawk War he returned to Springfield and engaged in various enterprises, including a furniture factory and a sawmill. He was also a railroad contractor. On October 14, 1835, he married Margret Wilson Keyes Backenstoe, a young widow with an infant daughter, Virginia. The Reeds had four more children; Martha Jane, James Frazier, Jr., and Thomas Keyes accompanied their parents to California, but an eleven-month-old son died in December 1845.

Reed was active in organizing the group that emigrated from Sangamon County in the spring of 1846, which was remembered in Springfield as the "Reed-Donner Party." Diaries of the 1846 emigration frequently refer to Reed; in addition to his public role, he was also conspicuously more wealthy than most of the other emigrants. Despite Reed's prominence, however, George Donner was elected captain of the party that formed on the Little Sandy, a fact which has been attributed to the latter's genial disposition rather than his ability. Donner's death left Reed the only surviving leader to face the blame for the disaster, but at least two sources attribute the catastrophe in the Sierra Nevada to the absence of Reed's leadership after his banishment.[1]

The criticism leveled at Reed probably had as much to do with his personality as with his leadership. Though a man of great ability, Reed rubbed some of his companions the wrong way and he has been described as "overbearing" and "aristocratic." A biographical sketch described him more thoroughly as "strong in his convictions, warm in his friendships, bitter in his hate; but honorable in apologising if satisfied that he has been in

---

1 John Breen, in the memoir cited, and William M. Boggs, "The Donner Party: Authentic Story of Their Trip Across the Plain," *San Francisco Examiner,* August 25, 1884; reprinted in *Crossroads* 6 (Winter 1995), 7–9.

the wrong."[2] However his manner may have struck some individuals, Reed was energetic in his efforts to direct the company while they were en route and to rescue them after they were trapped.

In 1847 the Reeds settled in San Jose, where they became prominent citizens. They had two more children, one of whom died young. Reed prospered in the gold rush and invested the proceeds in land and mining interests; he was also active in civic affairs. He died in San Jose at the age of seventy-three on July 24, 1874.

The Text

Reed had not commented on the Donner party in public before Frances McDougall's article provoked him to respond. Like other survivors' accounts, Reed's is self-serving, but understandably so: he had been attacked in print with false accusations. He is not entirely truthful in reporting that he went ahead to Sutter's only for supplies; however, mentioning the killing of Snyder would have given McDougall ammunition to use against him, in addition to opening old wounds. He is also careful to record that the decision to cut the trail through the Wasatch and to abandon the emigrants at Starved Camp was not his alone.

The *Pacific Rural Press* published Reed's rebuttal in two installments on March 25 and April 1, 1871, the second accompanied by William McCutchen's statement. Reed's memoir was reprinted in the *San Jose Pioneer* on April 28 and May 5, 1877; but since the *Pioneer* had not published McDougall's article, some of Reed's initial remarks became irrelevant and were omitted. His stylistic mannerisms were also much edited in the *Pioneer*'s version, but the sense was not materially altered.

Despite its late composition, Reed's memoir is of great value, especially when taken in conjunction with his other major contributions to the Donner story: letters written on the plains, the Miller-Reed diary, his diary of the Second Relief, and the J. H. Merryman article (all of which are published in Morgan, *Overland in 1846*). Despite the memoir's importance, it is surprisingly difficult to come by. In addition to the version in the *San Jose Pioneer,* a nearly complete version appeared in *History of Santa Clara County* (1881), and lengthy extracts can be found in other works, but it has not been reprinted in its entirety. The present text is that of the original *Pacific Rural Press* article of 1871.

---

2 Frederic Hall, *The History of San José and Surroundings* (San Francisco: A. L. Bancroft, 1871), 371.

James F. Reed (1800–1874). © Utah State Historical Society, all rights reserved, used by permission

The Snow-Bound, Starved Emigrants of 1846 Statement by Mr. Reed, One of the Donner Company

"The Donner Tragedy—A Thrilling Chapter
in Our Pioneer History."

Editors Press:—An article under the above quoted title appeared in your issue of January 21st, 1871. The preface contained the following:

"The sufferings of the Donner party, who were snowed in, and detained on the mountains more than three months, in the winter of 1846–47 has been much talked about, and some garbled stories have been published; but from the very nature of the case, anything like a true history was difficult to come at."

The writer of the above truly says that it has been much talked about, and some garbled stories have been published. But there never was a more garbled story that the one entitled the "Donner Tragedy," written by F. H. McDougal. After the lapse of 25 years the sad affair must be raked over and hashed up to furnish material for F. H. McDougal's "Tragedy."

F. H. McDougal's informant, Mrs. Curtis, never was a member of the Donner party, and she states herself that she never was. Then how could it be possible for her to give anything like a true history. "From the very nature of the case" she could know nothing about the company in the mountains. Nevertheless she vouches for her statement as being true, when it must have been derived from hearsay only, and the writer of the "Tragedy," knowing from the statement of Mrs. Curtis that the information she could give was only hearsay, must have exercised very little judgment in writing such garbled matter for a journal of the character of the Press.

I have never appeared voluntarily, and never wished to, before the public in reference to this sad affair; having gained the ill-will of parties who wished to write books with reference to it by refusing. Myself and family have always refused giving particulars, but were always willing to give general items; and it is with extreme reluctance that I publish the following statement of my connection with the Donner party, only giving the general outlines.

I have a diary containing all the particulars pertaining to the party in the mountains,[3] and my four children are living witnesses of the truth. Two of them were old enough at that time to remember all the circumstances. I have always "drawn the curtain over the revolting scenes."

I would do all again that I did do in the company, except two things: First, leaving my family and wagons in the desert to hunt water to gratify the desire of a number of the company, when there was a plain road traveled by companies before us. Second: No inducement could persuade me to leave my family to the tender mercies of a company.

"A touching little incident is related of these times. On the passage from the camp to Fort Sutter, Mr. Brein and one of this little daughters became very faint, and it was feared that they would die. It was proposed to Mr. Reid that they should stop and light fires, and try to restore them. He treated the matter coolly, not to say gruffly, saying that he did not think it worth while to take much trouble about it. On hearing this, his little girl took him by the hand, saying in the sweet earnestness of a grateful child, "Papa, if it hadn't been for Mr. Reed (Mr. Brein), we should all have been dead!" The sight of the sweet pleader brought the lesson home to his heart. He instantly ordered a halt; when they kindled fires on each side of them, administered remedies, and the sufferers were saved."

With what fine flow of language, and how smoothly the "touching little incident" is written. Surely the informant and writer, after being so particular in giving the conversation, could have located the place on the route from the emigrants' camp to Sutters Fort. No, that would not answer the purpose. I denounce it as wilfully and maliciously false, and the heart that could giver utterance to it, must be devoid of all the finer feelings of a woman. Referring to Mr. McCutchen's account for all the transactions at this place "Starved Camp" only stating that Mr. Brien was not sick, neither was it feared that he would die. He had only one daughter then, she was an infant not more that eighteen months old.

I thank Mr. and Mrs. Brien for giving shelter to my wife and children, but as to giving them of their stores they never did.[4]

The article "Donner Tragedy," reflecting with unmerited severity on me as a man and my efforts in carrying relief to the suffering party when I, without fear of contradiction, can say that myself with Mr. McCutchen did more

---

3 It is unclear whether Reed is referring to the Miller-Reed diary or the diary he kept of the Second Relief; he does not seem to have used either in writing this memoir. See note 11, below.

4 As mentioned in the introduction to Farnham's account, Virginia Reed Murphy reports that Margaret Breen slipped her a few bits of meat; but the Breens did not regularly share food with the Reed family.

for that party than all the members together, is my justification in publishing the following statement of my acts in connection with the Donner Party.

Any one wishing further information of myself is referred to Thornton's "Oregon and California," Bryant's "What I Saw in California," and Hall's "History of San Jose."

I left Springfield, Ill., with my family about the middle of April, 1846. George and Jacob Donner with their families accompanied me. We arrived at Independence, Mo., where I loaded two of my wagons with provisions, a third one being reserved for my family. Col. W. H. Russell's company had started from here before our arrival. We followed and overtook them in the Indian Territory. I made application for the admission of myself and others into the company, and it was granted. We traveled on with the company as far as the Little Sandy, here a separation took place. The majority of the members going to Oregon, and a few wagons, mine with them, going the Fort Bridger, [or] Salt Lake Route for California. The day after our separation from the Russel company, we elected George Donner captain, and from this time the company was known as "The Donner Company."

Arriving at Fort Bridger, I added one yoke of cattle to my teams, staying here four days. Several friends of mine who had passed here with pack animals for California, had left letters with Mr. Vasques—Mr. Bridger's partner—directing me to take the route by way of Fort Hall and by no means to go the Hastings cut-off. Vasques being interested in having the new route traveled, kept these letters. This was told me after my arrival in California.[5] Mr. McCutchen, wife and child joined us here.

Leaving Fort Bridger, we unfortunately took the new route, traveling on without incident of note, until we arrived at the head of Webber [Weber] canyon. A short distance before reaching this place we found a letter sticking in the top of a sage bush. It was from Hastings. He stated that if we would send a messenger after him he would return and pilot us through a route much shorter and better than the canyon. A meeting of the company was held, when it was resolved to send Messrs. McCutchen, Stanton and myself to Mr. Hastings;[6] also we were at the same time to examine the cañon and report at short notice. We overtook Mr. Hastings at a place we called Blackrock,[7] south end of Salt Lake, leaving McCutchen and Stanton

---

5 Edwin Bryant reports leaving such letters on July 18.

6 Here Reed identifies McCutchen as the third member of this party, where Thornton reports that it was Pike. McCutchen did not correct Reed's statement, but neither did he correct McGlashan's contradictory one.

7 This may be the formation called Black Rock located on the south shore of the lake, but Adobe Rock, a few miles to the south in Tooele Valley, is another possibility.

here, their horses having failed. I obtained a fresh horse from the company Hastings was piloting, and started on my return to our company, with Mr. Hastings. When we arrived at about the place where Salt Lake city is built,[8] Mr. Hastings, finding the distance greater than anticipated by him, stated that he would be compelled to return the next morning to his company. We camped this evening in a canyon.[9] Next morning ascending to the summit of the mountain where we could overlook a portion of the country that lay between us and the head of the cañon, where the Donner party were camped.[10] After he gave me the direction, Mr. Hastings and I separated. He returning to the companies he had left the morning previous, I proceeding on eastward. After descending to what may be called the table land, I took an Indian trail and blazed the route where it was necessary that the road should be made, if the company so directed when they heard the report. When McCutchen, Stanton and myself got through Webber cañon on our way to overtake Mr. Hastings, our conclusions were that many of the wagons would be destroyed in attempting to get through the cañon. Mr. Stanton and McCutchen were to return to our company as fast as their horses would stand it, they having nearly given out. I reached the company in the evening and reported to them the conclusions in regard to Weber cañon, at the same time stating that the route that I had blazed that day was fair, but would take considerable labor in clearing and digging. They agreed with unanimous voice to take that route if I would direct them in the road making, they working faithfully until it was completed. Next morning we started, under these conditions, and made camp that evening without difficulty on Bossman [East Canyon] creek. The afternoon of the second day, we left the creek, turning to the right in a cañon, leading to a divide. Here Mr. Graves and family overtook us.[11] This evening the first

---

8 In 1868 Reed traveled to Kansas in an attempt to locate Sarah Keyes's grave; this statement suggests that he passed through Salt Lake City on the way. See note 13, below.

9 Morgan suggests that the men spent the night "where Clyman had encamped on June 2,"–i.e., in Parleys Canyon–but does not indicate his reasons for this statement. Emigration Canyon is at least as likely a candidate for the campsite, particularly in light of Thornton's account; see Thornton, note 30, above.

10 Morgan identifies this peak as Big Mountain, which would have required an additional fifteen miles of travel, roundtrip, for Hastings. It seems unlikely that he would have agreed to go so far if he were intent on returning to his company, as Reed states; however, Morgan's closely reasoned argument is hard to beat. See Korns, *West from Fort Bridger,* 211–12, note 9.

11 Here it sounds as though the Graveses caught up with the Donner party two days after the latter left Henefer; in this case the upsetting of the wagon mentioned here would have happened on August 12 and would not be the same

accident that had occurred was caused by the upsetting of one of my wagons. The next morning the heavy work of cutting the timber commenced. We remained at this camp several days. During this time the road was cleared for several miles ahead. After leaving this camp the work on the road slackened and the further we advanced the slower the work progressed.[12] I here state that the number of days we were detained in road-making was not the cause by any means, of the company remaining in the mountains during the following winter.

We progressed our way, and crossed the outlet of the Utah, now called Jordan, a little below the location of Salt Lake city.[13] From this camp in a day's travel we made connection with the trail of the companies that Hastings was piloting through his cut-off. We then followed his road around the Lake without incident worthy of notice until reaching a swampy section of the country west of Black Rock, the name we gave it. Here we lost a few days on the score of humanity. One of our company, a Mr. Halloron being in a dying condition from consumption. We could not make regular drives owing to his situation. He was under the care of Mr. Geo. Donner, and made himself know to me as a Master Mason. In a few days he died. After the burial of his remains we proceeded on our journey, making our regular drives, nothing occurring of note until we arrived at the springs where we were to provide water and as much grass as we could for the purpose of crossing the Hastings desert, which was represented as 40 or 45 miles in length (but we found it at least 70 miles). We started to cross the desert traveling day and night only stopping to feed and water our teams as long as water and grass lasted. We must have made at least two-thirds of the way across when a great portion of the cattle showed signs of giving out. Here the company requested me to ride on and find the water and report. Before leaving I requested my principal teamster [Milt Elliott], that when my cattle became so exhausted that they could not proceed further with the wagons, to turn them out and drive them on the road after me until they reached the water, but the teamster misunderstanding unyoked them when they first showed symptoms of giving out, starting on with them for the water.

---

accident as the broken axletree recorded in the Miller-Reed diary on August 18; but Reed's memory may have been faulty.

12 A letter in the *California Star* of February 13, 1847, probably by George McKinstry based on information from Reed, reports "they were sixteen days making the road, as the men would not work one quarter of their time."

13 There were two fords across the Jordan, one at about North Temple and the other at about 2700 South in present-day Salt Lake City. Reed's description—"a little below the location of Salt Lake City"—obviously refers to the latter, for in his day the city did not extend as far as 2700 South. This passage also suggests Reed's familiarity with the area in later years.

I found the water about twenty miles from where I left the company and started on my return. About 11 o'clock at night I met my teamsters with all my cattle and horses. I cautioned them particularly to keep the cattle on the road, for that as soon as they would scent the water they would break for it. I proceeded on and reached my family and wagons. Some time after leaving the men one of the horses gave out and while they were striving to get it along, the cattle scented the water and started for it. And when they started with the horses the cattle were out of sight, they could not find them or their trail, as they told me afterward. They supposing the cattle would find water, went on to camp. The next morning they could not be found, and they never were, the Indians getting them, except one ox and one cow. Losing nine yoke of cattle here was the first of my sad misfortune[s]. I staid with my family and wagons the next day, expecting every hour the return of some of my young men with water, and the information of the arrival of the cattle at the water. Owing to the mistake of the teamsters in turning the cattle out so soon the other wagons had drove miles past mine and dropped their wagons along the road, as their cattle gave out, and some few of them reaching water with their wagons. Receiving no information and the water being nearly exhausted, in the evening I started on foot with my family to reach the water. In the course of the night the children became exhausted. I stopped, spread a blanket and laid them down covering them with shawls. In a short time a cold hurricane commenced blowing; the children soon complained of the cold. Having four dogs with us I had them lie down with the children outside the covers. They were then kept warm. Mrs. Reed and myself sitting to the windward helped shelter them from the storm. Very soon one of the dogs jumped up and started out barking, the others following making an attack on something approaching us. Very soon I got sight of an animal making directly for us; the dogs seizing it changed its course, and when passing I discovered it to be one of my young steers. Incautiously stating that it was mad, in a moment my wife and children started to their feet scattering like quail, and it was some minutes before I could quiet camp; there was no more complaining of being tired or sleepy the balance of the night.[14] We arrived about daylight at the wagons of Jacob Donner, the next in advance of me, whose cattle having given out, had been driven to water. Here I first learned of the loss of my cattle, it being the second day after they had started for the water. Leaving my family with Mrs. Donner, I reached the encampment. Many of the people were out hunting cattle, some of them had got their teams together and were going back into the desert for their wagons. Among them Mr. Jacob

---

14 Virginia Reed Murphy reports the same events, but in a different sequence. See her memoir, in this volume.

Donner, who kindly brought my family along with his own to the encampment. We remained here for days hunting cattle, some of the party finding all, others a portion, all having enough to haul their wagons except myself.

On the next day, or day following, while I was out hunting my cattle, two Indians came to the camp, and by signs gave the company to understand that there were so many head of cattle out, corroborating the number still missing; many of the people became tender-footed at the Indians coming into camp, thinking that they were spies. Wanted to get clear of them as soon as possible. My wife requested that the Indians should be detained until my return, but unfortunately before returning they had left. The next morning, in company with young Mr. [W. C.] Graves, he kindly volunteering, I started in the direction the Indians had taken; after hunting this day and the following, remaining out during the night, we returned unsuccessful, not finding a trace of the cattle. I now gave up all hope of finding them and turned my attention to making arrangements for proceeding on my journey.

In the desert were my eight [three] wagons; all the team remaining was an ox and cow. There was no alternative but to leave everything but provisions, bedding and clothing. These were placed in the wagon that had been used for my family.[15] I made a cache of everything else. Members of the company kindly furnishing team to haul the wagon to camp. I divided my provisions with those who were nearly out, and indeed some of them were in need.[16] I had now to make arrangement for sufficient team to haul that one wagon; one of the company kindly loaned me a yoke of cattle, and with the ox and cow I had, made two yoke. We remained at this camp from first to last, if my memory is right, seven days.

Leaving this camp we traveled for several days. It became necessary from some cause, for the party who loaned me the yoke of cattle to take them. I was again left with my ox and cow, but through the aid of another kind neighbor, I was supplied with a yoke of cattle.

Nothing transpired for some days of any note. Some time after this it became known that some families had not enough of provisions remaining to supply them through; as a member of the company, I advised them to make an estimate of provisions on hand and what amount each family would need to take them through. After receiving the estimate of each family, on paper, I then suggested that if two gentlemen of the company would

15 The Miller-Reed diary entry for September 9 confirms that the "family waggon" was salvaged.

16 Virginia Reed's letter of May 16, 1847, states that the Reeds had to divide their provisions with the other emigrants before the others would consent to carry them. McGlashan's correspondence from survivors suggests that this was a sore spot—the Reeds were convinced that they had fed their impoverished companions, while the latter felt that they had done the Reeds a favor.

volunteer to go in advance to Captain Sutters (near Sacramento), in California, I would write a letter to him for the whole amount of provisions that were wanted, and also stating that I would become personally responsible to him for the amount. I suggested that from the generous nature of Captain Sutter he would send them. Mr. McCutchen came forward and proposed that if they would take care of his family he would go. This the company agreed to. Mr. Stanton, a single man, volunteered, if they would furnish him a horse. Mr. McCutchen, having a horse and a mule, generously gave the mule. Taking their blankets and provisions they started for California. After their leaving us we traveled on for weeks, none of us knowing the distance we were from California. All became anxious for the return of McCutchen and Stanton.

Leaving the Company.

It was here suggested that I go in advance to California, see what had become of McCutchen and Stanton, and hurry up the supplies. They would take care of my family. That being agreed upon I started, taking with me about three days provisions, expecting to kill game on the way.[17] The Messrs. Donner were two days drive in advance of the main party when I overtook them. With George Donner there was a young man named Walter Herren [Herron], who joined me; with all the economy I could use, our provisions gave out in a few days; I supplied our wants by shooting wild geese and other game when we could find any. The next day after I was joined by Herren, I proposed to him—I having a horse and he none—that we would ride half the day about; it was thankfully accepted; no game to be seen; hunger began to be felt, and for days we traveled without hope or help. We reached the Sierra Nevada mountains; I could have stopped here, and hunting, found game. Then again I might not be successful. This would have delayed our progress and increased our hunger. The second day before we found relief, Herren wanted to kill the horse; I persuaded him from it by stating that we might find relief soon, but before we would perish I would kill the horse. Soon after this he became delirious; this afternoon, while walking, I found a bean, and gave it to him, and there never was a road examined more closely for several miles than was this. We found in all *five beans*. Herren's share was three of them. We camped that night in a patch of grass a short distance off the road. Next morning, after traveling a few miles, we saw some wagons.

---

17 Reed here omits any reference to Snyder's death, and there is no mention that he was banished without food or arms, as described by his daughter Virginia; see her memoir, this volume.

Eating Axle-Grease.

We soon reached and ransacked the wagons, hoping to find something to eat, but found nothing. Taking the tar bucket that was hanging under one of the wagons, I scraped the tar off and found a streak of rancid tallow at the bottom. I remember well that when I announced what I had found, Herren, who was sitting on a rack near by, got up, hollooing with all the strength he had, and came to me. I handed the tar paddle to him, having some of the tallow about the size of a walnut on it. This he swallowed without giving it a smell. I then took a piece myself, but it was very repulsive. He, craving more, I gave him another piece. Still wanting more, I positively refused stating that it would kill him. After leaving the wagons probably fifty yards, I became deadly sick and blind. I rested myself against a rock, leaning my head on the muzzle of my gun. Herren, seeing my condition came to me and said, "My God, Mr. Reed, are you dying!" After resting a few minutes, I recovered, much to his joy.

The wagons were within a short distance of the steep descent going down into Bear river Valley. After descending the first steep pitch, I discovered wagons in the valley below us. Herren, said I there are wagons in the valley, pointing to them. When he saw them, he gave vent to his joy, hallooing at the top of his voice, but could not be heard ten rods off, he being so weak. The sight of the wagons revived him and he descended the mountains with all his ability.[18]

On reaching the wagons we found several families of emigrants who supplied us with bread. I here met Mr. Stanton with provisions sent by Capt. Sutter, on receiving my letter. Next morning Mr. Stanton started for the company and myself for Capt. Sutter's.

Arrive at Capt. Sutter's.

When I arrived, making known my situation to him, asking if he would furnish me horses and saddle to bring the women and children out of the mountains (I expected to meet them at the head of Bear Valley by the time

---

18 This is the last Reed tells of his companion, Walter Herron, a twenty-seven-year-old native of Virginia. After he reached California Herron enlisted and took part in the Mexican War, attaining the rank of major. In the fall of 1847 he assisted Jasper O'Farrell in surveying the site of Stockton, where Herron settled. He was elected San Joaquin County surveyor in 1850 and also served as the first recorder for the city of Stockton. At the beginning of January 1853 Herron set off for Mexico; he wrote to a friend after arriving in Acapulco in February but was never heard from again.

I could return there), he at once complied with the request, also saying that he would do everything possible for me and the company. On the evening of my arrival at the Captain's, I found Messrs. [Edwin] Bryant, [Benjamin] Lippencott, [A. J.] Grayson, and [R. T.] Jacobs, some of the early voyagers in the Russel Company, they having left that company at Fort Laramie, most of them coming on horseback.

During the evening a meeting was held, in which I participated, adopting a memorial to the commander of Sutter's Fort, to raise one or more companies of volunteers, to proceed to Los Angeles, we being at war with Mexico at this time. The companies were to be officered by the petitioners. Being requested to take command of one of the companies, I declined, stating that it would be necessary for the Captain to stay with the company; also, that I had to return to the mountains for the emigrants; but that I would take a Lieutenantcy. This was agreed to, and I was on my return to the emigrants to enlist all the men I could between there and Bear Valley. On my way up I enlisted twelve or thirteen.

The second night after my arrival at Captain Sutter's, we had a light rain; next morning we could see snow on the mountains. The Captain stated that it was low down and heavy for the first fall of the season. The next day I started

On My Return

with what horses and saddles Capt. Sutter had to spare. He furnished us all the flour needed, and a hind quarter of beef, giving us an order for more horses and saddles at Mr. Cordway's, near where Marysville is located.[19] In the mean time, Mr. McCutchen joined me, he being prevented from returning with Mr. Stanton, on account of sickness. After leaving Mr. Johnson's ranch we had thirty horses, one mule, with two Indians to help drive.

Nothing happened until the evening before reaching the head of Bear Valley, when there commenced a heavy rain and sleet, continuing all night. We drove on until a late hour before halting. We secured the flour and horses, the rain preventing us from kindling a fire; next morning proceeding up the valley to where we were to take the mountain, we found a tent containing a

---

19 Theodor Cordua, a German settler, established Neu Mecklenburg at the forks of the Yuba and Feather rivers in 1843. The ranch became the site of Marysville, named for Donner party survivor Mary Murphy Covillaud. Cordua mentions the Donner party in "The Memoirs of Theodor Cordua," ed. and trans. by Edwin G. Gudde, *California Historical Society Quarterly* 12 (December 1933): 291–92.

Mr. Curtis and Wife.

They hailed us as angels sent for their delivery, stating that they would have perished had it not been for our arrival. Mrs. Curtis stated that they had killed their *dog,* and at the time of our arrival had the last piece in the Dutch oven baking. We told them not to be alarmed about anything to eat, for we had plenty, both of flour and beef; that they were welcome to all they needed. Our appetites were rather keen, not having eaten anything from the morning of the day previous. Mr. Curtis remarked that in the oven was a piece of the dog, and we could have it. Raising the lid of the oven, we found the dog well baked, and having a fine savory smell. I cut out a rib, smelling and tasting, found it to be good, and handed the rib over to Mr. McCutchen, who, after smelling it some time, tasted it and pronounced it *very good dog. We Partook of Curtis' Dog.* Mrs Curtis immediately commenced making bread, and in a short time had supper for all.

At the lower end of the valley, where we entered, the snow was eighteen inches in depth, and when we arrived at the tent, it was two feet. Curtis stated that his oxen had taken the back track; that he had followed them by the trail though the snow. In the morning before leaving, Mrs. Curtis got us to promise to take them into the settlement when on our return with the women and children. Before leaving, we gave them flour and beef sufficient to keep them until our return, expecting to do so in a few days.

We started, following the trail made by the oxen, and camped a number of miles up the mountain. In the night, hearing some of the horses going down the trail, we went to where the Indians had lain down, and found them gone. McCutchen mounted his horse and rode down the mountain to Curtis' camp; found that the Indians had been there, stopped and warmed themselves, and then started down the valley.

Next morning we started, still on the trail of the oxen, but unfortunately, the trail turned off to the left from our direction. We proceeded on, the snow deepening rapidly, our horses struggling to get through; we pushed them on until they would rear upon their hind feet to breast the snow, and when they would alight they would sink in it until nothing was seen of them but the nose and a portion of the head. Here we found that it was utterly impossible to proceed further with the horses. Leaving them, we proceeded further on foot, thinking that we could get in to the people, but found *that* impossible, the snow being soft and deep.

I may here state that neither of us knew anything about snow shoes, having always lived in a country where they never were used. We were here

Compelled to Return,

and with sorrowful hearts, we arrived that night at the camp of Mr. Curtis, telling them to make their arrangements for leaving with us in the morning. Securing our flour in the wagon of Mr. Curtis, so that we could get it on our return, we packed one horse with articles belonging to Mr. and Mrs. Curtis, and started down the valley to where the snow was light, and where there was considerable underbrush, so that our famished animals could browse, they not having eaten anything for several days.

After packing Mr. Curtis' horse for him the next morning, we started; in a short time, Mr. and Mrs. Curtis proceeded ahead, leaving the pack-horse behind for us to drive, instead of his leading him; we having our hands full in driving the loose ones, they scattering in all directions. The pack turned on the horse. Mr. Curtis was requested to return and help repack and lead his horse, but he paid no attention to us. We stood this for some time; finally, McCutchen became angry, started after him, determined to bring him back; when he got with him he paid no attention to McCutchen's request to return; Mc becoming more exasperated, hit him several times over the shoulders with his riatte. This brought him to his senses. He said that if Mc would not kill him, he would come back and take care of the pack animal, and he did.[20]

As soon as we arrived at Capt. Sutter's, I made a statement of all the circumstances attending our attempt to get into the mountains. He was no way surprised at our defeat. I also gave the Captain the number of head of cattle the company had when I left them. He made an estimate, and stated that if the emigrants would kill the cattle, and place the meat in the snow for preservation, there was no fear of starvation until relief could reach them. He further stated that there were no able bodied men in that vicinity, all having gone down the country with and after Fremont, to fight the Mexicans. He advised me to proceed to Yerba Buena, now San Francisco, and make my case known to the naval officer in command.

I left Capt. Sutter's, by the way of San Jose, for San Francisco, being unable to come by water. When I arrived at San Jose, I found the San Francisco side of the bay was occupied by the Mexicans. Here I remained

---

20 This is the last time Reed mentions Curtis, but the two apparently were at loggerheads a few months later. On January 29, 1847, R. F. Pinckney discharged "Jonathan" Curtis for being insubordinate and abusive to his superior officer, James F. Reed. Eberstadt, *A Transcript of the Fort Sutter Papers*, MS 106.

and was attached to a company of volunteers, commanded by Capt. Webber, until after the fight at Santa Clara.[21]

The road now being clear, I proceeded to San Francisco, with a petition for some of the prominent citizens of San Jose, asking the commander of the navy to grant aid to enable me to return to the mountains. Arriving at San Francisco, I presented my petition to Commodore Hull, also making a statement of the condition of the people in the mountains as far as I knew; the number of them, and what would be needed in provisions and help to get them out. He made an estimate of the expense that would attend the expedition, and said that he would do anything within reason to further the object, but was afraid that the department at Washington would not sustain him, if he made the general out-fit. His sympathy was that of a man and a gentleman.

I also conferred with several of the citizens of Yerba Bueno, their advice was not to trouble the commodore further. That they would call a meeting of the citizens and see what could be done. At the meeting, the situation of the people was made known, and committees were appointed to collect money. Over a thousand dollars was raised in the town, and the sailors of the fleet gave over three hundred dollars. At the meeting, midshipman Woodworth volunteered to go into the mountains. Commodore Hull gave me authority to raise as many men, with horses, as would be required. The citizens purchased all the supplies necessary for the out-fit, and placed them on board the schooner —, for Hardy's Ranch, mouth of Feather river. Midshipman [Selim E.] Woodworth took charge of the schooner, and was the financial agent of the government.

I left in a boat for Napa, by way of Sonoma, to procure men and horses, and when I arrived at Mr. [William] Gorden's, on Cache creek, I had all the men and horses needed. From here I proceeded to the mouth of Feather river for the purpose of meeting Mr. Woodworth with the provisions. When we reached the river the boat had not arrived. The water was very high in the river, the tule lands being overflowed. From here I sent a man to a point of the Sacramento river opposite Sutter's Fort, to obtain information of the boat with our provisions, he returned and reported the arrival of the boat at the Fort.

Before leaving Yerba Bueno, news came of a party of 15 persons having started from the emigrant encampment, and only 7 getting to Johnson's. I was here placed in a quandary—no boat to take us across the river, and no

---

21 Reed described this skirmish, which occurred on January 2, 1847, in a letter to Sutter. It came to light sixty-three years later in Edwin A. Sherman's article "An Unpublished Report of the Battle of Santa Clara, written by John [sic] Frazier Reed Using his Saddle Horn as a Desk," published in the *San Francisco Chronicle* on September 4, 1910.

provisions for our party to take into the mountains. We camped a short distance back from the river, were we killed a number of elk, for the purpose of using the skins in covering a skeleton boat. Early next morning we started for the river, and to our delight saw a small schooner, belonging to Perry McCan,[22] which had arrived during the night. We immediately crossed, McCutchen and myself, to the opposite bank of the river. I directed the men to cross and follow us to Johnson's ranch. We arrived there early that day. Making known our situation, he drove his cattle up to the house, saying "There are the cattle, take as many as you need." We shot down five head, staid up all night, and with the help of Mr. Johnson and his Indians, by the time the men arrived the next morning, we had the meat fire dried, and ready to be placed in bags. Mr. Johnson had a party of Indians making flour by hand mills, they making during the night, nearly 200 lbs.

Start for the Emigrants' Camp.

We packed up immediately and started. After reaching the snow, the meat and flour was divided into suitable packs for us to carry, we leaving the horses there. At Johnson's, I learned that a relief party had passed in a few days previous, being sent by Captain Sutter and Mr. Sinclair.

Leaving a man at this camp with all the extra provisions we could not pack, with instructions to prepare a camp for the parties coming out, we passed on and at the head of Bear Valley met the party returning with a party of women and children. Among them was my wife and two of my children. We delayed no time, only a few minutes, and pushed on until the snow became too soft for us to travel on. Then stopping until it froze sufficient to bear us, we traveled all this night, and about the middle of the next day we arrived at the first

Camp of Emigrants,

being Mr. Breen's. If we left any provisions here, it was a small amount. He and his family not being in want. We then proceeded to the camp of Mrs. Murphy, where Keysburg and some children were. Here we left provisions

---

22 Perry McCoon, an English sailor, had come to California about 1843. He first worked for Sutter; in 1845 he established a ranch near the Cosumnes River. On June 1, 1847, he married the orphaned Elitha Donner, then only fourteen years old. McCoon was dragged to death by a runaway horse in 1851.

and one of our company to cook [for] and attend them. From here we visited the camp of Mrs. Graves, some distance further east. A number of the relief party remained here, while Messrs. Miller, McCutchen, and one of the men and myself, proceeded to the camp of the Messrs. Donner's. This was a number of miles further east. We found Mrs. Jacob Donner in a very feeble condition. Her husband had died early in the winter. We removed the tent and placed it in a more comfortable situation. I then visited the tent of Geo. Donner, close by, and found him and his wife. He was helpless. Their children and two of Jacob's had come out with the party we met at the head of Bear valley.

I requested Mrs. George Donner to come out with us, as I would leave a man to take care of both Mr. George Donner and Mrs. Jacob Donner. Mrs. Geo. Donner positively refused, saying that as her children were all out she would not leave her husband in the situation he was in.[23] After repeatedly urging her to come out, and she as positively refusing, I was satisfied in my own mind that Mrs. Geo. Donner remained with her husband for pure love and affection, and not for money, as stated by Mrs. Curtis.

When I found that Mrs. Geo. Donner would not leave her husband, we took the three remaining children of Jacob Donner's leaving a man to take care of the two camps. Leaving all the provisions we could spare, and expecting the party from Sutter's Fort would be in in a few days, we returned to the camp of Mrs. Graves, where all remained during the night except McCutchen, Miller, and myself, we going to the cabin of Mr. Breen, where two of my children were. Notice was given in all the camps that we would

Start on Our Return

to Sutter's early the next day. About the middle of the day we started, taking with us all who were able to travel. In a short time we reached Donner Lake. Traveling on ice a short distance, we made camp on the eastern side. Here were several springs; in the water were many small fish. The next day we traveled up to the head of the Lake on the ice, making camp here for the night. From this camp I sent in advance of us two of our men, Jondrieux [Joseph Gendreau] and [Matthew] Dofar, good mountaineers, for the purpose of getting the provisions in our last cache and returning with them they to meet us on the road the next day.

When coming in we made three caches, or deposits of beef. Two of them were made by taking a bag of dried beef to the top of a pine sapling,

---

23 Actually, the George Donners' three youngest daughters had yet to be rescued.

then securing it, cutting all the limbs off the tree to prevent animals from getting up and destroying the meat.

The next morning we proceeded up the mountain and in the evening came to one of the camping places of the party we had met in Bear Valley.

Starved Camp.

With a little repairs everything necessary for building a fire on the snow, which was twenty feet at least in depth, was here. We camped for the night. During all this day the sky had been overcast, threatening a storm. This night a heavy snow storm burst upon us, continuing all this night and the following day and night, and up to the middle of the next day. Our provisions gave out, and one of the children [Isaac Donner] died. I expected the two men, Jondrieux and Dofar, at the latest, to be back in the morning after we made camp here. But the storm had overtaken them. They found the cache had been destroyed by animals and had proceeded on to the next one, finding that partly destroyed, there were they snow-bound, and were nearly perishing.

As soon as the storm abated we made preparations for leaving. All that were able started, with the exception of Mr. Breen and family. He stated that if he had to die, he would rather die in camp that on the way. A strange proceeding of Mr. Breen, when he and his family were all strong enough to travel. We remonstrated with him, advising him to come with us; that if we perished, let us all die together in the effort to get out. Finding that we could not prevail upon him, I asked some of the men standing by to witness, that I then told Mr. Breen, "that if his family died, their blood be upon his head, and not ours."[24]

We had not proceeded far before the weather became intensely cold and when we stopped for the night many of the party had their feet frozen. The next day our travel was slow, many in pain. When night came on those in advance camped, the next coming straggling in, making considerable noise. This gave the camp of Mr. Woodworth the first intimation of our proximity to them. He sent some of his party to us requesting that we would come down to his encampment; but the most of us having laid down for the night, declining going, but would be glad if he would sent us something to eat, which he did, and some of the party who had not

---

24 Here Reed seems to forestall criticism for having abandoned the refugees, but he actually had little choice. W. C. and Mary Graves apparently accepted the necessity, for they expressed no resentment towards Reed for leaving their family at Starved Camp, despite the fact that their mother and little brother died and were cannibalized there.

camped, went down. Next morning Mr. Woodworth proceeded on with all haste, and my impression is, that two or three of our party went back with them.

We proceeded slowly, and the second night, we reached the encampment at Bear valley, in company with Mr. Woodworth, he returning to Sutter's Fort. From here a majority of the party rode to Sutter's, I stopping at Mr. Sinclair's.

James F. Reed
San Jose, Santa Clara Co., Calif.

WILLIAM McCUTCHEN (1816-1895)

William McCutchen was born in 1816 in Davidson County, Tennessee, the youngest child of James and Elizabeth Deane McCutchen. The family moved to Morgan County, Missouri, some time prior to 1836. William McCutchen married Amanda Henderson about 1841. The McCutchens had been living in Jackson County, Missouri, when they decided to emigrate west in the spring of 1846 with their daughter Harriet, about one year old.

Little is known about the McCutchens' journey across the plains. Shortly after leaving the Missouri settlements one "McKetchem" offered to pull Heinrich Lienhard's aching tooth for fifty cents, and George McKinstry passed "McCutchens co" about 100 miles east of Fort Laramie.[1] Whether these incidents refer to the same McCutchen who joined the Donner party cannot be determined, especially as a John McCutchen is mentioned as traveling with the Harlan-Young party.[2] In any event, the William McCutchen family was at Fort Bridger, apparently without a wagon, when the Donner party arrived.

After her husband and Stanton went ahead to Sutter's Fort for supplies, Amanda McCutchen struggled along with Harriet to Donner Lake, where they lived in the Graves cabin. Amanda departed with the Forlorn Hope in mid-December, leaving Harriet with the Graveses; the child died at the beginning of February.

After they were reunited in California, the McCutchens lived for a time in Sonoma. They settled in Santa Clara County in 1848, living at San Jose and Gilroy. William served as county sheriff in the 1850s. Amanda died after giving birth to a son, Edward, in 1857; William remarried in 1860. The Great Register of Santa Clara County for 1866 lists him as a farmer,

---

1 Heinrich Lienhard, *From St. Louis to Sutter's Fort, 1846,* trans. and ed. by Edwin G. and Elisabeth K. Gudde (Norman: University of Oklahoma Press, 1961), 18; McKinstry, entry for June 21, in Morgan, *Overland in 1846,* 214.

2 "Biographical Obituary: Samuel C. Young," *San Jose Pioneer,* November 9, 1878; reprinted in *Crossroasds* 6 (Fall 1995): 9–12.

but the 1890 Great Register records his occupation as "Collector." He died April 17, 1895, after a stroke.

The Text

McCutchen, like Reed, responded to Frances H. McDougall's article in the *Pacific Rural Press*. Since Reed bore the brunt of Mrs. Curtis's irresponsible tale, McCutchen's answer is comparatively brief. He is chiefly concerned with the remarks about himself but also bolsters Reed's statement regarding events at Starved Camp.

McCutchen's account was published in the *Pacific Rural Press* on April 1, 1871, following the second installment of Reed's memoir. It was similarly appended to the version of Reed's memoir printed in the *San Jose Pioneer* of May 5, 1877. This later printing of McCutchen's statement, unlike that of Reed's, differs very little from the first version.

William McCutchen (1816–1895); photo of engraving from C. F. McGlashan, *History of the Donner Party: A Tragedy of the Sierra.* Special Collection, University of Utah Library

STATEMENT OF WILLIAM MCCUTCHEN

F. H. McDougal's "Donner Tragedy" contains the following:—"Reed and McCutchen came to their camp nearly starved, having made a meal of wagon grease and mustard taken from Mr. C–s wagon, which he had left on the mountain, intending to go back for it."

I left the Donner party in company with *Mr. Stanton* some distance west of Salt Lake desert for California, for the purpose of obtaining a supply of provisions, and to return with them to the company. I did not see *Mr. Reed* after leaving the company, until he arrived at Capt. Sutter's, therefore I could not have made a meal of wagon grease with him. My account of what the writer styles "a strange proceeding" is, that Mr. Reed and myself arrived at a camp at the upper end of Bear Valley, in the evening, finding a Mr. and Mrs. Curtis the sole occupants. They exhibited great emotion on our arrival. Mr. Curtis said it was a voice from heaven, and that we were angels sent to them, that they were out of provisions; and the only thing we found in their camp to eat, was a portion of a dog baking in a small oven. We supplied them from the provisions we were taking to the Donner party. It was storming when we arrived at Curtis' camp, and continued the next day.

The following day we started up the mountain following a track made by oxen, and camped about five or six miles from their camp. During the night our two Indians left us returning to the valley. I followed them as far down as Curtis camp. Finding they had been there and had left for Ordway's [Cordua's], I returned to our camp reaching there about 12 P.M. Next morning we proceeded still further on until finding it utterly impossible to proceed further, on account of the depth of the snow, we returned and in the evening reached the camp of Mr. Curtis. Here we remained for the night. Next morning after cacheing our provisions, and some of Curtis' goods, we proceeded down the valley to Johnson's, accompanied by Mr. and Mrs. Curtis.

I state that it was utterly impossible for any two men to have done more than we did in striving to get in to the people. A company of men might have succeeded.

The statement of Mrs. Curtis in regard to myself is a base falsehood. She never was in the mountains at the emigrant camp, and Mr. Curtis was never there to my knowledge. If Mr. Reed and myself had succeeded in packing to the party all the provisions we could have carried, what relief would it have been to the emigrants? It would not have been a mouthful for them, there being about 80 persons at the emigrants' encampment.

"About the middle of February, seven men and women, finding their situation intolerable, left the Donner camp, hoping to reach the valley in safety and out of the fourteen, only five women and two men came into Johnson's ranch, then the first house on this side of the mountains."

My wife came out with this party; they started from the emigrants' camp the last [15th] day of *December* and were 31 *days* getting through to Johnson's.

"There were left behind to their fate: a Dutchman by the name of Reesburg (Keysburg), old Mrs. Donner and a child that Mrs. McCutchen, one of the fourteen who went out, had left behind. The child died next day."

There were left behind, when we started on our return, Mr. and Mrs. Geo. Donner, Mrs. Jacob Donner, and Keysburg, with two of our men to take care of them.

My child was dead before the Glover party reached the emigrant camp, and when we succeeded in getting in, Mr. Reed and myself buried the remains.

Starved Camp.

We arrived at this camp about 3 o'clock in the afternoon; this camp was under the peak at the head of the Yuba River. The Glen [Glover] party had made it when returning from the Donner party. Every thing necessary for building a fire on the snow was here. A storm commenced this night and continued until about noon of the third day. The second night Mr. Reed became snow blind and chilled through; he had overexerted himself in securing shelter for the party. Now there was only Mr. Miller and myself who were able to do anything; the rest of the men were disheartened, and would not use any exertion; in fact they gave up all hope, and in despair, some of them commenced praying. I d–d them, telling them it was not time to pray but to get up, stir themselves and get wood, for it was a matter of life and death to us in a few minutes. The fire was nearly out; the snow in falling off the trees had nearly extinguished it before discovered; it was only rekindled by the exertion of Mr. Miller and myself. After we got the fire started I was so chilled that in getting warm I burned the back out of my shirts, having four on me; only discovering the mishap by the scorching of my skin.

On the third day about noon, the snow ceased falling, and it was agreed that all who were able should leave, all the provisions being consumed the day before. The day after our arrival at this camp Mr. Reed divided the remaining flour. A spoonful as each person's share, "young and old," and it was four days in all before we got anything to eat.

Persons may ask why we camped here. Simply, it was a good place to stop: all of us were fatigued with the exertion made in climbing the mountain and packing the children; and the adult portion of the emigrants were so weak, even if we had wished to proceed further, they could not. There was no proposition made to Mr. Reed to stop here or elsewhere, by Mr. Brien or anyone else on account of the sickness of himself or daughter. It was the general desire of all.

All who were able started to leave, except Mr. Brien and family. He said that if they had to die he would sooner die in camp than on the way; he was repeatedly urged to come, but positively refused. Then Mr. Reed called myself and others to witness, that if any of Mr. Brien's family died, their death be upon him and not upon us. Mr. Brien had only one daughter; she was an infant.

Before leaving, we did everything in our power for those who had to remain, cutting and leaving wood enough to last for several days.

After leaving here, we traveled about five miles, then stopped. During this five miles travel all of us were frost bitten except Mr. Miller. After traveling all the next day, making about ten miles, we camped on the Yuba river. At this camp Mr. Woodworth, hearing the noise made by the party in camping, sent a man to us, requesting that we should come down to his camp, but most of us having lain down, refused, only asking of him to send us something to eat, which he did. From here we made our way into Bear Valley, in company with Mr. Woodworth, he returning; but his party, Mr. Miller and two others of ours, whose names I have forgotten, returned to the Donner camp.

WM. McCUTCHEN.
Gilroy, Santa Clara Cty.

Frances H. McDougall

On April 29, 1871, Mrs. Curtis had the last word, at least in the *Pacific Rural Press:*

The Donner Tragedy Once More.
Reply to Mr. Reed.

In this regard I have very little to say. Having conscientiously done what I believed my duty, and that, too in the tenderest spirit of sympathy for the sufferers, and not intending to reflect severely on any one, I am content to know that, in the long run, truth and right will appear. Mr. Reed winces very sharply under a simple statement of truth; but strict justice in the historian would not have treated the subject quite so tenderly. All that he did afterward could never atone for what he neglected to do.

My informant was one of the general company, and traveled with, or near them, until the fatal mistake of attempting to cut a new road, when she and her companion pushed forward, getting over the mountains before the first heavy fall of snow. She was at Fort Sutter when the sufferers were brought in, and was in the habit of daily conversation with them and with the men who rescued them. She heard their stories when they first gushed forth from the heart in response to the look and words of sympathy. Was there not, then, a fair presumption that her account would be correct, especially when we consider the entire truthfulness and superior intelligence. No one who has ever seen her could doubt her word. Her character is, every way, above all suspicion. And as I know nothing of the facts myself I will briefly state what Mrs. C. gives me in reply to Mr. Reed.

"In the first place, I find truth so cunningly interwoven with falsehood it is difficult to separate them without making more words that the subject deserves.

"The assertion that we were in a state of starvation, made by Reed and McCutchen, is false. We had just killed a large ox; and besides, the bears had killed a fine cow, leaving part of her carcass behind. We had at the

207

time five other oxen, which were driven to San Francisco, and there sold. It would then have been absurd, though by no means disgraceful, as there seems to be an effort to represent, if we *had* fallen to eating dog; but at the same time we *had* killed one dog, on account of his howling so terribly. I made a mistake in regard to the name of the person who first came with Reed. It was not McCutchen, but another man. I am very forgetful of names.

"On my own personal knowledge I affirm that Reed and McCutchen were not out all night when they left our camp on their way over the mountains, nor did the two Indians leave their camp, as they assert, but ours. They (Reed and McCutchen) left a little before 9 o'clock in the morning and returned about sundown. We were greatly astonished at their return; and Mr. Curtis said, if he had a wife and children in so perilous a condition he would have got through. This, on one can doubt, would have been practicable if the men had so determined, for it was the first snow; and Reed's objection that the provision they had was insufficient is of no weight, because the company might then have been brought over with much greater ease than when the passage was made in the heaviest depth of the winter snows. McCutchen says that *'no two men could have got through.'* But months afterwards, six men, with heavy packs on their backs, *did* get through; and what is the reason two could not have gone, and at that more favorable time?

"The incident of Mr. Breen's sickness was related to me by Mrs. Breen herself; and the account of Mrs. Donner preferring her money to her life was given me by many witnesses. We gave the two travelers, Reed and McCutchen, all the aid we possibly could, socks, mittens, boots, etc., for which they have made but a poor return.

"The account of the altercation with Mr. Curtis about driving the cattle is generally false. We were behind, driving our cattle, and our mule got among theirs. We chose to keep behind, because Reed, the night before, had threatened to kill Mr. Curtis, for the reason that he would not submit to his overbearing behavior, and do the duty of a body servant. It is true that one of them struck Mr. Curtis with his *reata;* though, as it seemed, playfully. But when Mr. Curtis got out his pistols and loaded them, Mr. Reed found it convenient to take himself out of the way, and we saw no more of him till after arriving at Fort Sutter."

In conclusion I will just say, that they who are so ready to catch others had better mind how they are caught tripping.

Frances H. McDougal

WILLIAM C. GRAVES (1829-1907)

William Cooper Graves was born January 20, 1829, in Vicksburg, Mississippi, the eldest son of Franklin Ward and Elizabeth Cooper Graves. By the spring of 1846, when his family left Illinois for California, he was old enough to take an active part in the events of that year. Only a few weeks after his escape from Donner Lake with the First Relief in February 1847, Graves joined the failed relief party of March that was forced to turn back because of soft snow.

In June 1847 Graves went back to Illinois, but he returned to California in 1849, guiding a company of gold seekers from Pittsburgh.[1] After his return, he at first lived in the Napa Valley near his sister Eleanor but later moved to Lake County, where, in 1853, he helped build one of the first houses in the town of Clearlake. He also had a blacksmith shop there. It was presumably during this period that Graves took a Pomo Indian woman to wife; the couple had several children but later separated.

W. C. Graves lived near Visalia for a time in the 1860s and in Plumas County in the 1880s but spent much of his life in Sonoma and Napa counties. Standing 6'-3", Graves was correspondingly strong; he was also a skilled hunter. He generally supported himself as a blacksmith but was interested in mining as well, and in the 1890s talked of going to the Klondike.

In his later years, Graves took turns living with his sisters and their families, who had come to regard him as a ne'er-do-well; as a result of his stays with them, descendants of the Graves family acquired a fund of stories

---

1 When the party neared Donner Lake, Graves disappeared and did not rejoin his companions until after they passed the ruined cabins. "He preferred viewing the place of his unprecedented suffering alone, not wishing that the eye of unsympathising man should be a witness to his harrowed feelings." Vincent Geiger and Wakeman Bryarly, *Trail to California: The Overland Journal of Vincent Geiger and Wakeman Bryarly,* ed. by David Morris Potter (New Haven: Yale University Press, 1962), 203. John A. Markle gave a more prosaic reason: he, Graves, and another went in search of game. "The Diary of John A. Markle, Forty-niner," *Donner Trail Rider* 6 (1936), 26:1.

about gruff Uncle Will.[2] W. C. Graves died at the Sonoma County Hospital in Santa Rosa on March 5, 1907, and is buried in Calistoga.

The Text

W. C. Graves was living at Pine Flat in northeastern Sonoma County in 1875 when he visited the office of the *Russian River Flag,* a weekly paper published in Healdsburg. Graves chatted about his pioneer experiences with the editor, who wrote up the conversation and published it as "A Survivor of the Downer *[sic]* Horror" on December 30. In the spring of 1877 the *Flag* published Graves's first-person memoir, "Crossing the Plains in '46," in four installments appearing on April 26 and May 3, 10, and 17.

In early 1878 Graves moved to Calistoga in Napa County and was working there as a blacksmith the following February when he began a lengthy correspondence with C. F. McGlashan. The two men became friends and Graves visited Truckee, pointing out various sites, assisting in the excavation of the ruined cabins, and identifying artifacts. He sent McGlashan a map he had sketched of the vicinity, showing the relative locations of the camps to one another and to various landmarks. Early in the correspondence Graves sent McGlashan a book in which he had pasted a copy of his published memoir. McGlashan used several of Graves's anecdotes in his *History of the Donner Party.*

A few of Graves's recollections are quite accurate—the details of his family's losses to Indians along the Humboldt River are attested by Thornton's account and the Miller-Reed diary, for instance—but he garbles so many other incidents that his account is best taken with a grain of salt. As he points out in his memoir, the events he relates had happened thirty years previously. Despite the many errors of fact in his account, Graves took care to correct or explain several minor inaccuracies in his letters to McGlashan.

Though unreliable, Graves's account is strikingly honest: it represents his own memory, fallible though it was, and there is no sign that he relied on such earlier authors as Thornton and Bryant. This is in sharp contrast with the late reminiscent accounts by Virginia Reed Murphy and Eliza Donner Houghton, whose debt to earlier writers is readily apparent.

At the end of his memoir Graves published a version of Patrick Breen's diary which is, in the words of Dale Morgan, "grossly inaccurate & much

---

2 I am indebted to Karl Kortum for sharing a wealth of family lore; Donna Diehl also provided several anecdotes.

altered."[3] The person responsible for most of these errors was not Graves, however, but the author of an article in the *San Francisco Chronicle* of December, 3, 1876, which included the version of the diary printed with Graves's memoir.[4]

For the most part these changes are minor, but a more serious alteration is found in the entry for February 15, 1847. In the original manuscript this reads, "Mrs Graves refusd to give Mrs Reid any hides"; but an accurate transcription of the diary was not available until 1910. Writers had to rely on the 1847 *California Star* version, which tactfully replaced the names in this and other entries with dashes. The author of the 1876 *Chronicle* article, however, filled in the blanks, apparently by guesswork, and had Mrs. Murphy refusing the hides. Though Graves has been accused of deliberately falsifying this entry in order to make Levinah Murphy appear guilty of an uncharitable act committed by Graves's mother, it is clear that he merely repeated another's error. Whether he knew the real circumstances and chose not to correct the statement is another matter.

"Crossing the Plains in '46," unreliable in many details yet corroborated in others, is a problematic source, and secondary writers have approached it with due caution. Nevertheless, as a first-person, firsthand account told by a survivor who had been nearly an adult at the time of the disaster, it is surprising that the memoir has never been reprinted in its entirety since 1877, unless one counts an obscure genealogical compilation made by the California Daughters of the American Revolution in 1929.[5] The memoir is a useful addition to the available sources of the Donner story. The present transcription is from photostats of the *Russian River Flag* in the Madeleine R. McQuown papers, Marriott Library, University of Utah.

---

3 Handwritten note at the top of one of the photostats from which this transcription was made, signed "DLM." Madeleine R. McQuown papers, Marriott Library, University of Utah.

4 "A Tale of 1846: The Donner and Reed Expedition Across the Plains." *San Francisco Chronicle,* December 3, 1876. The *California Star* of May 22, 1847, was the source of this version of the diary and of that published by Thornton. Graves may have been inspired to write his own memoir after seeing the article in the *Chronicle.*

5 Daughters of the American Revolution. State Committee on Genealogical Research. "Franklin Ward Graves, California Pioneer," in *Unpublished Records of the Families of California Pioneers,* 1:77–83. Franklin Ward Graves's father, Zenas, had been a fifer in the Revolutionary War.

William C. Graves (1829–1907); date of photo, 1879. Courtesy, the
Bancroft Library

CROSSING THE PLAINS IN '46

PERSONAL NARRATIVE OF THRILLING ADVENTURE–ENCOUNTER WITH INDIANS–TRAGEDIES IN THE TRAIN–SNOW BOUND– FROZEN–STARVED

[The following is a personal narrative by W. C. Graves, who now resides with his family[6] at Pine Flat, 16 miles northeast of Healdsburg. Mr. Graves is one of the survivors of the Donner horror, and through this narrative the public will be enabled to gain the true story of all that occurred to the unfortunate company. We know Mr. Graves personally and that his integrity is unimpeachable; he writes conscientiously and fearless of consequences. We commend his contribution as being well and interestingly written; it cannot fail to interest the general reader.–Ed. Flag.]

NUMBER ONE

On the twelfth of April, 1846, my father, Franklin Ward Graves, started, with his family, consisting of my mother, and Sarah, Mary Ann, myself, Eleanor, Lavina [Lovina], Nancy, Jonathan, Franklin and Elizabeth, the latter only about nine months old, from Marshall county, Illinois, to come to California. My oldest sister, Sarah, had been married to Jay Fosdick a few weeks before we started;[7] he and a hired man by the name of John Snider [Snyder][8] completed our company from that place till we got to St.

---

6 It is unclear if "his family" here refers to Graves's Pomo wife and children, or to other family members.

7 Jay Fosdick had been courting Sarah Graves, who had not intended to accompany her family to California. At the last minute she decided to go and the couple married "a few days" before starting out. Spencer Ellsworth, *Records of the Olden Time, or, Fifty Years on the Prairies* (Lacon, IL: Home Journal Steam Printing Establishment, 1880), 589.

8 "The first we saw of Snider was in the winter before we started. He and a brother moved from Ohio into our neighbor-hood and on hearing that we were going to

213

Joseph, Missouri, where we joined a large party, some bound for Oregon and some for California. This was about the 25th of May. We crossed the river, called a meeting and elected a Captain and other officers, such as we deemed necessary in crossing the great plains.[9]

First Excitement in Camp

On the evening of the fourth day, I, with four or five others, was detailed to stand guard the forepart of the night, over our cattle while they grazed on the prairie. We were marched out by the sargeant of the guard, placed in a circle around the cattle and ordered to keep the stock in and the Indians out. About 9 o'clock a fire started from some cause unknown to me, in the prairie grass about half a mile to the north. The wind was in the west, and blew the flames so that they passed in a streak. In a few minutes I saw a man coming on a full run toward me; I recognized him to be my nearest neighbor guard, but to play the veteran, I yelled at him, "who comes there!" He answered, in a low tone, "friend." "Friend, advance and give the countersign;" to which he said, "don't talk so loud; hain't you seen them?" "Seen what;" said I. "Why, the Indians; they are setting the prairie on fire, and agoing to surround and kill us and take our stock. Let's go to camp and give the alarm." I must confess that I had begun to "tremble in my boots," but I feigned brave, and asked, "where are the Indians?" "Why, there, running along by the fire; there are hundreds of them." Then I saw how he was deceived. In that country there is a resin weed that grows in bunches to the height of four or five feet; and on a dark night like that we could see those weeds standing up between us and the fire, and the wind was blowing the flames along; but it appeared to him that the weeds were Indians running the other way. When I explained to him, he was satisfied; but in a few minutes we heard an uproar at camp. A little while longer brought nearly the whole company out armed and equipped to fight– what? why the resin weeds. Two of the guard on the other side of the cattle had seen the same Indians that my neighbor had, and rushed into camp without looking back, and gave the alarm. But they did not hear the last of the resin weed Indians for some time. My neighbor persuaded me to not

---

California he wanted to come along so father told him he wuld bord him for his work so they made a bargain to that effect." W. C. Graves to C. F. McGlashan, March 30, 1879.

9 Relatively little is known about this wagon train, the Smith company, which was the hindmost party of the emigration of 1846 until the Donner party was belated. Donner party rescuer Reason P. Tucker and his family also traveled with this group.

tell on him, so they never found out that he had seen any Indians. I did not know the exact number in the company at that time, but there were about 85 wagons, and I think would average about five persons to the wagon; about half were women and children.

Attacked By Indians–Two Men Killed

After we left the resin weed Indians, we got along smoothly till within about fifty miles of Scott's Bluffs;[10] here we found some real Pawnee Indians, or they found us, and stole some of our cattle and killed two men; one of them, Wm. [Edward] Trimble, left a wife and two or three children. She and some of her relatives turned back because they lost so many of their cattle, and we never heard any more of them.[11]

At Scott's Bluff we met a party of Mormons who had been in California and did not like it and were then returning to Illinois.[12] We got to Fort Laramie on the third of July and stayed there until the fifth, celebrating the fourth by giving the Indians a few presents. From here on to Fort Bridger we did not pay much attention to company; my father's three wagons, Mr. Daniel's one and Mr. McCracken's one left the rest and pushed to the South Pass; there we left them, for they talked of going to Oregon and we were bound for California.[13] With our three wagons we went on to Fort Bridger; here we heard of

The Donner Party,

some three or four days ahead of us. Bridger and Vascus had hired L. W. Hastings to pilot a company on a new route by their Fort[14] (or camp, for it

---

10 Scotts Bluff, a butte on the North Platte River, was a famous landmark on the overland trail. It is located in northwestern Nebraska, about fifteen miles from the Wyoming border.

11 The second man, Harrison, was not killed but captured by the Pawnees; members of his party rescued him. Trimble's family actually continued on to Oregon.

12 Morgan identifies this group as the party with which James Clyman was returning East; however, the travelers were not Mormons. Morgan, *Overland in 1846,* 758, note 95.

13 William Daniels and his family of four were from Jefferson County, Iowa. The seven members of the John McCracken family, from Walpello County, Iowa, went to Oregon but the following year moved to California. They lived first near present-day Marysville, later settling near Sonoma.

14 On the other hand, Virginia Reed Murphy reports that it was Bridger and Vasquez who were in Hastings's pay. It was in the interest of both parties to

was only a camp then) and the south side of Salt Lake, thence striking the Humboldt river (and the old road) near a hundred miles below its head. This company was several weeks ahead of the Donner party; he took them through the noted Webber [Weber] Cañon and left them close to where Ogden is now located; but he was dissatisfied with the Cañon road because it was so terribly rough and dangerous, so he hastened back to meet the Donners, pilot them around the Cañon and strike Salt Lake valley where Salt Lake City now stands. He met them before they got to the turning off place and took James F. Reed, of the Donner party, and showed him the way through then he went on and overtook his party, and Reed returned to his. Just then we overtook and joined the Donner Party.[15]

Here is what caused our suffering, for Reed told us if we went the Cañon road we would be apt to break our wagons and kill our oxen, but if we went the new way, we could get to Salt Lake in a week or ten days;[16] so we started on it and as near as I can remember it took us about forty days to get to Salt Lake.[17] Here, at the crossing of the river Jordan, we struck the other road and had no trouble till we got to the Salt Lake desert, on the south west side of the lake, which is about seventy-five miles without water. Reed, being an aristocratic fellow, was above working, so he had hired hands to drive his teams and he gave orders, although no one paid much attention to him; but his wife was a lady and the company humored him a good deal on that account.[18]

When we had been on the desert two nights and one day Reed started off—no one knew nor cared much where—and was gone about twenty

---

encourage travel on the cutoff, however, and no financial relationship need be inferred.

15 Morgan discounts this statement, believing that Graves's other inaccuracies render him unworthy of credence. Graves is supported, however, by his sisters Mary (in Farnham's account) and Lovina (whose memoir also appears in this volume), both of whom say that the Donner party was waiting for Reed to come back when the Graveses caught up with them.

16 "A casual reader wuld think we were the first to come a crost the plains But there had been over a thousand wagons come a head of us except in the one place that we were fools enough to leave the old road & suffer the consiquence But that was Reed's fault Oh I get mad evry time I think it and I will quit now till I get over it." W. C. Graves to C. F. McGlashan, February 28, 1879. Graves's resentment is based on a misunderstanding: the Graveses had been "fools enough to leave the old road" before they caught up with Reed.

17 Forty days is an exaggeration; Reed's diary records only eighteen.

18 Franklin Ward Graves was remembered by his neighbors as "a genuine back-woodsman and pioneer," "more hunter than farmer," who "despised the trammels of civilization"; see Ellsworth, 583. This attitude might explain some of his son's disdain for the wealthy Reed with his luxurious outfit.

hours; during this time his men turned the oxen loose and left Reed's three wagons on the desert with his family; they drove the oxen till they scented water, then they became unmanageable and the men neglected to look after them any more till Reed came, which was nearly twenty four hours; but the Indians looked after them so well that Reed never found them; so there he was, nine persons in his family besides himself, and eight hundred miles from California, with only one ox and one cow to haul them and their provisions. Father loaned him one ox and Mr. Breen one and with his cow and ox made two yoke to one wagon, and in that way they started on.

Here we began to be afraid our provisions would give out before we got through, so we held a meeting, and Mr. McCutchen and Mr. Stanton volunteered to go ahead and get provisions and meet us as far back as possible. Then we had no more trouble till we got to Gravelly Ford, on the Humboldt, where the Indians stole two of fathers oxen and in two days after they stole a horse; but we pushed on.[19]

We had a rule in traveling which we always observed, and that was, if one wagon drove in the lead one day it should fall in the rear the next, so as to allow every one his turn in the lead. This day of

A Terrible Tragedy

my father was in the lead, Jay Fosdick second, John Snider third, and Reed fourth; arriving at the foot of a short steep hill, my father's team was not able to pull the wagon up, so Fosdick took his team, doubled to father's and went up, then took both teams back and started up with Fosdick's. Snider said his team could pull up alone; just then Reed had got another team to double to his wagon, and started to pass Snider's wagon; but the leaders did not want to pass, and tangled in with Snider's oxen. Reed at this time was on the opposite side of the oxen from Snider, and said to Snider, "you have no business here in the way;" Snider said, "it is my place." Reed started toward him, and jumping over the wagon tongue, said, "you are a damned liar, and I'll cut your heart out!" Snider pulled his clothes open on his breast and said, "cut away." Reed ran to him and stuck a large six-inch butcher's knife into his heart and cut off two ribs. Snider then turned the butt-end of his whip stock and struck at him three times, but missed him the third and hit Mrs. Reed, who had in the meantime got

---

19 Here Graves's memory about his family's losses is very accurate, being supported by the Miller-Reed diary and Thornton's account. McGlashan misunderstood this passage, taking the reference to "trouble" at Gravelly Ford to be the Reed-Snyder fight.

hold of her husband.[20] Snider then started up the hill and went about ten steps, when he began to stagger; just then I got to him and kept him from falling, by laying him down easy, where he died in five minutes. We then went a little ways to a place where we could camp, and held a council to find out what to do with Reed and took affidavits from the witnesses with the view of giving him a fair trial when we got to civilization. But Mrs. Reed and I were the only witnesses that got through, the affidavits were all lost, and I went back to Illinois the next June;[21] so Reed, taking advantage of the circumstances, went before a Justice of the Peace, told his own story, and was acquitted for the lack of evidence.

Some of the company were opposed to allowing Reed to travel in the company; so they agreed to banish him instead of sending him after provisions, as he and others have erroneously stated. He left and persuaded one of his hired hands, Walter Herron, to go with him; they started, and that was the last we knew of them till in February; so that left Mrs. Reed with four children and two servants depending on the mercy and charity of the company, which must have been pretty good, for they all got through except one Balis Williams, her male servent, who died early in the Winter, before the provisions gave out.

NUMBER TWO

Another Murder

There was a German in our company by the name of Woulfinger [Wolfinger], who had a wife, two yoke of oxen and a wagon which was all that we knew of, but it was rumored that he had considerable money. One day he was driving in the rear; his wife, being on foot, kept along in company with the other women. Our oxen being so poor and weak it was necessary for all to walk that were able to do so; another German by the name of Keisburgh [Keseberg] staid behind with him; they traveled so slow they got out of sight, but we thought nothing of it till night and they did not come; and we became a little alarmed about their safety; so two of the men and myself mounted horses and started back after them, but we had gone

---

20 Even Graves does not deny that Snyder struck Margret Reed, contrary to the memory of John Breen.
21 Graves was one of the handful of civilians traveling with General Stephen Watts Kearny, who was returning to Fort Leavenworth for the court martial of Colonel John C. Fremont on charges of insubordination.

but a little ways till we met Keisburgh, and he said Woulfinger would be along soon, so we turned back. But as he did not come the next morning, two of the company and myself again went back and in about five miles found the wagon in the road; the oxen had been unhitched from it, but left (two yoke) chained together and were grazing along the Humboldt river bank, not far from the wagon but we could not find Woulfinger. There were no Indian tracks about nothing but what we supposed to be Keisburgh's and Woulfinger's; we hitched the oxen to the wagon and drove them on till we overtook the company and delivered them up to Mrs. Woulfinger; she hired another German by the name of Charles Berger to drive it, after that, and there was nothing more said about it, but I suppose the reason was because Mrs. Woulfinger did not understand any English at that time, and Keisburgh told her what suited him about the case, and she never knew any better; but it was the general supposition that he killed him for his money and threw him into the river.[22]

Nothing particular happened after that till we got to Truckee river; here we met Stanton, one of the men we had sent after provisions; he had two California Indians with him and five mules packed with flour and jerked beef; he told us to go slow and recruit our teams, so they could pull us over the mountains, for they were very rough; that there was no danger of snow, for others had crossed in midwinter and we could do the same; so we did as he said, and lost five days between there and the mountains, which would have put us over safely had we kept on and not taken his advice. We afterwards learned that Captain Sutter told him to make haste back and tell us not to lose a moment's time till we got over the mountains, and if the snow did come before we got over to save everything that was eatable for we would have to stay there all Winter.

Fatal Accident

One morning we were encamped near where Reno now is; two men, Wm. Foster and Wm. Pike, had agreed to got a head to Sutter's, get provisions and meet us as far back as possible. Foster was loading a pistol, which was accidentally discharged, shooting Pike in the back and killing him in about twenty minutes; so that was the end to their journey.

---

22 Graves, the only survivor who implicates Keseberg in Wolfinger's disappearance, has apparently conflated the incident with the abandoning of Hardcoop. Rheinhard confessed to having murdered Wolfinger (Thornton, note 54), but Patrick Breen saw fit to note on December 29, 1846, "Keysburg has Wolfings Rifle gun."

The Place of Horrors

On the 30th of October, 1846, we camped in a pretty little valley about five miles from Donner Lake; that night it snowed about eight inches deep.

Now this being the last place that we were all together, and the place where the two Donner families staid and died, I will give the names of the whole company as near as I can recollect, and also each one's age as near as I can guess.

I begin with Capt. George Donner, aged about 50; wife[;][23] Tabitha [Elitha], 14, Leanna, 12; Frances, 8; Georgia Ana, 6; Louisa [Eliza], 4; Jacob 50, wife, 45; Saul [Sol Hook], 19; William [Hook], 14; George, 12; Mary, 10.

Patrick Breen, 50, wife, 48; John, 17; James, 15; about 4 more children.

Franklin W. Graves, 57; wife, Elizabeth, 47; Mary Ann, 20; Wm. C. (myself), 18; Eleanor, 15; Lavina, 13; Nancy, 9; Jonathan, 7; Franklin, 5; Elizabeth, 1.

Jay Fosdick, 23; wife Sarah, 22; Keisburg, 36; wife, 34; infant, 1; Mrs. Murphy (widow), 50; William, 17; Landron, 15; Lemuel, 13; Mary, 12; Wm. Foster, 28; Mrs. Foster, 23; Mrs. Pike, 21; Mrs. McCutchen, 24; child, 1; Mr. Eddy, 28; wife, 25; child, 1; Mrs. Woulfinger, 23; Mrs. Reed, 30; Virginia, 15; James, 12; Mattie Reed, 8; Thomas Reed, 6; Miss [Eliza] Williams, 21; Balis [Baylis Williams], 24; John Denton, 28; Milton Elliott, 26; Noah James, 20; John Baptist[e], 23; Charles Berger, 30; Samuel [James] Smith, 25; Mr. [Joseph] Rhinehart, 30; Sam Shoemaker, 25; Antonio, Mexican, 23; Mrs. Pike's child, 1.

I may have forgotten two or three besides Reed, McCutchen, Stanton, Herron.

It seems to me that we made a count near Salt Lake and made the number seventy-four in all, but it could hardly be expected that I could remember so many names for thirty years.[24]

On the 31st, all but the two Donner families, Mrs. Woulfinger, and three or four of the men who had formerly been Reed's hands, started on to try to cross the Summit. We got about four miles past the lower end of the lake, but could not go any further because the snow was about four feet deep, and we could not find the road. We were within one mile of the top,

---

23 The omission of a semicolon here created a false impression, which Graves later corrects.

24 Graves has confused or omitted the names of several individuals. Where they can be checked, the ages he gives are sometimes quite accurate, sometimes quite wrong. Those he gives for his own family are generally off by one year; he seems to have subtracted their years of birth from 1847, rather than 1846. See the Roster at the end of this volume.

when some were obliged to give it up and go back to the lower end of the Lake, where the snow was not so deep; there was a cabin there that had been built two years before by some emigrants. Mrs. Breen and Mrs. Keisburgh took this. Father and Fosdick went about a half mile below, to a thick timber flat, at the outlet of the lake, and built two log cabins, one for us and one for Mrs. Reed.[25] Foster and Eddy built [one], not far from Breen's, for themselves, the widow Murphy and widow Pike; the latter and Mrs. Foster were Mrs. Murphy's daughters. Mrs. Reed wanted to make a bargain with father for some cattle to live on, for which she agreed to pay when we got through by giving two for one; father let her have two and Mr. Breen let her have two on these terms. We then butchered our cattle and piled the meat up where it froze and kept good until we consumed it. We had nothing else to eat, then, not even salt to put on our meat.

We spread the hides over our shanties, in the place of shingles. My father was a native of Vermont, near the Green mountains, and had some idea of the snow Mountains. He would not risk the snow going off, but kept trying to get over. About two weeks after we stopped here, the weather was clear and pretty, the snow nearly all gone in the valley, so father proposed trying to cross on foot; about 20 started with him; when they got to the top they found the snow so deep and soft they could not go any further and were obliged to turn back. My father was the only man in the company who had ever seen snow shoes; and upon his return, made fifteen pairs. He and Stanton, Fosdick and wife, Foster and wife; Mrs. Pike, Mrs. McCutchen, Mr. Eddy, Miss Mary Ann Graves, Wm. Murphy, the two California Indians, and two other men, whom I have forgotten, started on them (Dec. 15), and resolved to go through or die in the attempt. I may say they did both, for some died and some got through, after thirty-two days wallowing through snow, lost and most of the time without anything to eat. Wm. Murphy, however, came back the second day. Mr. Foster, Mr. Eddy, Mrs. Pike, Mrs. Foster, Mrs. Fosdick, Mrs. McCutchen, and Miss Graves got to Johnson's Ranch, on Bear river, and told their story to a few men who lived near there.

But here let us return to the camp and see what is going on there. A few days before Christmas, five men, Jack [Jake] Donner, Rhinehart,

---

25 This was actually a double cabin, the two halves separated by an internal wall. Patty Reed Lewis wrote tartly that Franklin Graves built so far away from the other emigrants "because he wished too, for he, & all of his family, had minds & wills of their own." She denied that the Graveses built the Reed half of the cabin and described the partition as "pretty well-chincked." Letter to C. F. McGlashan, April 15, 1879. Mary Graves Clarke wrote that "Father built his cabin where it was most sheltered from wind and storm and wood near by regardless of company interest, I supposed." Letter to C. F. McGlashan, April 16, 1879.

Shoemaker, Smith [and] Williams died, although they had had all the meat they could eat. But it is a fact (though I think not generally known) that some people can not subsist on meat alone, while others would not suffer any while they had what meat they wanted. I and a few others did not suffer at all as long as our meat lasted, but it gave out about the fifth of February,[26] and then we had nothing but the hides of our cattle, till relief came, on the 19th of February. We would take a piece of hide, singe the hair off, and then boil until it was tender enough to be eaten. But that kind of living weakened my knees a little. And now let me state here that up to this time (Feb. 19th) there had not been a word said in my hearing about eating human flesh, and I never thought of it till we got through, and they told us about the first company having to eat it in order to get through, and send relief to those left behind.

On the fourth of January, Mrs. Reed, Mr. Elliott, Eliza Williams, myself and three or four others started to cross the mountains. We went about four miles the first day, and made a fire in a dead pine tree; but did not sleep much that night for it was too cold. In the morning, Miss Williams returned to the cabins, but the rest of us pushed ahead to the top of the mountains; there we could see nothing but snow and the tops of pine trees sticking out of it, which discouraged us, and we returned.

Beasin [Reason P.] Tucker, John Rhodes [Rhoads], Daniel Rhodes [Rhoads], Edward Coffeemire, Jackson Foster, Mathew D. Ritchey, George Tucker, [William] Thompson, [Aquilla] Glover, and a sailor,[27] whose name I have forgotten, started as soon as possible with provision to relieve us; when they got to the snow they left George Tucker, M. D. Ritchey, and Mr. Thompson with the horses, and the other seven men took what provisions they could carry and pushed on, occupying five days to go about forty miles. Mr. Tucker said the men would get tired, sit down, and say, "we'll never get there, we had better turn back;" but he would say, "we must and shall get there," and start on, and when he was pretty near out of sight they would get up and follow.[28]

They arrived about 8 o'clock Saturday night, February 18, 1847, and told us that father and his party all got through alive, but they froze their

---

26 Graves told a reporter that he had spent his eighteenth birthday (January 20, 1847) digging a horse out of a snowbank; "Another Pioneer Gone," *Weekly Calistogan,* March 15, 1907. Breen's diary records that on February 10 John Denton tried to borrow meat for the Graveses, who had nothing but hides left.

27 Joseph Foster, or Sel, was also called "Jack the Sailor"; Graves has left out R. S. Moutrey and Adolf Brueheim, or "Greasy Jim."

28 The Tuckers, Graves's former traveling companions, were prominent early settlers of the Napa Valley and Graves kept up his acquaintance with them.

feet, and were so badly fatigued they could not come back with them. They said they would start back Monday or Tuesday and take all that were able to travel. Mother had four small children who were not able to travel, and she said I would have to stay with them, and get wood to keep them from freezing. I told her I would cut enough wood to last till we could go over and get provisions and come back and relieve them; to which she agreed, and I chopped about two cords.[29]

NUMBER THREE

A Struggle for Life–Great Disappointment–
A Horrible Death–Reaching Camp

Wednesday, Feb. 22, 1847, the relief party and Mrs. Reed, Virginia Reed, James Reed, Eliza Williams, John Denton, Saul Donner, Wm. Donner, George Donner, Jr., Tabitha Donner, Leannah Donner, Mrs. Keisburg and child, Mary Murphy, Wm. Murphy, Lemuel Murphy, Noah James, myself, Eleanor Graves, Lavina Graves and two Mexicans, John Baptiste and Antonio–started over the mountains and snow. The relief had left part of their provisions on top of the mountain, thinking to have it on their return and save packing it down and up the mountain; and leaving everything with those behind, made calculations to reach their deposit the first day, which we did, tired and hungry; but, lo, and behold! there was nothing there. The fishers (a mountain animal), had torn it down and devoured it, so the "children" had to got to bed without their supper. But the "bed!" what do you suppose it was? soft enough, deep enough and as white as any swan's down; but no blanket to cover; and we were in that fix for four more days, before we could see bare ground. The second day, Mrs. Keisburg offered twenty-five dollars and a gold watch to anyone who would carry her child through; but it died that night and was buried the next morning in the snow; about noon, the third day, John Denton got snowblind, and could not travel, so we had to leave him on the snow, to suffer the worst of deaths. On the fifth day, about ten o'clock, I and some of the stronger, reached camp where the provisions were; but the weaker ones did not get in till night. Wm. Donner [Hook] ate so much he died the next day about 10 o'clock.

---

29 This seems quite a feat for a half-starved youth; Virginia Reed Murphy commented wryly on it in a letter to McGlashan.

A Second Relief Party—Faithless Woodworth— Feet Frozen and Amputated

When the first party got to Johnson's and started the first relief to us, other settlers there got up a subscription, circulated it and got several hundred dollars signed to assist the sufferers, bought clothing, provisions, a keg of fourth-proof brandy and started; about that time Reed and one S. E. Woodworth, of San Francisco, came along, and volunteered to act as Commissary, to which they appointed Woodworth. They went to the first snow; there Reed should take nine men,—NAMES OF SECOND RELIEF: Charles Cady, Patrick [Henry] Dunn, Hiram Miller, Brit Greenwood, John Turner, [Nicholas] Clark, [Charles] Stone, Johndro Duphanse [Joseph Gendreau and Matthew Dofar], McCutchen—loaded with provisions and go over to the cabins, get all of the suffers and bring them up to the top of the mountain, arriving there on a set time; Woodworth was to keep three men and follow after, in time to meet Reed on the set day. Reed started into the snow the same day we with the first relief got out. So you see, Woodworth was at the camp with all these good and fine things; but we knew nothing of them, only we could see that he was drunk. Reed and his men brought Breens' whole family of ten or twelve persons, my mother, Nancy, Jonathan, Franklin and Elizabeth Graves, Mattie and Thomas Reed, and Mary Donner, up to the top of the mountain, according to agreement, but found no Woodworth there; they stayed that night, the next day and next night; no Woodworth yet, but a heavy storm came on that night the snow fell about four feet deep, and was so soft they could not travel in it.

Mr. John Stark and family lived on Johnson's ranch. He had been in the lower part of the State engaged in the Mexican war, during the Winter, but returned home a few days after Reed and Woodworth had gone. On learning how things were he started alone to go over and assist in helping us out; when he got to the snow, where Woodworth was, they told him how Reed had done, and how they had agreed to meet Reed on a certain day which had then passed two or three days. Stark then scolded them for not doing as they agreed to and took as much provision as he could carry, and started to meet Reed and company,[30] who by this time had left the sufferers and were making their way out the best they could, after being without food for four or five days, and their feet frozen so bad that some of them lost their toes. Mary Donner's feet were so badly frozen they had to be cut off; almost everyone of us had our feet frozen, but not so bad as hers were.

---

30 Much of this description of Stark's role in the relief is echoed in a letter by George Tucker to C. F. McGlashan, dated April 5, 1879.

Soon after Stark started, he met some of Reed's men, so he followed their tracks and by doing so had but little trouble to find where the sufferers had been left, but my mother and brother Franklin were dead; he carried some of the least, and led some and helped them all out. Reed had left George Donner and wife and Keisburg in the cabins alive, but Mr. Donner was not able to travel and his wife would not leave him. Keisburg could come out but would not because he knew Donner had considerable money and he wanted to stay there till they died so he could get it.

A Third Relief

When Stark got his party out, three or four men started after Mrs. Donner and Keisburg, supposing Mr. Donner would be dead. When they got to the cabins they found Keisburg had flayed Mrs. Donner, and had some of her flesh and blood cooked, and was eating of them; they thought he killed her to get her money, because he had been to her camp and got it and hid it in a tree; they asked him about the money, but he denied knowing anything about it; then they put a rope around his neck and choked him awhile and then told him if he did not tell, they would hang him outright; whereupon he told them to take his track, follow it to a dead tree and look on the north side between the bark and trunk, and find it; they did so and found the money as he stated. They then helped him out of the mountains to Sutter's Fort; when they got there, one of the men, Coffeemire, who helped him out, told the people he thought Keisburg killed Mrs. Donner. Keisburg went to Esq. Sinclay [Alcalde John Sinclair], and sued him for defamation of character.

NUMBER FOUR

Settlement of the Trial for Slander–Faithless Woodworth–Bear Valley Camp–Arrival in the Valley–Etc.

The case of Coffeemire was tried before a jury, who decided that he should pay Kiesburg one dollar for his character and Kiesburg should pay the cost of the suit.

Woodworth was the cause of my mother's and brother's death and of very great suffering. Aside from his eating up the provisions that were donated to us he sold all the clothing he could, put the money in his pocket, and did not give us any thing that he could sell; and then he had the audacity to write a description of how he suffered and our party and had it published in the "Annals of San Francisco," which was as bad as Munchausen's or Gulliver's big stories.[31]

The camp where Woodworth and the provisions were, was Bear Valley, not far from where Dutch Flat is now located.[32] There were about two feet of snow there, but the first relief party had shoveled it away from the ground in a circle of about twenty feet in diameter and then cut and spread down small pine boughs for us to sleep on, which was an improvement on the five previous nights. They had packed supplies to this camp on horses and mules and then took the animals back some twenty miles to grass. We staid at Bear Valley Camp two days, then went on to where the horses were; here was the main rendezvous. A man by the name of Kern, a Vaquero, and partner of Woodworth, reigned supreme and gave us a benefit by making some wild Indians drunk and allowing them to have a war dance. But, you say, where was the benefit. It was in giving the liquor all to the Indians and their keeping us from sleeping more than half the night. The Indians got some shirts there, too, but I don't know how; only I am satisfied they did not steal them. However, they needed them worse than we did, for they were entirely naked, and we were not quite.[33]

From here we were taken on horseback to Johnson's ranch, the first settlement in California; here we were left to look out for ourselves, but the

---

31 The account to which Graves so objects only implies that Woodworth reached the mountain camps; but the impression given is decidedly false. The book also repeats some of the familiar sensational tales about the Donner Party. Frank Soulé, John H. Gihon, and James Nisbet, *The Annals of San Francisco,* 794–98.

Woodworth provoked unfavorable comment months before his involvement with the Donner party. He was carrying dispatches to Oregon overland when he met emigrant John R. McBride, who recalled: "Because he was in command of the party he seemed to think it his duty to exercise his authority on all subjects, even if he were ignorant of them." Francis Parkman "rode to Westport with that singular character, Lieutenant Woodworth, who is a great busybody, and ambitious of taking command among the emigrants." These and other remarks are found in Morgan, *Overland in 1846,* 98–99 and 102–3.

Graves is the source of another Woodworth anecdote. John Stark told him that when Mrs. Breen was brought in she mentioned how they had suffered. "Woodworth said to her you may thank me Mrs. Breen for you safe delivery. Thank you I thank no boddy but God and Stark and the Vergin Mary she said. Putting Stark second best and I think he deserved it." Letter to C. F. McGlashan, February 28, 1879.

32 The camp near Dutch Flat was at Mule Springs, not in Bear Valley.

33 Edward Meyer Kern was a painter and draftsman who had been a topographer with John C. Fremont's third expedition. He was in charge of the finances of the Donner relief effort. Others remarked sharply on Kern's supplying "his" Indians with items intended for the emigrants; see Morgan, *Overland in 1846,* 336.

people were very kind to us and we got along very well; but our flesh swelled up as if we had been stung all over by bees, and it was equally as sore. Our only flour at that time was wheat, ground in a common coffee mill. Beef was very cheap; we could by a quarter of a full grown bullock for a dollar.

But now I have finished all that will be of interest to the general reader, and will close by appending the following diary. It was kept by Patrick Breen, and I will vouch for its correctness.[34] It was published in the San Francisco *Chronicle* in December last, but the author's name was not mentioned:

Patrick Breen's Diary

Truckee's Lake, November 20, 1846.

Came to this place on the 31st of last month; went into the pass; the snow was so deep we were unable to find the road, and turned back to the shanty on Truckee Lake. Stanton came up one day after we arrived here. We again took our teams and wagons and made another unsuccessful attempt to cross the mountains, as snow fell all the time. We now had killed the most of our cattle, having to remain here until next Spring and live on lean meat without bread or salt. It snowed during the space of eight days after our arrival, with little intermission, though now clear and pleasant, freezing at night; the snow nearly all gone from the valleys.

Nov. 21 Fine morning; wind north west; twenty-two of our company about starting to cross the mountains to-day, including Stanton.

Nov. 22. Cold and clear to day; no account of those on the mountains.

Nov. 23. Same weather, wind west; the expedition across the mountains returning after an unsuccessful attempt.

Nov. 24. Cloudy; looks like the eve of a snowstorm; our mountaineers are to make another attempt to-morrow, if fair.

Nov. 25. Began to snow last evening; now rains or sleets; the party do not start to-day.

Nov. 29. Still snowing; now about three feet deep; killed my last oxen today; wood hard to get.

Nov. 30. Snowing fast, and seems likely to continue for days; no living thing without wings can get about.

---

34 What exactly Graves means by "correctness" is a mystery, as the diary is not accurately transcribed and some of its statements are not true, as Graves must have known.

Dec. 1. Still snowing; snow about six and a half feet deep; very difficult to get wood, and we are completely housed up; our cattle all killed but two or three, and these with the horses and mules, all lost in the snow; no hopes of finding them alive.

Dec. 3. Ceases snowing; warm enough to thaw.

Dec. 4. Beautiful sunshine; thawing a little; snow seven or eight feet deep.

Dec. 6. The morning fine and clear; Stanton and Graves manufacturing snowshoes for another mountain scramble; no account of mules.

Dec. 8. Fine weather; froze hard last night; wind southwest; hard to find wood to cook our beef or keep us warm.

Dec. 9. Commenced snowing about 11 o'clock; took in Spitzer yesterday, who is so weak that he cannot rise without help, caused by starvation; some have a scant supply of beef; Stanton trying to get some for himself and Indians; not likely to get much.

Dec. 10. Snowed fast all night, with heavy squall of wind; continues to snow—about seven feet deep.

Dec. 14. Snows faster than any previous day; Stanton and Graves, with others, making preparations to cross the mountains on snow-shoes; snow eight feet on a level.

Dec. 16. Fair and pleasant; froze last night; the company started on snow-shoes to cross the mountains; wind southeast.

Dec. 17. Pleasant; William Murphy returned from the mountain party last night; Bayless Williams died night before last.

Dec. 19. Snowed last night; thawing to-day; wind northwest, a little singular for a thaw.

Dec. 20. Clear and pleasant; Mrs. Reed here; Charles Berger set out for Jacob Donner's, who is camped about a mile ahead of us;[35] turned back unable to proceed; tough times, but not discouraged. Our hope are in God. Amen!

Dec. 21. Milton arrived from Donner's last night; sad news; Jacob Donner, Samuel Shoemaker, Rhinehart and Smith are dead; the rest of them in a low condition; snowed all night, with a strong southwest wind.

Dec. 23. Clear to-day, Milton took some of his meat away; began to read the "Thirty Days' Prayer." Almighty God grant the request of unworthy sinners!

Dec. 24. Rained all last night, and still continues; poor prospect for any kind of comfort, spiritual or temporal.

Dec. 25 Began to snow yesterday; snowed all night, and snows yet extremely hard to find wood; offered our prayers to God this (Christmas) morning; the prospect is appalling, but we trust in Him.

---

35 The distance was actually about five miles away in a direct line, about seven miles by road; Graves corrects this error below.

Dec. 27. Cleared off yesterday and continues so; wood growing scarcer; a tree when felled sinks into the snow and is hard to be got at.

Dec. 30. Fine, clear morning; Charles Berger died last night about 10 o'clock.

Dec. 31. Last of the year; may we with the help of God spend the coming year better than we have the past, which we propose to do if it be the will of the Almighty to deliver us from our present dreadful situation. Amen. Morning fair but cloudy; wind east by south; looks like another snow storm; the snow at present is very deep.

Jan. 1, 1847. We pray the God of mercy to deliver us from our present calamity, if it be His holy will. Commenced snowing last night; provisions scant; dug up a hide from under the snow yesterday, but have not commenced on it yet.

Jan. 3. Fair during the day, freezing during the night; Mrs. Reed talks of crossing the mountains with her children.

Jan. 4. Fine morning; looks like Spring; Mrs. Reed, Milton Elliott and Eliza Williams started a short time ago, with the hopes of crossing the mountains; left the children here; it was hard for Mrs. Reed to part with them.

Jan. 6. Eliza Williams came back from the mountains yesterday evening, not able to proceed; the others kept ahead.

Jan. 8. Very cold this morning; Mrs. Reed came back, not being able to find her way over the mountains; they have nothing but hides to live on.

Jan. 10. Began to snow last night and still continues; wind west by northwest.

Jan. 13. Snowing fast; snow higher than the shanty; it must be thirteen feet deep; cannot get wood this morning; it is a dreadful sight for us to look upon.

Jan. 14. Cleared off yesterday; the sun shining brightly reinvigorates our spirits; praise be to the God of Heaven.

Jan. 15. Clear day again; Mrs. Murphy blind, and Lanthron not able to get wood; has but one ax between him and Kiesburg; it looks like another storm; expect to hear from Sutter's soon.

Jan. 17. Lanthrone became crazy last night; provisions scarce; hides our main subsistence; may the Almighty send us help.

Jan. 21. Fine morning; the women do not like hides, but must either eat them or die.

Jan. 22. Began to snow after sunset, and is likely to continue; wind north.

Jan. 23. Blew hard and snowed all night; the most severe storm we have experienced this winter; wind west.

Jan. 26. Cleared up yesterday; today fine and pleasant; wind south; in hopes we are done with snowstorms; those who went to Sutter's not yet returned; provisions scant, and living on small allowances of hides.

Jan. 28. Commenced snowing yesterday and still continues; one of Stanton's Indians died three days ago;[36] food growing scarcer; don't have fire enough to cook our hides.

Jan. 31. The sun does not shine out brilliant this morning; Murphy died last night; Mrs. Reed went to Grave's this morning to look after goods.

Feb. 5. Snowed hard until 12 o'clock last night; many uneasy for fear we shall all perish with hunger; we have but little meat left and three hides; Mrs. Reed has but one hide and that is on Graves' house; Milton lives there and likely will keep that; two children died last night.

Feb. 6. It snowed faster last night and to-day than it has done before this Winter, and continues without intermission; wind southwest; Murphy's folks and Kiesburg say that they cannot eat hides; I wish we had enough of them; Mrs. Eddy is very weak.

Feb. 7. Ceased to snow at last; to-day it is quite pleasant; McCutchen's child died on the second of this month.

Feb. 8. Fine clear morning. Spitzer died last night; we will bury him in the snow; Mrs. Eddy died on the night of the 7th.

Feb. 9. Mr. Pike's child died last night; Milton is at Murphy's, not able to get out of bed; Mrs. Eddy and child were buried to-day; wind southeast.

Feb. 10. Beautiful morning; thawing in the sun; Milton Elliot died last night at Murphy's shanty; Mrs. Reed went there to see after his effects; John Denton trying to borrow meat for the Graves but failed; they have nothing but hides; all are entirely out of meat, but we still have a little; our hides are nearly gone; with God's help Spring will soon smile upon us.

Feb. 12. Warm thawy morning.

Feb. 14. Fine morning, but cold; buried Milton in the snow; John Denton not well.

Feb. 15. Morning cloudy until 9 o'clock, then cleared off warm; Mrs. Murphy refused to give Mrs. Reed any hides; put Sutter's pack hides on her shanty, and would not let her have them.[37]

Feb. 16. Commenced to rain last evening, and turned to snow during the night, and continued until morning; weather changeable, sunshine, then light showers of hail and wind at times. We all feel very unwell; the snow is not getting much less at present.

---

36 Breen's diary notes the death of "Lewis Suitor," the Kesebergs' infant son; the version published in the *California Star* renders this "Lewis (Sutter's Indian)," which the author of the *Chronicle* article further garbled.

37 As noted in the introduction above, this entry is altered in Graves's source, the article in the *San Francisco Chronicle;* it was Elizabeth Graves, not Levinah Murphy, who denied Mrs. Reed the hides.

Feb. 19. Froze hard last night; seven men arrived yesterday from California with provisions, but left the greater part on the way; some of the men have gone to Donner's camp, and will start back on Monday.

Feb. 22. The Californians started this morning, accompanied by some of our party, who were in a very weak condition; Mrs. Kiesburg started with them, and left Keisburg here unable to go; buried Pike's child this morning in the snow; it died two days ago.

Feb. 23. Froze hard last night; to-day pleasant and thawy, and has the appearance of Spring; all but the deep snow; shot a dog to-day and dressed his flesh.

Feb. 25. To-day Mrs. Murphy says the wolves are about to dig up the dead bodies around her shanty, and the nights are too cold to watch them, but we can hear them howl.

Feb. 26. Hungry times in camp; plenty of hides, but the folks won't eat them; our little party eat them with tolerably good appetite, thanks be to the Almighty God. Mrs. Murphy said here yesterday that she would commence on Milton and eat him; I do not think she has done so yet; it is distressing. The Donners told the California folks four days ago that they would commence on the dead people if they did not find their cattle, then ten or twelve feet under the snow, and did not know the spot or anywhere near it; they have done so ere this.

Feb. 28. One solitary Indian passed by to-day; had a heavy pack on his back; gave me five or six roots resembling onions in shape; tasted like a sweet potato, but full of tough little fibers.

Feb. 29. Ten men arrived this morning from Bear valley with provisions; we all leave in two or three days, and cache our goods here; they say the snow till remain until June.

Thus ends the journal; the conclusion of the affair is as follows:

The above mentioned men started for the valley with seventeen of the sufferers. They traveled fifteen miles and a severe snow storm came on. They left fourteen of the emigrants, including the writer of the above journal and his family, and succeeded in getting in with but three children. Lieutenant Woodworth was immediately sent to the assistance of the others, but before he reached them they had eaten three of their number who died from hunger and fatigue. Woodworth brought in the remainder. The last of the unfortunate party reached Sutter's Fort in April, 1847. It is utterly impossible to give any idea of the sufferings of the company, and they can best be understood by perusing the diary.

[Conclusion]

Correction—In number two of this story, we inadvertently gave the age of Mrs. George Donner at 14, when the author wrote, 50. Also, in number two the name Beasin Tucker is given, instead of Reasin Tucker, as written. Mr. Graves says in the paragraph beginning "Dec. 20," it should read five miles behind, instead of a mile ahead. Thinks mistake was made in copying.—Ed. Flag.

JACOB WRIGHT HARLAN (1828–1902)

Jacob Wright Harlan was born October 14, 1828, in Wayne County, Indiana. His mother died when he was two, after which his father remarried. The family moved to Kosciusko County, where Harlan received a limited education. In 1838, at the age of ten, he was bound out to his uncle Elijah, for whom he labored until 1844. Overwork damaged his health to the point his life was despaired of, but he recovered and, in 1845, was sent to live with another uncle, George W. Harlan, in Michigan.

Not long after young Jacob joined his uncle, George Harlan decided to emigrate to California with his large extended family. The Harlans were among those who took Hastings Cutoff ahead of the Donner party. After arriving in California, Jacob Harlan met Hastings in San Jose and taxed him about the shortcut: "Of course he could say nothing but that he was very sorry, and that he meant well." This is the only recorded instance that Hastings apologized to one of his victims. Harlan enlisted in Hastings's company of Fremont's battalion and campaigned in southern California, doing a great deal of marching but little if any fighting.

Harlan returned north in 1847 and married Ann Eliza Fowler in Sonoma on November 22, Lilburn W. Boggs officiating. Harlan worked at various occupations over the next two decades; he had a livery stable, kept a store, prospected, ran San Francisco's first dairy business, farmed, and ranched in various locations in northern California. He went back east by sea in 1852, returning overland with livestock the following year. The Harlans did well until Ann died in 1866; after which, her widower wrote, "my prosperity has seemed to have left me." Harlan struggled along, but in the fall of 1886 he reluctantly entered the Alameda County Infirmary as a charity case. He applied for and received a pension as a veteran of the Mexican War, and also stayed for a time at the Napa Soldiers' Home, which was not to his liking. He died March 7, 1902, in San Leandro, California.

The Text

In 1888 the Bancroft Company published Harlan's *California, '46 to '88,* which, though often inaccurate, provides not only an intriguing view of life in early California but also personal glimpses of such figures as Lansford W. Hastings, William H. Russell, John C. Fremont, Sam Brannan, William A. Leidesdorff, and many others. Harlan reprinted the memoir himself in 1896 from the original plates; except for the title page and an additional preface, the second edition is identical to the first. The volume has not been republished in print since 1896, but microfilm and microfiche versions are available.

Harlan's narrative of the journey to California, written forty-two years after the event, is unreliable in many particulars. He reports, for instance, that his company had celebrated Independence Day before reaching Fort Laramie, a statement refuted by contemporary sources. Harlan also labors under the delusion that the Donner party had traveled with the Harlans as far as the Weber River but then backtracked and struck out on their own.[1] Needless to say, Harlan is quite wrong, but at least he is consistent. His account of the Donner party is a mixture of garbled hearsay and precise data.

In creating his account, Harlan, like W. C. Graves, seems to rely primarily on his own memory with little recourse to published accounts. Interestingly, Harlan appears to derive isolated details from McGlashan, but otherwise the text shows little influence from other sources. The story of the Fourth Relief's arrival at the lake was supplied by Louis Keseberg, whose acquaintance Harlan renewed in the early 1870s. Harlan's description of the Donner party's most notorious survivor is unique: though he is sympathetic and believes Keseberg innocent of murder, Harlan also suggests that the German suffered from longstanding mental instability.

Though his account is a more valuable source for the 1846 migration and early California than for the Donner party per se, that tragedy's historians have found Harlan useful despite his errors. He adds to the Inman and Old Bill Williams anecdotes told elsewhere and contributes to our understanding of the parties that took Hastings Cutoff ahead of the Donners. The Harlan-Young party's experiences on the cutoff parallel those of the Donner party in many respects: both companies buried members in the Tooele Valley, both had one member who lost most of his cattle on the Great Salt Lake Desert, both spent several days recuperating at Donner Spring, both sent two men ahead to Sutter's for supplies, of whom only one returned.

---

1 Among writers on the Donner party, only Zoeth Skinner Eldredge and Charles Kelly accepted this statement, which is unique to Harlan.

The text published here consists of chapters 3 to 15 of *California, '46 to '88*. In the preceding chapter Harlan had been diagnosed with incurable consumption and sent back to his uncle Elijah's to die, but his ailing grandmother assured him on her deathbed that would get well. A few days after her death Harlan had a remarkable dream of recovered health and a beautiful countryside, which he later associated with California.

Jacob Wright Harlan (1828–1902); photo of frontispiece from *California '46 to '88*. Special Collection, University of Utah Library

From *California, '46 to '88*

Chapter III.

A short time after this my uncle sent me to his brother, my Uncle George, who lived in Michigan and had a family consisting of his wife and six children. They all received me with great kindness and took the best care of me; in fact, except my relations with my grandmother, which I have described, this was about the first real sympathetic kindness that had yet been extended to me.

My father had died in 1843. After he had bound me out to my Uncle Elijah, he appeared to take but little interest in me. By his second wife he had five children. His widow, with this family and a debt hanging over the farm, had enough to do to make both ends meet, and we of the family of my father's first wife found that we had to depend upon ourselves. At least, I found it so, and that I had to depend on my own efforts in order to gain a livelihood.

Some time after my going to live with my Uncle George he sent his son Joel and me to Niles, Michigan, with a load of wheat. Joel and I were of about the same age. He was an excellent fellow and we were good friends. When at Niles we received from a friend of his father, *Hastings' Work on California and Oregon*. I believe my uncle had known Hastings, who had left Michigan in 1844.[2] When we had read the book, my uncle declared that as soon as harvest was over and his grain sold, he would sell his farm and leave for California. Accordingly, these sales having been made and necessaries provided for the journey, we all started on our pilgrimage toward the Pacific coast, on October 14th, 1845—my birthday. Our party consisted of fourteen persons, viz.: My uncle and his wife, his wife's mother, then ninety years of age and blind, his two small children, his two married daughters and their husbands, Ira and John Van Gordan, my two

---

2 According to John Bidwell, Hastings had returned to the Midwest from California, lecturing on temperance to raise money for his book, which was published in early 1845; see "Life in California before the Gold Discovery," *Century Illustrated Magazine* 41 (1890): 176. It was presumably on this lecture tour that Hastings met George Harlan.

sisters, Sarah and Malinda, his nephew, G. W. Harlan, some others, and myself.[3]

We had eleven wagons, ten of our teams being of oxen, and one of horses. At that time there was very little movement from that part of the country toward California. It was sometimes difficult to make people believe that that country was our destination. At Joliet, Ill., for instance, we were camped and had a large fire, for it was frosty. An Irishman drove up with a team and asked where we were going. One of our party said, "to California;" upon which he got into a rage and swore that he would not be made game of, and he threatened violence to our whole company. Some of our boys ran him off, and he escaped. He was not the only one who doubted our being bound for the Northwest coast. In passing through Hancock County, Ill., we met with an accident which detained us for a week. My uncle's son, Elisha, fell out of the wagon and a wheel passed over his body. A doctor who was called, in trying to bleed the boy, cut an artery, and the poor little fellow came near bleeding to death. In about a week he got well enough to travel.

Our stay in Hancock County gave us some experience of the Mormons. Nauvoo was not far off. A short time before we encamped here, several foraging parties–I think they called them "destroying angels"–were sent out by the Mormon leaders to gather corn belonging to the Gentiles. The Gentiles objected to having their corn thus taken, and the result was a fight in which the Gentiles lost seven men and the Mormons more. Near where we were camped was a well into which the Gentiles had thrown the bodies of seventeen saints who had been killed in the fight. The house of the farmer on whose land we were encamped was full of holes of bullets which had been fired into it during the engagement. At this time the Mormons had been driven out of Missouri, where their killing of many citizens, their

---

3 Harlan's count of fourteen people is undoubtedly wrong. In the next paragraph he states that the party had eleven wagons, which would have required that everyone but the blind mother-in-law and the two small children drive teams, an entirely improbable scenario. Family tradition records that the party actually numbered thirty-two individuals in a complex web of relationships; see Brent Galloway, "Editor's Note Number One," *San Leandro Recollections* 5 (September 1973): 11–14.

   Peter L. Wimmer had married Polly Harlan, Jacob's cousin; after her death Wimmer remained on good terms with his former father-in-law, though by 1846 he had remarried. His second wife, Elizabeth Jane Baiz, née Cloud, was known as Jennie. Legend has it that she was making soap at Coloma one day when John Marshall used her kettle to test a lump of metal which proved to be gold and sparked the gold rush that changed California's history forever. Though they were technically no relation to him, Harlan refers to the Wimmers as his aunt and uncle.

wounding of Gov. Boggs of that State and their other rascalities had made them odious. When we were near them in Hancock County, we learned that they had determined to leave Nauvoo; that their first intent was to go to Vancouver's Island, but their prophet and president had changed this, having had a revelation that they must go to Salt Lake, and there found a great people, who would in time wipe all Gentiles off from the face of the earth. This short experience of the Mormons I afterwards found useful when I had contact with many of them on the Pacific Coast. I have always found that when they have felt safe in doing so they have been ready to act in hostility to the Gentile. It may be that I err, but I believe that but for the discovery of gold and the consequent coming of so many people to California, the Mormons would have taken California.

When I first arrived in Yerba Buena—now San Francisco—the Mormons were strong there. If one needed a laborer to do a piece of work, the chance was that a Mormon would be on hand to do it. If one wished to have his clothes washed, a Mormon woman would be the washer-woman. When a ball was given to Com. Stockton, at Leidesdorff's house, at the corner of Kearny and Clay streets, the majority, if not all, of the females were Mormon women. All this was happily swamped and lost in the flood of immigration, which the discovery of gold directed to California, and the Mormons had to take a back seat.[4]

Chapter IV.

At Quincy, Ill., we remained a few hours to rest our teams, and to buy some necessary things, and we came near being taken for saints. Our wagon covers were painted to make them water-proof, and each had its driver's name painted on it. A green-looking Sucker came gawking along spelling these names. When he came to John Van Gordan's wagon, he began to spell, and got as far as V-a-n, Van, when he shouted, "Vancouver's Island!" "Why, that's where the — Mormons are going. These fellows are Mormons," which was not a very safe or pleasant accusation at the time and place. John, however, corrected his spelling and his notions by treating to a kind of cyclone in the shape of a strong application of a big ox-whip, and we had no trouble.

We crossed the Mississippi at Hannibal, and at Brunswick we met Mr. [William Squire] Clark, who had lost much of his property in a great

---

4 Harlan's description of the Mormon situation is distorted but relatively mild compared to much that had been written about the Latter-day Saints by his contemporaries. The Wimmers were said have been Mormons, but Harlan does not mention this.

flood, which had done much damage to the latter place. When told that we were bound for California, he vowed he would go too, which he did. He settled in San Francisco, and gave to "Clark's Point," the name which it bears to-day.

We wintered at Lexington, LaFayette County, Missouri. We had not been long there, when a steamboat arrived, bringing one hundred and fifty Sac and Fox Indians from Iowa, who were on their way to a reservation in Kansas Territory. Two of Black Hawk's sons were among them, fine-looking fellows. One, we found, weighed two hundred and fifty the other two hundred and fifteen pounds. My uncle made a contract with the agent to move them to Westport, on the boundary between Missouri and Kansas Territory. It took all our teams to haul their effects, their children and those who could not walk.

We started on Christmas day and travelled about five miles when there came on a severe snow storm. In a short time the road became covered so that we lost our way and we had to camp on a small creek among shrub oaks. We had attended to our animals and prepared for supper and were warming ourselves at the campfire when John Van Gordan, in pulling a pistol from his pocket accidentally discharged it, and shot my cousin G. W. Harlan who was stooping over the fire. The ball entered his right hip and passed upward. He cried out that he was killed and fell backward. This caused much confusion among the Indians. They were all on their feet in an instant. No interpreter was present to explain to them the cause of the shooting and matters were serious, as there were some seventy-five armed Indian warriors all under great excitement. Finally one of those sons of Black Hawk came forward. He could speak some English, and being informed about the accident he explained it to the Indians and pacified them. He then called the Indian medicine man, who carefully traced the course of the ball which he found under the right nipple, and said that by proper treatment the young man would get well. Next day a doctor came with an ambulance and took George back to Lexington. The rest of us with our Indian freight went on to Westport, and returning by way of Independence we found our patient rapidly getting well.

Chapter V.

During this winter, through the care and kind treatment of my uncle and his family, I had much improved health. They always had prevented my doing any hard work which they thought would injure me. With returning health and strength I began to think it time for me to do something toward my own maintenance. Much hemp was raised in the part of Missouri, where we were wintering, and I found a chance to earn wages in braking hemp. My uncle at first objected to my engaging in this, but finally said I might go at it, and he would watch me lest it might injure me. Far different this from his brother's conduct toward me.

One morning in January I began work for a farmer who had 400 slaves, a few of whom were nearly as white as any of us. The slave that I chose as my teacher in this new kind of work was named Jacob, the same as myself, and was of fairer complexion, than I, having reddish hair and blue eyes. He told me that his mother was a slave and a quadroon, and his father was his master. He also told me that three very pretty girls with his same complexion and who were in his mother's house, were his sisters, his master's daughters, and were the special servants of "Missus." The house in which this contraband family of "Massa" lived was much superior to the houses of the rest of the slaves. It was a comfortable log house, lined and neatly kept. The other slaves lived in common log-cabins. Jake made a wide distinction between his family and the other slaves. He called the latter "niggers."

Aside from this the master was a very good man, and kind to his slaves. Sometimes, however, when a slave would behave badly, Jake said, master would sell him to Louisiana people and the negro would not be heard of again.

The master's next neighbor had a large force of slaves and was very different in his treatment of them. This man, one night, came home drunk from town, and meeting one of his slaves, an old man, cursed him as good for nothing and killed him. My uncle found this to be true, as the murderer was arrested and fined $50, as punishment for doing it. He was a white "gentleman" and old Sam was only a "nigger." I learned also that Jake's master was permitting him to buy his freedom. His value was set at $1500, and Jake had already made and paid $1200, and would pay the balance in three years.

At first the work was very severe upon me, and I did not get through with a very great quantity of hemp. The "master," at the end of my first day, weighed my quantity and found it to be only forty-seven pounds. Jake being an old hand, his quantity was found to be two hundred pounds. The "master" then said to me that I had earned thirty-seven and one-half cents, but that Jake had earned one dollar and fifty cents, of which Jake's share was fifty cents; that in this way Jake was buying his freedom; that he hated to lose him, and could have sold him on the previous Saturday for two thousand dollars, but he preferred to let him buy his freedom in this way, and afterwards to let him work for wages as a free man.

On the succeeding Saturday I attended the slave auction. There was quite a large number of buyers. The slaves were in an enclosure, men, women, and children together, and they were sold off rapidly, without regard, evidently, to the separating of members of families. To me it looked very cruel and it affected me deeply. The last slave that was sold was a young girl. The auctioneer said: "Gentlemen, this girl is the last that we can offer you to-day, and I want you to bid up quickly on her. You can see that in form, color, and beauty she cannot be surpassed in La Fayette County. Her age is seventeen years and eight months, and she is an excellent servant." One of the bidders desired that her mouth be opened, that he might see her teeth. She was caused to do this, and a most beautiful set she had. Then the bidding went on; $400, $500, $600, $800, and so on until she was knocked down at $2,500. Her buyer asked how much negro blood she had, and was told that she had about one-eighth.

I never went to any more slave sales. The whole thing looked abominable to me. I came away with feelings of sadness and disgust.

I continued working among the hemp until Spring, and became quite handy at it. I earned enough to pay for my full outfit for the journey, and had forty dollars left. About my best investment was in a dapple grey mule, which afterwards proved a good friend when such a friend was much needed by me.

Chapter VI.

With the opening of Spring we made ready to start, and a very important part of our preparation was the marrying of two couples of our young folks, the natural result of a winter's close contact in camp.

Our first destination was Indian Creek, in Kansas, which was the place of rendezvous of California and Oregon emigrants. Here we found about five hundred wagons, two-thirds of which were bound for Oregon.

On April 5 [May 9], 1846,[5] we had a grand time. About five hundred people came from Missouri to see us off and bid us God-speed. Rev. Mr. Dunleavy, one of the emigrants, preached a sermon. He was quite eloquent, and his discourse had a powerful effect upon us all.[6]

On April 6 [May 12] we bade adieu to the "States" and started for our land of promise. The California emigration moved together for three days,

---

5 On May 8 Edwin Bryant recorded: "A party from Michigan, under the direction of Mr. Harlan, we learned, was encamped in a grove of timber about a mile beyond us....They had been in their present encampment more than a month, but appeared to be contented and happy, and, with the numerous women and children, who greatly outnumbered the men, to possess a persevering energy and confidence in the future, that would sustain them in a journey round the globe, whatever might be its difficulties." Bryant, *What I Saw in California.*

6 Bryant wrote on May 9: "Numerous parties of ladies and gentlemen from the neighboring villages visited our camp in the course of the day, and attended divine service, the exercises of which were performed by the Rev. Mr. Dunleavy of the Methodist Episcopal church, one of the emigrants to California."

Ex-Gov. Boggs, of Missouri, being captain; then we were divided into two parties. He went on in command of one-half. The other half, in which was our party, then elected Judge Moran [Josiah Morin], of Missouri, as captain. They wished to elect my uncle, but he refused the command.[7] For some time everything went on smoothly enough. In our company there was a preacher—for such he claimed to be—named [Peter] Inman. He thought that he was not recognized, but several of us knew him to be no preacher at all, but a man who had been imprisoned in Kosciusko County, Ind., for being a horse thief, and had broken jail and escaped by crawling through a stove-pipe hole in the roof. He became very wroth at our captain, because, as he said, the latter did not preserve proper discipline. He complained about this mostly to the young men, appearing afraid to approach the captain or my uncle. We young folks decided to gratify his ambition, and have some fun as well. At night our camp was made by drawing all the wagons into a circle, and after supper we held a meeting of some 30 or 40 youngsters. We had speeches and a great show of enthusiasm. Finally, it was moved and unanimously voted that Captain Moran had failed in his duty, by not keeping proper discipline, and that he should be turned out of office. Then Inman was nominated, and he was elected with a tremendous hurrah. The older men, startled by the noise, ran out to see what was up. I called my uncle and the captain aside and explained it to them. I begged them not to interfere with our fun, and told them that we boys had elected Inman to-night and to-morrow night we would put him out. The boys lifted him up and carried him in procession all about the camp, with great shouting and applause.

Next morning, Inman ordered every team to be ready to start at 6 A. M., and that any who were not then ready should be left behind, and not allowed to join the company again. Accordingly all were ready at the appointed time except one old man named [Edward Gantt] Pyle, whose oxen had strayed away, and could not be readily found. The order was to march in four platoons. Four wagons should start together, keeping twenty feet apart. Then four more should move in the same manner, and so on till all were under way.

My uncle had eighty head of two-year old cattle, and he was ordered to keep them half a mile to the rear. Inman rode back and forth all day giving orders, and was on the run most of the time, so that some time before we got to camp his horse gave out, when he was far in the rear seeing if the loose cattle were nearer than the half mile. Before he could get to the front

---

243

again the older men had camped and turned their stock loose to graze. He was in a great rage at this but could not help himself. That night he called a meeting of the young men, and stated his grievances to them, and asked their views and their advice. Just then old man Pyle came into camp, and said Inman had done him great wrong and had endangered the lives of himself and family, by making him camp half a mile away from the rest of us without any protection from the Sioux, who would like nothing better than to kill him and his wife and daughters. These daughters were nice pretty girls, and some of the young men had already begun to cast sheep's eyes in their direction; so the old man's talk made quite a sensation, and young Billy McDonald[8] moved that Inman should be forthwith turned out of office and Captain Moran reinstated. I seconded the motion, and it was carried unanimously. Inman was wrothy at me for this. As I got down from my wagon Inman was standing beside his wife, across the corral, armed with bowie knife and rifle. As he aimed at me, I thought I could see right down the barrel. He pulled the trigger, but his gun snapped. I quickly brought my rifle to bear on him, but my uncle knocked it upward as I fired, and my ball only cut a groove on the top of Inman's head. There was much excitement in camp, and some young men wanted to lynch him, but the wisdom of the older men prevented this. He was ordered to leave camp, and we got rid of him.[9]

Chapter VII.

We proceeded very happily till we reached the South Platte. Every night we young folks had a dance on the green prairie. Our musician was usually a young fellow named Frank Kellogg,[10] who played the fiddle pretty well, but from time to time, as our musician, we would get Ann Eliza Fowler. She was a young lady who afterwards became my wife, and in playing the fiddle she could just knock the hind-sights off Frank or any one in the train.[11]

---

8 Probably William McDonnell, age twenty-one, a teamster for the Kellogg brothers; he later married Eleanor Graves of the Donner party.

9 Heinrich Lienhard also tells a version of the Inman episode. See *From St. Louis to Sutter's Fort, 1846,* translated and edited by Erwin G. Gudde and Elisabeth K. Gudde (Norman: University of Oklahoma Press, 1961), 24–31.

10 Benjamin Franklin Ephraim Kellogg, traveling with his brother Florentine Erwin and Florentine's family. The Kelloggs first settled in the Napa Valley but later moved to southern California.

11 Jennie Wimmer reported, "Mrs. Jacob Harlan and her sister Minerva were expert violinists, and the character of music furnished the dancers was superb."

On the Platte we stayed a week, laying in a stock of buffalo meat. We encamped about two miles from a buffalo lick, to which thousands of those animals came to lick the salt with which the earth was impregnated. July 4th found us filled with buffalo meat and patriotism, and after our usual dance, we youngsters drew up in a line to fire a salute, which was done without other loss of killed or wounded than a young fellow named Bill Richardson, who, in order to make greater noise, had overloaded his yäger rifle and got knocked a rod or so out of line, his rifle flying forty feet away.

The lick was very large, extending for several miles. In hunting we would divide into squads of five or six, and when the animals came to the lick we would fire at them. In this way we killed twenty-two on our first day's hunt. We cut the meat into thin slabs about as large as a common-sized shingle, and dried it in the sun. One morning we came upon a bull much bigger than any that we had yet seen. He was a monster in size and in fierceness. My rifle was larger in the bore than any of the rest, and it fell to me to shoot him. There were several others with him, and for some little time I could not get a fair shot at him. Finally I got a bead on a vital spot on him and fired. He fell, but was on his feet again in an instant. He saw me, and immediately charged me. I ran for my life, expecting every moment to be lifted on his horns. At last, when my breath and strength were gone, I stumbled on a buffalo chip, and fell headlong. Turning my head, I saw that my bull had fallen about two rods behind me. I immediately rose and cut his throat, and received the congratulations of my companions. I did not wholly escape damage, however. My hands and knees were full of thorns of the prickly pear, which was abundant on the prairie, and in my eagerness to bag that big bull I had not observed that I was laying in a stock of thorns, which would give me much acute suffering.

In the afternoon of this day we witnessed a grand sight. Luckily we had just got into camp, when there came toward us a band of fully one thousand buffalos, running with great swiftness, and reckless of any obstacle which might be in their way. The ground fairly trembled under their tread. About one hundred mounted Sioux, armed with bows and arrows, were pursuing them. Four or five Indians would run up to a fat cow, and shoot arrows into her until she would fall dead. We saw them kill about a dozen in this manner. If our camp had happened to be in the course of their stampede, none of us could have escaped.

Having laid in our stock of buffalo meat, we proceeded to Fort Laramie.[12] Here we found encamped a large body of Sioux. About five

---

W. W. Allen and R. B. Avery, *California Gold Book* (San Francisco: Donohue and Heneberry, 1893), 64.

12 Harlan has gotten events out of sequence. The emigrants were past Fort Laramie by July 4.

hundred of their warriors had just returned from a fight with the Pawnees. We were told that they had killed about one hundred and fifty of their enemies, and had lost about eighty of their own warriors in the fight. They had also taken a great many ponies. When we were there these Sioux had their war dance. They were all in war paint, and danced around a big fire, with the Pawnee scalps in their hands. The one who had taken the most scalps received greatest honor. They were hideous to behold.

We had some fear that these savages would steal our animals, but the white men at the fort assured us that we need have no fear of their doing so. We made some presents to the old chief, which pleased him much, and he told us through an interpreter that our stock was safe, and that we need not guard it. We found this to be true, and lost no animals by those Indians.

Chapter VIII.

From Laramie we kept on to Fort Bridger, where we halted for three days. Here we met a man named L. W. Hastings, who had written the book which I have mentioned. He had just come from California, and professed to know all about the proper way to get there. He got all the emigrants together, and recommended that we leave the old trail and make a cut off from Bridger to pass round the south end of Salt Lake, and strike the Humboldt river one hundred and fifty miles above its sink. He said we would thus save three hundred miles of travel, it being that much nearer than the way by Fort Hall. There was a difference of opinion among our chief men. Governor Boggs and his company, our captain, Judge Moran, and some others were in favor of the Fort Hall route, but my uncle and old man Pyle, and James F. Reid, and George Donner were in favor of the cut-off recommended by Hastings.[13]

While at this place I got me a complete suit of buckskin, which with moccasins and my ornamenting myself with some Indian paint, made our young folks take me for Captain Bridger's half-breed son. I paid for my frolic rather dearly, as it took no little time and trouble to get the paint off. While here, also, an old mountaineer named Bill Williams came to us to buy a rifle. He examined nearly every rifle in camp. Mine was a good one—the same with which I killed that big buffalo. With him this rifle failed to pass inspection. He declared that the only good piece in our whole company was John Van Gordan's. I told Williams that the latter was an

---

13 Reed and Donner undoubtedly did deliberate about the route with the Harlans and others at some point; many years later Harlan may have confused such a discussion with a similar one at Fort Bridger, thus accounting for his peculiar notion that the Donner party was there at the same time he was.

unlucky gun, and that with it John had shot and nearly killed my cousin, and also had clipped a piece off the ear of another of our company, and that if he bought it he would get killed with it. He said to me: "See here, young man, I have hunted and trapped in these mountains for sixty years, and you need not think, for all of your buckskin dress, that you can teach me anything about a rifle. Just get back under your wagon and keep on mending your moccasins, and let me alone." So I said no more to him. He then stepped off one hundred and fifty yards, and put up a mark, came back and carefully examined the rifle, and asked John his price. John said $20. Williams paid him that sum, and then heavily loaded the gun to see, as he said, how she would carry for that distance. He aimed at his mark and fired. The rifle burst at the breech. A piece of the barrel ten inches long was split out, the stock torn to pieces. The lock flew across the corral fifty feet, and wounded me slightly on the leg. I ran across the corral and found old Williams lying flat on his back, and with his legs and body full of splinters. I helped him up, and after Bridger had restored him with some whiskey, he cried out that since he had hunted and trapped in the mountains he had been wounded a hundred times, and been struck by lightning twice, and that nothing, not even a — mean rifle, could kill him.[14]

Chapter IX.

Our journey from Fort Bridger to Salt Lake was both difficult and disagreeable, especially when we had to travel through the sage-brush and grease-wood. When we had come to within a half mile of the lake we halted at "Weber cañon," a pass which for about a half mile seemed impracticable. Our four head men[15] held a council. Reid and Donner declared it to be impossible for us to get through. My uncle and old man Pyle felt sure that we could; so there was a split. Reid and Donner turned, and trailed back for three days, and then crossed the mountains. We worked six days building a road, and got through on the seventh day. This put Reid and Donner ten days behind us. If they had helped us we would have got through on the fourth day. We then continued on round the south

---

14 Edwin Bryant recorded the incident on July 19: "Bill Smith, a noted mountain character, in a shooting-match burst his gun, and he was supposed for some time to be dead. He recovered, however, and the first words he uttered upon returning to consciousness were, that 'no d—d gun could kill him.'"

15 Harlan, Pyle, Reed, and Donner. Although writers frequently refer to the "Harlan-Young party," Harlan nowhere mentions Samuel C. Young, nor are the Harlans mentioned in the lengthy "Biographical Obituary: Samuel C. Young," *San Jose Pioneer,* November 9, 1878; reprinted in *Crossroads* 6 (Fall 1995): 9–12.

end of the lake, crossing the river Jordan, a small stream, which runs out of Utah lake into Salt Lake. We passed many beautiful springs, but on trial the water was found to be saltish, and we were distressed by want of good water till we reached a range of mountains, where we laid in a supply of fresh water for the ninety-mile desert. We started on our passage over this desert in the early morning, trailed all day and all night, and all next day and next night, and on the morning of the third day our guide told us that water was still twenty-five miles distant. Our teams were so exhausted that they could not haul the wagons. We had to unyoke them and drive them to the water, then back again to fetch the wagons. William Fowler[16] here lost his seven yoke of oxen. The man who was in charge of them went to sleep, and the cattle turned back and recrossed desert—or perhaps died there. Thus he was left with his two wagons, and no teams to haul them. It was a hard case, as he had a large family with him. He had married my sister, Malinda, after we left Fort Bridger. Then he had his mother, a half brother, and three sisters, one of whom was a Mrs. Hargrave (wife of John Hargrave, who died and was buried here),[17] and her four small children. Also, he had with him two brothers named Musgrave, one of whom was his stepfather.[18] The rest of our company helped him with teams, and he managed to keep with us.

After having passed the desert, we found it necessary to rest our animals for three days, they were so exhausted and spirit-broken. On arriving at the Humboldt river we found that Governor Boggs' party was some seventy miles in advance of us, the Fort Hall route being the better after all. My uncle searched all our wagons, and found that we had not half enough of provisions to take us through. He ordered me to mount my mule, which I had bought with the money earned in hemp-breaking; to take with me Tom Smith;[19] to go on quickly in advance to Sutter's Fort, in California; to get twelve head of Spanish cattle, and a supply of provisions, and to meet him and the party on the east side of the Sierra Nevada. He gave us a little flour and bacon to last till we should overtake Governor Boggs' party, and a letter to Sutter stating the condition of our company.

The Indians on the Humboldt were at this time hostile and very troublesome, killing the emigrants, and stealing their stock whenever they could

---

16 William Fowler captained the company in which the Curtises traveled; see Mc-Dougall, note 2.

17 Hargrave had actually been buried back in Tooele Valley, not at Donner Spring. His widow, Catherine, later married George Harlan, Sr.

18 Despite their misfortune, the family arrived safely at their destination; page 133 of the 1850 Napa County census lists six consecutive households of individuals named Musgrave, Harlin, Hardgrave, and Fowler.

19 Smith was a nephew of Elizabeth Duncan Harlan, George Harlan's wife.

get a chance. We managed to work our way down to the sink of the Humboldt without being attacked. A short time before we intended to camp, Smith having fallen a little behind, ran forward to me and said that some Indians had shot arrows at him. He was much frightened. I made him go back with me, and presently we saw some twenty Indians, who started to run. Tom and I both fired, and brought down two of them. We then rode around a point of willows, and having watched them for a while, we mounted, and after eight or ten miles' travel, we camped, eat our supper, and slept for two or three hours. We were awakened by the snorting of the mules. On the frontier a mule is better than any watch-dog. If an Indian, or a bear, or wolf approaches one's camp, the mule is sure to give the alarm. So we were up in an instant, with our rifles ready. The night was clear and bright, and we could plainly see a party of Indians a short distance off. There were thirty or forty of them, and they had no brush or other means of hiding or lying in ambush. I told my companion to be of good courage, and keep cool, and that we must advance toward the savages and fire upon them. We did so, and shot two more of them. Tom had two pistols, and I had three. These we also fired at them, and they all ran off in a general stampede. From the number of our shots, they doubtless thought that we had been reinforced. We immediately reloaded our arms, saddled up, and went forward. Having travelled about half a mile, we found a board sticking by the side of the trail warning emigrants that the Indians were hostile and dangerous. It stated that on the previous day Governor Boggs' party had a severe fight with the Indians; that one man named Salley was killed in the fight, and Ben Lippincott badly wounded; that they had killed about forty Indians; that the savages fought with poisoned arrows, tipped with the venom of the rattlesnake; that many Indians had concentrated at this point to steal stock, and murder emigrants, and that they had buried Salley in the road, and run the wagons over the grave to conceal it. Notwithstanding these precautions, a few rods past this notice we found poor Salley's body. The savages had found the grave, dug him up, scalped him, and mutilated his body in a cruel manner.[20]

Chapter X.

We had now to begin another desert journey, there being forty miles of desert from the sink of the Humboldt to the Truckee river. We started

---

20 Lienhard found a similar message, but in a note stuck on a bush; he does not mention Sallee's death or his grave; see *From St. Louis to Sutter's Fort,* 144. According to Bryant, Sallee was a member of West's emigrant company; see *What I Saw in California,* 249.

early in the morning and traveled all day. At night we encamped at seven miles distance from the Truckee, at some brackish springs called Steamboat Springs.[21] The grass was fair, and we found some wagons and people of Gov. Boggs's party. One of the men of this party named Savage[22] here lost his wife. She died that night and was buried next morning. Our seven miles hence to the Truckee was very difficult, being all the way through deep sand. About noon we arrived at that river, and there overtook Gov. Boggs's company in camp attending to their wounded. To us, this overtaking our old friends seemed like coming home. We reported to Gov. Boggs the condition of our company and about our difficulties on the Hastings cut off, and also about the secession from us of Reid and Donner at the Weber cañon. Also, we told him of our experience with the savages on our road. He commended us highly, saying that our march down the Humboldt through a country swarming with hostile savages, and our successful encounters with them, were most daring and showed true courage. In fact, he made heroes of us. He examined his wagons and found that he would spare our company 700 pounds of flour and some bacon, which I received, and hired a man named Bonsell[23] to watch these provisions till our party should arrive. I gave him one of my pistols for his protection. He was a giant and as brave as a lion. He guarded these provisions alone for about two weeks, when our party reached him. I also got what I thought was enough flour and bacon to take us to Sutter's Fort, and thanking the Governor for his great kindness we started on our way to that place. When we camped on the second night I found that Tom had lost his bacon, so I had to divide with him, and soon there was none left. For the last three days we had only a little flour and water. When we arrived at Johnson's rancho, forty miles from Sutter's Fort, and heard the cocks crowing, and saw the pastures covered with fat cattle and horses, and with the view of the grand Sacramento valley spread out before us, I was reminded of my dream, which I have described, and of my grandmother's having foretold on her death-bed that I should be cured of my consumption and be a well man. I traded my mule to Johnson for a pinto horse, and got from him some dried

---

21 Harlan has apparently confused Steamboat Springs with Brady's Hot Springs, but the latter is close to twenty miles from the Truckee river.

22 Probably mountain man James D. Savage, whom Lienhard (and others) regarded as a ruffian. Savage is said to have discovered the Yosemite Valley.

23 This is likely the "long-legged" man Lienhard refers to as Bunzel (or Buntsel), who took Hastings Cutoff; see *From St. Louis to Sutter's Fort,* 105, 110. Harlan is evidently mistaken in thinking him a member of Boggs's group. In 1849 Harlan crossed the San Joaquin River at Bonsell's ferry: "In many ways Bonsell was a good man, but he was terrible fellow when hostile. He had just finished hanging six men from the limb of a tree." *California '46 to '88,* 141.

beef, but we found the latter to be so spoiled that notwithstanding our hunger we could not stomach it, and we threw it away.

Having arrived at the Fort, I presented my uncle's letter to Capt. Sutter, and explained to him the condition of our company and what we needed. He said he could not help us with cattle, as he had none of the kind which were suitable. He gave us enough provisions to take us back to our company, and also a letter to Capt. [Theodor] Cordua, who lived where Marysville now is, requesting that gentleman to furnish us with twelve head of cattle, and he (Sutter) would be responsible for them. On our presenting this letter to Cordua, he caused [Michael C.] Nye, his vaquero, to rodeo the cattle and pick us out twelve of his choice oxen; and I have never seen a dozen finer cattle than he chose for us. I afterwards became intimate with Nye. He married a daughter of Mr. Graves.[24] Next morning, when I went to get my horse to take the cattle from the corral and start back with them, I was astounded by Tom Smith's saying to me, "Jake, I am not going back again across those mountains. I can get twenty-five dollars a month to enlist with the recruiting officer, and join Fremont's force and go with him to fight the Spaniards." I asked him what he supposed I could do without his help. He answered with an oath that he did not care what I should do, and that the company might all die before he would go back. For a time his answer stupefied me. I went to Capt. Cordua and told him how my comrade was treating me. Cordua declared that he ought to be shot. I answered that it would not do in this way to give Tom his deserts, as he had in our company a sister and her husband and their two children, and it would bring misery upon them. Cordua then made me turn my horse out, and gave me a fresh horse and two Indians to help me. Cordua was a German, and one of the best and most charitable men that I ever met.

Chapter XI.

On my return eastward over the mountains, I reached Johnson's rancho on the first night, and encamped there. Next day I started early, and drove till dusk, as I wished to tire the cattle so that they would lie down and give me a chance to sleep. They would rest for two or three hours, and then try to go back home to their former range. I did not unsaddle my horse, but lay with my rope in my hand, and slept, as it were, with one eye open. My Indians slept soundly all night. I could then speak no Spanish, and could not give them orders. So they left me to do the greater part of the work.

---

24 Actually, Nye married the widowed Harriet Murphy Pike of the Donner party. He had been a member of the Bidwell-Bartleson party of 1841, the first overland emigrant company to California.

On the third day I met Stanton and Pike [McCutchen][25] of the Reid and Donner party. They were going to Sutter's Fort for provisions, and told me that the Donner party was over one hundred miles behind my company. I told them what a Judas Tom Smith was, and asked them if they were going to return and save the lives of the members of their company as I was doing for mine. Stanton declared that he would do so, or die in the attempt. The poor man kept his word, and died in doing as he had promised. At Bear valley, on the west side of the mountains, we met a part of Governor Boggs' party, and camped with them. I told them of the beautiful land where I had been, and left them next morning full of desire to get there.

Upon the second bench of the mountains, about two miles from this camp, one of my largest steers suddenly became possessed of some evil spirit, and ran back to where we had passed the night. I tried every way to turn him and get him to go up the mountain with the rest, but without success. The parties with whom I had stayed the night previous were still in camp, and told me that if I would kill him they would buy the beef. I did so. The two Indians and I took what meat we needed, and that party paid me $80 for the rest. We crossed the mountain range without much further trouble, and met our company just beginning to come up with their teams so worn out that they could hardly walk. When my uncle saw me coming with such a fine lot of oxen, he ran to me, caught my hands in his, and wept for joy. He assembled the whole company, and told them that they should never forget the service which I had done them, but hold me in gratitude and respect during their whole lives. We yoked the Spanish cattle to the wagons, and got over the mountains with little trouble.

A few miles before we reached Johnson's rancho we met Stanton with two Indians, returning with supplies for the Reid and Donner party, and at night we encamped at that rancho, full of thanks, which we rendered where it was due, for our delivery from desert and mountain, and our happy arrival in our land of promise. The next morning, October 25, 1846, heavy rain fell. This rainfall must have been that, which in the shape of snow, stopped the Donner party on the east side of the Sierra. In the midst of the storm a man appeared riding slowly down the mountain toward our camp. On his reaching us, we recognized James F. Reid. He was nearly worn out with fatigue and suffering. We entertained and restored him as we best could. Reid gave us a full account of what had happened to the party of him and Donner after they left us at Weber cañon. He and Donner deeply regretted their not having stayed with us and helped us to build the road through that pass. He now saw that if they had done so, he and

---

25 Another confusion of Pike and McCutchen; see Thornton, note 26, and Reed, note 6.

their whole party would have been safe through all their difficulties, as we were. He told us that after leaving us they went back some two days' travel, turned to the southwest, and crossed over a low depression in the Wahsatch range. They had a very hard time in getting into Salt Lake valley, which they entered fifty miles south of where we did. In crossing the desert they were obliged to unyoke their cattle, drive them to water, and then return to bring on the wagons as we had done.

Reid's cattle got away like those belonging to Fowler of our company, and he thus lost sixteen head, leaving him with only a cow and a calf. The rest of the party furnished him with teams, and they all succeeded in reaching the Humboldt river. Here they took an inventory of their provisions, and found it necessary to put the whole party on short allowance, which must continue till Stanton could return from Sutter's Fort with supplies. This, together with their other troubles, made every one very irritable. They found the rocky ford of the Humboldt[26] to be so difficult that they were obliged to double the teams in crossing, yoking six oxen to each wagon. Reid was absent hunting game, and Elliott was driving his team. During the work of crossing John Snyder and Elliott were quarrelling, and nearly fighting, when Reid returned from hunting. Snyder was whipping his own team very severely, and Reid remonstrated with him for his cruelty. Snyder answered abusively, and said Reid and he might settle the dispute at once. Reid told him to wait till they got up the hill, but Snyder struck him on the head with the butt end of his oxwhip, and repeated his blows several times, drawing blood. Mrs. Reid ran toward them to stop the trouble, when Snyder struck her also. This so stirred Reid's Scotch-Irish blood, and enraged him so, that drawing his hunting-knife, he gave Snyder a thrust with it. The knife entered Snyder's left breast, cutting two ribs, entering the left lung, and inflicting a mortal wound, of which he died in about fifteen minutes. The whole company were much excited by this occurrence. Some of the members were for lynching Reid, and a wagontongue was put up, and other preparations made to hang him; but finally, after much discussion, it was determined not to hang him, but to make him leave the party without any food. He thereupon took his gray racing mare, bade his family farewell, and overtook us at Johnson's rancho, as I have stated. Reid told us he was bound for Sutter's Fort, and would return at once. He did not do so, however, but went to San José, and returned later.[27]

---

26 This apparent reference to Gravelly Ford as the location of the Reed-Snyder fight suggests that Harlan was familiar with McGlashan's history, though he obviously did not consult it during most of the writing of his memoir.

27 Harlan overlooks Reed and McCutchen's unsuccessful attempt to take supplies to the emigrants before Reed went to San Jose.

Chapter XII.

As to what afterwards happened to this Donner party, my information has been derived from the common report among us emigrants, and from conversations which I have had with many of those who were so fortunate to escape. Stanton got back to them in safety, but the amount of provisions which he was able to convey was soon consumed. The party was camped near a lake which we then knew as "Truckee Lake," but is now known as "Donner Lake." They there built cabins and were all snowed in. Some said that the snow was twenty feet deep. They lived upon their starving cattle until the snow buried them. After this they had no meat, but cooked and ate hides and bones and offal of cattle, whose flesh had been previously consumed. They were suffering all the pains of starvation, and at last the flesh of those who died was eaten by the starving survivors. In that way, only, could they save their lives. Stanton took supplies to them through the deep snow twice. The last time he tried to return with a party of the strongest of those in the Donner camp, and two Indians who had gone over with him, but he became snow-blind and died. The rest followed the two Indians who knew the way. One night the Indians slipped off and left them without other guide than the bloody tracks of the Indians' feet. When the party got out of the snow they overtook the Indians, one of whom was already dead, and the other died within an hour after. This party all escaped except Stanton and one or two others, and the two Indians.

Stanton was a true hero. He endured all these labors and privations, and gave his life in order to aid and save this Donner party, not one member of which was of kin to him.[28]

At last a relief party was sent by Commodore Sloat. There were seven men in this party. I knew most of them personally. There was Moultrey, Glover, the brothers Rhodes [Rhoads], Joe Still [Sel], Ned Copymire, and another whose name I forget [Tucker]. They started from Johnson's rancho, stopping at the snow line to make snow shoes. They then left their mules and all the provisions which they could not carry, and, with what they could carry on their backs, they made the journey of seventy miles over the snow to the Donner camps. The snow upon which they traveled was sometimes over fifteen feet deep. When they came near the camps they cried out to the survivors, and all who were able to move rushed out of the cabins. Moultrey told us that they were in a dreadful condition and reduced almost to skeletons. He said that some wept and others prayed and returned thanks for this partial relief. They told the relief party of their months of suffering,

---

28 Harlan's previous description of his own mission to bring back supplies is perhaps an unconscious attempt to draw a parallel between himself and Stanton,
who has been universally praised for his disinterested heroism.

with death constantly present with them. In some of the cabins the dead were lying unburied, and in many cases the flesh had been cut from them for food.[29] Ten were already dead, and others were in a dying condition and too weak to eat. So it was thought best to take care of those who were still strong enough to be capable of recovery. The relief party had to guard the provisions from the poor starving souls. They distributed the food here and at the Donner family's camp, which was some distance off, retaining barely enough to supply the returning party. They formed this party of about twenty persons, mostly women and children, choosing those who were strong enough to get over the mountains. Many of the weak cried and begged to go also, but it was impossible to take them. Having passed over the mountains they arrived safely at Sutter's Fort. On the west side they met James F. Reid, with fifteen men, going with provisions to relieve those who from necessity had been left in the camps. Reid and his party were delayed for several days by a severe snow storm, and when they reached the camps they found that three more of the sufferers had died.

Chapter XIII.

As I have stated, after Stanton died his party did not all get safely out of the mountains. They had nearly as bad a time a those who staid at the Donner camps. They got lost and were four days without food, and a fierce snow storm came on. They resolved that one of their number must be killed and his flesh used for food to save the lives of the rest. They cast lots to determine which one should be killed, and it fell upon Pat Dolan. He was a great favorite, and when it came to killing him not one of the party could do it. Just then F. W. Graves, who was of the party, became very sick and felt that he was about to die. He had three [two] daughters with him. He called them and the rest of the company to him and told them that after his death they might eat his flesh; that they must do so or they, also, would surely die; that there would be no impropriety in their doing so, as it was justifiable in order to save their lives.[30] Another of them, a young man named Foster, and also Mr. Fosdick, died and were eaten. It was a hard case, and a dreadful thing to think of or to do, but I judge it to be justifiable, as it was their only resource,

---

29 Thornton states that the emigrants had not resorted to cannibalism until after the First Relief left, and Daniel Rhoads confirms this in his 1873 memoir; see Morgan, *Overland in 1846,* 329. Riley Moutrey, Harlan's source, was convinced that the opposite was true; see "A Horror Revived," *Santa Cruz Sentinel,* August 31, 1884.

30 Farnham referred to Graves's behest obliquely in 1856, McGlashan straightforwardly in 1879.

after having eaten their moccasins and every other animal substance that they could find. While in this condition of hunger Mr. Eddy killed a deer, which was at once completely consumed. They again got into a desperate condition of hunger, when of a sudden they came upon Stanton's two Indians, as has been stated, and they got out of the snow and were saved.

A fourth relief party afterward crossed to the Donner camps, and found only L. Keeseburg alive. He has been a noted character in connection with these dreadful disasters and sufferings. He was a German by birth; a strong, good-looking man, about six feet high, and when I knew him in his health he weighed about one hundred and eighty pounds.[31] When this last relief arrived they found a horrible state of things. Bodies and parts of bodies in every condition of mutilation and decay lay scattered about. This party was believed to have gone over the mountains as much for gain as for charity to any who might still be surviving. Donner was reputed to be rich, and to have valuable goods in his wagons, and also a considerable sum of money; and it was known that one Halloran, who died on the desert, had left his money to Donner. This party could find no money in any of the cabins or tents. They concluded that the Donner tents had been robbed. Keeseburg was not at the lake camps when the party arrived; but they found his track leading to the Donner camp, and afterward tracked him back to the lake camp. They tried to force him to tell whether he had taken this money, and if so, what he had done with it. With a rope round his neck, they choked him, and threatened to hang him till he was dead, and at last he confessed that Mrs. Donner had intrusted him with $531 in gold and silver, and had charged him to give it to any of her family who might survive.

Chapter XIV.

I kept a hotel in Calistoga, Cal., in 1871. Keeseburg lived close by.[32] I had become well acquainted with him on the way to California, particularly

---

31 Johann Ludwig Christian Keseberg, a native of Bad Berleburg, Westphalia, Germany, was thirty years old when he and his wife emigrated to the United States in 1844. Keseberg was educated and intelligent but had a dark side, as Harlan and many others indicate. He confessed to Lienhard that he had a violent temper and several Donner party survivors remembered him as a wifebeater; he was tried for assault in 1856 and 1863; and in an incident reported by Virginia Reed Murphy, he struck a little girl who came to play with his daughters, scarring her for life. Keseberg's behavior at Donner Lake was suspicious, but nothing can be proven against him. While he did not deserve the opprobrium heaped upon him by his contemporaries, neither does he deserve admiration. Keseberg is a conundrum, and will likely remain one.

32 He was a partner in Sam Brannan's distillery.

when we were on the "Hastings' Cut-off." At Calistoga we renewed our acquaintance. I saw him, and spoke to him frequently, and had good opportunity to learn whatever he would tell about himself in connection with that Donner camp. He said that when Fallon and his party came to the camp, where he was sole survivor, they treated him from the very first with great cruelty, and as a criminal. Of the whole of that party, Mr. Tucker was the only one who in any way befriended or protected him. He declared to me that the members of this party showed by their actions that they were in pursuit of gain, and had not come from any motive of charity. They obtained many valuable packages of goods from the Donner camp consisting of silks, delaines, and calicoes, besides other things of value. Each man would carry a package a little way, then lay it down, and return for another, and in this way they went over the snow three times. Keeseburg said that in his weak state he could not keep up with them, but generally managed to get to their camp at night. He told me about finding the dead body of his little girl. He was dragging himself along far behind the others, and stopped to rest himself at a place which had been used as a camping-ground by one of the previous relief parties. He had with him some coffee, and having filled his little coffee-pot with snow, he set it on a fire which he had made, and sat waiting for the melted snow to boil. As he sat there he observed a little piece of calico which was uncovered by snow. Half thoughtlessly, partly from idle curiosity, he took hold of the cloth and pulled it. It did not come easily, and he gave it a strong pull. A heavy substance came toward him. It was the dead body of his little girl, who had been taken to cross the mountains by the previous relief party, and had died and been buried in the snow which, having somewhat melted, thus uncovered a part of her dress. This was the first information that he had received of his child's death. His residence in that dreary camp, and the dreadful necessities to which he and others had been reduced, had rendered him callous to death and suffering, but this brought home to him that he was yet a man, and with the affections and weaknesses and responsibilities of a human being.

Another story which he told me was not of so melancholy a character. He said that just as they were getting out of the snow he was sitting alone in camp. All the others were away hunting. He was feeling glad that his escape from his suffering was so near. Of a sudden he was startled by a snuffing, growling noise, and looking around, there was a big grizzly bear within a few feet of him. Keeseburg knew that he was too weak to escape, and so kept perfectly quiet where he sat. He was expecting every moment to be grabbed by the monster, when suddenly there was the sharp report of a rifle and the bear fell dead. Mr. [William M.] Foster, one of the party, had chanced to be returning to camp, and seeing the bear, he had crept up and killed it.

On arriving at Sutter's Fort, some of this party publicly reported Keeseburg had murdered Mrs. Donner. Sutter acted like a friend to him, and advised him to bring an action against them for slander, which he did, against Fallon, Ned Copymire, and some others. The case was tried before Alcalde Sinclair and a jury, and Keeseburg gained the case, the jury giving him the nominal damages of one dollar.

I have never believed, and I have not known any of the old emigrants to believe, the stories which have been told on this subject. For instance, Fallon's story about his finding in Keeseburg's cabin two kettles full of fresh human blood. He did not attempt to prove this at the trial before Alcalde Sinclair, and how could blood have been taken from the poor, starved, dead bodies? Keeseburg had no cause to murder Mrs. Donner. He had enough to eat without killing her. She had been dead for so much time before Fallon arrived that her blood could not have been fresh, but must have already been coagulated and stale, and her body does not appear to have been in any manner mutilated.[33] Keeseburg told me that she never eat of human flesh, but preferred to die of hunger, although he himself, offered her some, and urged her to eat it to save her life. His being forced to disgorge the $531 was the ugliest thing in his whole conduct, but he assured me that Mrs. Donner had intrusted him with that money, and charged him to deliver it to the surviving members of her family. When I knew Keeseburg on the desert, I observed him to be a man, I may say, of much eccentricity. He kept himself greatly to himself, and his unsociable ways made him unpopular with his fellow emigrants. I have thought him to have been predisposed to derangement of mind, and surely his dreadful suffering and experience at the starved camps might have unsettled almost anyone's mind. When I again became intimate with him, in Calistoga, his mind continually dwelt on the occurrences in that camp. In our conversations he would always recur to them.[34] He looked upon himself as a man predestined to misfortune. He would recall the fact that, in his business relations with Sutter, Brannan, Gen. Vallejo and others, no man could question his honesty and integrity.[35] Several times he had acquired a considerable amount of property, but had lost it by no fault or act of his own.

---

33 The reliquefaction of cadaveric blood has been discussed in Thornton, note 113. Contrary to Harlan's statement, Keseberg never denied eating Tamsen Donner's corpse.

34 In 1847 Keseberg had insisted on telling Heinrich Lienhard about the Donner party; see *A Pioneer at Sutter's Fort,* ed. and annotated by Marguerite Eyer Wilbur (Los Angeles: Calafia, 1941), 167–69. Twenty-five years later Keseberg's obsession continued unabated.

35 This may have been true of Keseberg's business relations, but Brannan was known to throw Keseberg's unsavory past up at him in the course of a quarrel; William R. Grimshaw, biographical notes appended to Daniel Rhoads's memoir, Bancroft MS C-D 144.

Once, in Sacramento City, from being rich he was ruined by the great flood, and again, in the same place, he was made a poor man by the fire of 1852, which destroyed nearly the whole of that city.

I have known several men who have become more or less insane from allowing their minds to dwell continually on some one subject—some real or fancied grievance. Such I believe to have been the case with Dr. Powers, whom I will mention hereafter in this book, and I believe that Keeseburg became unsettled in the same way. He said that the treatment which, from the first, he received from Fallon and some of his party made him refuse to tell them anything, till they choked him into it with a rope around his neck. He declared that he would have faithfully executed the trust with which Mrs. Donner encharged him. That he respected her greatly, and never did an evil thing in regard to her. He said she was a true, good woman, and might have got out with one of the first relief parties, but she refused to leave her husband and stayed to die with him. I have never believed in the truth of the terrible charges which were brought against this man, and I know that many of the old emigrants who, perhaps, knew the facts of his case better than myself, would give him the same verdict as myself—*Not guilty.*[36]

Chapter XV.

I have several times mentioned Mr. Pyle as "old man Pyle." He was one of the seniors of our emigrant company.[37] He and his family all arrived in California safely. His daughters were among the young ladies with whom we young men used to dance on the prairies, and who enlivened our otherwise tedious journey. His son, Edward, married one of the daughters of Mr. Graves, whom I have previously mentioned. Edward was an intimate friend of mine. The family settled in San José. One day, in looking for a stray mare, he found her in a corral among some horses belonging to a Mexican known as Mariano; at least, I never knew him by any other name. A son of this Mexican [Antonio Valencia] lassoéd the horse upon which young Pyle was riding, and threw it down, breaking its leg. The father then told his son to also lasso Pyle and kill him, or they would have to pay for the horse. The young man was mounted, and lassoed Pyle by the neck, starting his horse on the gallop, and dragging Pyle for about a mile toward a small creek that runs into the Guadalupe river. While dragging his victim,

---

36 While some "old pioneers" may have believed Keseberg innocent, a large number were quite willing to believe him guilty of just about anything.

37 Edward Gantt Pyle, Sr., was born September 22, 1785, in Virginia. He appears to have been a distant relation of Margret Reed.

he looked back and saw the face distorted and the tongue protruding, which horrified him, but he went on, and threw the body into the dry bed of the creek. Then he went and reported what he had done to his father, who went back with him, taking with them a bow and arrows. When they arrived at the place where the young Mexican had thrown the body, they found Pyle alive and sitting on a heap of drift-wood. He begged for his life, but they barbarously murdered and mutilated him, and shot a number of arrows into his dead body–probably to make it appear that Indians had done the deed.[38] The old Mexican died soon after, and thus escaped earthly punishment. The son ran away to Lower California, but his conscience so troubled him that in a few months he returned and confessed the whole matter. He said that the appearance of his victim's countenance never left him by day or night, and he wished to die. He was condemned in Alcalde Burton's court in San José, and hanged; that being, I believe, the first occasion of the infliction of capital punishment in San José.

Another man with whom I became well acquainted during our troubles in the mountains was John Stark. He went from California over to "starved camp" in the same relief party with McCutcheon and Stone, and the old mountaineer, Greenwood. When they got over to the camp they deliberated whether they should stay with the sufferers till another relief party should come, or take those who were able to travel and convey them across the mountains over the snow. All but Stark agreed on the latter course. He refused, and said that he would not abandon those people; that the rest might go if they liked, but he would stay with them. So he alone remained. To him many owed their lives. I think there was no man then in California who possessed the qualities of intelligence, determination, and at the same time, physical strength and courage in the same degree with John Stark. I believe he was stronger than any two of us, and as the common saying is, "he would do to tie to." What he did was done with so much good humor and willingness that his help was doubly agreeable to those who received it. It was said that in passing over the mountain snows he would carry a great part of the provisions and blankets, and sometimes also some of the weaker children. The latter he would take forward a little way, and return for others. He would cheer and encourage them and the rest, and would laugh and say they were so wasted and light that he believed if there was room on his back he could carry them all. While at the camp young James F. Breen's feet had been both frozen and burned, and he and Jonathan Graves, then little boys, were thus carried by Stark the greater part of the way over the mountains. On arriving at Sutter's Fort a surgeon was sought to amputate James' disabled feet. Fortunately for

---

38 This is one of several versions of Pyle's murder; see also the biographical sketch
    of Mary Ann Graves, above.

him, no doctor was at hand, and nature and youth effected the cure, in which, probably, professional skill would have failed.

Stark was of a Virginia family, which settled in Kentucky in Daniel Boone's time. In fact, I believe one of his family married a near relative of that noted pioneer. The family moved over to Wayne county, Indiana, where John was born in 1817, as was I myself eleven years afterward. Stark was a large, powerful man, weighing some two hundred and twenty pounds. He made his California home in Napa county, of which he was sheriff for several terms, and also represented that county in the state legislature. He died suddenly near Calistoga in 1875 of heart disease. His death was instantaneous, and occurred when he was at work pitching hay from a wagon. He left a large family, most or all of whom yet live in that county. Like Stanton, he was a true hero, and endured all the hardships incident to the rescue of the sufferers at "starved camp" without being connected by any family tie with any of them. In fact, I believe he was not even personally acquainted with any of them until he rendered them that great service.

Probably about twenty members of the Reid and Donner party yet survive. James F. Reid lived in San José, where he was much respected till his death, on Nov 24th, 1874. His wife died at the same place on July 24th, 1861.[39]

In dismissing this matter of the "starved camp" tragedy, I cannot but again advert to the fact that if Reid and Donner had stayed with Mr. Pyle and my uncle, and helped us to make the road through Weber cañon, they would have got through in safety, and both they and we, by arriving at the mountains so many days earlier, would have escaped many other troubles which afflicted us. Hastings was not to blame in this.[40] He told Reid and Donner that he did not know the route which they wished to take, having never been over it. The blunder of all of us lay in our leaving the Fort Hall road, which was a well known and an easier route, and this is an illustration of the truth of the adage,

> "While you have a highway
> never take a bye way,
> E'en tho' it be a nigh way."

---

39 Harlan's version of Starved Camp is much confused when compared with other sources, but the information about Stark and the Reeds is from McGlashan. Harlan has garbled McGlashan's dates, however; Margret Reed died on November 25, 1861, James Reed on July 24, 1874.

40 Except for Thornton, early Donner party sources hardly mention Hastings, let alone blame him. After about 1930 it became fashionable to see the disaster as Hastings's fault; although this oversimplification is untenable, his irresponsible promotion of an untried cutoff was a significant factor in the deaths of more than forty people and in the sufferings of many others.

VIRGINIA REED MURPHY (1833–1921)

On September 13, 1832, Margret Wilson Keyes married Lloyd C. Back-enstoe in Springfield, Illinois. Backenstoe died of cholera the following year, leaving his widow with an infant daughter, Virginia Elizabeth, who had been born on June 28, 1833. Margret Backenstoe married James F. Reed on October 14, 1835. Reed was a kind stepfather who regarded Virginia as his own, never treating her any differently than he did his other children. She went by his name, signing her early letters "Virginia E. B. Reed."

In the spring of 1846 Virginia was twelve, old enough to observe and take part in the events of that year. After the family settled in San Jose, she attended school for a few years, but ran off to marry John M. Murphy on January 26, 1850.[1] John Murphy was active in the early administration of Santa Clara County, serving as treasurer, recorder, and sheriff at various times. He kept a store for some time but later went into the real estate and insurance trades. When her husband became ill, Virginia assisted him with his enterprises, successfully continuing them after his death in 1892. She was the first woman on the Pacific Coast to engage in the fire insurance business. The Murphys had nine children, three of whom died young. Virginia Reed Murphy died in 1921 at the age of eighty-seven.

The Text

Virginia's contributions to the literature of the Donner party are varied. On July 12, at Independence Rock, she wrote a letter describing the journey to a young cousin in Springfield. Ten months later she had quite a tale to tell the folks back home: a second letter, dated May 16, 1847, contains an often misspelled, ungrammatical, but remarkably vivid account of her family's sufferings to which James Reed added his own corrections. A much-edited version of this missive appeared in the *Illinois Journal* under

---

1 John Murphy had been a member of the Townsend-Stephens-Murphy party of 1844, not the Donner party.

the headline "Deeply Interesting Letter" on December 16, 1847. The letter has been published in many forms over the years and is widely available; both it and Virginia's earlier letter are printed in *Overland in 1846*. Her vivacity undimmed by the years, Mrs. Murphy also carried on a voluminous correspondence with C. F. McGlashan.

That same vivacity appears in the following account which was published in the popular *Century Illustrated Magazine* in July 1891, signed "Virginia Reed Murphy." Preserved in the Bancroft Library's McGlashan Collection is an early but undated version of this memoir which relates the journey only as far as Fort Bridger. Expanded and much edited, it became the account published below.

This document is one of the most popular in the Donner canon. Lively, unpretentious, and full of human interest, it tells the story of the Donner party as seen by a young girl, and has the additional virtues of being comprehensive yet relatively brief. Its very readability is a serious drawback to its usefulness as a historical text, however, as this leads one to forget that it is a late memoir, written forty-five years after the event. In addition, its apparent accuracy is deceptive, for some passages indicate that the author has referred to McGlashan's history. This is not to suggest that it is without merit as a historical document, only that it should be used warily. "Across the Plains in the Donner Party" has been published several times, most recently by Outbooks in 1989, but without a critical apparatus.

Virginia Reed Murphy (1833–1921); date of photo, 1880. Courtesy, the Bancroft Library

ACROSS THE PLAINS IN THE
DONNER PARTY (1846)
A PERSONAL NARRATIVE OF THE
OVERLAND TRIP TO CALIFORNIA

I was a child when we started to California, yet I remember the journey well and I have cause to remember it, as our little band of emigrants who drove out of Springfield, Illinois, that spring morning of 1846 have since been known in history as the "Ill-fated Donner party" of "Martyr Pioneers." My father, James F. Reed, was the originator of the party, and the Donner brothers, George and Jacob, who lived just a little way out of Springfield, decided to join him.

All the previous winter we were preparing for the journey—and right here let me say that we suffered vastly more from fear of the Indians before starting than we did on the plains; at least this was my case. In the long winter evenings Grandma [Sarah] Keyes used to tell me Indian stories. She had an aunt who had been taken prisoner by the savages in the early settlement of Virginia and Kentucky and had remained a captive in their hands five years before she made her escape. I was fond of these stories and evening after evening would go into grandma's room, sitting with my back close against the wall so that no warrior could slip behind me with a tomahawk. I would coax her to tell me more about her aunt, and would sit listening to the recital of the fearful deeds of the savages, until it seemed to me that everything in the room, from the high old-fashioned bedposts down even to the shovel and tongs in the chimney corner, was transformed into the dusky tribe in paint and feathers, all ready for the war dance. So when I was told that we were going to California and would have to pass through a region peopled by Indians, you can imagine how I felt.

Our wagons, or the "Reed wagons," as they were called, were all made to order and I can say without fear of contradiction that nothing like our family wagon ever started across the plains.[2] It was what might be called a two-story wagon or "Pioneer palace car," attached to a regular immigrant

---

2 Virginia is exaggerating. Several pioneers of 1846 mention wagons with features similar to the Reeds' family wagon.

train. My mother, though a young woman, was not strong and had been in delicate health for many years, yet when sorrows and danger came upon her she was the bravest of the brave. Grandma Keyes, who was seventy-five years of age,[3] was an invalid, confined to her bed. Her sons in Springfield, Gersham and James W. Keyes, tried to dissuade her from the long and fatiguing journey, but in vain; she would not be parted from my mother, who was her only daughter.[4] So the car in which she was to ride was planned to give comfort. The entrance was on the side, like that of an old-fashioned stage coach, and one stepped into a small room, as it were, in the centre of the wagon. At the right and left were spring seats with comfortable high backs, where one could sit and ride with as much ease as on the seats of a Concord coach. In this little room was placed a tiny sheet-iron stove, whose pipe, running through the top of the wagon, was prevented by a circle of tin from setting fire to the canvas cover. A board about a foot wide extended over the wheels on either side the full length of the wagon, thus forming the foundation for a large and roomy second story in which were placed our beds.[5] Under the spring seats were compartments in which were stored many articles useful for the journey, such as a well filled work basket and a full assortment of medicines, with lint and bandages for dressing wounds. Our clothing was packed—not in Saratoga trunks—but in strong canvas bags plainly marked. Some of mama's young friends added a looking-glass, hung directly opposite the door, in order, as they said, that my mother might not forget to keep her good looks, and strange to say, when we had to leave this wagon, standing like a monument on the Salt Lake desert, the glass was still unbroken. I have often thought how pleased the Indians must have been when they found this mirror which gave them back the picture of their own dusky faces.

We had two wagons loaded with provisions. Everything in that line was bought that could be thought of. My father started with supplies enough to last us through the first winter in California, had we made the journey in the usual time of six months. Knowing that books were always scarce in a

---

3 Sources from 1846 invariably give the age as seventy.

4 Edwin Bryant and George McKinstry report that Mrs. Keyes hoped to meet her youngest son on the trail; see Thornton, note 12.

5 In this passage, the basis of the "pioneer palace car" legend, Virginia Reed Murphy does not describe the wagon as large, nor did her sister Patty Reed Lewis in later recollections; see Katherine Wakeman Cooper, "Patty Reed," *Overland Monthly* 69 (June 1917): 518 and Wells, "The Tragedy of Donner Lake," June 13, 1919. The few emigrants who mentioned the wagon remark only on its comforts and conveniences, not its size; see Thornton, note 13, and William M. Boggs's 1884 account.

new country, we also took a good library of standard works.[6] We even took a cooking stove which never had had a fire in it, and was destined never to have, as we cachéd it in the desert. Certainly no family ever started across the plains with more provisions or a better outfit for the journey;[7] and yet we reached California almost destitute and nearly out of clothing.

The family wagon was drawn by four yoke of oxen, large Durham steers at the wheel.[8] The other wagons were drawn by three yoke each. We had saddle horses and cows, and last but not least my pony. He was a beauty and his name was Billy. I can scarcely remember when I was taught to sit on a horse. I only know that when a child of seven I was the proud owner of a pony and used to go riding with papa.[9] That was the chief pleasure to which I looked forward in crossing the plains, to ride my pony every day. But a day came when I had no pony to ride, the poor little fellow gave out. He could not endure the hardships of ceaseless travel. When I was forced to part with him I cried until I was ill, and sat in the back of the wagon watching him become smaller and smaller as we drove on, until I could see him no more.

Never can I forget the morning when we bade farewell to kindred and friends. The Donners were there, having driven in the evening before with their families, so that we might get an early start. Grandma Keyes was carried out of the house and placed in the wagon on a large feather bed, propped up with pillows. Her sons implored her to remain and end her days with them, but she could not be separated from her only daughter. We were surrounded by loved ones, and there stood all my little schoolmates who had come to kiss me good-by. My father with tears in his eyes tried to smile as one friend after another grasped his hand in a last farewell. Mama was overcome with grief. At last we were all in the wagons, the drivers cracked their whips, the oxen moved slowly forward and the long journey had begun.

Could we have looked into the future and have seen the misery before us, these lines would never have been written. But we were full of hope

---

6 The earlier version of the memoir gives a different impression: "a small library of select books."

7 William Boggs concurred: "James F. Reed had the best equipped outfit of any man with a family in the train."

8 Milt Elliott had driven the wheel oxen, Bully and George, while previously employed at Reed's factory. The animals died in July after drinking bad water at the Dry Sandy, to Reed's great regret; he mentions their deaths several times in his writings.

9 Virginia Reed Murphy won prizes for her horsemanship at county fairs; see D. Alexander Brown, "A Girl with the Donner Pass Party," *American History Illustrated* 1 (October 1966): 48.

and did not dream of sorrow. I can now see our little caravan of ten or twelve wagons as we drove out of old Springfield, my little black-eyed sister Patty sitting upon the bed, holding up the wagon cover so that Grandma might have a last look at her old home.

That was the 14th day of April, 1846. Our party numbered thirty-one, and consisted chiefly of three families, the other members being young men, some of whom came as drivers. The Donner family were George and Tamsen Donner and their five children, and Jacob and Elizabeth Donner and their seven children. Our family numbered nine, not counting three drivers—my father and mother, James Frazier and Margaret W. Reed, Grandma Keyes, my little sister Patty (now Mrs. Frank Lewis, of Capitola), and two little brothers, James F. Reed, Jr., and Thomas K. Reed, Eliza Williams and her brother Baylis, and lastly myself. Eliza had been a domestic in our family for many years, and was anxious to see California.

Many friends camped with us the first night out and my uncles traveled on for several days before bidding us a final farewell. It seemed strange to be riding in ox-teams, and we children were afraid of the oxen, thinking they could go wherever they pleased as they had no bridles. Milt Elliott, a knight of the whip, drove our family wagon. He had worked for years in my father's large saw-mill on the Sangamon River. The first bridge we came to, Milt had to stop the wagon and let us out. I remember that I called to him to be sure to make the oxen hit the bridge, and not to forget that grandma was in the wagon. How he laughed at the idea of the oxen missing the bridge! I soon found that Milt, with his "whoa," "haw," and "gee," could make the oxen do just as he pleased.

Nothing of much interest happened until we reached what is now Kansas. The first Indians we met were the Caws, who kept the ferry, and had to take us over the Caw river. I watched them closely, hardly daring to draw my breath, and feeling sure they would sink the boat in the middle of the stream, and was very thankful when I found they were not like grandma's Indians. Every morning, when the wagons were ready to start, papa and I would jump on our horses, and go ahead to pick out a camping-ground. In our party were many who rode on horseback, but mama seldom did; she preferred the wagon, and did not like to leave grandma, although Patty took upon herself this charge, and could hardly be persuaded to leave grandma's side. Our little home was so comfortable, that mama could sit reading and chatting with the little ones, and almost forget that she was really crossing the plains.

Grandma Keyes improved in health and spirits every day until we came to the Big Blue River, which was so swollen that we could not cross, but had to lie by and make rafts on which to take the wagons over. As soon as we stopped traveling grandma began to fail, and on the 29th day of May she died. It seemed hard to bury her in the wilderness, and travel on, and we were afraid that the Indians would destroy her grave, but her death here, before our troubles began, was providential, and nowhere on the whole road could we have found so beautiful a resting place. By this time many emigrants had joined our company, and all turned out to assist at the funeral. A coffin was hewn out of a cottonwood tree, and John Denton, a young man from Springfield, found a large gray stone on which he carved with deep letters the name of "Sarah Keyes; born in Virginia," giving age and date of birth. She was buried under the shade of an oak, the slab being placed at the foot of the grave, on which were planted wild flowers growing in the sod.[10] A minister in our party, the Rev. J. A. Cornwall, tried to give words of comfort as we stood about this lonely grave. Strange to say, that grave has never been disturbed; the wilderness blossomed into the city of Manhattan, Kansas, and we have been told that the city cemetery surrounds the grave of Sarah Keyes.[11]

As the river remained high and there was no prospect of fording it, the men went to work cutting down trees, hollowing out logs and making rafts on which to take the wagons over. These logs, about twenty-five feet in length, were united by cross timbers, forming rafts, which were firmly lashed to stakes driven into the bank. Ropes were attached to both ends, by which the rafts were pulled back and forth across the river. The banks of this stream being steep, our heavily laden wagons had to be let down carefully with ropes, so that the wheels might run into the hollowed logs. This was no easy task when you take into consideration that in these wagons were women and children, who could cross the rapid river in no other way. Finally the dangerous work was accomplished and we resumed our journey.

The road at first was rough and led through a timbered country, but after striking the great valley of the Platte the road was good and the

10 On July 12, at Independence Rock, Virginia described her grandmother's death in a letter to to a cousin back in Springfield: "she became spechless the day before she died. We buried her verry decent We made a nete coffin and buried her under a tree we had a head stone and had her name cutonit and the date and yere verry nice, and at the head of the grave was a tree we cut some letters on it the young men soded it all ofer and put Flores on it We miss her verry much every time we come into the Wagon we look at the bed for her." Morgan, *Overland in 1846,* 278.

11 In 1868 Reed and his brother-in-law James W. Keyes visited Kansas in an attempt to locate Mrs. Keyes's grave, intending to have the remains reinterred elsewhere. The grave was near the confluence of the Big and Little Blue rivers, close to present-day Marysville, but Reed mistakenly believed that the burial was at the confluence of the Big Blue and Kansas rivers, some forty miles to the south near the town of Manhattan. See Wm. H. Van Doren, "That Old Grave," *Blue Rapids Times* (Blue Rapids, Kansas), August 15, 1895. I am indebted to Alan Feldhausen for this reference.

country beautiful. Stretching out before us as far as the eye could reach was a valley as green as emerald, dotted here and there with flowers of every imaginable color, and through this valley flowed the grand old Platte, a wide, rapid, shallow stream. Our company now numbered about forty wagons, and, for a time, we were commanded by Col. William H. Russell, then by George Donner. Exercise in the open air under bright skies, and freedom from peril combined to make this part of our journey an ideal pleasure trip. How I enjoyed riding my pony, galloping over the plain, gathering wild flowers! At night the young folks would gather about the camp fire chatting merrily, and often a song would be heard, or some clever dancer would give us a barn-door jig on the hind gate of a wagon.

Traveling up the smooth valley of the Platte, we passed Court House Rock, Chimney Rock and Scott's Bluffs, and made from fifteen to twenty miles a day, shortening or lengthening the distance in order to secure a good camping ground. At night when we drove into camp, our wagons were placed so as to form a circle or corral, into which our cattle were driven, after grazing, to prevent the Indians from stealing them, the camp-fires and tents being on the outside. There were many expert riflemen in the party and we never lacked for game. The plains were alive with buffalo, and herds could be seen every day coming to the Platte to drink. The meat of the young buffalo is excellent and so is that of the antelope, but the antelope are so fleet of foot it is difficult to get a shot at one. I witnessed many a buffalo hunt and more than once was in the chase close beside my father. A buffalo will not attack one unless wounded. When he sees the hunter he raises his shaggy head, gazes at him for a moment, then turns and runs; but when he is wounded he will face his pursuer. The only danger lay in a stampede, for nothing could withstand the onward rush of these massive creatures, whose tread seemed to shake the prairie.

Antelope and buffalo steaks were the main article on our bill-of-fare for weeks, and no tonic was needed to give zest for the food; our appetites were a marvel. Eliza soon discovered that cooking over a camp fire was far different from cooking on a stove or range, but all hands assisted her. I remember that she had the cream all ready for the churn as we drove into the south fork of the Platte, and while we were fording the grand old stream she went on with her work, and made several pounds of butter. We found no trouble in crossing the Platte, the only danger being in quicksand. The stream being wide, we had to stop the wagon now and then to give the oxen a few moments' rest. At Fort Laramie, two hundred miles farther on, we celebrated the fourth of July in fine style.[12] Camp was

---

12 In her 1846 letter Virginia wrote that the family had spent Independence Day "on plat at Bever crick." The Donner party was a week out from Fort Laramie on July 4; it was the Graves family who spent the holiday at the fort. This passage

pitched earlier than usual and we prepared a grand dinner. Some of my father's friends in Springfield had given him a bottle of good old brandy, which he agreed to drink at a certain hour of this day looking to the east, while his friends in Illinois were to drink a toast to his success from a companion bottle with their faces turned west, the difference in time being carefully estimated; and at the hour agreed upon, the health of our friends in Springfield was drunk with great enthusiasm.[13] At Fort Laramie was a party of Sioux, who were on the war path going to fight the Crows or Blackfeet. The Sioux are fine looking Indians and I was not in the least afraid of them. They fell in love with my pony and set about bargaining to buy him. They brought buffalo robes and beautifully tanned buckskin, pretty beaded moccasins, and ropes made of grass, and placing these articles in a heap alongside several of their ponies, they made my father understand by signs that they would give them all for Billy and his rider.[14] Papa smiled and shook his head; then the number of ponies was increased and, as a last tempting inducement, they brought an old coat, that had been worn by some poor soldier, thinking my father could not withstand the brass buttons!

On the sixth of July we were again on the march. The Sioux were several days in passing our caravan, not on account of the length of our train, but because there were so many Sioux. Owing to the fact that our wagons were strung so far apart, they could have massacred our whole party without much loss to themselves. Some of our company became alarmed, and the rifles were cleaned out and loaded, to let the warriors see that we were prepared to fight; but the Sioux never showed any inclination to disturb us. Their curiosity was annoying, however, and our wagon with its conspicuous stove-pipe and looking-glass attracted their attention. They were continually swarming about trying to get a look at themselves in the mirror, and their desire to possess my pony was so strong that at last I had to ride in the wagon and let one of the drivers take charge of Billy. This I did not like, and in order to see how far back the line of warriors extended, I picked up a large field-glass which hung on a rack, and as I pulled it out with a click, the warriors jumped back, wheeled their ponies and scattered. This pleased me greatly, and I told my mother I could fight the whole

---

demonstrates that the author must have referred to McGlashan, who used W. C. Graves's description of the celebration.

13 Virginia described the incident in 1846: "severel of the gentemen in Springfield gave paw a botel of licker and said it shouden be opend till the 4 day of July and paw was to look to the east and drink it and they was to look to the West an drink it at 12 o clock paw treted the compiany and we all had some lemminade."

14 As mentioned in Farnham, note 3, accounts of Indian attempts to buy white girls appear to be apocryphal.

Sioux tribe with a spy-glass, and as revenge for forcing me to ride in the wagon, whenever they came near trying to get a peep at their war-paint and feathers, I would raise the glass and laugh to see them dart away in terror.[15]

A new route had just been opened by Lansford W. Hastings, called the "Hastings Cut-off," which passed along the southern shore of the Great Salt Lake rejoining the old "Fort Hall Emigrant" road on the Humboldt. It was said to shorten the distance three hundred miles. Much time was lost in debating which course to pursue; Bridger and Vasques, who were in charge of the fort, sounded the praises of the new road. My father was so eager to reach California that he was quick to take advantage of any means to shorten the distance, and we were assured by Hastings and his party that the only bad part was the forty-mile drive through the desert by the shore of the lake. None of our party knew then, as we learned afterwards, that these men had an interest in the road, being employed by Hastings.[16] But for the advice of these parties we should have continued on the old Fort Hall road. Our company had increased in numbers all along the line, and was now composed of some of the very best people and some of the worst.[17] The greater portion of our company went by the old road and reached California in safety. Eighty-seven persons took the "Hastings Cut-off," including the Donners, Breens, Reeds, Murphys (not the Murphys of Santa Clara County), C. T. Stanton, John Denton, Wm. McClutchen [sic], Wm. Eddy, Louis Keseburg, and many others too numerous to mention in a short article like this. And these are the unfortunates who have since been known as the "Donner Party."

On the morning of July 31[18] we parted with our traveling companions, some of whom had become very dear friends, and, without suspicion of impending disaster, set off in high spirits on the "Hastings Cut-off"; but a few days showed us that the road was not as it had been represented. We were seven days in reaching Weber Cañon, and Hastings, who was guiding a party in advance of our train, left a note by the wayside warning us that the road through Weber Cañon was impassable and advising us to select a road over the mountains, the outline of which he attempted to give on paper. These directions were so vague that C. T. Stanton, William

---

15 Patty Reed Lewis describes her father frightening the Indians off with the telescope; see Wells, "The Tragedy of Donner Lake," June 18, 1919.

16 As W. C. Graves heard it, Hastings was in the pay of Bridger and Vasquez.

17 This sentence echoes a line from a letter by Tamsen Donner, published by McGlashan.

18 The emigrant companies had separated ten days earlier, but the Donner party did set out on the cutoff on July 31, the day they left Fort Bridger.

Pike,[19] and my father rode on in advance and overtook Hastings and tried to induce him to return and guide our party. He refused, but came back over a portion of the road, and from a high mountain endeavored to point out the general course. Over this road my father traveled alone, taking notes, and blazing trees, to assist him in retracing his course, and reaching camp after an absence of four days.[20] Learning of the hardships of the advance train, the party decided to cross towards the lake. Only those who have passed through this country on horseback can appreciate the situation. There was absolutely no road, not even a trail. The cañon wound around among the hills. Heavy underbrush had to be cut away and used for making a road bed. While cutting our way step by step through the "Hastings Cut-off," we were overtaken and joined by the Graves family, consisting of W. F. Graves, his wife and eight children, his son-in-law Jay Fosdick, and a young man by the name of John Snyder. Finally we reached the end of the cañon where it looked as though our wagons would have to be abandoned. It seemed impossible for the oxen to pull them up the steep hill [Donner Hill] and the bluffs beyond, but we doubled teams and the work was, at last, accomplished, almost every yoke in the train being required to pull up each wagon. While in this cañon Stanton and Pike came into camp; they had suffered greatly on account of the exhaustion of their horses and had come near perishing. Worn with travel and greatly discouraged we reached the shore of the Great Salt Lake. It had taken an entire month, instead of a week, and our cattle were not fit to cross the desert.

We were now encamped in a valley [Tooele Valley] called "Twenty Wells." The water in these wells was pure and cold, welcome enough after the alkaline pools from which we had been forced to drink. We prepared for the long drive across the desert and laid in, as we supposed, an ample supply of water and grass. This desert had been represented to us as only forty miles wide but we found it nearer eighty. It was a dreary, desolate, alkali waste; not a living thing could be seen; it seemed as though the hand of death had been laid upon the country. We started in the evening, traveled all that night, and the following day and night—two nights and one day of suffering from thirst and heat by day and piercing cold by night. When

---

19 Here Virginia has Pike as the third member of this party, not McCutchen, agreeing with the accounts of Thornton and McGlashan but not her father's published memoir.

20 Some details of the foregoing passage agree with Reed's diary—setting out on the cutoff on July 31, seven days' travel to reach the Weber, and Reed's absence of four days—but they either contradict or are absent from Thornton and McGlashan. Murphy does not appear to have used the diary for other dates, however.

the third night fell and we saw the barren waste stretching away apparently as boundless as when we started, my father determined to go ahead in search of water. Before starting he instructed the drivers, if the cattle showed signs of giving out to take them from the wagons and follow him. He had not been gone long before the oxen began to fall to the ground from thirst and exhaustion. They were unhitched at once and driven ahead. My father coming back met the drivers with the cattle within ten miles of water and instructed them to return as soon as the animals had satisfied their thirst. He reached us about daylight. We waited all that day in the desert looking for the return of our drivers, the other wagons going on out of sight. Towards night the situation became desperate and we had only a few drops of water left; another night there meant death. We must set out on foot and try to reach some of the wagons. Can I ever forget that night in the desert, when we walked mile after mile in the darkness, every step seeming to be the very last we could take! Suddenly all fatigue was banished by fear; through the night came a swift rushing sound of one of the young steers crazed by thirst and apparently bent upon our destruction. My father, holding his youngest child in his arms and keeping us all close behind him, drew his pistol, but finally the maddened beast turned and dashed off into the darkness. Dragging ourselves along about ten miles, we reached the wagon of Jacob Donner. The family were all asleep, so we children lay down on the ground. A bitter wind swept over the desert, chilling us through and through.[21] We crept closer together, and, when we complained of the cold, papa placed all five of our dogs around us, and only for the warmth of these faithful creatures we should doubtless have perished.[22]

At daylight papa was off to learn the fate of his cattle, and was told that all were lost, except one cow and an ox. The stock, scenting the water, had rushed on ahead of the men, and had probably been stolen by the Indians, and driven into the mountains, where traces of them were lost. A week was spent here on the edge of the desert in a fruitless search. Almost every man in the company turned out, hunting in all directions, but our eighteen head of cattle were never found. We had lost our best yoke of oxen before reaching Bridger's Fort from drinking poisoned water found standing in pools, and had bought at the fort two yoke of young steers, but now all were gone, and my father and his family were left in the desert,

---

21 The incidents are strikingly similar to Reed's 1871 memoir but are given in a different order. Virginia's letter of May 16, 1847, relates very similar details of the Salt Desert crossing but omits the incident of the thirst-maddened ox; see Morgan, *Overland in 1846*, 281–82.

22 In editing Virginia's 1847 letter Reed recorded the dogs' names for posterity: Tyler, Barney, Trailer, Tracker, and Cash.

eight hundred miles from California, seemingly helpless. We realized that our wagons must be abandoned. The company kindly let us have two yoke of oxen, so with our ox and cow yoked together we could bring one wagon, but, alas! not the one which seemed so much like a home to us, and in which grandma had died.[23] Some of the company went back with papa and assisted him in cacheing everything that could not be packed in one wagon. A cache was made by digging a hole in the ground, in which a box or the bed of a wagon was placed. Articles to be buried were packed into this box, covered with boards, and the earth thrown in upon them, and thus they were hidden from sight.[24] Our provisions were divided among the company. Before leaving the desert camp, an inventory of provisions on hand was taken, and it was found that the supply was not sufficient to last us through to California, and as if to render the situation more terrible, a storm was came on during the night and the hill-tops became white with snow. Some one must go on to Sutter's Fort after provisions. A call was made for volunteers. C. T. Stanton and Wm. McClutchen bravely offered their services and started on bearing letters from the company to Captain Sutter asking for relief. We resumed our journey and soon reached Gravelly Ford on the Humboldt.[25]

I now come to that part of my narrative which delicacy of feeling for both the dead and the living would induce me to pass over in silence, but which a correct and lucid chronicle of subsequent events of historical importance will not suffer to be omitted. On the 5th day of October, 1846, at Gravelly Ford, a tragedy was enacted which affected the subsequent lives and fortunes of more than one member of our company. At this point in our journey we were compelled to double our teams in order to ascend a steep, sandy hill. Milton Elliott, who was driving our wagon, and John Snyder, who was driving one of Mr. Graves's became involved in a quarrel over the management of their oxen. Snyder was beating his cattle over the head with the butt end of his whip, when my father, returning on horse-back from a

---

23 Reed's diary entry for September 9, 1846, and his 1871 memoir state that the family wagon had been salvaged from the Salt Desert, yet Virginia was convinced that it had been abandoned there. It is difficult to reconcile these contradictions, but Reed's contemporary testimony gives him the advantage. If he is correct, the "palace car" was abandoned twice—once, temporarily, on the Salt Desert, and again, permanently, along the Humboldt. It seems likely that Murphy confused the memory of the first, presumably more traumatic, abandoning with the later one.

24 As previously stated (Thornton, note 41), it is unlikely that the emigrants would have taken the time for such elaborate precautions, which the thick mud would have hampered considerably.

25 The reference to Gravelly Ford as the site of Snyder's death is another indication that the author resorted to McGlashan's history; see Thornton, note 48, above.

hunting trip, arrived, and, appreciating the great importance of saving the remainder of the oxen, remonstrated with Snyder, telling him that they were our main dependance[26] and at the same time offering the assistance of our team. Snyder having taken offense at something Elliott had said declared that his team could pull up alone, and kept on using abusive language. Father tried to quiet the enraged man. Hard words followed. Then my father said: "We can settle this, John, when we get up the hill." "No," replied Snyder with an oath, "we will settle it now," and springing upon the tongue of a wagon, he struck my father a violent blow over the head with his heavy whip-stock. One blow followed another. Father was stunned for a moment and blinded by the blood streaming from the gashes in his head. Another blow was descending when my mother ran in between the men. Father saw the uplifted whip, but had only time to cry: "John, John," when down came the stroke upon mother. Quick as a thought my father's hunting knife was out and Snyder fell, fatally wounded. He was caught in the arms of W. C. Graves, carried up the hill-side, and laid on the ground.[27] My father regretted the act, and dashing the blood from his eyes went quickly to the assistance of the dying man. I can see him now, as he knelt over Snyder, trying to stanch the wound, while the blood from the gashes in his own head, trickling down his face, mingled with that of the dying man. In a few moments Snyder expired. Camp was pitched immediately, our wagon being some distance from the others. My father, anxious to do what he could for the dead, offered the boards of our wagon, from which to make a coffin. Then, coming to me, he said: "Daughter, do you think you can dress these wounds in my head? Your mother is not able, and they must be attended to." I answered by saying: "Yes, if you will tell me what to do." I brought a basin of water and sponge, and we went into the wagon, so that we might not be disturbed. When my work was at last finished, I burst out crying. Papa clasped me in his arms, saying: "I should not have asked so much of you," and talked to me until I controlled my feelings, so that we could go to the tent where mama was lying.

We then learned that trouble was brewing in the camp where Snyder's body lay. At the funeral my father stood sorrowfully by until the last clod

---

26 Interestingly, Virginia Reed Murphy describes Reed's reaction as pragmatic, while her sister saw it as affectionate. A late account derived from the testimony of Patty Reed Lewis stresses Reed's love of animals, which caused "the tragedy of his life, for he had never been able to see an animal abused." Wells, "The Tragedy of Donner Lake," June 13, 1919; see also the installments of June 20 and 23. Reed's frequent references to animals by name certainly suggest concern for them.

27 This reference is another sign of McGlashan's influence; in an early letter to the historian, Mrs. Murphy wrote that she did not remember W. C. Graves.

was placed upon the grave. He and John Snyder had been good friends, and no one could have regretted the taking of that young life more than my father.

The members of the Donner party then held a council to decide upon the fate of my father while we anxiously awaited the verdict. They refused to accept the plea of self-defense and decided that my father should be banished from the company and sent into the wilderness alone. It was a cruel sentence. And all this animosity towards my father was caused by Louis Keseburg, a German who had joined our company away back on the plains. Keseburg was married to a young and pretty German girl, and used to abuse her, and was in the habit of beating her till she was black and blue. This aroused all the manhood in my father and he took Keseburg to task—telling him it must stop or measures would be taken to that effect. Keseburg did not dare to strike his wife again, but he hated my father and nursed his wrath until papa was so unfortunate as to have to take the life of a fellow-creature in self-defense. Then Keseburg's hour for revenge had come. But how a man like Keseburg, brutal and overbearing by nature, although highly educated, could have such influence over the company is more than I can tell. I have thought the subject over for hours but failed to arrive at a conclusion. The feeling against my father at one time was so strong that lynching was proposed. He was no coward and he bared his neck, saying, "Come on, gentlemen," but no one moved. It was thought more humane, perhaps, to send him into the wilderness to die of slow starvation or be murdered by the Indians; but my father did not die. God took care of him and his family, and at Donner Lake we seemed especially favored by the Almighty as not one of our family perished, and we were the only family no one member of which was forced to eat of human flesh to keep body and soul together. When the sentence of banishment was communicated to my father, he refused to go, feeling that he was justified before God and man, as he had only acted in self-defense.

Then came a sacrifice on the part of my mother. Knowing only too well what her life would be without him, yet fearful that if he remained he would meet with violence at the hands of his enemies, she implored him to go, but all to no avail until she urged him to remember the destitution of the company, saying that if he remained and escaped violence at their hands, he might nevertheless see his children starving and be helpless to aid them, while if he went on he could return and meet them with food. It was a fearful struggle; at last he consented, but not before he had secured a promise from the company to care for his wife and little ones.

My father was sent out into the unknown country without provisions or arms—even his horse was at first denied him. When we learned of this decision, I followed him through the darkness, taking Elliott with me, and carried him his rifle, pistols, ammunition and some food. I had determined to stay with him, and begged him to let me stay, but he would listen to no argument, saying that it was impossible. Finally, unclasping my arms from around him, he placed me in charge of Elliott, who started back to camp with me—and papa was left alone.[28] I had cried until I had hardly strength to walk, but when we reached camp and I saw the distress of my mother, with the little ones clinging around her and no arm to lean upon, it seemed suddenly to make a woman of me. I realized that I must be strong and help mama bear her sorrows.

We traveled on, but all life seemed to have left the party, and the hours dragged slowly along. Every day we would search for some sign of papa, who would leave a letter by the way-side in the top of a bush or in a split stick, and when he succeeded in killing geese or birds would scatter the feathers about so that we might know that he was not suffering for food. When possible, our fire would always be kindled on the spot where his had been. but a time came when we found no letter, and no trace of him. Had he starved by the way-side, or been murdered by the Indians?

My mother's despair was pitiful. Patty and I thought we would be bereft of her also. But life and energy were again aroused by the danger that her children would starve. It was apparent that the whole company would soon be put on a short allowance of food, and the snow-capped mountains gave an ominous hint of the fate that really befell us in the Sierra. Our wagon was found to be too heavy, and was abandoned with everything we could spare, and the remaining things were packed in part of another wagon.[29] We had two horses left from the wreck, which could hardly drag themselves along, but they managed to carry my two little brothers. The rest of us had to walk, one going beside the horse to hold on my youngest brother who was only two and a half years of age. The Donners were not with us when my father was banished, but were several days in advance of our train. Walter Herron, one of our drivers, who was traveling with the Donners, left the wagons and joined my father.

On the 19th of October,[30] while traveling along the Truckee, our hearts were gladdened by the return of Stanton, with seven mules loaded with provisions. Mr. McClutchen was ill and could not travel, but Captain Sutter

---

28 Eddy had claimed to Thornton that he was the one who took provisions to Reed, but Virginia makes no mention of him. Her courage in this undertaking inspired George Wharton James to write two articles about her. He collected materials for a contemplated biography of Virginia, including a photostatic copy of her famous letter of May 16, 1847—providentially, as it turned out, for the original has since disappeared.

29 In her 1847 letter Virginia says this occurred two or three days after Reed left the company, or about October 8; see Thornton, note 50.

30 The date is from Thornton, repeated by McGlashan.

had sent two of his Indian vaqueros, Luis and Salvador with Stanton. Hungry as we were, Stanton brought us something better than food—news that my father was alive. Stanton had met him not far from Sutter's Fort;[31] he had been three days without food, and his horse was not able to carry him. Stanton had given him a horse and some provisions and he had gone on. We now packed what little we had left on one mule and started with Stanton. My mother rode on a mule, carrying Tommy in her lap; Patty and Jim rode behind the two Indians, and I behind Mr. Stanton, and in this way we journeyed on through the rain, looking up with fear towards the mountains, where snow was already falling although it was only the last week in October. Winter had set in a month earlier than usual. All trails and roads were covered; and our only guide was the summit which it seemed we would never reach. Despair drove many nearly frantic. Each family tried to cross the mountains but found it impossible. When it was seen that the wagons could not be dragged through the snow, their goods and provisions were packed on oxen and another start was made, men and women walking in the snow up to their waists, carrying their children in their arms and trying to drive their cattle. The Indians said they could find no road, so a halt was called, and Stanton went ahead with the guides, and came back and reported that we could get across if we kept right on, but that it would be impossible if snow fell. He was in favor of a forced march until the other side of the summit should be reached, but some of our party were so tired and exhausted with the day's labor that they declared they could not take another step; so the few who knew the danger that the night might bring yielded to the man, and we camped within three miles of the summit.

That night came the dreaded snow. Around the camp-fires under the trees great feathery flakes came whirling down. The air was so full of them that one could see objects only a few feet away. The Indians knew we were doomed, and one of them wrapped his blanket about him and stood all night under a tree. We children slept soundly on our cold bed of snow with a soft white mantle falling over us so thickly that every few moments my mother would have to shake the shawl—our only covering—to keep us from being buried alive. In the morning the snow lay deep on mountain and valley. With heavy hearts we turned back to a cabin that had been built by the Murphy-Schallenberger party two years before. We built more cabins and prepared as best we could for the winter. That camp, which proved the camp of death to many in our company, was made on the shore of a lake, since known as "Donner Lake." The Donners were camped in Alder

---

31 George W. Tucker, in an 1879 memoir written for McGlashan, said that his company was at Bear Valley when Stanton came by with the Indians and provisions, the same day that Reed passed, going in the opposite direction.

Creek Valley below the lake, and were, if possible, in a worse condition than ourselves. The snow came on so suddenly that they had no time to build cabins, but hastily put up brush sheds, covering them with pine boughs.

Three double cabins were built at Donner Lake, which were known as the "Breen Cabin," the "Murphy Cabin," and the "Reed-Graves Cabin."[32] The cattle were all killed, and the meat was placed in snow for preservation. My mother had no cattle to kill, but she made arrangements for some, promising to give two for one in California. Stanton and the Indians made their home in my mother's cabin.

Many attempts were made to cross the mountains, but all who tried were driven back by the pitiless storms. Finally a party was organized, since known as the "Forlorn Hope." They made snow-shoes, and fifteen started, ten men and five women, but only seven lived to reach California; eight men perished. They were over a month on the way, and the horrors endured by that Forlorn Hope no pen can describe nor imagination conceive. The noble Stanton was one of the party, and perished the sixth day out, thus sacrificing his life for strangers. I can find no words in which to express a fitting tribute to the memory of Stanton.

The misery endured during those four months at Donner Lake in our little dark cabins under the snow would fill pages and make the coldest heart ache. Christmas was near, but to the starving its memory gave no comfort. It came and passed without observance, but my mother had determined weeks before that her children should have a treat on this one day. She had laid away a few dried apples, some beans, a bit of tripe, and a small piece of bacon.[33] When this hoarded store was brought out, the delight of the little ones knew no bounds. The cooking was watched carefully, and when we sat down to our Christmas dinner mother said, "Children, eat slowly, for this one day you can have all you wish." So bitter was the misery relieved by that one bright day, that I have never since sat down to a Christmas dinner without my thoughts going back to Donner Lake.[34]

The storms would often last ten days at a time, and we would have to cut chips from the logs inside which formed our cabins, in order to start a

---

32 The only double cabin was the Graves-Reed cabin; Keseberg built a shed against the Breen cabin.

33 Lovina Graves also remembered having tripe and beans for Christmas dinner; see her memoir, below. The Murphys had oxtail soup.

34 As might be expected, survivors had strong feelings about food. Several could not abide calves'-foot jelly or similar dishes which reminded them of the gluey boiled hide they ate at Donner Lake. Jacob Donner's son George could never sit down to a large family meal; abundant food reminded him of the days when there was none.

fire. We could scarcely walk, and the men had hardly strength to procure wood. We would drag ourselves through the snow from one cabin to another, and some mornings snow would have to be shoveled out of the fireplace before a fire could be made. Poor little children were crying with hunger, and mothers were crying because they had so little to give their children. We seldom thought of bread, we had been without it so long. Four months of such suffering would fill the bravest hearts with despair.

During the closing days of December, 1846, gold was found in my mother's cabin at Donner Lake by John Denton. I remember the night well. The storm fiends were shrieking in their wild mirth, we were sitting about the fire in our little dark home, busy with our thoughts. Denton with his cane kept knocking pieces off the large rocks used as fire-irons on which to place the wood. Something bright attracted his attention, and picking up pieces of the rock he examined them closely; then turning to my mother he said, "Mrs. Reed, this is gold." My mother replied that she wished it were bread. Denton knocked more chips from the rocks, and he hunted in the ashes for the shining particles until he had gathered about a teaspoonful. This he tied in a small piece of buckskin and placed in his pocket, saying, "If we ever get away from here I am coming back for more." Denton started out with the first relief party but perished on the way, and no one thought of the gold in his pocket.[35] Denton was about thirty years of age; he was born in Sheffield, England, and was a gunsmith and gold-beater by trade. Gold has never been found on the shore of the lake, but a few miles from there in the mountain cañons, from which this rock possibly came, rich mines have been discovered.

Time dragged slowly along till we were no longer on short allowance but were simply starving. My mother determined to make an effort to cross the mountains. She could not see her children die without trying to get them food. It was hard to leave them but she felt that it must be done. She told them she would bring them bread, so they were willing to stay, and with no guide but a compass we started—my mother, Eliza, Milt Elliott and myself. Milt wore snow shoes and we followed in his tracks. We were five days in the mountains; Eliza gave out the first day and had to return, but we kept on and climbed one high mountain after another only to see others higher still ahead. Often I would have to crawl up the mountains, being too tired to walk. The nights were made hideous by the screams of wild beasts heard in the distance. Again, we would be lulled to sleep by the moan of the pine trees, which seemed to sympathize with our loneliness. One morning we awoke to find ourselves in a well of snow. During the

---

35 James F. Reed described Denton's discovery in a letter published in the *Illinois Journal* on July 4, 1849.

night, while in the deep sleep of exhaustion, the heat of the fire had melted the snow and our little camp had gradually sunk many feet below the surface until we were literally buried in a well of snow. The danger was that any attempt to get out might bring an avalanche upon us, but finally steps were carefully made and we reached the surface. My foot was badly frozen, so we were compelled to return, and just in time, for that night a storm came on, the most fearful of the winter, and we should have perished had we not been in the cabins.

We now had nothing to eat but raw hides and they were on the roof of the cabin to keep out the snow; when prepared for cooking and boiled they were simply a pot of glue. When the hides were taken off our cabin and we were left without shelter Mr. Breen gave us a home with his family, and Mrs. Breen prolonged my life by slipping me little bits of meat now and then when she discovered that I could not eat the hide. Death had already claimed many in our party and it seemed as though relief never would reach us. Baylis Williams, who had been in delicate health before we left Springfield, was the first to die; he passed away before starvation had really set in.

I am a Catholic although my parents were not. I often went to the Catholic church before leaving home, but it was at Donner Lake that I made the vow to be a Catholic. The Breens were the only Catholic family in the Donner party and prayers were said aloud regularly in that cabin night and morning. Our only light was from little pine sticks split up like kindling wood and kept constantly on the hearth. I was very fond of kneeling by the side of Mr. Breen and holding these little torches so that he might see to read. One night we had all gone to bed—I was with my mother and the little ones, all huddled together to keep from freezing—but I could not sleep. It was a fearful night and I felt that the hour was not far distant when we would go to sleep—never to wake again in this world. All at once I found myself on my knees with my hands clasped, looking up through the darkness, making a vow that if God would send us relief and let me see my father again I would be a Catholic. That prayer was answered.

On his arrival at Sutter's Fort, my father made known the situation of the emigrants, and Captain Sutter offered at once to do everything possible for their relief. He furnished horses and provisions and my father and Mr. McClutchen started for the mountains, coming as far as possible with horses and then with packs on their backs proceeding on foot; but they were finally compelled to return. Captain Sutter was not surprised at their defeat. He stated that there were no ablebodied men in that vicinity, all having gone down the country with Frémont to fight the Mexicans. He advised my father to go to Yerba Buena, now San Francisco, and make his case known to the naval officer in command. My father was in fact conducting parties there—when the seven members of the Forlorn Hope arrived from across the mountains. Their famished faces told the story. Cattle were killed and men were up all night drying beef and making flour by hand mills, nearly 200 pounds being made in one night, and a party of seven, commanded by Captain Reasen P. Tucker, were sent to our relief by Captain Sutter and the alcalde, Mr. Sinclair. On the evening of February 19th, 1847, they reached our cabins, where all were starving. They shouted to attract attention. Mr. Breen, clambered up the icy steps from our cabin, and soon we heard the blessed words, "Relief, thank God, relief!" There was joy at Donner Lake that night, for we did not know the fate of the Forlorn Hope and we were told that relief parties would come and go until all were across the mountains. But with the joy sorrow was strangely blended. There were tears in other eyes than those of children; strong men sat down and wept. For the dead were lying about on the snow, some even unburied, since the living had not had strength to bury their dead. When Milt Elliott died,—our faithful friend, who seemed so like a brother,—my mother and I dragged him up out of the cabin and covered him with snow. Commencing at his feet, I patted the pure white snow down softly until I reached his face. Poor Milt! it was hard to cover that face from sight forever, for with his death our best friend was gone.

On the 22d of February the first relief started with a party of twenty-three—men, women and children. My mother and her family were among the number. It was a bright, sunny morning and we felt happy, but we had not gone far when Patty and Tommy gave out. They were not able to stand the fatigue and it was not thought safe to allow them to proceed, so Mr. Glover informed mama that they would have to be sent back to the cabins to await the next expedition. What language can express our feelings? My mother said that she would go back with her children—that we would all go back together. This the relief party would not permit, and Mr. Glover promised mama that as soon as they reached Bear Valley he himself would return for her children. Finally my mother, turning to Mr. Glover said, "Are you a Mason?" He replied that he was. "Will you promise me on the word of a Mason that if we do not meet their father you will return and save my children?" He pledged himself that he would. My father was a member of the Mystic Tie and mama had great faith in the word of a Mason. It was a sad parting—a fearful struggle. The men turned aside, not being able to hide their tears. Patty said, "I want to see papa, but I will take good care of Tommy and I do not want you to come back." Mr. Glover returned with the children and, providing them with food, left them in the care of Mr. Breen.

With sorrowful hearts we traveled on, walking through the snow in single file. The men wearing snow-shoes broke the way and we followed in their tracks. At night we lay down on the snow to sleep, to awake to find our clothing all frozen, even to our shoe-strings. At break of day we were again on the road, owing to the fact that we could make better time over the frozen snow. The sunshine, which it would seem would have been welcome, only added to our misery. The dazzling reflection of the snow was very trying to the eyes, while its heat melted our frozen clothing, making them cling to our bodies. My brother was too small to step in the tracks made by the men, and in order to travel he had to place his knee on the little hill of snow after each step and climb over. Mother coaxed him along, telling him that every step he took he was getting nearer papa and nearer something to heat. He was the youngest child that walked over the Sierra Nevada. On our second day's journey John Denton gave out and declared it would be impossible for him to travel, but he begged his companions to continue their journey. A fire was built and he was left lying on a bed of freshly cut pine boughs, peacefully smoking. He looked so comfortable that my little brother wanted to stay with him; but when the second relief party reached him poor Denton was past waking. His last thoughts seemed to have gone back to his childhood's home, as a little poem was found by his side, the pencil apparently just dropped from his hand.

Captain Tucker's party on their way to the cabins had lightened their packs of a sufficient quantity of provisions to supply the sufferers on their way out. But when we reached the place where the cache had been made by hanging the food on a tree, we were horrified to find that wild animals had destroyed it, and again starvation stared us in the face. But my father was hurrying over the mountains, and met us in our hour of need with his hands full of bread. He had expected to meet us on this day, and had stayed up all night baking bread to give us. He brought with him fourteen men. Some of his party were ahead, and when they saw us coming they called out, "Is Mrs. Reed with you? If she is, tell her Mr. Reed is here." We heard the call; mother knelt on the snow, while I tried to run to meet papa.

When my father learned that two of his children were still at the cabins, he hurried on, so fearful was he that they might perish before he reached them. He seemed to fly over the snow, and made in two days the distance we had been five in traveling, and was overjoyed to find Patty and Tommy alive. He reached Donner Lake on the first of March, and what a sight met his gaze! The famished little children and the death-like look of all made his heart ache. He filled Patty's apron with biscuits, which she carried around, giving one to each person. He had soup made for the infirm, and rendered every assistance possible to the sufferers. Leaving them with about seven days' provisions, he started out with a party of seventeen, all that were able to travel. Three of his men were left at the cabins to procure wood and assist the helpless. My father's party (the second relief) had not traveled many miles when a storm broke upon them. With the snow came a perfect hurricane. The crying of half-frozen children, the lamenting of the mothers, and the suffering of the whole party was heart-rending; and above all could be heard the shrieking of the Storm King. One who has never witnessed a blizzard in the Sierra can form no idea of the situation. All night my father and his men worked unceasingly through the raging storm, trying erect shelter for the dying women and children. At times the hurricane would burst forth with such violence that he felt alarmed on account of the tall timber surrounding the camp. The party were destitute of food, all supplies that could be spared having been left with those at the cabins. The relief party had cached provisions on their way over to the cabins, and my father had sent three of the men forward for food before the storm set in; but they could not return. Thus, again, death stared all in the face. At one time the fire was nearly gone; had it been lost, all would have perished. Three days and nights they were exposed to the fury of the elements. Finally my father became snow-blind and could do no more, and he would have died but for the exertions of William McClutchen and Hiram Miller, who worked over him all night. From this time forward, the toil and responsibility rested upon McClutchen and Miller.

The storm at last ceased, and these two determined to set out over the snow and send back relief to those not able to travel. Hiram Miller picked up Tommy and started. Patty thought she could walk, but gradually everything faded from her sight, and she too seemed to be dying. All other sufferings were now forgotten, and everything was done to revive the child. My father found some crumbs in the thumb of his woolen mitten; warming and moistening them between his own lips, he gave them to her and thus saved her life, and afterward she was carried along by different ones in the company. Patty was not alone in her travels. Hidden away in her bosom was a tiny doll, which she had carried day and night through all of our trials. Sitting before a nice, bright fire at Woodworth's Camp, she took dolly out to have a talk, and told her of all her new happiness.[36]

There was untold suffering at that "Starved Camp," as the place has since been called. When my father reached Woodworth's Camp, a third relief started in at once and rescued the living. A fourth relief went on to Donner Lake, as many were still there—and many remain there still, including George Donner and wife, Jacob Donner and wife and four of their children. George Donner had met with an accident which rendered him unable to travel; and his wife would not leave him to die alone. It would take pages to tell of the heroic acts and noble deeds of those who lie sleeping about Donner Lake.

---

36 The doll is currently on display at the Sutter's Fort State Historic Park in Sacramento; a replica is at Donner Memorial State Park in Truckee. *Patty Reed's Doll* (1989), a children's book by Rachel K. Laurgaard, tells the story of the Donner party from the doll's point of view.

Most of the survivors, when brought in from the mountains, were taken by the different relief parties to Sutter's Fort, and the generous hearted captain did everything possible for the sufferers. Out of the eighty-three persons who were snowed in at Donner Lake, forty-two perished, and of the thirty-one emigrants who left Springfield, Illinois, that spring morning, only eighteen lived to reach California. Alcalde Sinclair took my mother and her family to his own home, and we were surrounded with every comfort. Mrs. Sinclair was the dearest of women. Never can I forget their kindness. But our anxiety was not over, for we knew that my father's party had been caught in the storm. I can see my mother now, as she stood leaning against the door for hours at a time, looking towards the mountains. At last my father arrived at Mr. Sinclair's with the little ones, and our family were again united. That day's happiness repaid us for much that we had suffered; and it was spring in California.

Words cannot tell how beautiful the spring appeared to us coming out of the mountains from that long winter at Donner Lake in our little dark cabins under the snow. Before us now lay, in all its beauty, the broad valley of the Sacramento. I remember one day, when traveling down Napa Valley, we stopped at noon to have lunch under the shade of an oak; but I was not hungry; I was too full of the beautiful around me to think of eating. So I wandered off by myself to a lovely little knoll and stood there in a bed of wild flowers, looking up and down the green valley, all dotted with trees. The birds were singing with very joy in the branches over my head, and the blessed sun was smiling down upon all as though in benediction. I drank it in for a moment, and then began kissing my hand and wafting kisses to Heaven in thanksgiving to the Almighty for creating a world so beautiful. I felt so near God at that moment that it seemed to me that I could feel His breath warm on my cheek. By and by I heard papa calling, "Daughter, where are you? Come, child, we are ready to start, and you have had no lunch," I ran and caught him by the hand, saying, "Buy this place, please, and let us make our home here." He stood looking around for a moment, and said, "It *is* a lovely spot," and then we passed on.

Virginia Reed Murphy

San José, Cal.

EDNA MAYBELLE SHERWOOD (1885–1951)

E dna Maybelle Sherwood was born in 1885 in Elk Grove, California, the daughter of Seth P. Sherwood and Mary Anna Cyrus, a daughter of Lovina Graves Cyrus of the Donner party. Edna Sherwood married Theodore Tracey Fairchild in 1911, living for a time in Nevada but moving back to Calistoga by 1919. They had three children. Edna Sherwood Fairchild married Arthur Wing in 1948; she died May 10, 1951, in Larkspur, California.

Edna's grandmother, Lovina Graves Cyrus, was born in Steuben, Indiana, on July 3, 1834. After her rescue from Donner Lake, Lovina was cared for by her older sisters. She and her younger sister Nancy lived for a time with Mary Graves Pyle in San Jose, where they attended school. Lovina also stayed with Sarah Fosdick Ritchie and Eleanor Graves McDonnell, who lived in the Napa Valley (Eleanor moved to nearby Knights Valley, Sonoma County, in 1850). On June 5, 1855, Lovina married John Cyrus, also a veteran of Hastings Cutoff, with whom she had six children. She died in Oakland on July 27, 1906.

The Text

Like her sister Nancy, Lovina was reluctant to talk about the Donner party and did not correspond with C. F. McGlashan, though her brother William and sister Mary did. W. C. Graves consulted her on some of the questions McGlashan posed, but wrote the historian that Lovina was "a little childish" about discussing the tragedy. She later relented and gave her granddaughter a brief account of the Donner party. This story is not a major contribution to the Donner literature, being late and secondhand, but it contains several interesting details.

Edna Sherwood wrote down her grandmother's memoir and sent it to the San Francisco *Chronicle*. The memoir is said to have appeared on the children's page of that newspaper about 1900 but this version has not been located. The memoir was incorporated into a Daughters of the American Revolution publication in 1929, taken from an equally elusive version which appeared in a Calistoga newspaper about 1910. The present account is from the *Weekly Calistogan* of June 14, 1940, and published with the kind permission of editor Pat Hampton. I thank Maxine Durney for bringing the memoir to my attention.

Edna Maybelle Sherwood (1885–
1951); date of photo, circa 1900.
Courtesy, Marilyn Kramer

Lovina Graves Cyrus (1834–
1906); date of photo, circa 1850.
Courtesy, Marilyn Kramer

Tragic Story of the Donner Party

Calistoga, Calif.

Dear Editor—I have finished my story, but perhaps you will not like it. I did the best I could. Grandma told it to me, then I wrote what I could remember of it to suit myself, but she says I did not put in a thing that was not true, and I have left our a great deal that is too sad to tell—the way they suffered and the things they had to eat. I am sure I did not want to. I have tried to write it just as I would tell it, but I am afraid I have made a great many mistakes. If you do not think it is good enough or it is too long, please send it back to me just as it is for I want to keep it. This the first time I ever wrote to any paper like this. But I wrote a composition on California at one time and received a first prize. I remain

> Your Interested Reader,
> E. Maybelle Sherwood

The Story

In the spring of 1846, F. W. Graves sold his home near Lacon, Marshall county, Illinois, to a Mr. Sparr and left with his family for California. His reason for coming was the desire to find a warmer climate. His home in Illinois was a good one, and after it became the property of Mr. Sparr, was laid off into a town, now Sparland.

Mr. Graves was the father of eleven children, two of whom died before they started for California. Grandma was the fifth child. Her name was Lovina. When she left her home she was nearly twelve years old. She now has one brother [W. C. Graves] and one sister [Nancy Graves Williamson] living.

They traveled alone until they reached St. Josephs a town on the Missouri river. All this side of the Missouri river was then Indian country. The families tried to form in companies, so that travel would not be so dangerous. From there they came on in company with other families: The Tuckers and Richies [Ritchies] being among them. Both families now live in Napa county.[1]

The party divided at Fort Bridger, part going to Oregon and the remainder coming to California. It seems the families that started to Oregon again divided, part coming to California, the rest going on to Oregon. In the first division Grandma's people came on toward California and overtook the Donner party about four days travel with heavy wagons from Fort Bridger. The captain of the Donner party was then seeking the new road or shortcut to California, when they overtook heavy wagons from his company. It was not exactly a short-cut they were seeking, but an easier and more pleasant road. Their plan was to avoid the steep and disagreeable Weaver [Weber] canyon.[2] Grandpa Cyrus came to California just a few days ahead of the Donner party, but through the Weaver canyon.[3] He said they had to lift their wagons over boulders and even over fallen trees in coming through the canyon, this road was so rough.

The principal reason the Donner party had such a hard time was because they were taking a new road that had never been used, and they had to cut trees and clear it. Many bridges had to be built. All this, of course, took time. They were delayed for months in making the road. One entire week was spent in camp, the men going ahead building the road and bridges, then returning to the camp at night.

After joining the Donner party, all was trouble. Being so delayed, they were caught in the deep snow at the Sierras and were compelled to camp at a large lake, which is now known as Donner lake. Here they built their cabins and prepared to spend the winter, if necessary, but hoped that the snow would thaw and thus enable them to reach California before spring. Their cabins were built of logs, shed fashion, with oxen hides stretched over them (for they had been compelled to kill their oxen on entering camp, and to salt the meat and pack it in the snow for their winter's use, having no other way to keep it). This made than a passably good shelter. The snow was so deep it more than covered their cabins and the occupants had to cut steps in it to get out and get their wood. They cut the trees off close to the snow. After it thawed, they could see tall stumps from fifteen to

---

1 They were members of the Smith company. Reason P. Tucker and Matthew Dill Ritchie were active in the Donner relief efforts. Lovina's sister, the widowed Sarah Graves Fosdick, married Ritchie's son William in 1848; the name is generally spelled "Ritchie" in early sources, but "Ritchey" is favored by descendants.

2 This is the third statement from a member of the Graves family that they overtook the Donner party while Reed was off seeking Hastings.

3 The Enoch Cyrus family, accompanied by two married daughters and their husbands, seem to have traveled with the Pyles.

twenty feet and higher from the ground. By this, they could see plainly how deep the snow had been during the winter. Five feet of snow fell on Christmas night.

Grandma says she distinctly remembers going with one older brother and sister to the lake to fish. The ice was so thick they had to cut a hole in it about a foot and a half square, through which they dropped their lines, but they could not catch a thing. They could see the fish plainly, but caught nothing. It was very hard for them to go away without any fish for they were very hungry.[4]

They spent Christmas in camp and made an attempt to celebrate it. Being farmers, they had a supply of beans for seed. As their provisions were nearly gone, they used some of these, and with boiled tripe, had a very good dinner. They fared far worse before they reached the level plains of California.

A party of about eighteen strong men and women left the camp soon after the cabins were built to bring aid to their friends. These people suffered very much, and only a few survived to report their condition and send aid to the camp.

During this time those remaining at the camp were suffering for provisions and several died. They were very glad when the relief party reached them. As soon as possible about twenty of the stronger came out of the mountains with the first relief party and met the second relief party going in after the others. Grandma and one brother [William C.] and sister [Eleanor] came out with the first relief party.

This was about February, but her father, two sisters and brother-in-law came out in the first party that left the camp, hunting relief. Her father and brother-in-law died, but both sisters survived.

Her mother and younger brother [Franklin] were in the last party that came out. Both died. Mrs. Graves had with her money they had received for their farm, and when she felt she could not go any farther she hid the money under a big rock near a tree. Several of the party returned to where they had seen her stop, and searched for the money, but they could not find it. It was found several years ago by some men who were prospecting. Grandma has some of it, because it was divided among the children of the Graves family.

There was much suffering in the last party coming out, because a heavy storm came upon them and they had no shelter, therefore several died. The party before did not have such a hard time, although the snow was very deep, and they were often cold and tired because they had to walk.

---

4 The question of why the members of the Donner party failed to catch any fish in the lake has never been resolved, but whatever the problems initially may have been, the emigrants eventually became too weak to make the effort.

The Donner party consisted of (as near as can be stated) ninety persons, of which forty-two died. The remainder reached the level of California, after many days of suffering and almost starvation.

After leaving the mountains, most of the survivors suffered with mountain fever. Johnathan and Elizabeth Graves had it and both died.[5] They were on the American river near Sacramento at the time. Many of the people in the camp died from cold as much as hunger.

After coming out of the mountains, the survivors went all over California, so I will not attempt to follow them any farther.

---

5 In 1875 W. C. Graves told the editor of the *Russian River Flag* that the two youngest Graves children died in the summer of 1847.

Roster of the Donner Party

Members of the Donner party are listed by name, family groups first. The ages given are as of July 31, 1846, the day the emigrants committed themselves to Hastings Cutoff. Ages reckoned from known dates of birth are unmarked; bracketed ages are approximations; questionable approximations are also marked ?; and unknown ages are given as [?]. Survivors' names are in plain text, those who perished in italics; all but those marked * were trapped in the mountains.

Families

Breen

> Patrick, [51]. Taken out by the Second Relief; left at Starved Camp; came in with Stark.
>
> Margaret Bulger, [40]. Taken out by the Second Relief; left at Starved Camp; came in with Stark.
>
> John, 14. Taken out the by the Second Relief; left at Starved Camp; came in with Stark.
>
> Edward, [13]. Rescued by the First Relief.
>
> Patrick, Jr., 9. Taken out by the Second Relief; left at Starved Camp; came in with Stark.
>
> Simon Preston, [8]. Rescued by the First Relief.
>
> James Frederick, [5]. Taken out by the Second Relief; left at Starved Camp; came in with Stark.
>
> Peter, 3. Taken out by the Second Relief; left at Starved Camp; came in with Stark.
>
> Margaret Isabella, [1]. Taken out by the Second Relief; left at Starved Camp; came in with Stark.

Donner

> *George,* [62]. Died at the Alder Creek camp, March 1847.
>
> *Tamsen Eustis Dozier,* 44. Died at the Breen cabin, March 1847.
>
> Elitha Cumi, 14. Rescued by the First Relief.

Leanna Charity, 12. Rescued by the First Relief.
Frances Eustis, 6. Rescued by the Third Relief.
Georgia Ann, 4. Rescued by the Third Relief.
Eliza Poor, 3. Rescued by the Third Relief.

Donner

Jacob, [65]. Died at the Alder Creek camp, December 1846.

Elizabeth Blue Hook, [45]. Died at the Alder Creek camp, March 1847.

George, Jr., [9]. Rescued by the First Relief.

Mary, [7]. Taken out by the Second Relief; left at Starved Camp; came in with Stark.

Isaac, [5]. Taken out by the Second Relief; died at Starved Camp, March 1847.

Samuel, [4]. Died at the Alder Creek camp, March 1847.

Lewis, [3]. Died at the Alder Creek camp, March 1847.

Also Elizabeth Donner's sons by her first husband:

Hook

Solomon Elijah, [14]. Rescued by the Second Relief.

William, [12]. Died after overeating en route with the First Relief, February 1847.

Eddy

William Henry, [28]. Survived the Forlorn Hope.

Eleanor Priscilla, [25]. Died at the Murphy cabin, February 7, 1847.

James, [3]. Died at the Murphy cabin, March 1847.

Margaret, [1]. Died at the Murphy cabin, February 3, 1847.

Graves

Franklin Ward, [57]. Died en route with the Forlorn Hope, December 25, 1847.

Elizabeth Cooper, 45. Taken out by the Second Relief; died at Starved Camp, March, 1847.

Mary Ann, 19. Survived the Forlorn Hope.

William Cooper, 17. Rescued by the First Relief.

Eleanor (Ellen), 14. Rescued by the First Relief.

Lovina, 12. Rescued by the First Relief.

Nancy, 9. Taken out by the Second Relief; left at Starved Camp; came in with Stark.

Jonathan, [7]. Taken out by the Second Relief; left at Starved Camp; came in with Stark.

Franklin Ward, Jr., [5]. Taken out by the Second Relief; died at Starved Camp, March 1847.

Elizabeth [1]. Taken out by the Second Relief; left at Starved Camp; came in with Stark.
Also a daughter and son-in-law:

Fosdick
  Jay, [23]. Died en route with the Forlorn Hope, January 1847.
  Sarah Graves, 21. Survived the Forlorn Hope.

Keseberg
  Johann Ludwig Christian (Louis), 32. Rescued by the Fourth Relief.
  Elisabeth Philippine Zimmerman, 23. Rescued by the First Relief.
  Ada, [3]. Died en route with the First Relief, February 1847.
  Louis, Jr., [1]. Died in Keseberg's lean-to, December 24, 1846.

McCutchen
  *William, [30]. Went ahead to Sutter's Fort for supplies.
  Amanda Henderson, [25]. Survived the Forlorn Hope.
  Harriet, [1?]. Died at the Graves cabin, February 2, 1847.

Murphy
  Levinah W. Jackson, 36. (A widow.) Died at the Murphy cabin, March 1847.
  John Landrum, 16. Died at the Murphy cabin, January 3, 1847.
  Meriam M. (Mary M.), 14. Rescued by the First Relief.
  Lemuel B., 12. Died enroute with the Forlorn Hope, December 1846.
  William Green, 10. Rescued by the First Relief.
  Simon Peter, 8. Rescued by the Third Relief.
  Also Mrs. Murphy's two married daughters and their families:

Foster
  William McFadden, 30. Survived the Forlorn Hope.
  Sarah Ann Charlotte Murphy, 19. Survived the Forlorn Hope
  George, [4?]. Died at Murphy cabin, March 1847.

Pike
  * *William M.,* [25?]. Accidentally killed along the Truckee River, late October 1846.
  Harriet Frances Murphy, 18. Survived the Forlorn Hope.
  Naomi Lavina, 2. Rescued by the First Relief.
  Catherine, [1?]. Died at the Murphy cabin, February 20, 1847.

Reed

> *James Frazier, 45. Banished after killing Snyder; went ahead to Sutter's Fort for supplies.
> Margret Wilson Keyes Backenstoe, 32. Rescued by the First Relief.
> Virginia Elizabeth Backenstoe, 13. Rescued by the First Relief.
> Martha Jane (Patty), 9. Taken out by the First Relief; brought back to the Breen cabin; rescued by the Second Relief.
> James Frazier, Jr., 6. Rescued by the First Relief.
> Thomas Keyes, 4. Taken out by the First Relief; brought back to the Breen cabin; rescued by the Second Relief.

Wolfinger

> *Mr. ——, [?]. Disappeared along the Humboldt River, October 1846; foul play suspected.
> Doris, [20?]. Rescued by the First Relief.

Unmarried Individuals

Antonio, [23?]. Hired on with the Donners at Fort Laramie; died en route with the Forlorn Hope, December 1846.

Burger, Charles (Dutch Charley), [30?]. Teamster for the Donners; died in Keseberg's lean-to, December 29, 1846.

Denton, John, [28?]. From Sheffield, England, traveling with the Donners; died en route with the First Relief, February 1847.

Dolan, Patrick, [35?]. Bachelor, friend of the Breen family; died en route with the Forlorn Hope, December 1846.

Elliott, Milford (Milt), [28]. Teamster for Reed; died at the Murphy cabin, February 9, 1847.

Luis, [?]. One of Sutter's vaqueros; killed en route with the Forlorn Hope, January 1847.

**Halloran, Luke,* [25?]. Traveling with the Donners; died in Utah, September 25, 1846.

**Hardcoop,* ——, [60?]. Belgian, traveling with Keseberg; abandoned in the desert, October 1846.

*Herron, Walter, [27]. Teamster for Reed; went ahead with Reed for supplies.

James, Noah, [20?]. Teamster for the Donners; rescued by the First Relief.

Rheinhard, Joseph, [30?]. Said to be partner of Augustus Spitzer; died at the Alder Creek camp, December 1846.

Salvador, [?]. One of Sutter's vaqueros; killed en route with the Forlorn Hope, January 1847.

Shoemaker, Samuel, [25?]. Teamster for the Donners; died at the Alder Creek camp, December 1846.

Smith, James, [25?]. Teamster for Reed; died at the Alder Creek camp, December 1846.

* Snyder, John, [25?]. Teamster for Graves; killed by Reed in Nevada, October 5, 1846.

Spitzer, Augustus, [30?]. Said to be partner of Joseph Rheinhard; died at the Breen cabin, February 7, 1847.

Stanton, Charles Tyler, 35. Traveling with the Donners; died en route with the Forlorn Hope, December 1846.

Trudeau, Jean Baptiste (Baptiste), [16]. Hired on with the Donners at Fort Bridger; rescued by the Third Relief.

Williams, Baylis, [25?]. Working for Reed; died at the Reed cabin, December 14, 1846.

Williams, Eliza, 31. Baylis's half-sister, working for Reed; rescued by the First Relief.

Traveling with the Reeds was Sarah Hanley Keyes, [70?], Mrs. Reed's mother, who died May 29, 1846, near present-day Marysville, Kansas.

Traveling with the Donners was Hiram Owens Miller, [28], who left on July 2 to join the Bryant-Russell party.

Bibliography

Unpublished Sources

[Covillaud, Mary Murphy]. Letter to relatives, May 25, 1847, Tennessee State Library and Archives, MS 72–29. A version of this letter is published in Steed, *The Donner Party Rescue Site.*

Daughters of the American Revolution, State Committee on Genealogical Research. "Ancestry of Franklin Ward Graves, California Pioneer." In *Unpublished Records of the Families of California Pioneers: Gathered by the Various Chapters from Original Sources in the Years 1925–1926–1927.* Circa 1929. 1:66–76. Family History Library, Salt Lake City, microfilm 844,436.

———. "Franklin Ward Graves, California Pioneer." In *Unpublished Records of the Families of California Pioneers: Gathered by the Various Chapters from Original Sources in the Years 1925–1926–1927.* Circa 1929. 1:77–83. Family History Library, Salt Lake City, microfilm 844,436.

Grimshaw, William Robinson. Biographical notes appended to Daniel Rhoads's memoir, Bancroft MS C-D 144, Bancroft Library, University of California, Berkeley.

Kortum, Karl, comp. The McDonnell Ranch. Unpublished oral history of the Graves family collected in the 1950s, 1960s, and 1970s.

McGlashan, Charles Fayette. Letters and papers, Bancroft MS C-B 570, Bancroft Library, University of California, Berkeley.

Rabbeson, Antonio B. Growth of Towns: Olympia, Tumwater, Portland and San Francisco, Bancroft MS P-B 17, Bancroft Library, University of California, Berkeley.

Rhoads, Daniel. Relief of the Donner Party (1873), Bancroft MS C-D 144, Bancroft Library, University of California, Berkeley. A lengthy excerpt appears in Morgan, *Overland in 1846,* 325–31.

Thornton, J. Quinn. Jessy Quinn Thornton autobiography. Bancroft MS P-A 69, Bancroft Library, University of California, Berkeley.

———. Oregon history: Salem, Ore., and related materials. Bancroft MS P-A 70, Bancroft Library, University of California, Berkeley. Interview with H. H. Bancroft, June 15, 1878; recorded by Amos Bowman.

Anonymous Newspaper Articles

"Another Pioneer Gone." *Weekly Calistogian,* March 15, 1907.

"Astounding Disclosure." *Alta California* (San Francisco), May 10, 1849.

"Biographical Obituary: Samuel C. Young–A Pioneer of 1846–An Enterprising Citizen." *San Jose Pioneer,* November 9, 1878. Reprinted in *Crossroads* 6 (Fall 1995): 9–12.

"California Emigrants." *California Star* (San Francisco), March 22, 1847.

"Carrie Carpenter, Early California Native, Is Dead." *Sacramento Union,* December 25, 1940.

"Correction" *California Star* (San Francisco), June 12, 1847.

"Distressing News." *California Star* (San Francisco), February 13, 1847. Also in Morgan, *Overland in 1846,* 702–5

"The Fate of the Late Emigrants." *Californian* (Monterey), April 24, 1847. Also in Morgan, *Overland in 1846,* 721–22.

"Half a Century Buried. The Lost Treasure of the Donner Lake Party Found at Last." *San Francisco Examiner,* May 24, 1891.

"A Horror Revived." *Santa Cruz Daily Sentinel,* August 31, 1888.

"Later from the California Mountains" *California Star* (San Francisco), March 13, 1847. Also in Morgan, *Overland in 1846,* 707–10.

"A more shocking scene cannot be imagined..." *California Star* (San Francisco), April 10, 1847. Also in Morgan, *Overland in 1846,* 719–20.

"Nicholas Clarke: One of the Rescuers of the Donner Party." *Truckee Republican,* October 24, 1885.

"A Survivor of the Downer Horror of 1846–7." *Russian River Flag* (Healdsburg, CA), December 30, 1875.

"Sutter's Fort is Given Donner Party Papers." *Sacramento Bee,* March 16, 1946.

"A Tale of 1846: The Donner and Reed Expedition Across the Plains." *San Francisco Chronicle,* December 3, 1876.

Books and Articles

Adams, Oscar Fay. *A Dictionary of American Authors.* Boston: Houghton Mifflin, 1904.

Allen, W. W. and R. B. Avery. *California Gold Book: Its Discovery and Discoverers.* San Francisco: Donohue & Henneberry, 1893.

American Authors, 1600–1900: A Biographical Dictionary of American Literature. Edited by Stanley J. Kunitz and Howard Haycraft. New York: H. W. Wilson, 1949.

American Reformers: An H. W. Biographical Dictionary. Edited by Alden Whitman. New York: H. W. Wilson, 1985.

Bagley, Will. "Lansford Warren Hastings: Scoundrel or Visionary?" *Overland Journal* 12 (Spring 1994): 12–26.

Bancroft, Hubert Howe. *Pioneer Register and Index*. Baltimore: Regional Publishing Co., 1964.

Bidwell, John. "Life in California before the Gold Rush." *Century Illustrated Magazine* 41 (1890): 163–92.

"Big Bill and the Donner Ordeal." *McCutchen* 3 (November 1978): 6–9.

Bigler, Henry W. *Bigler's Chronicle of the West*. Edited by Edwin G. Gudde. Berkeley: University of California Press, 1962.

Boggs, Lilburn W. "Emigrants to California." *Oregon Spectator* (Oregon City), July 8, 1847. Reprinted in *Crossroads* 6 (Winter 1995): 6–7.

Boggs, William M. "The Donner Party: Authentic Story of Their Trip Across the Plains." *San Francisco Examiner,* August 25, 1884. Reprinted in *Crossroads* 6 (Winter 1995): 7–9.

Breen, John. Memoir: Letter of November 19, 1877 to H. H. Bancroft. Published as "Memories of a Pioneer," *Pony Express Courier* (January 1941): 3, 7, 13, 16. Also in Stookey, *Fatal Decision,* 176–89; and excerpted in King, *Winter of Entrapment* (1994), 204–10.

[Breen, Patrick.] "Copy of a Journal Kept by a Suffering Emigrant on the California Mountains, from Oct. 31st, 1846, to March 1st, 1847." *California Star* (San Francisco), May 22, 1847.

Breen, Patrick. "Diary of Patrick Breen: One of the Donner Party." Edited by Frederick J. Teggart. *Publications of the Academy of Pacific Coast History* 1:6 (July 1910) 271–84; this version also available as a monograph. Other transcriptions of this diary are published in Stewart, *Ordeal by Hunger,* and Morgan, *Overland in 1846.*

Brown, D. Alexander, "A Girl with the Donner Pass Party," *American History Illustrated* 1 (October 1966); 48.

Browne, J. Ross. "A Dangerous Journey." *Harper's Monthly Magazine* (May 1862): 741–56; (June 1862): 6–19.

Bryant, Edwin. *What I Saw in California*. 1848. Reprint, Lincoln: University of Nebraska Press, 1985.

Burnett, Peter H. *Recollections and Opinions of an Old Pioneer*. New York: D. Appleton, 1880.

California Star, Yerba Buena and San Francisco. Berkeley: Howell-North, 1965.

Camp, Charles L., ed. "William Allen Trubody and the Overland Pioneers." *California Historical Society Quarterly* 16 (June 1937): 122–43.

Chapman, Mabel. "Jake Harlan of San Leandro." *San Leandro Recollections* 5 (September 1973): 1–10.

Cooper, Katherine Wakeman. "Patty Reed." *Overland Monthly* 69 (June 1917): 517–20.

Cordua, Theodor. "The Memoirs of Theodor Cordua." Edited and translated by Edwin G. Gudde. *California Historical Society Quarterly* 12 (December 1933): 279–311.

Cross, Ralph Herbert. *The Early Inns of California, 1844–1869.* San Francisco: L. Kennedy, 1954.

Croy, Homer. *Wheels West.* New York: Hastings House, 1955.

DeLafosse, Peter H., ed. *Trailing the Pioneers: A Guide to Utah's Emigrant Trails, 1829–1869.* Logan: Utah State University Press/Utah Crossroads, Oregon-California Trails Association, 1994.

DeVoto, Bernard. *Year of Decision, 1846.* Boston: Houghton Mifflin, 1943.

Diamond, Jared. "Living Through the Donner Party." *Discover* 13 (March 1992): 100–7.

Dictionary of American Biography. Edited by Allen Johnson & Dumas Malone. New York: Charles Scribner's Sons, 1931.

Duyckinck, Evert A., and George L. Duyckinck. *Cyclopædia of American Literature.* Edited by M. Laird Simons. 1875. Reprint, Detroit: Gale, 1965.

Eberstadt, Edward, ed. *A Transcript of the Fort Sutter Papers, Together with the Historical Commentaries Accompanying Them.* New York: De Vinne Press, 1921.

Eldredge, Zoeth Skinner. *The Beginnings of San Francisco from the Expedition of Anza, 1774 to the City Charter of April 15, 1850: With Biographical and Other Notes,* note 33: The Donner Party, 627–59. San Francisco: Z. S. Eldredge, 1912.

——, ed. *History of California.* Vol. 3: 120–49. New York: Century History Company, 1915.

Ellsworth, Spencer. "The Graves Tragedy." In *Records of Olden Times; or, Fifty Years on the Prairies.* Lacon, IL: Home Journal Steam Printing Establishment, 1880.

Fallon, William O. "Extracts from a Journal Written by a Member of the Party Latest from the California Mountains." *California Star* (San Francisco), May 22, 1847.

Farnham, Eliza W. "Narrative of the Emigration of the Donner Party to California, in 1846." In *California, In-doors and Out.* New York: Dix, Edwards, 1856. Facsimile edition, Nieuwkoop: B. de Graaf, 1972.

Foley, Doris. "Mary Graves, A Heroine of the Donner Party," *Nevada County Historical Society* 8 (July 1954)

Foote, H. S. *Pen Pictures From the Garden of the World, or Santa Clara County, California.* Chicago: Lewis Pub. Co., 1888.

Galloway, Brent. "Editor's Note Number One." *San Leandro Recollections* 5 (September 1973): 15–16.

——. "Editor's Note Number 2." *San Leandro Recollections* 5 (September 1973): 17–20.

——. "Sidelights: The Harlan Party of 1846." *San Leandro Recollections* 5 (September 1973): 11–14

Geiger, Vincent, and Wakeman Bryarly. *Trail to California: The Overland Journal of Vincent Geiger and Wakeman Bryarly.* Edited by David Morris Potter. New Haven: Yale University Press, 1962.

Graves, Mary Ann. "Letter from California." *Illinois Gazette* (Lacon, IL), September 9, 1847.

Graves, William C. "Crossing the Plains in '46." *Russian River Flag* (Healdsburg, CA), April 26, May 3, 10, 17, 1877. Photostat in the Madeleine R. McQuown Papers, Marriott Library, University of Utah.

Graydon, Charles K. *Trail of the First Wagons Over the Sierra Nevada.* 3rd. ed. Tucson: Patrice Press, 1894.

Grayson, Donald K. "Donner Party Deaths: A Demographic Assessment." *Journal of Anthropological Research* 46 (Fall 1990): 223–42.

——. "Historic Archaeology and the Donner Party." In *The Desert's Past: A Natural Prehistory of the Great Basin.* Washington, D.C.: Smithsonian Insititution Press, 1993. 277–96.

——. "Previous Donner Party Research." *Western Journal of Medicine* 161 (July 1994): 92.

Gregson, Eliza. "Mrs. Gregson's 'Memory.'" *California Historical Society Quarterly* 19 (June 1940): 114–30.

Haines, Francis, Sr., "Goldilocks on the Oregon Tail," *Idaho Yesterdays* 9 (Winter 1965–66): 26–30.

Hall, Carroll D., ed. *Donner Miscellany: 41 Diaries and Documents.* San Francisco: Book Club of California, 1947.

Hall, Frederic. *The History of San José and Surroundings, With Biographical Sketches of Early Settlers.* San Francisco: A. L. Bancroft, 1871.

Hancock, Levi. "Sooter's Fort to Salt Lake Valley: The 1847 Trail Journal of Levi Hancock." Transcribed and edited by Robert Hoshide and Will Bagley. *Crossroads* 4 (Winter 1993): 3–9.

Hardesty, Donald L. "The Archaeology of the Donner Party Tragedy." *Nevada Historical Quarterly* 30 (Winter 1987): 246–68.

——. "Donner Party Archaeology." *Overland Journal* 10 (1992): 19–26.

Harlan, Jacob Wright. *California, '46 to '88.* San Francisco: Bancroft, 1888.

Hastings, Lansford W. *Emigrants' Guide, to Oregon and California.* Cincinnati: G. Concklin, 1845. Facsimile reprint, Bedford, MA: Applewood Books, 1994.

Hawkins, Bruce, and David Madsen. *Excavation of the Donner-Reed Wagons: Historic Archaeology Along the Hastings Cutoff.* Salt Lake City: University of Utah Press, 1990.

Heffernan, William Joseph. *Edward M. Kern: The Travels of an Artist-Explorer.* Bakersfield: Kern County Historical Society, 1953.

Herr, Pamela. "Reformer." In Western Writers of America, *The Women Who Made the West*. New York: Avon, 1980.

History of Napa and Lake Counties, California. San Francisco: Slocum, Bowen, & Co., 1881.

History of Santa Clara County, California. San Francisco: Allen, Bowen & Co., 1881.

Hoshide, Robert K. "Salt Desert Trails Revisited." *Crossroads* 5 (Spring 1994): 5–8.

Houghton, Eliza Poor Donner. *The Expedition of the Donner Party and Its Tragic Fate*. Chicago: McClurg, 1911.

Hunt, Rockwell D. "Virginia Reed Murphy: Midnight Heroine." In *Personal Sketches of California Pioneers I Have Known*. Stockton: University of the Pacific, 1962.

James, George Wharton. "A Heroine of Our Own Land." *Ave Maria* 72 (January 7, 14, 21, 28, 1911): 12–15, 42–46, 75–78, 106–8.

——. "The Midnight Heroine of the Plains, Virginia Reed." In *Heroes of California: The Story of the Founders of the Golden State as Narrated by Themselves or Gleaned from Other Sources*. Boston: Little, Brown, 1910.

Johnson, Kristin. "The Pioneer Palace Car: Adventures in Western Myth-making." *Crossroads* 5 (Summer 1994): 5–8.

Johnson, Theodore T. *Sights in the Gold Region*. New York: Baker and Scribner, 1850.

Kelly, Charles. *Salt Desert Trails*. Salt Lake City: Western Printing Company, 1930.

——. *Salt Desert Trails*. Rev. ed. Salt Lake City: Western Epics, 1996.

King, Joseph A. *Winter of Entrapment: A New Look at the Donner Party*. Toronto: P. D. Meany, 1992.

——. *Winter of Entrapment: A New Look at the Donner Party*. Rev. ed. Walnut Creek: K & K, 1994.

Korns, J. Roderic, comp. "West from Fort Bridger." Edited by Dale Morgan. *Utah Historical Quarterly* 19 (1951).

Korns, J. Roderic, comp. *West from Fort Bridger: The Pioneering of Immigrant Trails Across Utah, 1846–1850*. Edited by J. Roderic Korns and Dale Morgan; revised and updated by Will Bagley and Harold Schindler. Logan: Utah State University Press, 1994.

Laurgaard, Rachel K. *Patty Reed's Doll: The Story of the Donner Party*. Fairfield, CA: Tomato Enterprises, 1989.

LeBaron, Gaye. "Sonoma County Home to Several Donner Survivors." *Santa Rosa Press Democrat*, May 23, 1993.

Lienhard, Heinrich. *From St. Louis to Sutter's Fort, 1846*. Translated and edited by Erwin G. and Elisabeth K. Gudde. Norman: University of Oklahoma Press, 1961.

——. *A Pioneer at Sutter's Fort*. Translated, edited, and annotated by Marguerite Eyer Wilbur. Los Angeles: Calafia, 1941.

Markle, John. "Diary of John Markle, Forty-niner." *Donner Trail Rider* 6 (1936): 24: 1; 25: 1, 5; 26: 1, 3, 5.

McCurdy, Stephen A. "Dr. McCurdy Responds." *Western Journal of Medicine* 161 (July 1994): 92.

——. "Epidemiology of Disaster: The Donner Party (1846–1847)." *Western Journal of Medicine* 160 (April 1994): 338–42.

McCutchen, William. "Statement of Wm. McCutchen." *Pacific Rural Press,* April 1, 1871, 195–96

McDougal, Frances H. "The Donner Tragedy: A Thrilling Chapter in Our Pioneer History." *Pacific Rural Press.* January 21, 1871.

——. "The Donner Tragedy Once More: Reply to Mr. Reed." *Pacific Rural Press.* April 29, 1871.

McGlashan, C. F. *History of the Donner Party: A Tragedy of the Sierra.* Rev. ed. Edited by George Henry Hickle and Bliss McGlashan Hinkle. Stanford: Stanford University Press, 1947.

——. *From the Desk of Truckee's C. F. McGlashan.* Edited by M. Nona McGlashan and Betty H. McGlashan. Fresno: Truckee-Donner Historical Society, 1986.

McGlashan, M. Nona. *Give Me a Mountain Meadow: The Life of Charles Fayette McGlashan (1847–1931).* Fresno: Valley Publishers, 1977.

McKinstry, George. Letter of April 29, 1847. *California Star* (San Francisco), May 22, 1847. Also in Morgan, *Overland in 1846,* 722–26.

Menefee, C. A. *Historical and Descriptive Sketch Book of Napa, Sonoma, Lake and Mendocino.* Napa: Reporter Publishing House, 1873.

Merryman, J. H. "Narrative of the Sufferings of a Company of Emigrants in the Mountains of California, in the Winter of '46 and '7, by J. F. Reed, Late of Sangamon County, Illinois." *Illinois Journal* (Springfield), December 9, 1847. Also in Morgan, *Overland in 1846,* 289–301.

Morgan, Dale L., ed. *Overland in 1846: Diaries and Letters of the California-Oregon Trail.* 2 vols. 1963. Reprint: Lincoln: University of Nebraska Press, 1993.

Murphy, Virginia Reed. "Across the Plains in the Donner Party (1846): A Personal Narrative of the Overland Trip to California." *Century Illustrated Magazine* 42 (July 1891): 409–26.

Nugget Editions Club, C. K. McClatchy Senior High School. *Early Day Romances: Sutter's Fort 1847–1848.* Sacramento: Nugget Press, 1943.

Perkins, Elisha Douglass. *Gold Rush Diary, Being the Journal of Elisha Douglass Perkins on the Overland Trail in the Spring and Summer of 1849.* Edited by Thomas D. Clark. Lexington: University of Kentucky Press, 1967.

Pigney, Joseph. *For Fear We Shall Perish: The Story of the Donner Party Disaster.* New York: Dutton, 1961.

Poulsen, Richard C. "The Donner Party: History, Mythology, and the Existential Voice." In *Misbegotten Muses: History and Anti-History.* New York: Peter Lang, 1983.

Power, John Carroll. *History of the Early Settlers of Sangamon County, Illinois: "Centennial Record."* Springfield: E. A. Wilson, 1876.

Ramey, Earl. "The Beginnings of Marysville, Part I." *California Historical Quarterly* 14 (September 1935): 195–229.

Reed, James F. Letter from Fort Bridger, July 31, 1846. Published as "From a California Emigrant" in the *Illinois Journal* (Springfield), November 5, 1846. Also in Morgan, *Overland in 1846,* 279–80.

——. "From California." *Illinois Journal* (Springfield), July 4, 1849.

——. Letter from Napa Valley to Gersham Keyes, July 2, 1847. In Morgan, *Overland in 1846,* 301–5.

——. Miller-Reed diary. In Hall, *Donner Miscellany,* 7–27; Morgan, *Overland in 1846,* 245–68; and excerpted in Korns, *West from Fort Bridger* (1994), 197–239.

——. "The Snow-Bound, Starved Emigrants of 1846." *Pacific Rural Press.* March 25, April 1, 1871. A slightly different version was reprinted in the *San Jose Pioneer,* April 28 and May 5, 1877.

Reed, Virginia. Letter to Mary C. Keyes, July 12, 1846. In Morgan, *Overland in 1846,* 278–79.

——. Letter to Mary C. Keyes, May 16, 1847. Published as "Deeply Interesting Letter." *Illinois Journal* (Springfield), December 16, 1847. Other transcriptions of this letter appear in Stewart, *Ordeal by Hunger,* 277–88; and Morgan, *Overland in 1846,* 278–79.

Sangamon County Genealogical Society. *An Index of Surnames.* Springfield: Sangamon County Genealogical Society, 1980.

——. *Sangamon County, Illinois, Marriage Records, 1821–1840.* Springfield: Sangamon County Genealogical Society, 1987.

Sherman, Edwin A. "An Unpublished Report of the Battle of Santa Clara, Written by John *[sic]* Frazier Reed Using his Saddle Horn as a Desk." *San Francisco Chronicle,* September 4, 1910.

Sherwood, Edna Maybelle. "Tragic Story of the Donner Party." *The Weekly Calistogan,* June 14, 1940.

Shipman, Pat. "Life and Death on the Wagon Trail." *New Scientist* 131 (27 July 1991): 40–42.

Soulé, Frank, John H. Gihon, and James Nisbet. *The Annals of San Francisco.* New York: D. Appleton, 1855.

Spedden, Rush. "The Fearful Long Drive." *Overland Journal* 12 (Summer 1994): 2–16.

——. "The Hastings Cutoff." In *Trailing the Pioneers: A Guide to Utah's Emigrant Trails, 1829–1869.* Edited by Peter H. DeLafosse. Logan: Utah State University Press/Utah Crossroads, California-Oregon Trails Association, 1994.

Stanton, Charles Tyler. Letter to Sidney Stanton, July 12, 1846. In Morgan, *Overland in 1846.*

Steed, Jack. *The Donner Party Rescue Site: Johnson's Ranch on Bear River.* Santa Ana: Graphic, 1993.

Steed, Jack, and Richard Steed. "The Rediscovery of Johnson's Ranch." *Overland Journal* 4 (Winter 1986): 18–32.

Stewart, George R. *Ordeal by Hunger: The Story of the Donner Party.* New York: H. Holt, 1936.

——. *Ordeal by Hunger: The Story of the Donner Party.* New ed., with a supplement and three accounts by survivors. Lincoln: University of Nebraska Press, 1986.

Stookey, Walter M. *Fatal Decision: The Tragic Story of the Donner Party.* Salt Lake City: Deseret Book, 1950.

[Tea, Roy D.] "Floating Island to Donner Spring: Post-Convention Tour." Salt Lake City: Utah Crossroads Chapter, Oregon-California Trails Association, 1994.

——. "Hastings Cutoff Tour: Donner Spring to Big Springs." Salt Lake City: Utah Crossroads Chapter, Oregon-California Trails Association, 1995.

Tea, Roy D., Rush Spedden, and Lyndia Carter. "Hastings Cutoff: The 'Long Drive' across the Great Salt Lake Desert." Salt Lake City: Utah Crossroads Chapter, Oregon-California Trails Association, 1994.

Thornton, Jessy Quinn. *Oregon and California in 1848.* 2 vols. New York: Harper & Bros., 1849. Donner party material reprinted as *The California Tragedy.* Oakland: Biobooks, 1945; and *Camp of Death: The Donner Party Mountain Camp, 1846–47.* Golden: Outbooks, 1986.

Van Doren, Wm. H. "That Old Grave." *Blue Rapids Times* (Blue Rapids, KS), August 15, 1895.

Wells, Evelyn. "The Tragedy of Donner Lake." *San Francisco Call,* June 11–July 5, 1919.

Wise, H. A. *Los Gringos, or, An Inside View of Mexico and California, with Wanderings in Peru, Chili, and Polynesia.* New York: Baker & Scribner, 1850.

Woodworth, Selim E. Letter of April 1, 1847. *California Star* (San Francisco), April 3, 1847. Also in Morgan, *Overland in 1846,* 715–18.

Wright, Rachel Elizabeth Cyrus. "The Early Upper Napa Valley." *Pacific Historian* 19 (Spring 1975): 33–49.

——. *The Early Upper Napa Valley.* Calistoga: Sharpsteen Museum, 1991.

INDEX